Intrusion Detection Systems

Intrusion Detection Systems

Editor

Beata Akselsen

scitus
academics

Intrusion Detection Systems
Edited by **Beata Akselsen**

ISBN: 978-1-68117-266-8
Library of Congress Control Number: 2016937434

SCITUS Academics LLC,
www.scitusacademics.com
Box No. 4766, 616 Corporate Way,
Suite 2, Valley Cottage,
NY 10989

Notice

Printed in United States of America on Acid Free Paper

Preface

An intrusion detection system inspects all inbound and outbound network activity and identifies suspicious patterns that may indicate a network or system attack from someone attempting to break into or compromise a system. Intrusion detection (ID) is a type of security management system for computers and networks. An intrusion detection system gathers and analyzes information from various areas within a computer or a network to identify possible security breaches, which include both intrusions (attacks from outside the organization) and misuse (attacks from within the organization). Intrusion detection and prevention systems (IDPS) are primarily focused on identifying possible incidents, logging information about them, and reporting attempts. In addition, organizations use IDPSes for other purposes, such as identifying problems with security policies, documenting existing threats and deterring individuals from violating security policies. IDPSes have become a necessary addition to the security infrastructure of nearly every organization Intrusion detection system uses vulnerability assessment (sometimes refered to as scanning), which is a technology developed to assess the security of a computer system. The safeguarding of security is becoming increasingly difficult, because the possible technologies of attack are becoming ever more sophisticated; at the same time, less technical ability is required for the novice attacker, because proven past methods are easily accessed through the Web.This book,Intrusion Detection Systems,presents the practical application and results obtained for existing networks as well as results of experiments confirming efficacy of a synergistic analysis of anomaly detection and signature detection, and application of interesting solutions, such as an analysis of the anomalies of user behaviors and many others.

Table of Contents

1

CHAPTER

FEEDBACK RELIABILITY RATIO OF AN INTRUSION DETECTION SYSTEM

Usha Banerjee[1*], Gaurav Batra[1], K. V. Arya[2]

[1]*Department of Computer Science and Engineering, College of Engineering Roorkee (COER), Roorkee, India*

[2]*Department of ICT, Atal Bihari Vajpayee Indian Institute of Information Technology and Management, Gwalior, India*

ABSTRACT

The behavior and nature of attacks and threats to computer network systems have been evolving rapidly with the advances in computer security technology. At the same time however, computer criminals and other malicious elements find ways and methods to thwart such protective measures and find techniques of penetrating such secure systems. Therefore adaptability, or the ability to learn and react to a consistently changing threat environment, is a key requirement for modern intrusion detection systems. In this paper we try to develop a novel metric to assess the performance of such intrusion detection systems under the influence of attacks. We propose a new metric called feedback reliability ratio for an intrusion detection system. We further try to modify and use the already available statistical Canberra distance metric and apply it to intrusion detection to quantify the dissimilarity between malicious elements and normal nodes in a network.

Keywords: Attacks; Canberra Metric; Feedback; Intrusion Detection; Performance; Reliability

1. INTRODUCTION

Nowadays the risk of attacks in data networks is exponentially rising. Thus, the area of network security is gaining importance for researchers and practioners. Attack could be either from outside or from the inside of a network. Further compared to wired networks, mobile ad-hoc networks have several disadvantages with respect to security the most important being the dynamic nature of such networks. In such networks node act as routers and participate in the routing process following some routing protocol. Till date several routing protocols have been formulated for such networks. However, attackers have been always successful to penetrate and harm such networks. Attacks have been classified by several researchers [1] based on the behavior of attacks. Attacks might be internal or external [2]. External attackers try to hamper network performance using any one of the technique like eavesdropping, message intercepting, replay etc. However, the problem is more severe in case of an internal attacker [3] and thus in such a situation the task to detect the misbehaving node becomes daunting. A single intruder can manage to create havoc in a network. This is referred as an intrusion in the system, where a node or malicious element from within a network tries to hamper the normal functioning of the network. To resolve this cumbersome task various Intrusion Detection Systems (IDS) have been developed, which uses different techniques to identify threats in a network. All the available algorithms are based on some assumptions and consider some measure which determine the misbehaving nature of a node. Different approaches are used to determine an intruder in a system, with every approach having its own merits and demerits [4]. One of the approaches used in intrusion detection system maintains a pre-defined knowledge of intrusion with it. Every time an abnormal activity is encountered, this predefined list of intrusions is checked for a match. But this type of technique can determine only a specified number of intrusions. While this list for intrusions can be updated from time to time, but this static approach known as signature-based intrusion detection [5], is not considered an efficient approach for real time network systems. Another approach used for the detection of misbehavior of an insider node considers a measure in which a threshold value is set on the basis of normal activities. Then value of the measure is determined for the node considering all of its parameters. If this calculated value shows some deviation from the threshold value, then the node is declared as an intrusion for the system. This kind of approach known as anomaly based detection helps in detecting new threats introduced in the network. Similarly, various other intrusion detection systems are available, but there is no particular measure available which can successfully rank these presently available IDS on the basis of their capability and performance.

In this paper, a novel approach has been proposed which can predict the performance level of an Intrusion Detection System on the basis of its activities recorded for a particular interval. For this purpose, real time data packets information are captured on a network of both types: pure network data, and data containing various attacks. A statistical approach is adopted in this proposal, known as Canberra metric. Canberra Metric is used to determine dissimilarity between different groups of elements based on various parameters.

Prior Work

Various attempts have been made in the past to define a reasonable measure which can measure the level of trust for an IDS such that the reliability of an IDS can be calculated and a confidence level can be defined for a particular network. The biggest problem that is yet to be resolved is to decide the key factors to be taken into account for describing and analyzing the performance of an IDS. Various options like false positive, false negative, number of packets observed, number of detections, cost of the maintenance, confidence value etc. have been proposed by researchers. Numerous techniques and methodologies have been adopted by researchers to illustrate and benchmark an IDS.

In [6] a survey of IDS technologies available have been analyzed and the authors have proposed an evaluation scheme which considered false positive rate, false negative rate, vulnerability etc. as the key dimensions of an intrusion detection system. And showed that these parameters are to be taken into account to analyze and improve the quality of Network IDS. [7] proposed a new measure metric called Intrusion Detection Capability, which considered ratio of the mutual information between the IDS input and output to the entropy of the input and proved it to be a better measuring tool to determine the capability of an IDS. The authors in [7] showed an analysis comparing previously available cost-based approaches and the proposed metric results in a scenario.

The authors in [8] summarize and present a few test cases to demonstrate various evaluation environment methodologies. A new technology has also been proposed with open source environment which is based on both Artificial Intelligence and real network traffic data. The approach included injecting artificial attacks in the isolated test environment to realize the capability of a system. A similar approach has been adopted by the authors in [9] in which a TCL script is executed in a set environment a TELNET environment and can reveal important information about an IDS and capabilities.

Benchmarking an IDS is not a fully evaluative task and cannot be accomplished by applying some logical technique. Hence, no perfect evaluation methodology has been developed so far to analyze an IDS to be installed on a system [10]. Approaches adopted so far lack depth in one or in another aspect and need some modification looking at the challenges present in real environment at present scenario [11]. Some of those challenges faced in the real-time network are: 1) ever increasing network traffic; 2) the use of encrypted messages to transport malicious information; 3) use of more complex, subtle, and new attack scenarios and many more.

[12] presented a brief description comparing different avail able approaches to evaluate the performance of an Intrusion Detection System. This article concluded on a note that there is lot of scope for further research in this field, as the best suitable approach is yet to be discovered. In this paper, a statistical approach has been proposed to untie the node of the problem explained above. This paper aims at presenting a metric based solution for the evaluation and analysis of the performance and reliability of an IDS. And provide a tool to network intrusion detection system analyst with a tool, which can be used to judge an IDS before installing it on a system. And predictions can be made for IDS regarding its reliability and trust level of its detections and security of data. [13] has previously shown that Canberrra and Chi Square are metrics which could be used in intrusion detection.

The rest of the paper is organized as follows. Section 2 discusses various statistical techniques available to evaluate similarities and dissimilarities and goes on to discuss how these statistical techniques could be applied to the field of intrusion detection. Section 3 presents the approach that we have followed. In Section 4 we present the mathematical and programmatical implementation of the problem. Section 5 deals with results and discussions.

2. STATISTICAL TECHNIQUES

Statistics deals with huge volumes of data and has several established techniques to analyze the data based on their similarity or dissimilarity. In huge volumes of data a small anomaly can be easily identified from historical data. This phenomenon can be adapted to network intrusion detection. Since warnings are based on actual usage patterns, statistical systems can adapt to behaviors and therefore create their own rule usage-patterns. The usage-patterns are what dictate how anomalous a packet may be to the network.

Anomalous activity is measured by a number of variables sampled over time and stored in a profile. Based on the anomaly score of a packet, the reporting process will deem it an alert if it is sufficiently anomalous; otherwise, the IDS will simply ignore the trace. The IDS will report the intrusion if the anomalous activity exceeds a threshold value.

Statistical techniques of intrusion detection usually measure similarities or dissimilarities between network variables like users logged in, time of login, time of logout, number of files accessed in a period of time, usage of disk space, memory, CPU, IP addresses, number of packets transferred etc. The frequency of updating can vary from a few minutes to, for example, one month. The system stores mean values for each variable used for detecting exceeds that of a predefined threshold.

Similarity is defined as a quantity that reflects the strength of relationship between two objects or two features. This quantity is usually having range of either −1 to +1 or normalized into 0 to 1. If the similarity between feature and feature is denoted by δ, we can measure this quantity in several ways depending on the scale of measurement (or data type) that we have. On the other hand, dissimilarity measures the discrepancy between the two objects based on several features. Dissimilarity may also be viewed as measure of disorder between two objects. These features can be rep resented as coordinate of the object in the features space. There are many types of distance and similarity. Each similarity or dissimilarity has its own characteristics. Let the dissimilarity between object i and object j is denoted by δ_{ij}. The relationship between dissimilarity and similarity is given by

$$S_{ij} = 1 - \delta_{ij} \tag{1}$$

for similarity bounded by 0 and 1. When the objects are similar, the similarity is 1 and dissimilarity is 0 and vice versa. If similarity has a range of −1 to +1 and the dissimilarity is measured with range of 0 and 1, then

$$S_{ij} = 1 - 2\delta_{ij} \tag{2}$$

There are several distance metrics available for measuring the similarity or dissimilarity between quantitative variables. The simplest distance variable is the Euclidean Distance [14]. Euclidean distance or simply "distance" examines the root of square differences between coordinates of a pair of objects and is given by

$$d_{ij} = \sqrt{\sum_{k=1}^{n} \left(x_{ik} - x_{jk}\right)^2} \tag{3}$$

Manhanttan distance metric is another such metric. It represents distance between points in a city road grid. It examines the absolute differences between coordinates of a pair of objects and is given by

$$d_{ij} = \sqrt{\sum_{k=1}^{n} \left| x_{ik} - x_{jk} \right|} \tag{4}$$

Chebyshev distance [15] is another such statistical distance metric and is also called maximum value distance. It examines the absolute magnitude of the differences between coordinates of a pair of objects and is given by

$$d_{ij} = \max_k \left| \left(x_{ik} - x_{jk}\right) \right| \tag{5}$$

Chebyshev metric is actually a special case of the Minowski metric with λ = ∞ and has been used to calculate the dissimilarities between normal events and malicious events in networks. In this paper we use the Canberra metric. Canberra distance was proposed by Lance and Williams in 1967. It examines the sum of series of a fraction differences between coordinates of a pair of objects. Each term of fraction difference has value between 0 and 1. The Canberra distance itself is not between zero and one. If one of coordinate is zero, the term become unity regardless the other value, thus the distance will not be affected. Note that if both coordinate are zeros, we need to be defined as $\frac{0}{0} = 0.$ This distance is very sensitive to a small change when both coordinates are near to zero.

$$d_{ij} = \sum_{k=1}^{n} \frac{\left| x_{ik} - x_{jk} \right|}{\left| x_{ik} \right| + \left| x_{jk} \right|} \tag{6}$$

3. OUR APPROACH

We start with selection of the key factors which can best describe a system in words of capability and vulnerability.

Using these key factors, a formula based approach is used to calculate a reliability value, which shows the level to which a user can rely on IDS. A Threshold value is defined in accordance with the normal functioning of an Intrusion detection system in a real time environment. A distance measuring metric known as Canberra metric is applied to determine the similarity or dissimilarity between the predefined threshold value and the observation value. Comparison results are provided by the Canberra metric, which depict the trust level of the IDS. If the observed value is less than the defined threshold value, it shows that IDS under consideration is not a reliable one.

Now these similarity based values generated by Canberra metric are passed to an evaluation tool which generates the receiver operating characteristics (ROC) graph showing the comparison between the observed value and the predefined value.

3.1. Feedback Reliability Ratio (FRR)

The primary task of our approach is the selection of the attribute on which the evaluation of IDS is to be classified.

For this purpose four parameters are taken into consideration namely: True Positive (TP), False Positive (FP), True Negative (TN), and False Negative (FN). True Positive depicts the number of detections caught by IDS when the detections are actually a threat to the system. False Positive value shows the incorrect decision made by IDS about a threat, while they were not actually involved in any threatening event. True Negative is the condition when IDS correctly determine an activity about its harmless nature. False Negative is the situation when IDS declares an activity as harmless, while the activity was a threat and was capable of causing harm to a system.

The fundamental property of a good Intrusion Detection System is not only to detect a threat but is also to provide a correct and reliable decision about an activity. Performance of a system degrades if the IDS installed on the system provide an improper feedback about an activity. So, the reliability factor converges to the False Positive (FP) and False Negative (FN) values of IDS, and these two attribute can describe the capability of an IDS to a reasonable extent. Lower the FP and FN values indicate better reliability on feedback provided by IDS. Mathematically, Reliability on a feedback provided by an IDS can be shown as:

$$\text{Feedback Reliability Value} = \alpha * \frac{1}{\text{FP} + \text{FN}} \tag{7}$$

Total value of both the factors (FP and FN) represents the number of incorrect decisions declared by the IDS. So, a feedback ratio can be determined on the basis of these two factors which can describe the reliability value of IDS on the basis of its past judgments. Hence,

$$\text{Feedback Reliability Value} = \frac{(\alpha * \text{FP}) + (\beta * \text{FN})}{\text{Total No. of Activities Observed}} \tag{8}$$

where α = Coefficient of false positives and β = Coefficient of false negatives.

Depending upon the environment in which the IDS is installed, expectations from an IDS varies in terms of performance. In some situations a very low value of FN is desired, as a high value of FN can harm a system if a strong attack passes through the IDS filter. However, in some cases a high value of FP can drastically degrade the system performance, as the user will not be able to execute any task if the IDS blocks most of the activities by marking them as a threat. Hence, the coefficients (α and β) used in the above equations can take values between 0 and 1 depending upon the expectation of the environment on which IDS is to be applied on. Figure 1 shows a flowchart of our approach.

3.2. Canberra Metric to Predict the Performance of an IDS

Canberra metric is a measure used for determining the distance between groups in terms of similarity between the elements. Canberra metric operates as a rectangular metric having numerical values, with different cases as its rows and variations observed in a case as its column values. A square symmetric matrix is generated as the output of the metric algorithm with zero's as its diagonal elements. The values of the output matrix represent the distance between the variations of cases. The distance between any two elements is determined using the formula shown below:

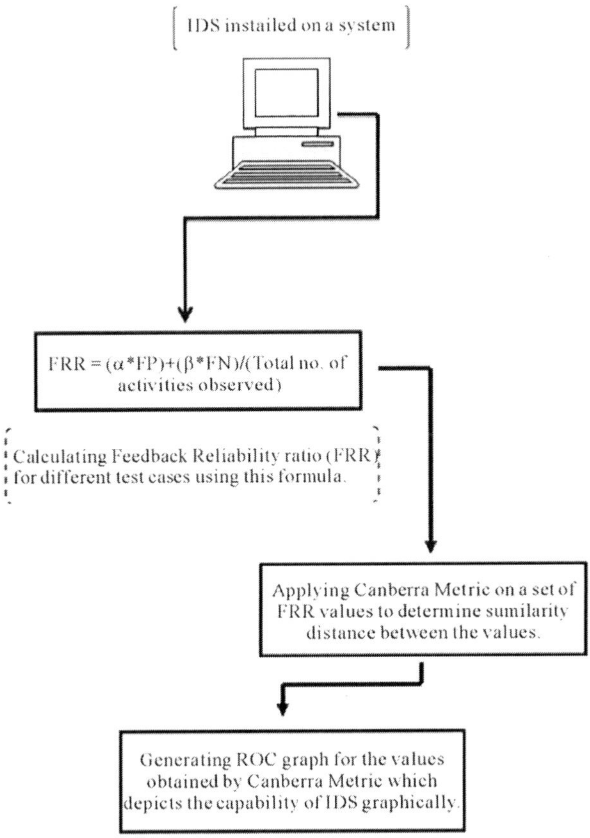

Figure 1. Flowchart.

$$d_{ij} = \sum_{k=1}^{n} \frac{|x_{ik} - x_{jk}|}{|x_{ik}| + |x_{jk}|} \qquad (9)$$

where, i and j are the cases for which distance is to be determined, and k is the variation index for the cases. For the evaluation of an Intrusion Detection System using the Canberra distance metric various test cases are taken under consideration which provide us with the numerical values to be passed as the input to Canberra metric. To generate different test cases for evaluation of computer network intrusion detection systems, the Dataset made available by MIT Lincoln Laboratory, under Defense Advanced Research Projects Agency (DARPA ITO) and Air Force Research Laboratory (AFRL/SNHS) sponsorship in 1998 and 1999 [16] and [17] evaluation is used. These data sets contain examples of both attacks and background traffic. Canberra metric determine the distance between the FRR values using the above equation and finally output the distance values in a square symmetric matrix form. These output values shows the distance or dissimilarity in our case for different test cases. Canberra metric provides a mathematical representation of the similarity/dissimilarity between various cases available, the values of different columns can be compared to see the different trust levels of IDS. This observation helps an analyst to decide upon the IDS to be used on a system for securing data and to protect it from any external threat.

3.3. Weka

To demonstrate the results obtained by Canberra metric graphically, any graphical tool can be used. In our case a famous tool named Weka [18] is used. Waikato Environment for Knowledge Analysis (Weka) is an evaluation Tool used for Data Mining for data analysis and predictive modeling purposes. Present version of Weka is built on Java programming language, so provides better flexibility and can be deployed on any platform [19]. The values generated by Canberra Metric are passed as an input to Weka through a file in Comma separated values (CSV) format. Weka use these values in CSV file to output a Receiver operating characteristics (ROC) graph which shows a deviation between different curves, more the deviation observed shows less capability of the IDS.

4. IMPLEMENTATION OF CANBERRA METRIC

A slightly modified form of Canberra Metric is implemented for the evaluation of distance measure. Pseudocode for modified Canberra Metric algorithm is given below: Consider "C" is the number test cases generated and "v" is the number of variation observed in a test case. And "X" is a temporary variable. Let "M" (of order C*v) is the input matrix containing all the data required to be processed by the algorithm. And "O" (of order C*C) is the output matrix, which is a square symmetric matrix.

CANBERRA-DETERMINE (C, v)

1) For i = 0 to C

2) Begin

3) For j = 0 to C

4) Begin

5) Val = 0

6) For k = 0 to v

7) Begin

8) Yik = M[i][k];

9) Yjk = M[j][k];

10) X = (Yik – Yjk)/(Yik + Yjk)//Standard formula for Canberra metric

11) End

12) O[i][j] = Val; //Save this value in the output matrix

13) End

14) End

15) Output 'Matrix O'

This output matrix "O" provides us with the values depicting the deviation between performances of the IDS in different cases, which helps us in determining overall capability of the IDS. The values passed to the Canberra algorithm are obtained by applying Feedback Reliability Ratio (FRR) formula on various test cases (By taking moderate value for both the constants a and SS as 0.5 in Equation (2)). After applying Canberra algorithm on these values of the test cases, a square matrix is obtained that clearly depicts the effective value for every case. Figure 2 shows the structure of the matrices, input values and the output matrix generated.

Finally, a graphical representation of the observed values is generated. The sum of the effective value for every case from the output matrix is used to locate points in the graph on y-axis, along with the intervals given on the x-axis. Joining these points in the graph generates a polyline graph, which shows the capability of an Intrusion Detection System for various test cases.

5. RESULTS AND DISCUSSION

The peak point of the ROC graph shown in Figure 3 shows the poor performance of IDS in real time environment. While a point at lower level shows better feedback results provided by the IDS. Thus, from the ROC graph for an IDS it can easily be predicted that in what scenario an IDS can perform efficiently. The ROC can also predict at what situation IDS does not provide a reliable detections and the trust level of the IDS.

The approach followed in this paper makes use of easily available attributes like False Positive (FP), False Negative (FN) and Total number of activities that helps in determining the Feedback Reliability Ratio (FRR). Further a distance based metric is used to determine the similarity or dissimilarity in the behavior of an IDS. In our case, Canberra Metric is implemented for this purpose on the data set provided by DARPA analysis in 1999 for the evaluation of Intrusion Detection Systems. Finally the results produced by Canberra Metric are shown graphically using a Java based data mining tool by drawing a ROC graph.

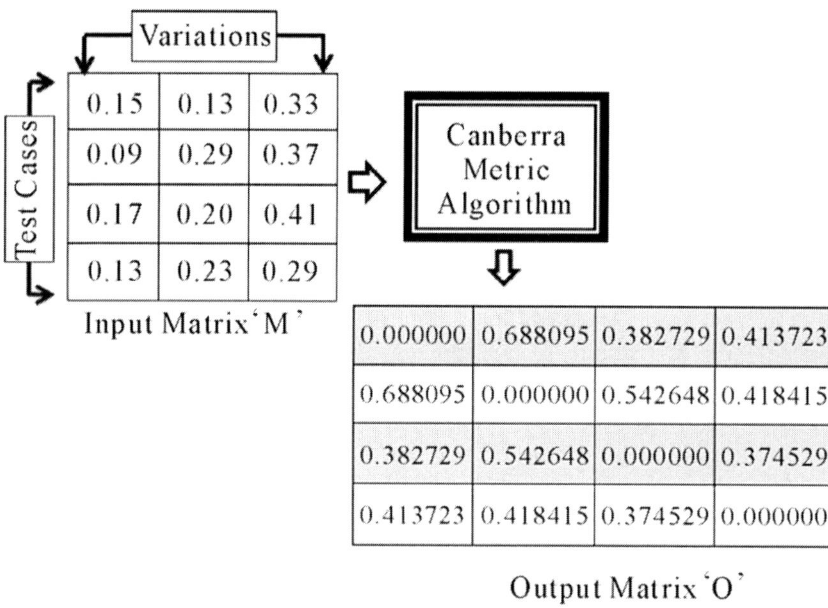

Figure 2. Structure of matrices.

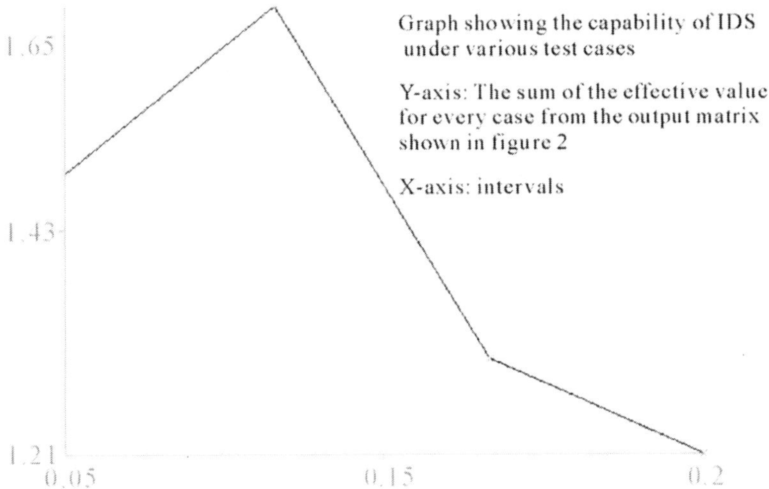

Figure 3. ROC curve.

The approach shown in this paper proved its importance in the field of network security as data security is a crucial factor in networks, where many sites interact with each other for data sharing and transaction of information. In such areas, a single threat can hamper the whole system due to its malicious nature. And hence need of a reliable Intrusion Detection System rises, which can secure both data and transactions on a system. But for this purpose, there should be a proper evaluation methodology which can predict the nature and performance of an IDS before installing it on a real time scenario. Our approach accomplishes that purpose by defining an evaluation technique for IDS using information of its behavior in the past.

6. FUTURE WORK

Unlike the norm that an IDS should be executed as often as possible to minimize the effects of intrusions we have shown that the IDS should be operated at optimum times with a view to maximize reliability o the IDS. The optimal position at which reliability is a maximum depends n several factors like attacker types, network characteristics etc. Thus, our aim should be to optimize performance and hence reliability of IDS in such varying circumstances. In future we hope to devise methods to increase performance and predict more accurate reliability of intrusion detection systems.

7. ACKNOWLEDGEMENTS

The first author wishes to acknowledge the support of a WOS-A project (ref. no. : SR/WOS-A/ET-20/2008) funded by the Department of Science and Technology, Government of India.

REFERENCES

1. M. Mahoney, "Computer Security: A Survey of Attacks and Defenses," 2000.
2. U. Banerjee and A. Swaminathan, "A Taxonomy of Attacks and Attackers in MANETs," International Journal of Research and Reviews in Computer Science, Academy Publishers, Vol. 2, 2011, pp. 437-441.
3. P. Ning and K. Sun, "How to Misuse AODV: A Case Study of Insider Attacks against Mobile Ad-Hoc Routing Protocols," Journal Ad Hoc Networks, Vol. 3, No. 6, 2005, pp. 60-67.
4. S. E. H. Smaha, "An Intrusion Detection System," Proceedings of the IEEE Fourth Aerospace Computer Security Applications Conference, Orlando, December 1988, pp. 37-44.
5. H. Debar, M. Dacier and A. Wespi, "Towards a Taxonomy of Intrusion Detection Systems," Computer Networks, Vol. 31, No. 8, 1999, pp. 805-822.
6. J. Allen, A. Christie, W. Fithen, et al., "State of the Practice of Intrusion Detection Technologies," Carnegie Mellon University, Software Engineering Institute, CMU/ SEI-99-TR-028 ESC-TR-99-028, 2000. http://citeseerx.ist.psu.edu/viewdoc/summary?doi=10.1.1.155.4719
7. G. F. Gu, P. Fogla, D. Dagon, W. Lee and B. Skori, "Measuring Intrusion Detection Capability: An Information-Theoretic Approach," Proceedings of the 2006 ACM Symposium on Information, Computer and Communications Security, New York, 2006, pp. 90-101.
8. A. Nicholas, A. Randal, L. John, O. Henry and R. George, "Intrusion Detection Testing and Benchmarking Methodologies," Proceedings of the First IEEE International Workshop on Information Assurance, Washington DC, 2003.

9. N. J. Puketza, K. Zhang, M. Chung, B. Mukherjee and R. A. Olsson, "A Methodology for Testing Intrusion Detection Systems," IEEE Transactions on Software Engineering, Vol. 22, No. 10, 1996, pp. 719-729.

10. M. Ranum, "Experiences Benchmarking Intrusion Detection Systems," 2001. http://www.nfr.com/

11. Anonym, "Testing Intrusion Detection Systems: A Critique of the 1998 and 1999 DARPA Intrusion Detection System Evaluations as Performed by Lincoln Laboratory," ACM Transactions on Information and System Security, Vol. 3, No. 4, 2000, pp. 262-294.

12. Wilkison, "Intrusion Detection FAQ: How to Evaluate Network Intrusion Detection Systems?" http://www.sans.org/security-resources/idfaq/eval ids.php

13. S. M. Emran, and N. Ye, "Robustness of Chi-Square and Canberra Distance Metrics for Computer Intrusion Detection," Quality and Reliability Engineering International, Vol. 18, No. 1, 2002, pp. 18-28.

14. R. A. Johnson and D. W. Wichern, "Applied Multivariate Statistical Analysis," Prentice Hall, New Jersey, 1998, pp. 226-235.

15. T. P. Ryan, "Statistical Methods for Quality Improvement," John Wiley & Sons, New York, 1989.

16. R. Lippmann, D. J. Fried, I. Graf, J. W. Haines, K. R. Kendall, D. McClung, D. Weber, S. H. Webster, D. Wyschograd, R. K. Cunningham and M. A. Zissman, "Evaluating Intrusion Detection Systems: The 1998 DARPA Off-Line Intrusion Detection Evaluation," IEEE Computer Society Press, Vol. 2, 2000, pp. 12-26.

17. R. Lippmann, J. W. Haines, D. J. Fried, J. Korba and K. Das, "The 1999 DARPA Off-Line Intrusion Detection Evaluation," Springer, Berlin Heidelberg, New York, 2000, pp. 162-182.

18. Weka. http://www.cs.waikato.ac.nz/ml/weka/

19. Z. Markov and I. Russell, "An Introduction to the WEKA Data Mining System," Proceedings of the 11th Annual SIGCSE Conference on Innovation and Technology in Computer Science Education, 2006, pp. 367 368.

2

CHAPTER

A MULTI-LEVELED APPROACH TO INTRUSION DETECTION AND THE INSIDER THREAT

Rita M. Barrios

Computer Information Systems, Cyber Security, University of Detroit Mercy Detroit, Detroit, USA

ABSTRACT

When considering Intrusion Detection and the Insider Threat, most researchers tend to focus on the network architecture rather than the database which is the primary target of data theft. It is understood that the network level is adequate for many intrusions where entry into the system is being sought however it is grossly inadequate when considering the database and the authorized insider. Recent writings suggest that there have been many attempts to address the insider threat phenomena in regards to database technologies by the utilization of detection methodologies, policy management systems and behavior analysis methods however, there appears to be a lacking in the development of adequate solutions that will achieve the level of detection that is required. While it is true that Authorization is the cornerstone to the security of the database implementation, authorization alone is not enough to prevent the authorized entity from initiating malicious activities in regards to the data stored within the database. Behavior of the authorized entity must also be considered along with current data access control policies. Each of the previously mentioned approaches to intrusion detection at the database level has been considered individually, however, there has been limited research in producing a multileveled approach to achieve a robust solution. The research presented outlines the development of a detection framework by introducing a process that is to be implemented in conjunction with information requests. By utilizing this approach, an effective and robust methodology has been achieved that can be used to determine the probability of an intrusion by the authorized entity, which ultimately address the insider threat phenomena at its most basic level.

Keywords: Bayesian Belief Network; Database; Insider Threat; Intrusion Detection

1. INTRODUCTION

As far back as the 1970's, detection of a data breach at the database level by an authorized insider (also known as the insider threat), has been an issue that has plagued the information technology community. The research put forth addresses the insider threat issue by presenting a multileveled approach to Database Intrusion Detection.

1.1. The Insider Threat

The theft and exposure of the critical data components that resides in a relational database by the authorized insider is on the rise [1].

An authorized insider can be defined as an individual who has been granted privileges to utilize or modify the critical data components. This entity can be characterized as an entity that chooses to abuse their role to perform malicious activities. It is because of this type of threat that has given visibility to the need for an automated solution that enables detection of this type of breach [10,20]. While the insider threat presents a trust issue that cannot be solved with this research, the framework as presented did, however, aid in the reduction of exposure when the motivations and subsequent actions of the trusted user can no longer be relied upon.

Finding those trusted entities that are capturing the confidential data components is a task that is difficult at best [1,2]. Identification can encompass a complex decision making process on several levels of abstraction which includes having an understanding of the daily non-threatening, functional actions of the users as identified in the usage logs as well as the measuring those actions against the defined access control policies associated with the related user classification [3]. The challenge within this scope becomes how identification can be successfully accomplished to distinguish between the dynamic and valid usages of the data components vs. the abuse situation. With the introduction of an automated and robust extension to the current research in database Intrusion Detection Systems (IDS), it is possible to overcome this challenge.

With this challenge in mind, the research presented focused on a novel combination of established methodologies in data mining, policy identification and abuse identification in an attempt identify inappropriate behavior as demonstrated by the authorized users of a relational database. Additionally, there are two secondary objectives presented in this research. The first being the creation of a supervised learning component of the presented Database Intrusion Detection Systems (dIDS) to determine the validity of the "normal" behavior and the latter is to develop the definition of the behaviors that were needed to identify, classify and respond to the introduction of new transactions. These objectives are realized by the pairing of the defined access control and security policies with the usage behaviors as found in the database logs.

1.2. Relevance

When the theft of critical data components is successfully executed by the authorized insider, corporate trust begins to deteriorate among its consumer base as well as exposes the organization to various legal issues due to the violation of local, state and/or federal laws and regulations.

This phenomena occurred recently when [4] reports that the data breach of 2008 at T. J. Maxx is expected to realize costs of more than 10 times the original estimate to a record $4.5 billion. This is about $100 per consumer record for each of the 45 million credit card account numbers stolen over an 18-month period [4]. It is expected that the cost associated with the breach to lower profits by $118 million in the first quarter of FY 08 [4].

The insider threat is considered significant, since there have been many cases presented in the literature where a security breach had been successfully accomplished by the actions of an internal user when there has been an advanced level of authorization granted. Statistics as presented in a study by [1], which had been conducted by the FBI in 2006 identified approximately 52% of the respondents had reported unauthorized use of information resources by internal users along with 10% of the respondents unsure if they had been exposed. Further, judicial proceedings as presented by [5] as well as is documented in industry publications as presented by [4] suggests that there is a significant degree of loss to those victim organizations where there has been an exposure of data as a result of inside. Reference [5] also presents a case where a senior database administrator (DBA) had pled guilty to stealing 8.5 million consumer information records over a five-year period, which subsequently had been sold for approximately $580 k. Reference [5] further exposes the problem of the insider threat by presenting a case where the directors of admissions and computer center operations at a Manhattan college were indicted on charges of fraud after setting up an operation where people who had never attended the college paid between $3 k and $25 k to obtain forged academic transcripts. As can been seen, the anomaly of the insider threat is consider a cross-cutting concern as it is not restricted to a single industry but can encompass all types information systems.

Many researchers tend to focus on a single aspect of the overall solution to database intrusion detection. It is not clear as to why the merging of the two critical components of transaction validation and abusive activity validation has not been attempted to create a wellrounded and complete solution even though many researchers do recognize the need for both components [2,3,6-8]. With this obvious omission, it appears as if this type of multileveled solution may in and of itself, pose a task that is too difficult to accomplish.

1.3. Guide to the Paper

The research presented takes on the following progresssion. Section 2 presents a brief but through review of the literature associated with research on database intrusion detection, digital rights management and data mining for behavior patterns. Section 3 presents a brief account of the methodologies that were employed to successfully implement the framework while Section 4 presents the post implementation findings. Section 5 concludes this work with a summary of research presented along with an examination of future works to be achieved.

2. PRIOR RESEARCH

2.1. Access Controls

Although advancement in database access controls has made significant progress towards securing data that resides within the database, there are still limitations of how much can be prevented when considering the insider threat phenomena. This becomes apparent given that the majority of the strides made thus far are focused on addressing the functions of proper authorizations. Since the insider is already authorized these methods will not prevent the theft and/or exposure of the data components [9].

2.2. Intrusion Detection Methodologies

Intrusion Detection Systems (IDS) have been a focused research subject for decades with significant attention given at the start of the 21st century. It was at this time that [10,11] as well as others began to present the foundational concepts in formalized research and publications. Because of the clarity presented in the [11] research, the discussions presented in the following paragraph are centralized around this work however; the seminal works are identified as well as the basis for [11] study. It should be noted that the research presented in the [10] study follows the same presentation as [11] whereby the seminal works form the foundational concepts.

IDS can be defined as a system with a goal to defend a system by raising an alarm when the protocol detects that there has been a security violation [11,12]. With this in mind, [10,11] as well as the seminal works in intrusion detection, identify two primary principles in the IDS model, anomaly detection and signature detection [12,13]. Anomaly detection is defined as flagging all abnormal behavior as an intrusion [10,12-14]. While Signature detection is defined as flagging behavior that is relatively, close in comparison of some defined, known pattern of an intrusion that has been previously defined to the IDS [10-13].

2.3. IDS Implementation

When implementing IDS the focus must be on the three primary components: the audit data, detector model and output that will be used in the follow-up process. The detector model and its underlying principles is the primary component of the system [10-19]. Additionally, IDS protocol is further categorized base on the type of intrusion recognized by the system. These categorizations are defined as follows: The Well-Known intrusion that identifies a static well-defined pattern discernible with the intrusion being executed in a predictable fashion. The Generalized intrusion is similar to the Well-Known category but is variable by nature. Lastly, the Unknown intrusion is identified by a weak coupling between the intrusion and a system flaw. This intrusion category is the most difficult to understand [5]. It is this category, the Unknown Intrusion that is the focal point of the presented research when coupled with the insider threat phenomena.

2.4. Database Intrusion Detection Systems

Historic as well as current research in the area of IDS and access control methodologies does not support the identification of intrusions at the database level [3,6,7,16]. As can been seen, most notably in a study presented by [11] on threat monitoring, there are three classes of database users: 1) The masquerader who has gained access to the system by impersonating an authorized user; 2) The legitimate user who misuses his/her authority; 3)The clandestine user who is operating in stealth mode and nearly undetectable. As [11] notes, the legitimate user can be most difficult to detect using standard audit trail data, as abnormal behavior is difficult to detect when the occurrence is minimal or when the standard rules of operation are often subject to exceptions and modifications. If the access control methods are the focal point, a misconception that simply having the right levels of access control applied to the data components as defined by [16] is sufficient to protect the data or that these methods will function as a deterrent to abusive access behavior. However, given statistics as noted previously on data breaches involving the legitimate user, it is understood in the industry that standard IDS with standard access control is not enough to prevent the insider threat risk. When taken in context with a legitimate user, these forms of detection and access control often fall short in detecting the abusive behavior [3,6,7,16].

Often, the developers of the common IDS make a false assumption that an entity accessing critical data is authenticated and authorized via external supporting automated security measures. These external authentication/ authorization methods reside primarily at the networking and/or operating system level. Another assumption is that authorization and authentication is a failsafe and always successfully identifies the entity as behaving in a trustworthy manner based on the high user database level access [6,7].

To aid in the closure of the gap between access rights, information protection and levels of responsibility, research in the area of the authorized insider threat risk as it relates to the capture of the critical data components has started to take shape. As seen in the [1] study an attempt is made to identify the person making a request for information via usage of the DBMS audit logs to determine whether the requestor is functioning within the boundaries of their security capacity. Again, as presented by [8] an attempt is made at identifying suspect actions via the usage of a quantitative measurement of transaction violations as had been mapped from the Database Management System (DBMS) audit logs. This measurement determines whether the requestor is making a "legal" request [8]. However, both of these studies fall just short of the proactive, dynamic and automatic identification of an abusive use of the data components by the authorized insider.

As previously noted, [20] attempts to identify the unauthorized insider by constructing a Networked Bayesian Network (NBN). This was done in an attempt to project the probability of an intrusion when critical data components are linked within a transaction. The deficient factors identified in this study are the authors' base assumption that 50% of all insiders are attempting to breach the system, leading the reader to conclude that the assumption is an unrealistic expectation given that there are no documented references in the study that lends itself to this percentage. In addition, the authors [4] realize that their proposed method is ineffective when applied to the authorized insider threat risk. However, if applied properly and with additional controls such as the use of the corporate access controls and security policies, this deficiency may be resolved. In addition to the inability of being able to identify an intrusion when executed by the authorized insider, the current research as demonstrated above produces a mutually exclusive view on abuse identification of the authorized user and the identification of a potentially harmful transaction when in actuality the two components should be working to compliment one another's strengths [1,6,7,8,20]. Therefore, the research put forth begins to fill the gap that exists between the concepts of malicious transaction and abusive action identification by expanding these concepts to incorporate the defined access control, security policies as well as the behavior of the authorized user to identify a viable, proactive solution that is both dynamic and automated.

3. METHODOLOGY

The foundations of this study were focused on three primary facets. The first was the research proposed by [21] with their methodologies of mining association rules within a large set of data using the Apriori Hybrid Algorithm. The methodologies put forth by [14] in the area of utilizing the Stochastic Gradient Boosting and the Bayesian Belief Network algorithms to determine probabilities was the second pillar for this study. Thirdly, current methodologies utilized in the dynamic maintenance area of security policy, known as Digital Rights Management (DRM) served as the final pillar to secure the foundation of this research. Along with the novel approach to database intrusion detection that guided the presented research, a series of modified Intrusion Detection System heuristics has been presented to provide a solid foundation for the acceptance of the results of the approach. The following paragraphs outline how these objectives were achieved.

3.1. Development Approach

The process began with the Trusted User initiating a transaction. Within the context of this study, whether the transaction is initiated via internal or external means has not been addressed but is considered in future work. Once the transaction has entered the presented dIDS system, several processes were initiated to determine the probability of an intrusion. The results from the probability assessment were stored in the dIDS repository for future reference by the dIDS. At this time, the transaction continued on to its completion since this study was focused on intrusion detection and not intrusion prevention. Future work focuses on extending the work presented into the intrusion prevention research area within the context of the database environment.

3.2. Association Rules

Following the building of the data repository that housed the various dIDS signatures, generation of the dIDS training data dependencies signatures was the next logical step. As in most organizations, certain data components are dependent upon other data components. Often usage outside of the normal transactional scope is an anomaly in and of itself. For instance, the retrieval of only a consumer name data component really does not garner one much information however if that same consumer name component is used in tandem with the corresponding consumer address component, one can make inferences about the data that was retrieved. It then makes sense if the selection of certain data components is without their complimentary counterpart, one can reasonably conclude that an intrusion may be occurring. However, obtaining the data dependencies can be a daunting task given that there may be thousands of various data component combinations open to selection. As [22] have reasoned, often times, in intrusion detection, the training data is developed utilizing a significant amount of expert information about the system and often times this domain knowledge is difficult to obtain. Continuing with the implementation of the [21] Apriori Hybrid Algorithm to mine the association rules, the difficulty of the domain expertise is greatly reduced. Following the acquisition of the training data, it is then subsequently used to identify known intrusions. As [5] point out there is a direct relationship between the quality of the intrusion detection model and the quality of the training data obtained thru various data mining techniques. With this quality concern in mind, the study presented in this research utilized an Apriori Hybrid Algorithm in order to determine the most appropriate data dependency signatures (or rule associations) since there can be a high correlation between the combinations of the data components. Utilization of this type of algorithm is common during a data mining operations when obtaining a selection of relevant facts (data components) where the members have a high degree of correlation [21]. Application of the algorithm in this regard helped to limit the creation of data component combinations to only those where the historical pattern has been consistently demonstrated throughout the data. Once developed, the application of the algorithm to the TPC-C data occurs in order to determine which data components appear to be of significance for the processing environment of the prototype dIDS. Since the creation of the training data is a generic process, utilization of the algorithm to process the historical data in order to determine the data component significance is appropriate. As such, it is also appropriate to apply the training algorithm to a variety of input data following the definition of the components within the pool of information to develop newly identified association rules.

To begin this novel approach to database intrusion detection, an unsupervised learning process was initially employed in a data-mining environment to establish the baseline rules, which developed the data association rules that established the behavior correlations. Rule associations algorithms are well researched as noted above. These methods are considered the standard in data mining when trying to establish data correlations. The Apriori Algorithm as implemented by [23] is said to be the most popular of these types of mining operations [24]. However, an extension to this algorithm as developed by [23], called the Apriori Hybrid was utilized in the development of the initial data signatures because of its wide acceptance within the data mining community. This is due in part to the algorithm's quality levels when mining user behavior, patterns of access and the assigned classifications from historical data [24]. To implement the Association Rule algorithm, two steps are taken into account to satisfy the user-specified minimum support and the user-specified minimum confidence in parallel [23]. These two steps are as follows:

Ÿ Apply the minimum support to find all frequent item sets in the database

Ÿ Form the rules using the frequent item sets as defined in the first step and minimum confidence constraint.

Typically, the first step is more challenging since it involves searching all item combinations. Given the growth rate of the item set can be expressed as a potential for exponential growth depending on the number of items in the item set, a method of deterring this growth can be found with the implementation of the downward-closure property of the support constraint [23,24]. This property guarantees that for a frequent item set, all of its subsets are frequent and therefore for an infrequent item set, all of its supersets must be infrequent.

Since the Apriori Hybrid Algorithm exploits the best features of both the Apriori and the Apriori TID in addition to being one of the most popular of the Association Rules algorithms as noted by [24], its foundational properties have been employed in the presented research.

3.3. Probability of Intrusion

As evidenced in historical and current research, fuzzy logic and/or neural networks have been successfully used to determine whether an intrusion has been encountered [3]. Since "normal" behaviors are often known within the data processing environments and patterns of behavior can be established from the historical information, the utilization of a similar approach to the neural network IDS solution can be implemented utilizing the more defined decision tree methodology to determine the probability of an intrusion.

The data gathered during the data mining process as outlined above was then utilized to refine the prototype system by utilizing the supervised Stochastic Gradient Boosting decision tree process to establish the probability of whether a given signature as created by the Apriori Hybrid Algorithm is considered an intrusion [14,25].

It should be noted that the recommend practice as suggested by [25], is to perform both the Stochastic Gradient Boosting tree creation as well as a single tree. This is because the Stochastic Gradient Boosting method is more like a "black box" methodology that is highly accurate however; it is difficult to visualize the relationships established during the process [25]. This recommendation of running both methods has been followed in the presented research to ensure the most complete information can be realized in building the model's accuracy as well as being able to fully understand the relationships.

Once the prototype had been successfully built with the association rules based on the Apriori Hybrid Algorithm as well as the detection signatures as identified in the Stochastic Gradient Boosting methodology, this same learning process was employed to account for new entities making requests for information. Upon the discovery of a new entity, the behavior signature repository was updated accordingly with relevant data.

3.4. Current Security Policies

In most organizations, the ability to dynamically create and maintain acceptable use policies tends to be an extensive and resource intensive process. For most, the development life cycle goes thru an iteration of steps ultimately ending up at the point where the policy must be published [12]. Today, most organizations' view on publishing the policy's modifications requires the updating of web pages, hard copy documents as well as applying any needed updates to the information systems via physical code modifications. Since a process so resource intensive can take weeks or even months to realize, often times, it is near impossible to determine if a violation of policy has occurred until sometime later. In recent times, the application of digital rights management systems (DRM) to allow for policy development and distribution is taking shape [26]. A DRM system is a system that allows for the management of the actions and entity can perform on a digital resource (the data) as well as controlling the usages of the resource within the information system. As [26] notes the ability to specify and manage the rights of an entity is one of the most important features of the DRM. Unlike standard authorization mechanisms, the DRM is meant to give specific rights to specific entities for a specific amount of time [26]. Bringing this notion of the DRM into the context of this research by building a DRM-like repository allowed for dynamic, real-time policy development that can be accessed at will by the presented intrusion detection system.

3.5. Detection of Abusive Activities with the Bayesian Approach

Since the Bayesian Belief Network (BBN) methodology employs a reasoning mechanism that the enables the determination of the probability of an event occurring when various factors are present, usage of the BBN is the most effective method of detection for this study.

The usage of BBN has been supported in recent literature as a viable method of intrusion detection. In [27] study, the Bayesian approach combined with a visualizetion component is defined to create an interactive intrusion detection system in an attempt to reduce the number of false positives presented in current intrusion detection systems. Again, in the [28] study, the Bayesian approach is applied to improve the effectiveness of the detection mechanism in the presented intrusion detection system for a mobile ad hoc network. Reference [20] used the Bayesian approach to expand the independent environment variables often present in intrusion detection to propose a networked Bayesian Network to understand the correlation between these environmental variables which may be used to identify an intrusion within a relational database. Therefore, with the objectives of this research endeavor in mind and in keeping with current research, the probabilistic approach of utilizing the BBN where the conditional probability and the causality relationships between the variables as defined have been applied to the presented intrusion detection system. Since the dIDS does have knowledge of the acceptable behaveiors, relevant security polices as well as the data dependencies, the BBN can make a reasonable assumption of the probability that an intrusion has occurred even when presented with new information.

Implementation of the BBN took the following path in the research presented. Initially, the data mined as described in the preceding paragraphs was used to identify the variables (nodes) of concern for the detection model as well as their association rules. With this information, the Directed Acyclic Graphs (DAG) was developed to visualize the conditional properties of the relationships presented. Following the creation of the DAGs the probabilities for each node was developed.

3.6. Information Flow Overview

The flow of information within the presented research and identified in **Figure 1** is as follows which is similar to the [20] study. Each of the contributing factors, which include environment, policy as well as data component combinations were given a conditional probability. If the computed probability of the information request, (given the identified variables), fell within an acceptable range, the transaction was identified as not being an intrusion. However, if the probability fell outside of the acceptable range, the transaction was defined, as a potential intrusion where by further steps were completed in an attempt to make a determination as to whether or not the "true" intrusion flag is accurate. These further steps include looking into the system to determine if there are any new applications as well as users accessing the system. Should this situation present itself where the dIDS encounters a "new" entity, the signatures of the entity were stored for utilization in future detection processes. Should the system identify an actual intrusion, in addition to storing the intrusion signatures, the transaction was flagged as an intrusion that should be further examined.

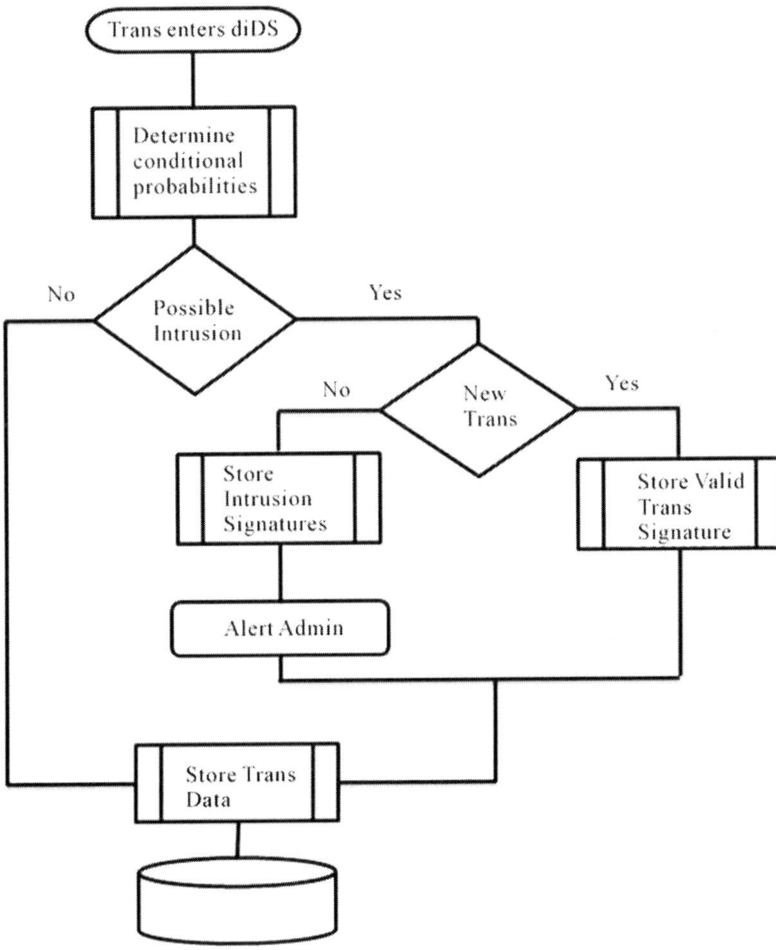

Figure 1. Information flow diagram.

It should be noted that in order to determine the most optimal thresholds, various probability thresholds were utilized. This aided in the determination of the level that the presented research is most effective with the goal being that the model should employ the most restrictive threshold possible while maintaining an acceptable level of detection.

3.7. Management of New Information

The research as is presented does not suggest that the flagged transactions should be prevented from completing its processing cycle. This decision should be left the system administrators given the business model in which the database operates. Future work focuses on extending this research into an intrusion prevention model to facilitate the prevention of potentially harmful transactions from reaching the database.

Continuing on to the acceptance of the new information within the dIDS, "new" data was collected via the development of a simulated payment processing application, where the necessary data components were established and persisted in a relational database. In addition, this subset of "new" data was utilized to develop the intelligent features needed to enable the system to automatically identify the new entity and "learn" from that new relationship for future reference.

To begin, a SQL Server 2008 Enterprise Edition database was created modeling the TPC-97 data structures. Give that one of the objectives of this research was to implement the Database Intrusion Detection System (dIDS) in an environment that supports the very large database (VLDB) concepts, the TPC-97 was selected as the data model of choice given its ability to support large amounts of data and transactions.

In order to generate a significant amount of data for the TPC-97 model, a data-generator software product was purchased under a research license via Red Gate Software, Ltd., a private limited company located in the UK. This software, called Data Generator, was specifically developed for the SQL Server environment to generate meaningful test data. To support this functionality, the generation of 1 million customer accounts as well as supporting order entry information, which included the customer order history using the primary keys of the schema's table object occurred. Following the build of the baseline TPC-97 objects, the specific tables for the intrusion detection system were generated along with the incoming transactions. The policy and entity information was manually entered using standard INSERT statements of the SQL query language given that the data was not complex in nature. To support incoming transactions to the TPC-97 database, 925 random transactions were generated based on the policies of the database. Following the requirements definition of the experiment the Apriori Hybrid algorithm was implemented in the Java programming language and applied against the TPC-97 database to determine the most common patterns of data contained within the data. These patterns served as the baseline patterns used in the dIDS.

To begin the process, the generated transactions were sequentially read into the dIDS where an attempt was made to seek out any existing patterns previously identified as well as any policies that may be set in place to govern the transaction processing. If the policy and pattern were found within the signature repository, the transaction was identified as being proper. However, if only a portion or no information was gathered about the transaction, it was subjected to further scrutiny by first going thru the Stochastic Gradient Boosting algorithm to understand the probability of an intrusion based on the transactional statically defined components such as the data relationships and defined policies. If the transaction continued to be identified as an intrusion by exceeding the pre-defined threshold, the transaction was then subjected to the Bayesian Belief Net algorithm to determine the probability that an intrusion was occurring based on the uncertainty of the environment and the prior behavior of the requestor. It should be understood that the requestor could be either a human or an electronic source. Should the transaction continue to be identified as an intrusion, it was flagged as an intrusion then logged as such in the signature table to be used in the analysis of future transactions. Manual verification and validation was then applied to determine whether the transaction was a true intrusion or classified as a false positive.

To support the learning component, if the transaction was not classified as an intrusion, it was also logged in the signature table along with the information to identify the transaction as a potential new signature. Like the intrusions that were identified during the probability of intrusion calculations, a manual verification and validation process was applied to determine the validity of the new log entry.

Since the availability of a standardized set of metrics used to measure intrusion detection at the level of the database are not readily available, the NIST algorithms that are used to measure network intrusion detection systems were modified to consider the database environment.

Instead of using the network packet as the focus of the measurements as is done in network intrusion detection systems, this research focused the attention on the incoming transaction that are requesting database services. This insider entity was defined to take on the role of an authorized application user, a Database Administrator or an automated program that requests database resources. These roles were defined in the additional database objects that were built to support the intrusion detection system. No programmatic distinction was made during the development of the functional dIDS as to which entity was requesting the information meaning that the policy definitions were the driving force in the identification of the requesting entity.

4. FINDINGS

Intrusion detection at the database level remains a new concept within industry and research. Attempting to find a relevant study to measure the presented research against was difficult. That said, the [5] study was selected as a measurement due to similarities in methodology. In the [5] study, the authors built user profiles of normal behavior as a baseline to detect anomalies. In addition, included in the [5] study was the deployment of the Bayesian approach to estimate probabilities to strengthen their intrusion detection process. Given these commonalities, the information presented in this study served to create the goal measurements for the presented work. Other studies on database intrusion detection identified in this research had a significant enough difference in approach and methodology that they could not be used to create a reasonable and like objective value.

The metrics identified in [7] are presented at a degree of abstraction higher than what was useful for this study. Therefore, the data identified in [7] was expanded and mined in an effort to make visible enough natural detail to provide a reasonable comparison to the presented work. Given that in [7] the successful detection rate was identified at 38.38%, it also served as the baseline for successful detection in this study. The presented study achieved similar results that fell within the range of <61.62% for false responses and ≥38.38% positive responses.

Additionally and where applicable, specific baseline measurement values identified in [7] were adopted and included in accordance with the Information Assurance Directorate (IAD)-US Government Protection Profile for Intrusion Detection Systems as described in [7,28,29,31]. Specifically, these measurements inclusive as quailtative measurements that relate directly to the accuracy of the detection model as defined in the following.

4.1. Coverage

Coverage (c) is determined by the rate which IDS can successfully identify an attack under ideal conditions. The original measurement as identified by [29] is concerned with detecting and measuring the number of unique attacks. This measurement, in a signature-based system, is achieved by verifying the number of valid signatures (s) and mapping them to a standard naming schema. The entering transaction (t) is then measured against the known signatures to determine if the transacttion exists within the signature baseline. If the transaction does exist, it is then considered a valid request for information since it meets the criteria of an authorized entity. If the signature does not exist, it is considered a successful recognition of an anomaly and counted in the measurement as noted in Equation (1). To support database intrusion detection in regards to the authorized insider, the measurement presented was adapted to focus attention on the rate by which IDS can identify an anomaly that has been initiated by authorized insiders at various levels of authorization. Therefore, only transactions that are initiated by a trusted user are considered in the measurement. This measurement achieved a rate of ≥38.38% as is indicated using the data presented in [7].

$$c = \sum (t \notin s)/s \tag{1}$$

4.2. Probability of Detection

This measurement determines the detection rate (d) of attacks correctly detected (b) by an IDS in a given environment during a particular period (T) in minutes [29]. As with the Coverage measurement, probability of detection assumes that various types of attacks were measured. Given that this study is focused on one type of attack, the measurement was adjusted to focus on the various levels of authorization of the information requestor as opposed to the various types of attacks. Given that the false positive rate is directly related to the detection rate, care must be given to ensure that the scenarios are exact and consistent when used in both measurements. This measurement, in accordance with the baseline data set as presented in [7] achieved a rate of measurement of ≥38.38% of correctly identified attacks.

$$d = \left(\frac{b}{t}\right) * T \tag{2}$$

4.3. Volume of Data

This measurement determines the difference in the volume of data (v) the dIDS can manage when presented with a large mass of transactions as compared with the pre IDS implementation. While data as presented in the NIST IR-7007 identifies the number packet/second for the network IDS, when put into the context of this study, the transaction will be the unit of measure. Additionally, this measurement will identify the change of data volume pre and post dIDS implementation in order to identify any latency issues that may be present.

Given that this measurement is very subjective to the system environment, the initial transaction sets were processed without the implementation of the dIDS to capture the rate of processing using the maximum (m) volume of data. This measurement was considered the baseline processing rate. Following the establishment of the baseline measurement, the same transaction set was processed through the implementation of the dIDS (i) to determine the change in processed transactions through the dIDS implementation. The pre and post IDS expressions used to calculate this measurement, m and i can be defined as follows:

Ÿ m = Tpre/s where Tpre is the number of pre-IDS transactions and s is the elapsed processing time (in seconds) for the transaction set

Ÿ i = Tpost/s where Tpost is the number of post-IDS transactions and s is the elapsed processing time (in seconds) for the transaction set Pre-IDS results show 408.38 as the volume of data transactions per second. Overall the system performed as expected with the greatest latency observed at iteration 4 with 309.67 as the volume of data transactions per second or a delta of 98.71 transactions.

$$v = m - i \tag{3}$$

4.4. Adaptability Rate

The Adaptability (a) Rate measurement determines the rate by which the presented dIDS was able to identify new, valid (v) transactions and new, authorized users (u). It is presented, as an aggregate and identified as total new (n) transactions. Note that new information always carries a higher rate of false positives when introduced to the dIDS and this will be reflected in the development of this measurement. The anticipated adaptability rate was achieved at ≥25% of new transactions identified.

The threshold values for the Adaptability Rate were manually modified in the code as the iterations progressed through the testing phase. The policy tables were also modified manually to test the response of the dIDS and its ability to recognize changes and permissions.

Transaction volume was not considered in the intrusion probability calculation in an effort to keep the intrusion process independent from the input. This allowed the system to recognize a normalized range of probabilities regardless of transaction volume during the intrusion detection process. As the metrics contained within this research demonstrate, the probability range remained stable and consistent throughout the testing phase.

Using the generated data, the Apriori Hybrid data mining Algorithm was deployed using the SPMF software created by [30]. The resulted in an in the generation of 13,199 patterns of data. Examination of these patterns reflect a support of <0.8 and creating less meaningful information. Often patterns were generated that had no value in the intrusion detection process. To avoid this, the threshold of pattern utilization was set at ≥0.8. The results were 14 common behavior patterns and 95 data patterns. Within the data patterns 14 common fields were identified. These results were then utilized as the baseline signature of the dIDS system.

To support the incoming transaction set, 925 incoming transactions were generated using the Data Generator software. However, the study only used 115% or 12.5% of the amount of input that [7] used, the sample reduction did not affect the testing since the study is focused on the percentage of transactions identified as an intrusion and not the volume. Additionally, the following results can further be inferred to account for the larger dataset.

The data was generated based on the behaviors identified in the Apriori Hybrid data mining process. The patterns mined were determined to be the valid signatures while the remaining. Using the valid signatures patterns as the catalyst, both valid and invalid transactions were generated.

Monitoring and subsequent analysis of incoming transactions will determine probability of intrusion by identifying the tokens in a transaction. Tokens are included the action SELECT, INSERT, UPDATE, DELETE as well as the individual columns, with the identity of the requesting entity and WHERE and SET clauses, (when present). Once identified, these tokens were then compared to policy tables to determine if they were contained in an existing policy. If the transaction is validated based on the information in the policy tables, the transaction was considered a non-intrusion. If not validated, the intrusion process will be triggered.

Once triggered, the intrusion process will compare the incoming transaction to the database transaction logs in an attempt to identify a new, valid signature. The method of identifying the information contained within the logs was implemented by way of a dynamically generated SELECT statement where a probability was computed based on how many of the tokens were found on a single log entry when taking into account the environmental factors (as previously noted). Next a probability was generated using the Stochastic Gradient Boosting algorithm. If the result was greater than 0.75, the transaction was marked as a new signature;

otherwise it was subjected to further scrutiny. The 0.75 probability threshold used to identify a new signature was established at a high value since a transaction that is not yet considered valid can hold a higher degree of risk.

If the transaction was not validated in the new signature identification process, the transaction was subjected to the intrusion detection process. Unlike the new signature identification process, logs do not support the intrusion transaction. To refine the intrusion probability the transaction's probability of intrusion was computed by the Stochastic Gradient Boosting algorithm. This allowed control over the refinement of the threshold level. Then the transaction was subjected to further refinement using the Bayesian Belief Net algorithm. If the probability of this primary review was below the threshold, it was deemed as a non-intrusion event and added to the signature table as a validated signature. Should the incoming transaction require further analysis the same principle as identified for the stochastic Gradient Boosting Algorithm was applied to the application of the Bayesian Belief Net algorithm. If this probability computation resulted in a value that was above the control threshold, the transaction was deemed an intrusion and logged to the intrusion table to be used in the on-going signature identification process. There were six (6) iterations of the transaction cycle performed during the testing phase using the various threshold values.

$$a = (u + v)/n \tag{4}$$

5. CONCLUSIONS AND FUTURE WORK

5.1. Conclusions

Based on the information provided to the dIDS model, the following conclusions have been drawn. Identification of "good" vs. "malicious" transactions is greatly dependent upon the information contained within the transaction itself, the log information, the number of rows being impacted by the database request and the policies pertaining to the entity making the request and the behavior of the requesting entity. Without consideration of each of these components within the context of each other, it cannot be accurately determined if the authorized insider is behaving as expected.

When using the Stochastic Gradient Boosting algorithm alone, when compared to using both algorithms to reach a finer degree of analysis, is less effective than use both algorithms together in a single process when attempting to identify an intrusive transaction. By using both algorithms within the same intrusion process, the number of false-positives was markedly reduced.

Several types of transactions were introduced to indicate a new entity; the system was able to identify the new entity as the testing iterations progressed regardless of what the threshold rate was set at. When policy changes were introduced, the system correctly identified the intrusion and non-intrusion state.

Overall, the system presented proved very successful. Each goal with the exception of the maintaining the latency factor at a steady rate was met. Further research in the area of maintaining or reducing the latency of a Database intrusion detection system is warranted.

As has been observed, to use one methodology in an attempt to identify the insider threat phenomena in the context of the database environment, that supports a reasonable probability measurement, cannot be considered a complete solution. The uncertainty of the requestor's prior behavior must take into consideration along with the complete set of data and environmental factors in order to reach the conclusion that the insider is behaving beyond the boundaries as stated within defined security policies.

This research also observed that it is possible to leave the system in unattended learning environment in order to determine the probability of intrusion when the system is presented with new information as long as the other factors as noted are considered.

5.2. Future Works

The success of this research was based upon the research of many other researchers in not only intrusion detection but in the database technologies as well.

This research simply laid the foundations for future work to be investigated with respect to Database intrusion detection systems. To further the positive results presented, it can be expected that research in the following areas will build upon what has been presented in the preceding sections.

The presented research was based upon current research in intrusion detection models. Some of these models are utilized at the network level while others are at the database level. While intrusion detection does aid in the discovery of potential intrusions, it still requires a manual decision to be made by an intrusion administrator as to whether the incoming database request can be definitively considered a non-intrusion event. This is most often accomplished by some form of human intervention. Expansion of this study to move from an intrusion detection model to an intrusion prevention model allows for an expansion in the research area which enables the next generation of database security to be realized.

Latency continues to be a concern whenever one considers the implementation of a component that forces extra work on the database. This is unavoidable as every layer of security requires some degree of computing power. At the database level of the technology stack, this latency is most often evident in the response times associated with the database request given that the system is asking the database for more information in an attempt to make a sustainable decision as to the state of the intrusion event.

In addition, since this study assumed that the database environment must be a complete system, more information on history, behavior and policy will need to be maintained in order to have a robust database intrusion model. By the nature of more data, latency will continue to grow, as more resources in terms of data and input/output processes will be utilized during the detection process. By moving the intrusion model to the database engine level, the system will be inherently faster since there will be less of the technology stack to traverse which ultimately reduces the latency time.

6. ACKNOWLEDGEMENTS

The author would like to thank Dr. Cannady for his guidance in the development of this research and Anthony Beshouri for his keen eye for refinement.

REFERENCES

1. J. Fonseca, M. Vieira and H. Madeira, "Online Detection of Malicious Data Access Using DBMS Auditing," Association for Computing Machinery, New York, 2008.
2. A. Kamra, E. Bertino and G. Lebanon, "Mechanisms for Database Intrusion Detection and Response," Association for Computing Machinery, New York, 2008.
3. S. Castano, M. Fugini, G. Martella and P. Samarati, "Database Security", Association for Computing Machinery, New York, 1994.

4. S. Gaudin, "Computer Crimes Charged in College Cashfor-Grades Scheme, 2007. http://www.informationweek.com/story/showArticle.jhtml?a

5. J. Vijayan, "DBA Admits to Theft of 8.5m Records," 2007.http://www.computerworld.com/action/article.do?command=viewArticleBasic&articleId=308611&source=rss_topic82

6. Y. Hu and B. Panda, "A Data Mining Approach for Database Intrusion Detection," Association for Computing Machinery, New York, 2004.

7. K. Ilgun, A. Kamra, E. Tertzi and E. Bertino, "Detecting Anomalous Access Patterns in Relational Databases," The VLDB Journal, Vol. 17 No. 5, 2007, pp. 1603-1077.

8. G. Lu, J. Yi and K. Lü, "A Dubiety-Determining Based Model for Database Cumulated Anomaly Intrusion," Association for Computing Machinery, New York, 1997.

9. E. Shmueli, R. Vaisenberg, Y. Elovici and C. Glezer, "Database Encryption: An Overview of Contemporary Challenges and Design Considerations", ACM SIGMOD Record, Vol. 38 No. 3, 2009, pp. 29-34.

10. J. Allen, A. Christie, W. Fithen, J. McHugh, J. Pickel and E. Stoner, "State of Practice of Intrusion Detection Technologies," Carnegie Mellon University, Pittsburgh, 2000.

11. S. Axelsson, "Intrusion Detection Systems: A Survey and Taxonomy," Chalmers University of Technology, Goteborg, 2000.

12. S. Kumar and E. H. Spafford, "An Application of Pattern Matching in Intrusion Detection," Purdue University, Lafayette, 1994.

13. S. E. Smaha, "Tools for Misuse Detection," Information Systems Security Association, Portland, 1993.

14. G. E. Leipins and H. S. Vaccaro, "Anomaly Detection: Purpose and Framework," Proceedings of 12th National Computer Security Conference, 1989, pp. 495-504.

15. H. Debar, M. Becke and D. Siboni, "A Neural Network Component for an Intrusion Detection System," Proceedings of IEEE Computer Society Symposium on Security and Privacy, Oakland, 4-6 May 1992, pp. 240-250.

16. D. E. Denning, "An Intrusion Detection Model", IEEE Transactions on Software Engineering, Vol. 13 No. 2, 1993, pp. 222-232.

17. T. F. Lunt, A. Tamru, F. Gilham, R. Jagannathan, C. Jalai, P. G. Newman, H. S. Javitz, A. Valdes and T. D. Garvey, "A Real-time Intrusion Detection Expert System (IDES)", Final Technical Report for SRI Project 6784, 1992.

18. R. A. Kemmerer and P. A. Porras, "State Transition Analysis: A Rule-based Intrusion Detection Approach," IEEE Transactions on Software Engineering, Vol. 21 No. 3, 1995, pp. 181-199.

19. H. S. Venter, M. S. Oliver and J. H. P. Eloff, "PIDS: A Privacy Intrusion Detection System" Internet Research, Vol. 14 No. 5, 2004, pp. 360-365.

20. X. An, D. Jutla and N. Cercone, "A Bayesian Network Approach to Detecting Privacy Intrusion," Proceedings of 2006 International Conferences on Web Intelligence and Intellgent Agent Technology Workshop, Hongkong, 18-22 December 2006, pp. 73-76.

21. R. Agrawal and P. Srikant, "Fast Algorithms for Mining Association Rules in Large Databases," Morgan Kaufmann Publishers, San Francisco, 1994.

22. Z. Yu, J. J. Tsai and T. Weigert, "An Adaptive Automatically Tuning Intrusion Detection System," ACM Transactions on Autonomous and Adaptive Systems, Vol. 3, No. 3, 2008, pp. 1-25.

23. R. Agrawal, T. Imielinski and A. Swami, "Mining Association Rules between Sets of Items in Large Databases," Proceedings of ACM International Conference on Management of Data (SIGMOD 93), Washington DC, 1993, pp. 207-216.

24. J. Hipp, U. Guntzer and G. Nakhaeizadeh, "Algorithms for Association Rule Mining—A General Survey and Comparison," ACM SIGKDD Explorations Newsletter, Vol. 2 No. 1, 2000, pp. 58-64.

25. P. H. Sharrod, "TreeBoost: Stochastic Gradient Boosting," 2003. http://www.dtreg.com/treeboost.htm

26. P. J. Windley "Digital identity," O'Reilly, Sebastopol, 2005.

27. S. Axelsson, "Combining a Bayesian Classifier with Visualization: Understanding the IDS," Proceedings of ACM Workshop on Visualization and Data Mining for Computer Security, New York, 2004, pp. 99-108.

28. A. H. R. Karim, R. M. Rajatheva and K. M. Ahmed, "An Efficient Collaborative Intrusion Detection System for MANET Using Bayesian Approach," Proceedings of 9th ACM International

Symposium on Modeling Analysis and Simulation of Wireless and Mobile Systems (MSWiM 06), New York, 2006, pp. 187-190.

29. P. Mell, V. Hu, R. Lippman, J. Haines and M. Zissman, "An Overview of Issues in Testing Intrusion Detection Systems" 2003. http://csrc.nist.gov/publications/PubsNISTIRs.html

30. P. Fournier-Viger, "Computer Software Documentation," 2008. http://www.philippe-fournierviger.com/spmf/

31. United States of America (USA), "US Government Protection Profile: Intrusion Detection System for Basic Robustness Environments," National Security Agency (NSA), Washington DC, 2007.

3
CHAPTER

AN INTRUSION DETECTION SYSTEM BASED ON MULTI-LEVEL CLUSTERING FOR HIERARCHICAL WIRELESS SENSOR NETWORKS

Ismail Butun [1,2,*], In-Ho Ra [3,*] and Ravi Sankar [2]

[1]*Department of Mechatronics Engineering, Bursa Technical University, Gaziakdemir M. Mudanya C. No:4/10, Osmangazi 16190, Turkey*

[2]*Department of Electrical Engineering, University of South Florida, 4202 E. Fowler Avenue, Tampa, FL 33620, USA*

[3]*School of Computer, Information and Communication Engineering, Kunsan National University, Gunsan 573-701, Korea*

ABSTRACT

In this work, an intrusion detection system (IDS) framework based on multi-level clustering for hierarchical wireless sensor networks is proposed. The framework employs two types of intrusion detection approaches: (1) "downward-IDS (D-IDS)" to detect the abnormal behavior (intrusion) of the subordinate (member) nodes; and (2) "upward-IDS (U-IDS)" to detect the abnormal behavior of the cluster heads. By using analytical calculations, the optimum parameters for the D-IDS (number of maximum hops) and U-IDS (monitoring group size) of the framework are evaluated and presented.

Keywords: intrusion detection; neighborhood watching; clustering; WSN; IDS; hierarchical

1. INTRODUCTION AND RELATED WORK

A group of sensing devices team up to form a wireless network to be named as wireless sensor network (WSN). WSNs constitute a challenging research area of engineering and still continue to attract scientists who are working in the following application areas: monitoring physical phenomena, such as fire, earthquakes, pollution; gathering information in military operations, such as reconnaissance and surveillance; gathering information for healthcare systems; building and construction safety; manufacturing machinery performance; *etc* [1,2].

WSNs have specific challenges due to low transmission bandwidth, constrained power supplies, tiny memory sizes and, finally, limited power [3,4]. This brings the fact that the security solutions devised for traditional networks cannot be applied to WSNs directly [5]. Therefore, new ideas and approaches (algorithms) are needed in order to increase the security of WSNs. In this paper, we propose security enhancements (especially on intrusion detection) for WSNs that are deployed in a hierarchical topology (clustered).

Intrusion is an active (e.g., packet dropping) or passive (e.g., eavesdropping) activity in a network without having permission to do so. While securing networks, "intrusion prevention" constitutes the first and "intrusion detection" constitutes the second line of defense. If authorized network members represent any misbehavior (e.g., packet dropping), intrusion prevention systems cannot stop this activity. Therefore intrusion detection systems come into play.

A typical hierarchical WSN consists of clusters, as shown in Figure 1. Each cluster is a group of interconnected sensor nodes with a dedicated node called the cluster head (CH). CHs are responsible for managing the member (subordinate) sensor nodes; such as scheduling of the medium access, dissemination of the control messages and, most importantly, data aggregation. Clustering methods devised for WSNs are out of the scope of this paper. Interested readers may refer to Abbasi and Younis's work [6] and Butun *et al.*'s work [7], as they provide thorough literature surveys in the mentioned field.

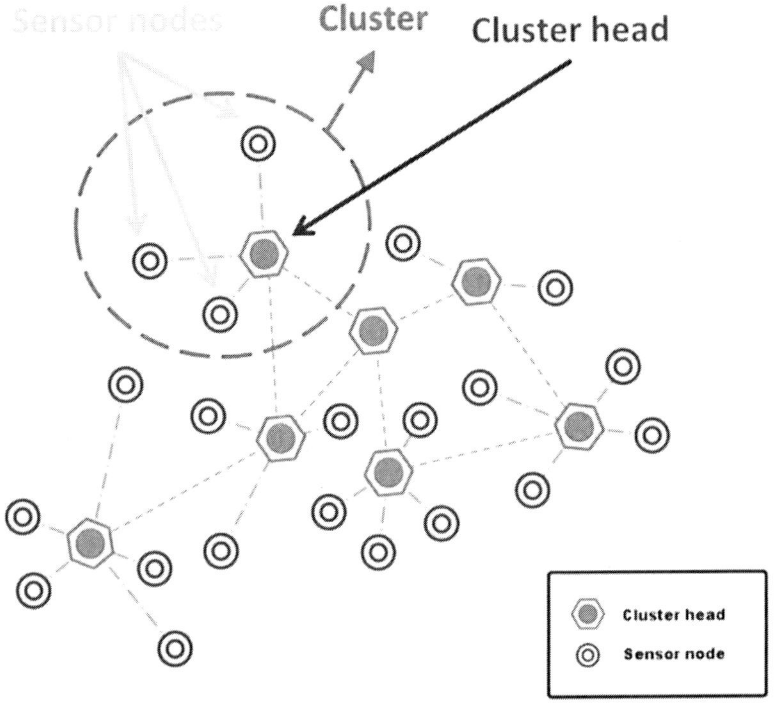

Figure 1. A typical clustered WSN.

In some practical configurations of hierarchical WSNs, CHs may also form a higher level of cluster in which one of the CHs is assigned as the CH (Level 2) of all other CHs (Level 1). This leveled architecture is shown in Figure 2. In a leveled and clustered WSN; the detection of abnormal behaviors of bottom level nodes (sensor nodes) is not enough to detect all of the intrusions of the network. This is because of the fact that CHs and upper level clusters may also be compromised. Following the deployment of the nodes and the formation of the clusters and the CHs, CHs may constitute a single point of failure. Therefore, in order to have a complete intrusion detection system (IDS) for hierarchical WSNs, intrusions through CHs need to be detected, as well.

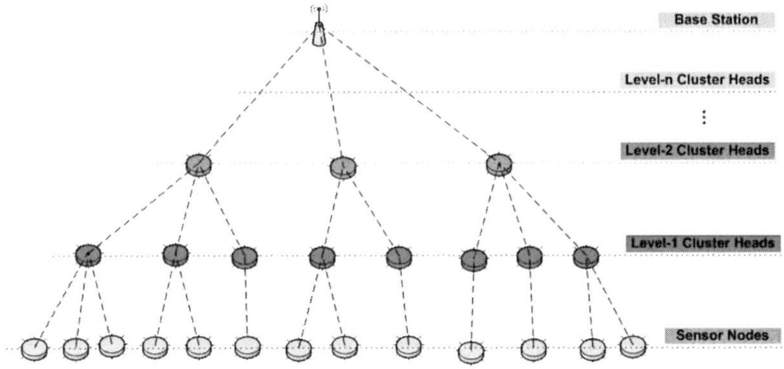

Figure 2. Multi-level clustering for our proposed IDS framework.

It is important to emphasize that our focus in this research is on the hierarchical WSNs, meaning that sensor nodes are gathered into groups called "clusters". Here, we will discuss only the references that are directly related to our paper. In the IDS approaches proposed by [8,9,10], the direction of the alert propagation is from subordinates through CHs, leaving the following question unanswered for the detection part: "What happens if a malicious upper level CH (Level 2) drops the packet that is coming from a member (subordinate) node (Level 1) and is about to alert an upper level CH (Level 3) concerning the misbehavior of the mentioned CH (Level 2)?". This is an open gap in the security of the mentioned schemes. In the IDS approaches proposed by Agah *et al.* [11,12], only one of the clusters of the network is monitored at a time. This leaves the rest of the network vulnerable. In the IDS approach of Su *et al.* [13], both downward and upward protections are provided. This means that CHs monitor subordinate nodes for downward protection and subordinate nodes monitor CHs for upward protection. However, the proposed scheme uses symmetric key cryptography, and therefore, new nodes cannot be added to the network after the deployment, which makes the proposed scheme impracticable for use.

For our IDS framework, we adopt the idea of downward and upward protection proposed by Su *et al.* [13]. For our downward (D)-IDS scheme, we adopted the "isolation table" concept that was suggested by Chen *et al.* [9] and also the "watchdog" concept that was suggested by Krontiris *et al.* [14]. For our upward (U)-IDS scheme, we adopted the "monitoring group" concept that was presented by Su *et al.* [13]. For both D-IDS and U-IDS schemes, as a detection algorithm, we adopt the "sequential probability ratio test (SPRT)" algorithm that was proposed by Brown and

Du [15]. Finally, for the decision making step, the "decision engine" algorithm is used, which was proposed by Patcha *et al.* [16]. Table 1 provides an overview of our proposed IDS framework. Our proposed framework is one of a kind; hence, it provides all of the required building steps of an IDS scheme for hierarchical WSNs.

Table 1. Our proposed IDS framework for WSNs.

Proposed IDS Framework		
	D-IDS	**U-IDS**
Detection methodology	Isolation table [9] Watchdog [14]	Monitoring group [13]
Detection algorithm	SPRT [15]	
Decision making	Decision engine [16]	

The rest of the paper is organized as follows: Section 2 presents the system model of the proposed IDS framework. Section 3 and Section 4 present the details of the D-IDS and U-IDS schemes, respectively. Details of the SPRT that is used in our proposed D-IDS and U-IDS schemes is presented in Section 5.1, whereas Section 5.2 summarizes the decision making process following the SPRT for each scheme. In Section 6, the effect of cluster size (maximum hops between cluster head and cluster members) on the detection probability of our intrusion detection system is investigated, when the IDS is located on the CH (D-IDS). In the reverse manner, in Section 7, the effect of the total number of monitoring nodes on the detection probability of a malicious cluster head is investigated, when the IDS is located on the member nodes of a cluster (U-IDS). Finally, Section 8 concludes the paper.

2. SYSTEM MODEL

As the name implies, the proposed IDS is based on multi-level clustering, meaning that Level 1 CHs are the CHs for sensor nodes and at the same time subordinates for Level 2 CHs, in the same manner, Level 2 CHs are the CHs for Level 1 CHs and at the same time subordinates for Level 3 CHs, and so on, as shown in Figure 2.

For the selection of the cluster heads, our proposed power and connectivity-aware clustering algorithm (for details, refer to [7,17]) can be used as follows:

- Level 1 CHs would be selected by selecting the maximum hop size as "1".
- Level 2 CHs would be selected by selecting the maximum hop size as "2"....
- Level-*n* CHs would be selected by selecting the maximum hop size as "*n*".

Our proposed IDS framework provides two types of intrusion detection approaches for the presented multi-level clustered WSN:

1. Downwards intrusion detection system (D-IDS): CHs are responsible for monitoring all of the activities of their subordinates by using watchdogs and recording their activities in a table called the "isolation table".
2. Upwards intrusion detection system (U-IDS): A certain number of (monitoring group size,*m*) subordinates coordinately monitor the activity of the CH and report any abnormal activity to an upper level CH.

Intrusions through subordinates of the network are detected by the D-IDS, and intrusions through CHs of the network are detected by the U-IDS. In this way, our overall proposed IDS framework (D-IDS and U-IDS) covers the entire network in terms of detecting intrusions.

3. DOWNWARDS INTRUSION DETECTION SYSTEM (D-IDS)

CHs hold watchdog counters with abnormality counters for each subordinate. Since the intrusion detection direction is from CHs towards subordinates, we call this scheme D-IDS. For example, consider the network shown in Figure 3. Here, Node A is the Level 1 CH of the remaining nodes. Therefore, it has a watchdog counter (that counts the pre-defined abnormalities) for each subordinate node, namely Node 1, Node 2, ..., Node 6.

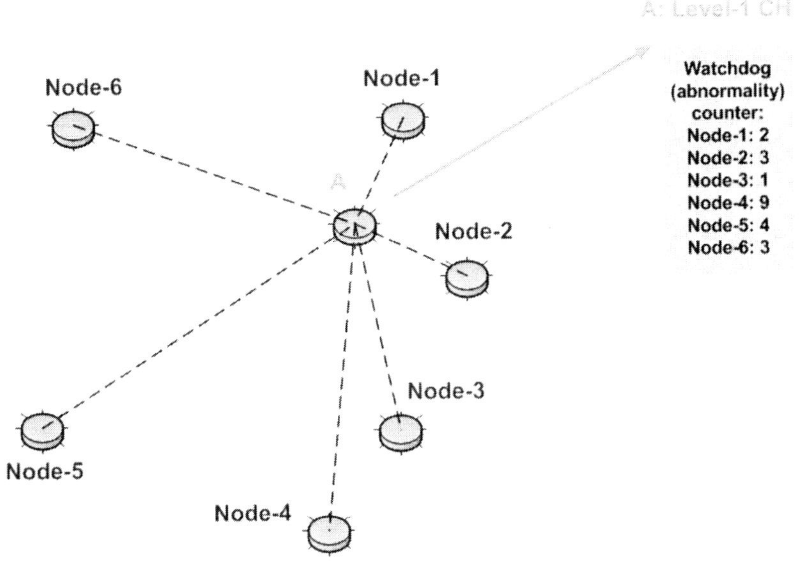

Figure 3. The usage of the watchdog counter concept for our D-IDS.

Whenever any watchdog counter reaches a certain threshold, the associated node is flagged and included in the isolation table. Then, as a mitigation step, any communication with this node is blocked (packets to be forwarded to this node, as well as the packets coming from this node are dropped). For example, consider again the same network shown in Figure 3. However, this time, assume that the watchdog counter of Node 4 is "10" and also assume that the threshold level for the watchdog counters is "10", as well. Since the watchdog counter of Node 4 has reached the threshold, Node 4 is marked as an abnormal node in the isolation table, as shown in Figure 4. Then, finally, all communications with Node 4 are blocked by the Level 1 CH (Node A).

The mentioned D-IDS is applicable to all levels. For example, consider the network shown inFigure 5. This time, Node A is a subordinate of Node X (an upper level node, Level 2), just like Node B and Node C. Node X holds watchdog counters for the abnormal behaviors of Node A, Node B and Node C. As mentioned above, if any watchdog counter reaches a certain threshold, the associated entry in the isolation table will be marked, and a mitigation technique is issued (revocation of the node from the network).

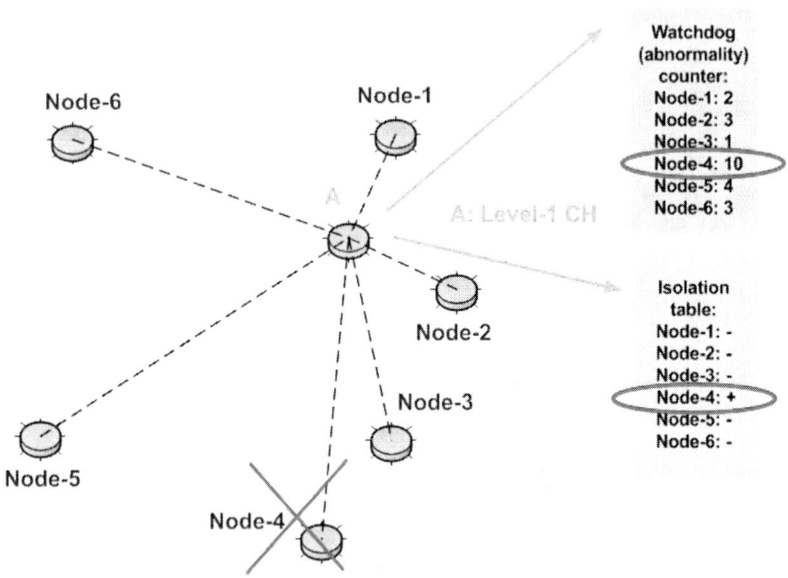

Figure 4. The usage of the isolation table concept in our D-IDS.

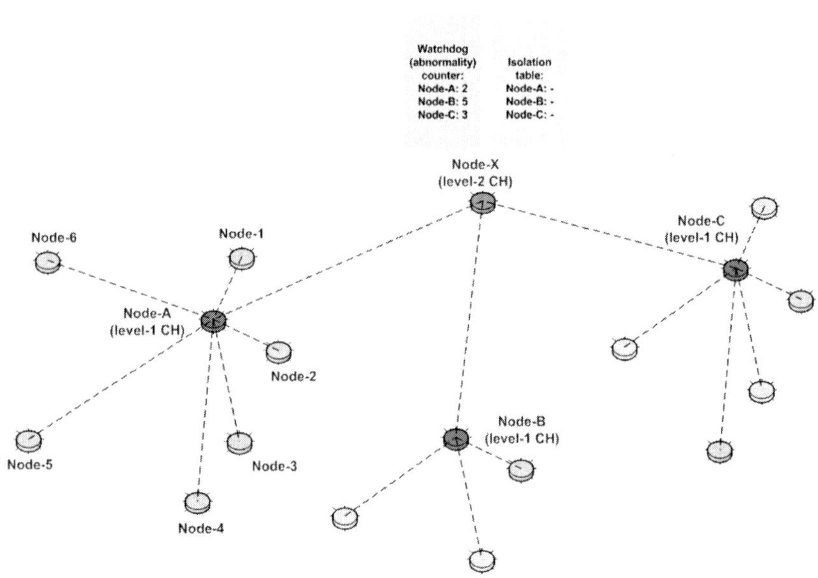

Figure 5. Implementation of D-IDS for upper levels of the network.

4. UPWARDS INTRUSION DETECTION SYSTEM (U-IDS)

A certain number of (monitoring group size, m) subordinates coordinately monitor the activity of the CH and report any abnormal activity to an upper level CH. Abnormal activity is determined when the watchdog counter reaches or exceeds a certain threshold. In accordance with the coordination concept, the total value of the abnormal cases is calculated by the logical "OR(+)" operation; individual watchdog results of each monitoring node are OR'ed with the rest of the watchdog results. As a result, the final decision associated with the abnormal behavior of the CH is concluded by the coordinated effort of all monitoring nodes.

The rationale for using the OR operation is as follows: In some specific time interval, some of the monitoring nodes might be in "sleep mode", and therefore, these nodes might miss the abnormal behavior of the CH. However, in that specific time frame, the other monitoring nodes possibly would be in "awake mode" and catch the incidence. Therefore, after a certain period of time (update interval), each monitoring node sends its individual result to the rest of the monitoring nodes, and a final decision is made.

In order to catch most of the incidences (high probability of detection), the sleep/awake cycles of the monitoring nodes should be assigned accordingly. For instance, if there are three monitoring nodes in a cluster and if one of them is in sleep mode in a specific time frame, then in order to catch the incidences, the rest of the monitoring nodes should be in awake mode.

Consider the cluster of a network shown in Figure 6. Here, Node A is again the Level 1 CH of the remaining nodes. Subordinate nodes are, namely, Node 1, Node 2, ..., Node 5 and Node 6. Among those, Node 1, Node 3 and Node 5 constitute the monitoring group. Their responsibility is to monitor the abnormal activity of Node A (consider that Node A is showing abnormal behavior for all time frames t1,t2,t3,t4). At a specific time frame, if the monitoring nodes are in awake mode and detect any abnormality, they update their watchdog counters, accordingly. For example, at the specific time frame of t1, Node 1 was in sleep mode, and therefore, it was not able to detect any abnormality. However, Node 3 and Node 5 were in awake mode, detected an abnormality of Node A and updated their own watchdog counters, accordingly (associated with the time frame of t1). At the end of the time frame t4, it is observed that out of four instances, Node 1 detected two instances, Node 3 three instances and Node 5 two instances.

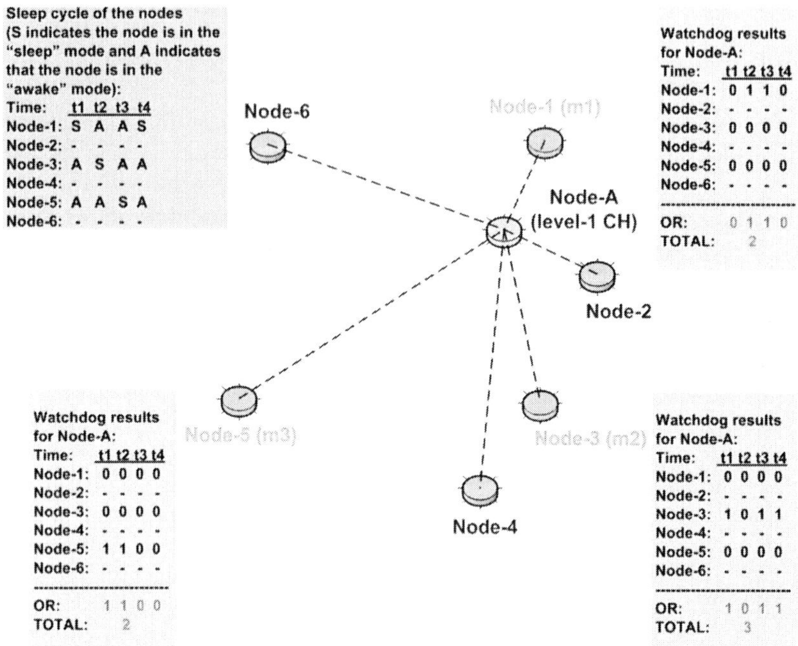

Figure 6. The usage of the monitoring group concept in our U-IDS.

The monitoring nodes share the entries of their watchdog counters among each other in certain time intervals. In the specific case shown in Figure 6, assume that the monitoring nodes share the entries of their watchdog counters after the time frame t4. This is shown in Figure 7. Here, as a result of the arrival of the watchdog counter entries from Node 3 and Node 5, Node 1 (*m1*) updates the watchdog counter entries associated with them, and finally, the total number of encounters is calculated by the OR operation, as mentioned earlier. In accordance with the updates from Node 3 and Node 5, Node 1 has refreshed its watchdog counter and calculated the total number of incidences as "4". In the same manner, Node 3 and Node 5 will update their watchdog counter entries and calculate the total number of incidences as "4".

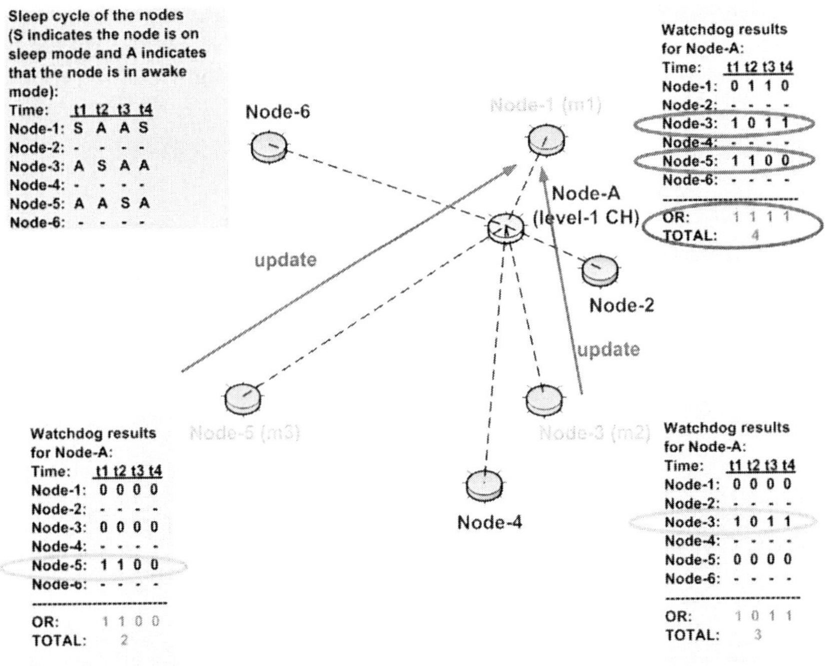

Figure 7. Watchdog update propagation in our U-IDS.

After each update interval, monitoring nodes check their updated counter values. Whenever their watchdog counter reaches a certain threshold ("15" in our example), they send an encrypted alert message to an upper level CH. The reason for the encryption is to hide the alert message from the CH that is under investigation (Node A in our example).

These alert messages are sent directly to the upper level cluster head. In order to do so, we assume that the radios of the nodes have two different operation modes: "normal mode" and "alert mode". In the normal mode, since CHs are generally one hop away, the radios operate to transmit in a short range. This energy-saving mode helps nodes to increase their life time. In the alert mode, the radios operate to transmit in a long range. In this way, without the help of intermediate nodes, a monitoring node can directly send the alert messages to an upper level CH.

Consider the case shown in Figure 8. Here, as mentioned above, in each update interval, each monitoring node updates the other monitoring nodes and also check its watchdog counter. After a certain period of time, watchdog counters of all of the monitoring nodes reach the threshold value of "15". Therefore, they change their radio's mode of operation to "alert mode" and send an encrypted alert message directly to an upper level CH, namely a Level 2 CH. In this specific example, Node 1 has a higher probability to alert Level 2 CH, since its location is closer than Node 3 and Node 5.

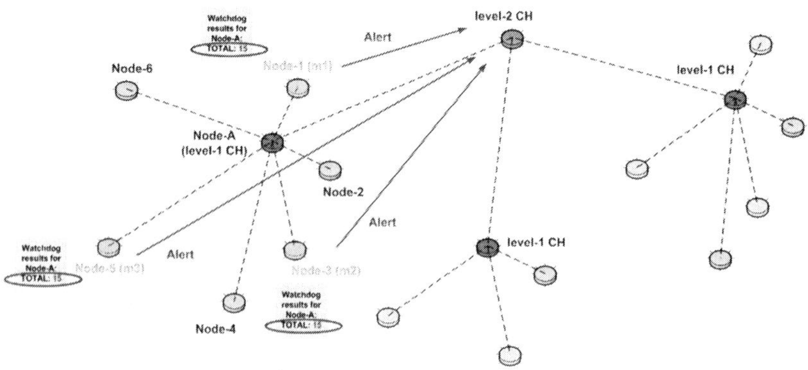

Figure 8. Alert propagation towards upper levels in our U-IDS.

5. DETECTION OF DOS ATTACKS IN WSNS BY USING SPRT

Wald's sequential probability ratio test (SPRT) for the detection of selective forwarding attacks (a denial of service (DoS) attack in the network layer of WSNs) was used in [15]. This method detects intentional packet drops with a high probability of detection rate. Therefore, it can be applied to any packet drop attack towards the security of WSNs, for example DoS attacks in the network layer (black hole attacks, sinkhole attacks, *etc.*).

5.1. SPRT

According to SPRT, a random variable p is used to define the status of packet forwarding, where 0 denotes successful transmission of the packet (good) and 1 denotes a packet drop (bad). p is calculated as the percentage of dropped packets over all packets to be transmitted. p′is defined as the acceptable probability of dropped packets. A node is considered as legitimate if p≤p′ holds, and it is considered as compromised if p>p′ holds. p0<p′<p1 defines the "gray region" for the decision making, where the decision is inconclusive regarding the legitimacy of the node. Figure 9 illustrates the decision boundaries for the SPRT, namely; white, gray and black regions.

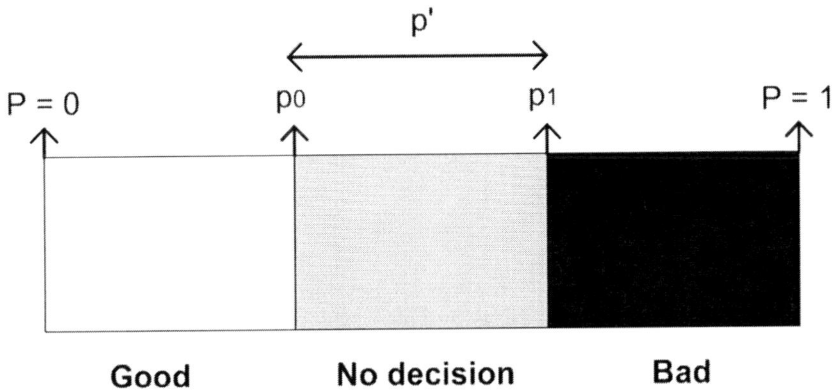

Figure 9. Thresholds for the decision making.

Note that 1,2,...,m represents the sample number. The ultimate goal is to minimize the missed detection rate, α=P1(|Dm=0) and the false alarm rate, β=P0(|Dm=1), where Dm stands for the decision at step *m* (P1 denotes that a failure occurred and the packet is dropped; P0 denotes that the packet is transmitted successfully; whereas, (Dm=0) means that the decision of the SPRT for the packet transmission is positive (the packet is concluded to be transmitted); and (Dm=0) means that the decision is negative (the packet is concluded to be dropped)). At the same time, we need to achieve this in the minimum number of samples (mmin). SPRT calculates this number as shown in Equation (1):

$$m_{min} = \frac{L(p)\log(\beta) + (1 - L(p))\log(\alpha)}{p\log(\frac{p_1}{p_0}) + (1 - p)\log(\frac{1-p_1}{1-p_0})} \qquad (1)$$

where L(p) is calculated as shown in Equation (2),

$$L(p) = \frac{\left(\frac{1-\beta}{\alpha}\right)^h - 1}{\left(\frac{1-\beta}{\alpha}\right)^h - \left(\frac{\beta}{1-\alpha}\right)^{-h}} \tag{2}$$

and *h* can be determined by solving Equation (3):

$$p = \frac{1 - \left(\frac{1-p_1}{1-p_0}\right)^h}{\left(\frac{p_1}{p_0}\right)^h - \left(\frac{1-p_1}{1-p_0}\right)^h} \tag{3}$$

After setting all of the parameters (p0,p1,α,β) and collecting *m* samples, the acceptance threshold (am) and the rejection threshold (rm) can be found by using Equations (4) and (5), respectively:

$$a_m = \frac{\log(\frac{\beta}{1-\alpha})}{\log(\frac{p_1}{p_0}) - \log(\frac{1-p_1}{1-p_0})} + m\frac{\log(\frac{1-p_0}{1-p_1})}{\log(\frac{p_1}{p_0}) - \log(\frac{1-p_1}{1-p_0})} \tag{4}$$

$$r_m = \frac{\log(\frac{1-\beta}{\alpha})}{\log(\frac{p_1}{p_0}) - \log(\frac{1-p_1}{1-p_0})} + m\frac{\log(\frac{1-p_0}{1-p_1})}{\log(\frac{p_1}{p_0}) - \log(\frac{1-p_1}{1-p_0})} \tag{5}$$

Let ⌈am⌉ denote the upper bound for am and ⌊rm⌋ denote the lower bound for rm. For each sample, ⌈am⌉ and ⌊rm⌋ should be revised according to new values of am and rm, respectively.

Let dm denote the number of packets dropped in the *m* number of samples. Then, the SPRT test needs to be continuously performed as long as Equation (6) holds:

$$\lceil a_m \rceil < d_m < \lfloor r_m \rfloor \tag{6}$$

At each round of the SPRT test, there are three possible outcomes based on the result of the comparison shown in Equation (6):

1. If dm≤⌈am⌉, then the conclusion is that the node is legitimate.
2. If ⌈am⌉<dm<⌊rm⌋, then the SPRT test needs to be continued.
3. ⌊rm⌋≤dm, then the conclusion is that the node is compromised.

5.2. Decision Making Process of IDS Following the SPRT

According to Patcha *et al.* [16], the decision engine (*i.e.*, decision making algorithm) of an IDS concludes either one of four decisions (with non-zero probabilities) as a result of the decision making process over a triggered alarm (event):

- Intrusive, but not anomalous (false-negative): there is an intrusion into the system, but IDS fails to detect it and concludes the event to be a non-anomalous one.
- Not intrusive, but anomalous (false-positive): there is no intrusion into the system, but IDS mistakenly concludes a normal event to be an anomalous one.
- Not intrusive and not anomalous (true-negative): there is no intrusion into the system, and IDS concludes the event to be an non-anomalous one.
- Intrusive and anomalous (true-positive): there is an intrusion into the system, and IDS concludes the event to be an anomalous one.

Figure 10 summarizes the mentioned possibilities regarding the legitimacy assessment of a node. Eventually, we expect the selected decision making algorithm to generate a greater percentage of true-positives and true-negatives and a lesser percentage of false-positives and false-negatives.

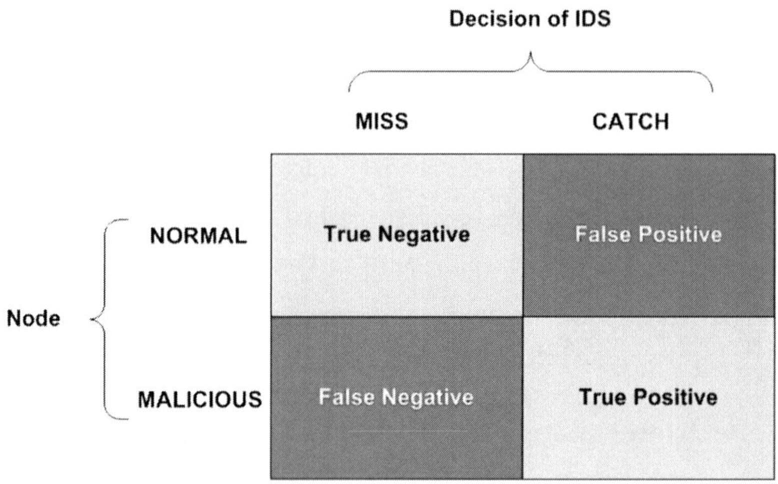

Figure 10. All possible detection results of an IDS.

6. THE EFFECT OF CLUSTER SIZE ON THE DETECTION PROBABILITY OF THE D-IDS

In this section, we followed Shin *et al.*'s approach [8] to evaluate the effect of clustering on the detection probability of D-IDS. Our main focus is to calculate the effect of the maximum distance (hops) between CH and cluster members on the intrusion detection probability.

In Figure 11, a WSN is divided into clusters. The maximum distance of each cluster is two hops, meaning that in a cluster, a CH (denoted as red nodes in the figure) is a maximum of two hops away from its member nodes. As an example, node *A* is a CH, and nodes *B* and *C* are its member nodes. A two-hop cluster does not mean that node *C* is in direct communication range of *A* (as we can see in the figure, *C* is outside of the communication range of *A*), but it means that *A* can connect and monitor the behavior of *C* through node *B* (since *B* is in communication range of both *A* and *C*, *B* performs as a relaying node between nodes *A* and *C*).

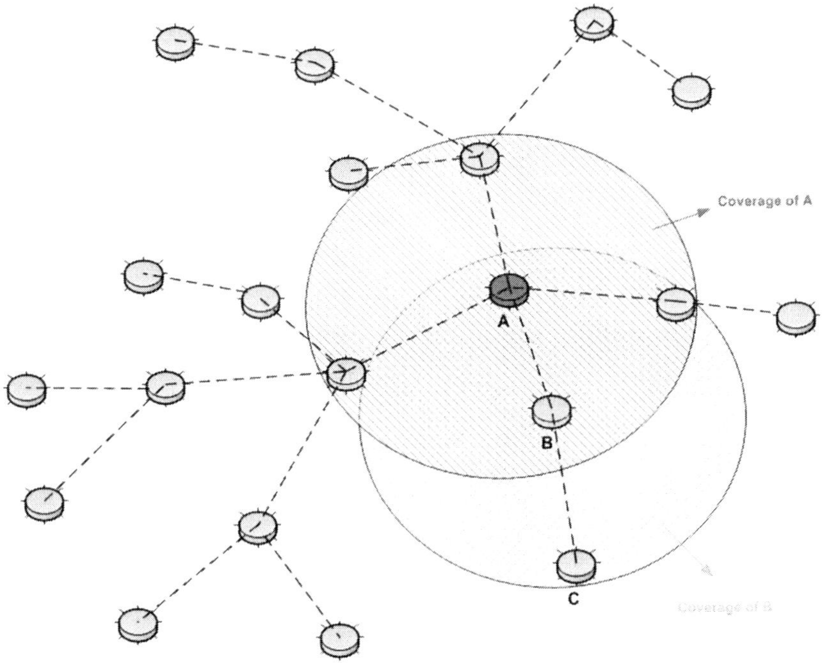

Figure 11. An example of a clustered network with a maximum hop distance of two.

CHs (such as node A) can use indirect monitoring (A monitors node C through node B) through intermediate nodes (such as node B) to detect intrusions that would happen at the end nodes (such as node C). However, this kind of monitoring definitely will increase the network overhead. Besides, the reliability of the intermediate nodes, such as the sleep rate and error rate, would certainly change the overall performance of the intrusion detection system.

Let us define the average sleep rate and the average error rate of all of the nodes (except the CH and the malicious node) to be s and e, respectively. Here, the error rate is due to packet losses caused by transmission problems, such as packet collisions. We assume the probability distributions of these random variables (s and e) to be Gaussian with means $0 \leq E(s) \leq 1$ and $0 \leq E(e) \leq 1$ and variances σ_s^2 and σ_e^2.

If a CH detects a malicious node that is located at j-hops away from the CH in an i-hops cluster, where i is the cluster size in terms of the number of hops, and if $0 \leq j \leq i$ holds, then the detection probability (pi,j) of each node is given by:

$$p_{i,j} = [(1 - E(s))(1 - E(e))]^{j-1} \tag{7}$$

In Table 2, different values of pi,j are shown as *i* and *j* are varied. Here, note that the value of *j* cannot exceed the value of *i*.

Table 2. Detection probability (pi,j) for different values of *i* and *j*.

	$j=1$	$j=2$	$j=3$	$j=4$
$i=1$	1	N/A	N/A	N/A
$i=2$	1	$(1-E(s))(1-E(e))$	N/A	N/A
$i=3$	1	$(1-E(s))(1-E(e))$	$[(1-E(s))(1-E(e))]^2$	N/A
$i=4$	1	$(1-E(s))(1-E(e))$	$[(1-E(s))(1-E(e))]^2$	$[(1-E(s))(1-E(e))]^3$

Finally, the average detection probability (Pi) of the *i*-hops cluster is given by:

$$P_i = \frac{1}{i}\sum_{j=1}^{i} p_{i,j} = \frac{1}{i}\sum_{j=1}^{i} \{(1 - E(s))(1 - E(e))\}^{j-1} \tag{8}$$

Figure 12 and Figure 13 show different values of Pi as the maximum number of hops (*i*) changes according to Equation (8). There are five plots in each figure, for various values of E(e) in Figure 12 and E(s) in Figure 13, respectively.

In Figure 12, E(s) is fixed at E(s)=0.6, meaning that the average sleep rate of the nodes is 60%. Each plot represents a different value of E(e) with a variance of 10%. From the plots, it can be observed that as the packet loss rate of each node increases, the average intrusion detection probability of the D-IDS decreases, which is expected. As the error rate increases, it becomes difficult for the D-IDS to determine if the loss of a packet was caused by a channel error (natural causes) or an outside (intruder) effect.

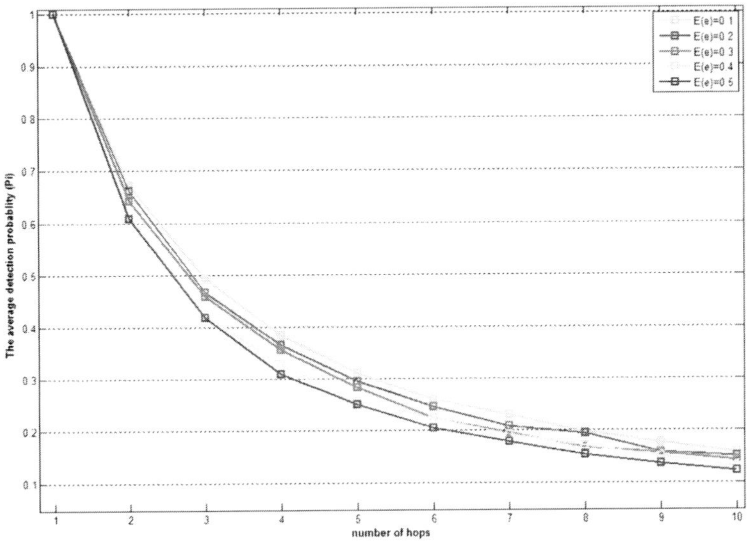

Figure 12. The effect of cluster size on the detection probability of the D-IDS for various packet loss rates while the sleep rate is 60%.

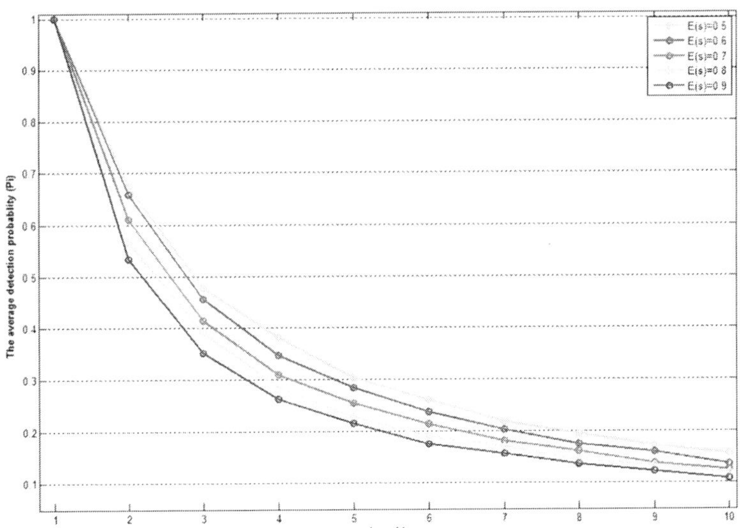

Figure 13. The effect of cluster size on the detection probability of the D-IDS for various sleep rates while the packet loss rate is 30%.

In Figure 13, E(e) is fixed at E(e)=0.3, meaning that the average packet drop rate of the nodes is 30%. Each plot represents a different value of E(s) with a variance of 10%. From the plots, it can be observed that as the sleep rate of each node increases, the average intrusion detection probability of the D-IDS decreases, which is also expected. As the sleep rate increases, the chance of the D-IDS for catching an intrusion decreases. Hence, the fewer the number of nodes that are awake in the network, the less intrusions will be caught by the D-IDS. In other words, an intrusion that would be caught by an intermediate node would be simply missed, because the node was sleeping at the exact time that the intrusion happened.

From the plots of Figure 12 and Figure 13, we can conclude that as the number of the maximum range of a cluster (maximum number of hops from a CH and a member node in a cluster) increases, the average intrusion detection probability of the D-IDS decreases. In other words, indirect monitoring of the intrusions has a bad effect on the overall intrusion detection probability of the IDS.

7. THE EFFECT OF MONITORING GROUP SIZE ON THE DETECTION PROBABILITY OF THE U-IDS

In this section, we follow Yang *et al.*'s work [18] to investigate the effect monitoring group size (*m*) on the detection probability of malicious cluster heads in our U-IDS. Here, we assume that *m* of the member nodes of a cluster have an intrusion detection scheme that is running in a collaborative manner. Thus, cluster members periodically give a decision regarding the trustworthiness of a cluster head.

Consider the clustered WSN (one-hop distance) shown in Figure 14. Node *A* (marked in red color) is the cluster head, and it has 15 member nodes, which are in the radio coverage of *A*. Among these member nodes, four of them ($m = 4$; marked in green color and denoted as m1, m2, m3 and m4) are collaborating to monitor the activity of *A*.

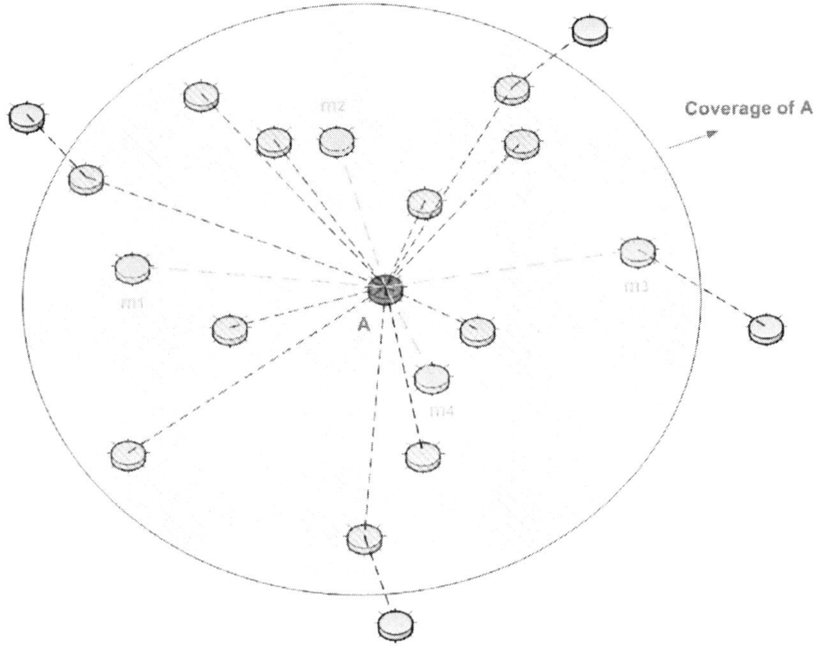

Figure 14. A typical 15-node clustered WSN (one-hop distance).

In order to calculate the effect of monitoring group size (*m*) on the detection probability of a malicious cluster head, assume that the size of a cluster is *N* (15 in our case) and the probability of each member node to detect the malicious cluster head is Pd. Then, the total probability of the malicious cluster head to be detected PD, as a result of the collaboration size (= monitoring group size = *m* number of the nodes) is calculated as shown in Equation (9):

$$P_D = \sum_{k=m}^{N} \binom{N}{k} P_d^k (1 - P_d)^{N-k} \qquad (9)$$

Figure 15 shows the change of the overall detection probability (PD) with respect to the collaboration size for various values of Pd, for a cluster size of 15 (N=15). Accordingly, it can be observed that collaboration is useful in increasing the overall detection rate (PD). As the collaboration size increases, overall detection probability increases and approaches one (100%).

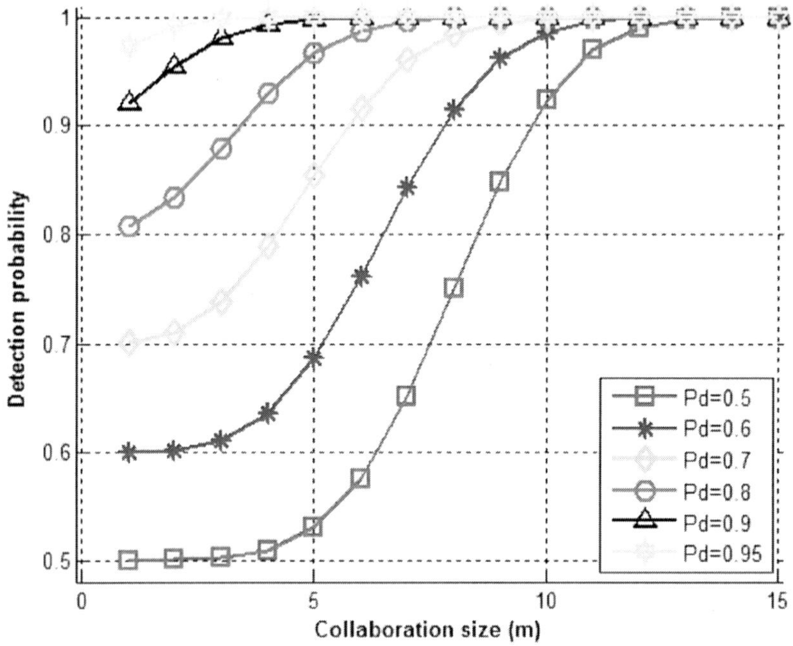

Figure 15. Detection probability (PD) *vs.* collaboration size (*m*) for various values of Pd.

Again, assume that the size of a cluster is *N* and that the probability of each member node to fail (false-alarm) in detecting the malicious cluster head is Pf. Then, the total probability of the malicious cluster head goes undetected (false-alarm) PF, as a result of the collaboration size (*m*number of the nodes) being calculated as shown in Equation (10):

$$P_F = \sum_{k=m}^{N} \binom{N}{k} (1 - P_f)^k (P_f)^{N-k} \tag{10}$$

Figure 16 shows the change of overall false-alarm probability (PF) with respect to the collaboration size for various values of Pf, for a cluster size of 15 (N=15). Accordingly, it can be observed that collaboration is useful in decreasing the overall false-alarm rate (PF). As the collaboration size increases, the overall false-alarm probability decreases and approaches zero (0%).

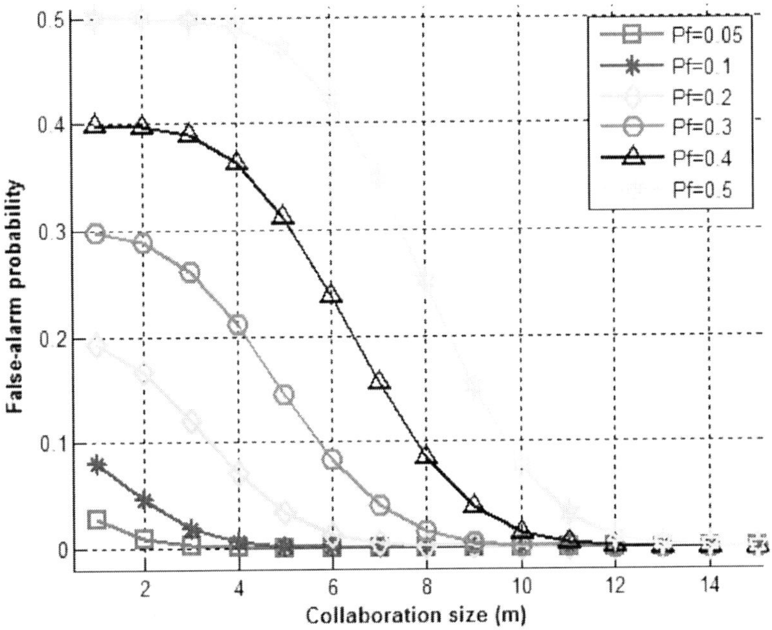

Figure 16. False-alarm probability (PF) *vs.* collaboration size (*m*) for various values of Pf.

8. CONCLUSIONS AND SUGGESTIONS FOR FUTURE RESEARCH

This work presents an intrusion detection system (IDS) framework based on multi-level clustering for hierarchical wireless sensor networks. Our proposed IDS framework provides two types of intrusion detection approaches, namely "downwards-IDS" to detect the abnormal behavior (intrusion) of the subordinate (member) nodes and "upwards-IDS" to detect the abnormal behavior of the cluster heads.

The effect of cluster size (maximum hops between the cluster head and cluster members) on the detection probability of a malicious node was evaluated, when the IDS is located on the CH (downwards-IDS). In the same manner, the effect of the total number of monitoring nodes on the detection probability of a malicious cluster head was evaluated, when the IDS is located on the member nodes of a cluster (upwards-IDS).

There is a trade-off between "maximum hop count" and "intrusion detection probability". As the maximum hop count increases, the intrusion detection probability (of an IDS) decreases and *vice versa*. According to the results of the analytical calculations presented in Section 6, the following recommendations are provided for the maximum hop count: Figure 12 and Figure 13suggest keeping the maximum hop distance lower than "4". The maximum hop distance should be selected as "2" or "3", depending on the "sleep rate" of the nodes and the "average packet loss rate" of the network (1.0 represents 100% probability of a node to be sleeping or a packet to be lost): if the "sleep rate" and/or "average packet loss rate" are higher than 0.7, then the maximum hop distance should be selected as "2"; otherwise, it should be selected as "3".

As in most technologies, nothing comes for free. By using a greater number of monitoring members, higher detection rates and lower false alarm rates can be achieved. The cost for this achievement is the loss of scarce resources (e.g., energy). The security solutions should bring minimum extra packets to the transmission, since every extra packet causes the depletion of the batteries faster and causes the network to have less life time. Therefore, a proper trade-off point needs to be determined in finding the right number for the monitoring group size (m).

As Figure 15 in Section 7 suggests, out of 15 nodes in each cluster, by selecting $m = 7$, a very satisfactory detection probability (>95%) can be achieved if the individual detection probabilities are higher than 70%. Again, out of 15 nodes in each cluster and for the same monitoring group size ($m = 7$), Figure 16 suggests that the false-alarm probability will be lower than 5% if the individual false-alarm rates are lower than 30%.

By evaluating the performance of our proposed IDS algorithms analytically, we were able to demonstrate their benefits in detecting the intrusions towards WSNs. Evaluation of the proposed algorithms via simulation tools (ns-3 [19], *etc.*) is left as future work.

ACKNOWLEDGMENTS

This research was supported by the Basic Science Research Program through the National Research Foundation of Korea (NSF), funded by the Ministry of Education, Science and Technology (2012R1A1A2044504).

AUTHOR CONTRIBUTIONS

The work has been primarily conducted by Ismail Butun. Extensive discussions about the algorithms and techniques presented in this paper have been carried between the author and In-Ho Ra among with Ravi Sankar in recent years.

APPENDIX

Table A1 summarizes the abbreviations used in the paper.

Table A1. List of abbreviations.

CH	cluster head
D-IDS	downwards IDS
DoS	denial of service
IDS	intrusion detection system
SPRT	sequential probability ratio test
U-IDS	upwards IDS
WSN	wireless sensor network

REFERENCES

1. Akyildiz, I.F.; Su, W.; Sankarasubramaniam, Y.; Cayirci, E. A survey on sensor networks.*IEEE Commun. Mag.* **2002**, *40*, 102–114.
2. Butun, I.; Morgera, S.; Sankar, R. A survey of intrusion detection systems in wireless sensor networks. *IEEE Commun. Surv. Tutor.* **2014**, *16*, 266–282.
3. Akyildiz, I.F.; Su, W.; Sankarasubramaniam, Y.; Cayirci, E. Wireless sensor networks: A survey. *Comput. Netw.* **2002**, *38*, 393–422.

4. Akyildiz, I.F.; Kasimoglu, I.H. Wireless sensor and actor networks: Research challenges.*Ad Hoc Netw.* **2004**, *2*, 351–367.
5. Butun, I.; Wang, Y.; Lee, Y.; Sankar, R. Intrusion prevention with two-level user authentication in heterogeneous wireless sensor networks. *Int. J. Secur. Netw.* **2012**, *7*, 107–121.
6. Abbasi, A.A.; Younis, M. A survey on clustering algorithms for wireless sensor networks. *Comput. Commun.* **2007**, *30*, 2826–2841.
7. Butun, I.; Ra, I.H.; Sankar, R. PCAC: Power-and Connectivity-Aware Clustering for Wireless Sensor Networks. *EURASIP J. Wirel. Commun. Netw.* **2015**, *1*, 1–15.
8. Shin, S.; Kwon, T.; Jo, G.Y.; Park, Y.; Rhy, H. An experimental study of hierarchical intrusion detection for wireless industrial sensor networks. *IEEE Trans. Ind. Inform.* **2010**,*6*, 744–757.
9. Chen, R.C.; Hsieh, C.F.; Huang, Y.F. A new method for intrusion detection on hierarchical wireless sensor networks. In Proceedings of the 3rd International Conference on Ubiquitous Information Management and Communication, Suwon, Korea, 15–16 January 2009; pp. 238–245.
10. Rajasegarar, S.; Leckie, C.; Palaniswami, M.; Bezdek, J.C. Distributed anomaly detection in wireless sensor networks. In Proceedings of the 10th Singapore International Conference on Communication Systems (ICCS), Singapore, 30 October–1 November 2006; pp. 1–5.
11. Agah, A.; Das, S.K.; Basu, K.; Asadi, M. Intrusion detection in sensor networks: A non-cooperative game approach. In Proceedings of the 3rd Singapore International Symposium on Network Computing and Applications (NCA), Cambridge, MA, USA, 30 August–1 September 2004; pp. 343–346.
12. Agah, A.; Das, S.K. Preventing DoS attacks in wireless sensor networks: A repeated game theory approach. *Int. J. Netw. Secur.* **2007**, *5*, 145–153.
13. Su, C.C.; Chang, K.M.; Kuo, Y.H.; Horng, M.F. The new intrusion prevention and detection approaches for clustering-based sensor networks [wireless sensor networks]. In Proceedings of the 2005 IEEE Wireless Communications and Networking Conference, New Orleans, LA, USA, 13–17 March 2005; pp. 1927–1932.

14. Krontiris, I.; Dimitriou, T.; Giannetsos, T.; Mpasoukos, M. Intrusion detection of sinkhole attacks in wireless sensor networks. *Algorithm. Asp. Wirel. Sens. Netw.* **2008**, 150–161.

15. Brown, J.; Du, X. Detection of selective forwarding attacks in heterogeneous sensor networks. In Proceedings of the IEEE International Conference on Communications (ICC), Beijing, China, 19–23 May 2008; pp. 1583–1587.

16. Patcha, A.; Park, J.M. An overview of anomaly detection techniques: Existing solutions and latest technological trends. *Comput. Netw.* **2007**, *51*, 3448–3470.

17. Butun, I. Prevention and Detection of Intrusions in Wireless Sensor Networks. Ph.D. Thesis, University of South Florida, Tampa, FL, USA, 2013.

18. Yang, H.; Shu, J.; Meng, X.; Lu, S. SCAN: Self-organized network-layer security in mobile ad hoc networks. *IEEE J. Sel. Areas Commun.* **2006**, *24*, 261–273.

19. ns-3—Network Simulator and Emulator. Available online: https://www. nsnam.org/ (accessed on 15 April 2015).

4

CHAPTER

DETECTION OF INTELLIGENT INTRUDERS IN WIRELESS SENSOR NETWORKS

Yun Wang *, William Chu, Sarah Fields, Colleen Heinemann and Zach Reiter

Department of Computer Science and Information Systems, Bradley University, 1501 W Bradley Ave, Peoria, IL 61625, USA

ABSTRACT

Most of the existing research works on the intrusion detection problem in a wireless sensor network (WSN) assume linear or random mobility patterns in abstracting intruders' models in traversing the WSN field. However, in real-life WSN applications, an intruder is usually an intelligent mobile robot with environment learning and detection avoidance capability (*i.e.*, the capability to avoid surrounding sensors). Due to this, the literature results based on the linear or random mobility models may not be applied to the real-life WSN design and deployment for efficient and effective intrusion detection in practice. This motivates us to investigate the impact of intruder's intelligence on the intrusion detection problem in a WSN for various applications. To be specific, we propose two intrusion algorithms, the pinball and flood-fill algorithms, to mimic the intelligent motion and behaviors of a mobile intruder in detecting and circumventing nearby sensors for detection avoidance while heading for its destination. The two proposed algorithms are integrated into a WSN framework for intrusion detection analysis in various circumstances. Monte Carlo simulations are conducted, and the results indicate that: (1) the performance of a WSN drastically changes as a result of the intruder's intelligence in avoiding sensor detections and intrusion algorithms; (2) network parameters, including node density, sensing range and communication range, play a crucial part in the effectiveness of the intruder's intrusion algorithms; and (3) it is imperative to integrate intruder's intelligence in the WSN research for intruder detection problems under various application circumstances.

Keywords: Artificial intelligence; Intrusion detection; Mobile intruder; Performance evaluation; Simulation; Wireless sensor networks

1. INTRODUCTION

Wireless sensor networks (WSNs) and their applications have moved to the forefront of research interest due to the tremendous potential in both civil and military environments [1,2]. Typical application scenarios include battlefield surveillance [3], illegal border crossing [1], malicious vehicle tracking [4], search and rescue [5], civilian vehicle tracking and autonomous interception [6], object tracking [7,8], wild animal tracking [9], *etc.* As an important problem in WSNs, intrusion detection is defined as a WSN system for detecting mobile intruders that are trying to traverse the WSN's field of interest (FoI) and reach the destination. The goal of intrusion detection using a WSN is to detect or prevent the intruder(s) from traversing the monitored FoI.

1.1. Related Works and Research Motivation

The research literature has extensively addressed the intrusion detection problem in WSNs under different metrics and assumptions [10]. On the one hand, the problem is addressed from the perspective of WSN design and deployment based on the assumption that an intruder follows a linear intrusion path and moves inside the WSN FoI at a constant speed [10,11,12,13,14,15,16,17,18]. The focus of the research is to investigate the tradeoff between WSN settings and detection probability and to identify critical network parameters for achieving the application-specific detection probability, while minimizing network cost and/or power consumption. Under the linear intrusion model, Cai *et al.* [19] derive the closed form formula of detection probability and the average detection delay of mobile intruder(s), taking into consideration the sensor sleeping pattern for energy efficiency. Gui *et al.* [11] study the tradeoff between intrusion detection quality and power conservation and derive the mean time when a linear mobile intruder is first detected. They also provide sleep-scheduling algorithms to guarantee a minimum response time for intrusion detection and power conservation. Lazos *et al.* [10,13] formulate the intrusion detection problem as a line-set intersection problem and utilize integral geometry to derive the intrusion detection probability for both random and deterministic WSNs. Wang *et al.* [15] derive the detection probability of a linear intruder that is detected by *k* sensors within the maximum allowable intrusion distance in homogeneous and heterogeneous WSNs. Further, Wang *et al.* [20] analyze the linear intruder detection problem in a Gaussian-distributed WSN with respect to a counterpart uniformly-distributed WSN and characterize the detection probability in both single-sensing detection and multiple-sensing detection scenarios.

On the other hand, the intrusion detection problem is addressed under the assumption that sensors and/or intruders are both mobile and follow some random mobility model [18]. Camp *et al.*[21] provide a comprehensive survey on a number of mobility models, including the random walk mobility model, the random way point mobility model, the random direction mobility model, the Gaussian-Markov mobility model, *etc.* The mobility model is to mimic the random movements of mobile sensors and/or intruders for network simulation and performance evaluations. Based on these random mobility models, Liu *et al.* [22] study the impact of sensor mobility on the network sensing coverage and intrusion detection probability. Their results show that sensor mobility can be exploited to improve the network sensor sensing coverage and reduce the detection time of a stationary intruder. For mobile intruders, the detection time depends on the mobility strategies of the sensors and the intruders. Keung *et al.* [23] address the mobile intruder detection problem in a mobile sensor network by formulating the problem as a *k*-barrier coverage problem. They derive the dynamic relationship for the *k*-barrier coverage performance in terms of the density of mobile sensors, sensing range, sensor mobility, intruder mobility, *etc.* This is done by utilizing the classical kinetic theory of gas molecules in physics for system modeling and analysis.

However, to the best of our knowledge, no prior research on the intrusion detection problem in sensor networks considers the intelligence of a mobile intruder that is capable of detecting nearby sensors and attempts to circumvent detected sensors for detection avoidance. In real-life applications, an intruder is usually an intelligent mobile robot with environment learning and detection avoidance capability. This motivates us to propose two intrusion algorithms that mimic the intelligent motion and behaviors of a mobile intruder in terms of detecting and avoiding nearby sensor(s) utilizing artificial intelligence (AI) strategies. The two proposed algorithms are integrated into a framework for intrusion detection analysis in WSNs, which enables us to examine the impact of intruder's intelligence on the intrusion detection capability of a WSN under various circumstances.

1.2. Paper Organization

The remainder of this paper is organized as follows. Section 2 presents assumptions, models and definitions for intrusion detection analysis in a WSN. Section 3 describes three intrusion algorithms, including the widely-adopted linear intrusion algorithm and the two proposed AI-enabled intrusion algorithm, pinball and flood-fill. Section 4 presents simulation, performance evaluation and discussions. Finally, the paper is concluded in Section 5 with remarks on future work.

2. SYSTEM MODELING AND DEFINITIONS

In this section, we first present the assumptions and system models for the examination of the intelligent intruder detection problem in a WSN under various circumstances. We then systematically formulate the problem and define performance evaluation metrics to capture the interplay between the intruder's intelligence and the WSN's detection capability.

2.1. Assumptions and Models

For system modeling and problem formulation, assumptions are unavoidable. In this work, we consider a homogeneous WSN model with N uniformly- and randomly-distributed sensors in a fixed square plane A (*i.e.*, FoI). The side length of A is L, and the area is $|A|=L*L$. The purpose of the WSN is to detect undesired or unexpected intruder(s) within a given application-defined time duration (Tmax). More specifically, we assume:

- All sensors have a sensing range of rs and a communication range of rc, both following the Boolean sensing/communication model;
- The Base Station (BS) is located in the center of A and has a communication range of rc;

- Any intruder is not aware of the layout of the sensors' placement;
- Sensors deployed in the WSN are not aware of the intrusion path or strategies adopted by any intruder;
- An intruder will enter the WSN FoI from any point along the left peripheral and move toward the right peripheral, aiming to traverse the WSN FoI and arrive at its destination outside of the FoI, as illustrated in Figure 1;
- An intruder is able to detect nearby sensor(s) within its sensing range Irs;
- Irs>rs, which ensures that an intelligent intruder is able to sense nearby sensor(s) and perform detection avoidance before being detected by the WSN;
- The terrain within the FoI will not affect sensor placement or the intruder's intrusion path.

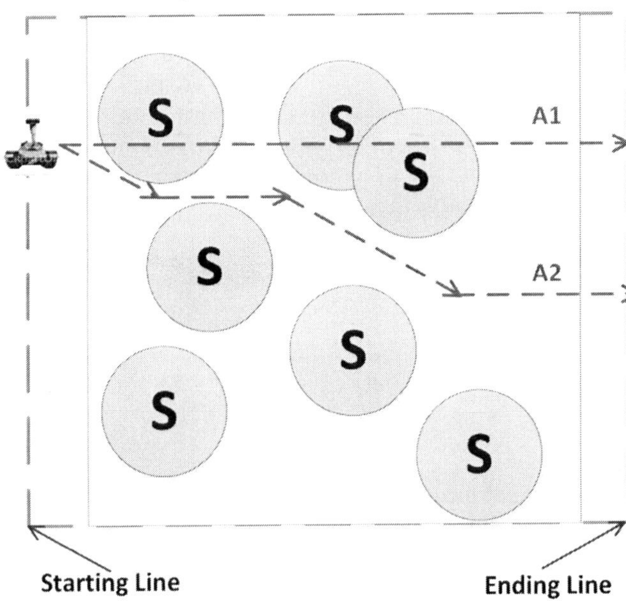

Figure 1. Illustration of an intelligent intruder detection problem formulation in a WSN. The intruder starts from a random point on the imaginary left periphery and moves toward another random point on the imaginary right periphery, which is the intruder's destination. The intruder may adopt an AI-enabled intrusion algorithm (like A2) for detection avoidance.

2.2. Problem Formulation

The intelligent intruder detection problem in a WSN system can be formulated as a "game" according to "game theory" [24], which can be roughly abstracted as "a set of tools and a language for describing and predicting strategic behavior" [25], helping us abstract and understand how decision makers, *i.e.*, the intelligent intruders, interact with the target WSN. In this paper, the interactions between an intruder and a WSN are terminated when either the intruder or the WSN wins. To be specific, the WSN is considered the "winner" if (1) the intruder is detected by a connected sensor before reaching its destination or (2) the intruder is still inside the WSN when the allotted time Tmax expires. Otherwise, the intruder is considered the "winner". In other words, the intruder, modeled as an intelligent decision maker, is able to detect nearby sensors and take actions to circumvent the sensing coverage area of the WSN while heading for its destination.

Without loss of generosity and for the similarity of analysis and boundary effects' avoidance, we formulate the given WSN field of interest *A* as a slightly bigger area with horizontal side length $L+\delta L$ ($\delta L \ll L$), while the vertical side length remains the same as *L*, as shown in Figure 1. The intruder will start from a random point on the imaginary left periphery and move toward another random point on the imaginary right periphery, which is the intruder's destination.

2.3. Performance Evaluation Metrics

Based on the assumptions, models and problem formulation, we define the following performance metrics to study the impact of intruder's intelligence on the intrusion detection capability of a WSN for various applications.

- Detection probability Pdet: the probability that an intruder is detected by a connected sensor in a WSN within the maximum allowable intrusion time Tmax.
- Prevention probability Pprevt: the probability that an intruder is not detected, however is prevented from reaching its destination within the maximum allowable intrusion time Tmax.
- WSN win probability Pwsn: the sum of the detection probability Pdet and the prevention probability Pprevt, and Pwsn=Pdet+Pprevt.

- Escape probability Pintru: the probability that an intruder manages to escape the WSN FoI and arrives at the destination within the allotted Tmax.

In addition, we include the definitions for general WSN evaluation metrics including coverage, connectivity and connected coverage for the purpose of comparison [5]:

- Coverage: Any point in the field of interest is said to be covered if it is within the sensing range of a sensor. The network coverage is defined as the probability of a random point in *A*being covered by at least one sensor.
- Connectivity: Consider two random sensors si and sj located inside *A*; si and sj are connected if there exists a communication path between them. The network connectivity is defined as the probability of a random sensor that can communicate with the base station through a direct or multi-hop communication path, *i.e.*, a connected sensor.
- Connected coverage: An intruder is considered to be detected when it enters the sensing coverage area of a connected sensor (to the BS). The network connected coverage is thus defined as the probability of a random point in *A* that is covered by at least one connected sensor.

The notations used in this work are summarized in Table 1.

3. INTRUSION ALGORITHMS

In this section, three intrusion algorithms, including the linear intrusion, pinball intrusion and flood-fill intrusion algorithms, are presented.

3.1. Linear Intrusion Algorithm

Following the linear intrusion algorithm, the intruder will start from a source point on the imaginary starting line on the left side of the WSN FoI and follow a straight-line path toward the ending line on the right side. In Figure 1, A1 illustrates an example linear intrusion path of a linear intruder.

Table 1. Notation table.

Notation	Description
L	Side length of the field of interest
N	Number of sensors deployed
r_s	Sensing range
r_c	Communication range
I_{rs}	Intruder sensing range
λ	Node density
P_{det}	Detection probability
P_{prevt}	Prevention probability
P_{wsn}	WSN win probability
P_{intru}	Intruder escape probability

3.2. Pinball Intrusion Algorithm

Motivated by the kinetic theory behind billiards or pinball balls rebounding off a collision with equal kinetic energy [26,27], we propose the pinball algorithm for detection avoidance. Intruders following this detection avoidance strategy, called pinball intruders, will bounce away with a constant speed after encountering the boundaries of WSN FoI or detecting the sensing coverage area of a sensor within its sensing range Irs.

To be specific, the intruder starts its intrusion from the left periphery of the WSN FoI and moves toward the right periphery, aiming to safely pass the WSN and reach its destination in a timely manner. During its traversal, the intruder might sense a nearby sensor (within distance Irs) or an edge of the FoI. If the intruder senses the left, upper, or bottom edge of the FoI, it will invert the x or y component of its velocity as if a ball hits the vertical or horizontal edges, respectively. On the other hand, if the intruder senses the sensing coverage area of a sensor that is modeled as a circular disk with radius rs, the normal of the reflection surface becomes the line between the intruder and the sensor. As illustrated in Figure 2, let $\vec{I}$ and $\vec{S}$ be the position vectors of the intruder and sensor detected. The *x* and *y* components of any vector $\vec{A}$ are denoted as Ax and Ay, respectively. The normal of the reflection surface is thus the mirror vector $\vec{M} = \vec{I} - \vec{S}$. Assume the intruder's initial velocity is $\vec{v_i}$, and the resulting velocity is $\vec{v_f}$ after bouncing off the sensor for collision avoidance. Using some vector math, $\vec{v_f}$ can be computed by calculating the angle $\theta$and performing a rotation on $\vec{v_i}$, as shown below.

$$\theta = \text{atan2}(M_y, M_x) - \text{atan2}(-v_{iy}, -v_{iy}) \quad (1)$$

$$\text{atan2}(y, x) = \begin{cases} \arctan \frac{y}{x}; & (x > 0) \\ \arctan \frac{y}{x} + \pi; & (y \geq 0, x < 0) \\ \arctan \frac{y}{x} - \pi; & (y < 0, x < 0) \\ \frac{\pi}{2}; & (y > 0, x = 0) \\ -\frac{\pi}{2}; & (y < 0, x = 0) \\ \text{undefined}, & (y = 0, x = 0) \end{cases} \quad (2)$$

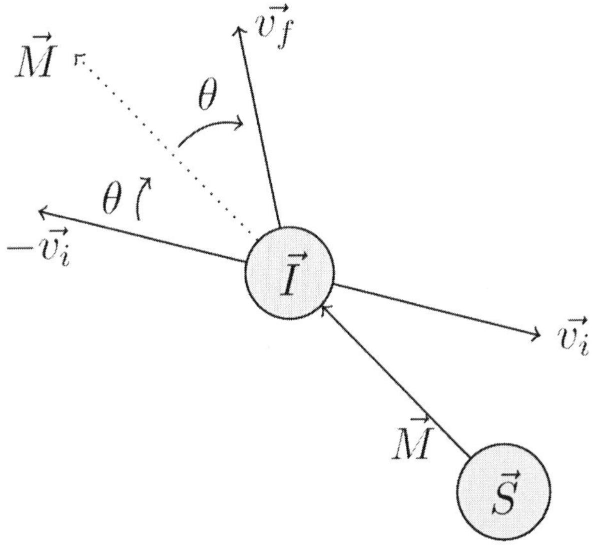

Figure 2. Pinball algorithm.

After solving for θ, twice that value is the angle that $-\vec{v}_i$ is to be rotated. Rotating $-\vec{v}_i$ by 2θ gives the resultant velocity $\vec{v}_f$.

$$\begin{aligned} v_{fx} &= (-v_{ix})cos(2\theta) - (-v_{iy})sin(2\theta); \\ &= -v_{ix}cos(2\theta) + v_{iy}sin(2\theta) \end{aligned} \tag{3}$$

$$\begin{aligned} v_{fy} &= (-v_{ix})sin(2\theta) + (-v_{iy})cos(2\theta); \\ &= -v_{ix}sin(2\theta) - v_{ix}cos(2\theta) \end{aligned} \tag{4}$$

$$\vec{v}_f = v_{fx}\hat{x} + v_{fy}\hat{y} \tag{5}$$

By setting the velocity to $\vec{v}_f$ upon the intruder's detection of any sensor or wall, the intruder avoids sensors by reflecting off of potential detection points. The pseudocode of the pinball intrusion algorithm is also described in Algorithm 1.

Note that some functionality is simplified into several functions to improve readability in Algorithm 1. To be specific:

- normalize($\vec{v}$) performs vector normalization. It returns a vector that points in the same direction as the input vector, but with a length of one.
- collides($\vec{p}, obj$) performs sensor/wall detection between the entity's original position and the next position $\vec{p}$ against the detected obj (*i.e.*, a sensor or an FoI boundary). In the case of an FoI boundary, the function will check for the intersection of two line segments. Additionally, in the case of a sensor, the function will check if $\vec{p}$ lies within the sensor's circular disk of radius rs.
- angleBetween($\vec{v}_1, \vec{v}_2$) finds the angle between the vectors $\vec{v}_1$ and $\vec{v}_2$ The resulting value will utilize the atan 2 function defined in Equation (2).

$$\theta = atan2(\vec{v}_{2y}, \vec{v}_{2x}) - atan2(\vec{v}_{1y}, \vec{v}_{1x})$$

- vectorRotate($\vec{v}, \theta$) returns the result of $\vec{v}$ rotated by θ around its origin.

Algorithm 1 Pinball.

```
while position! = destination do
    velocity ← normalize(destination − position)
    nextPosition ← position + velocity
    if collides(nextPosition, horizontalWall) then
        velocity.y ← −velocity.y
    if collides(nextPosition, verticalWall) then
        velocity.x ← −velocity.x
    for all sensor in sensors do
        if collides(nextPosition, sensor) then
            mirror ← position − sensorPosition
            angle ← angleBetween(mirror, velocity)
            negativeV ← −velocity
            velocity ← vectorRotate(negativeV, 2 * angle)
```

3.3. Flood-Fill Intrusion Algorithm

The pinball algorithm simply avoids collisions by bouncing off nearby sensors detected within its sensing range Irs. It does not estimate the cost to the destination for each state or efficiently store-and-update environment information with backtracking costs. In other words, while a pinball intruder can efficiently avoid sensor detection, it may become stuck or time-out inside the WSN FoI, *i.e.*, it may not be able to reach the destination in a timely manner. In most WSN applications, an intruder's primary goal is to safely traverse the WSN FoI and to arrive at its destination within a certain time. Hence, we propose a flood-fill intrusion algorithm that integrates environment learning, map building, updating, backtracking and path replanning for detection avoidance and timely destination arrival.

Different from the traditional flood-fill algorithms for maze-solving problems that require full prior knowledge of the environment, our proposed flood-fill algorithm assumes no prior knowledge of the WSN FoI. Instead, the flood-fill algorithm involves dividing the WSN FoI into a virtual m∗m grid map, and all cells in the map are initially "empty", which represents no prior knowledge of the WSN FoI, as illustrated in Figure 3. The algorithm attempts to update the status of the cells by measuring and updating the WSN FoI status in terms of "safe" or "unsafe" and utilizes the learning information to direct the next move, until reaching the destination or experiencing a time-out.

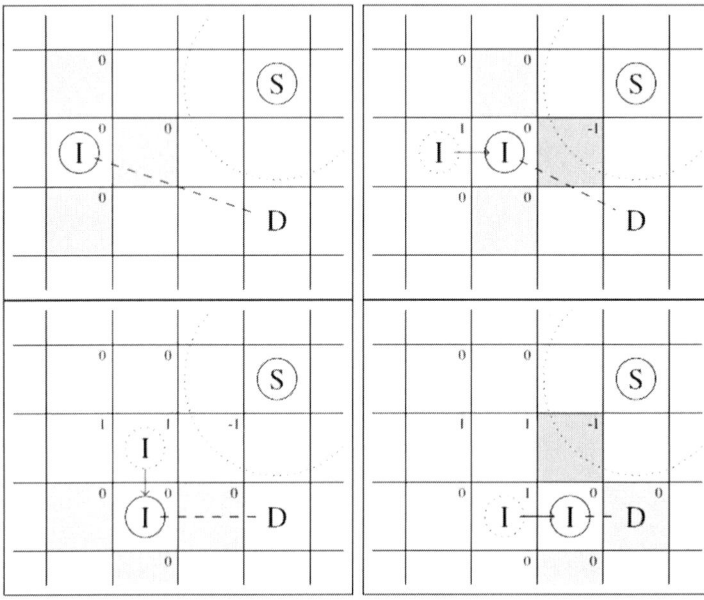

Figure 3. An illustration of the flood fill algorithm.

To start the algorithm, the intruder will choose a start position on the left extended periphery and a target position on the right extended periphery and will restrict all movements to the virtual grid, *i.e.*, move from the center of one cell to the next one. On each move, as illustrated in Figure 3, the intruder must check its adjacent cells and update the cell values in the map to represent their sensing coverage status and the status of "visits". To be specific:

- If a cell ci is fully or partially covered by a detected sensor within rs, then the cell receives a value of −1. Assume c(xi,yi) and s(xj,yj) are the locations of the cell ci, and the detected sensor sj. Cell ci will be considered as "unsafe" and receive a value of −1 if $\sqrt{(x_i - x_j)^2 + (y_i - y_j)^2} < r_s + \sqrt{2}/2.$ Otherwise, cell ci is considered "safe" and receives a value of zero.
- For a safe cell with a value of zero, the value will be incremented by one each time the intruder visits it. For instance, a cell with a value of three means the cell is visited by the intruder three times. This is

because the intruder might have to backtrack under certain conditions.

During traversal, while the intruder has not reached its target position or experienced a time-out and when it comes to make a move, it will check all cells adjacent to it to see which one is should head to next. More specifically:

- If a cell adjacent to the intruder has not been visited by the intruder before, it will check to see its coverage status first. Once the intruder has checked all adjacent cells, the intruder will proceed in the direction of the cell with the lowest value.
- If multiple cells have the same value, the intruder will decide which direction to move based on the distance from each cell to its target position. For example, if the intruder needs to travel six units along the *x*-axis and three units along *y*-axis to reach its target position, it will first attempt to travel along the *x*-axis.
- If that cell is not amongst those with the lowest value, then the intruder will go clockwise, checking the other cells for the lowest value, and will travel along the direction of the first lowest value cell it finds. Before the intruder leaves a cell, it will increment the value of that cell by one.

The pseudocode of the flood-fill intrusion algorithm is shown in Algorithm 2. Some critical functions and data structures are described as follows:

- directions is an array containing the four basic directions: up (<0,1>), down (<0,−1>), left (<1,0>) and right (<−1,0>).
- steps is an array generated every loop containing the position of the intruder if it were to take each of the directions in directions
- Count(array) counts the number of elements in an array
- map is a data structure mapping keys (cell positions) to values (cell values). Accessing a cell's value is expressed as map [position].

Algorithm 2 Flood-fill.

```
while position! = intruderDestinationPosition do
    for i = 0; i < Count(directions); i + + do
        steps[i] ← position + directions[i] ∗ cellSize
    for i = 0; i < Count(directions); i + + do
        if !map.containsKey(directions[i]) then
            map[steps[i]] ← IsCovered(steps[i])
    for i = 0; i < Count(directions); i + + do
        hits[i] ← map[steps[i]]
    targetVector ← targetPosition - position
    maxDot ← −∞
    generalDirection ← −1
    for i = 0; i < Count(directions); i + + do
        dot ← targetVector · directions[i]
        if dot > maxDot then
            maxDot ← dot
            generalDirection ← i
    min ← ∞
    minHit ← −1
    for i = 0; i < Count(directions); i + + do
        j ← (generalDirection + i)%4
        if hits[j]! = −1 then
            if hits[j] < min then
                min ← hits[j]
                minHit ← j
    if minHit! = −1 then
        position ← position + directions[minHit] ∗ cellSize
        map[steps[minHit]] ← map[steps[minHit]] + 1
```

4. DEMONSTRATION, SIMULATION AND DISCUSSION

This section presents the simulation results and evaluates the impact of different intrusion algorithms on the intrusion detection problem of a WSN under various environments. We developed two simulators using the Unity platform [28,29] and C++ for demonstration and statistical analysis, respectively. Both simulators implement the three intrusion algorithms described in Section 3, capture the critical aspects of various

WSNs and enable the interactions between intruders and WSNs. A screenshot of the simulator interface using Unity is demonstrated in Figure 4. The interface provides flexibility in selecting intrusion algorithms and configuring different WSN parameters for various settings. Moreover, Monte Carlo simulations are designed and conducted using the C++ simulator, aiming to examine the impact of different intrusion algorithms on the intrusion detection problem of a random WSN under various circumstances.

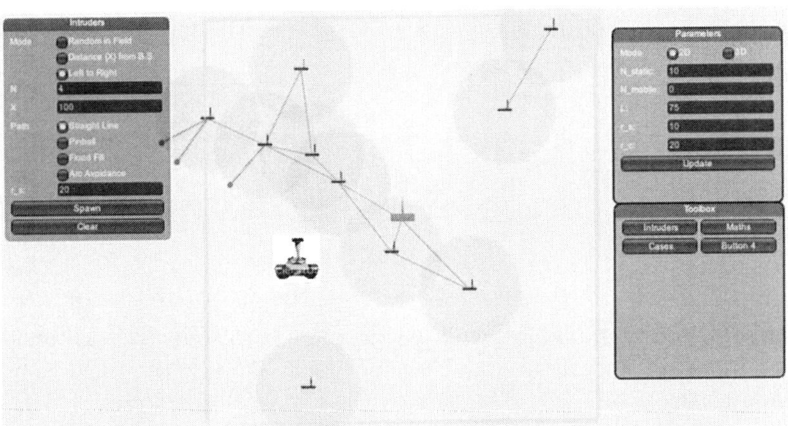

Figure 4. A screenshot of the simulator using the Unity platform.

4.1. Impact of Node Density λ

First, we examine the impact of node density on the WSN win probability and the intruder's escape probability, considering the three proposed intrusion algorithms. In this simulation, we fix L=500 m, rs=50 m and rc=100 m and vary *N* from five to 45 to generate different node densities and network topologies. The intruder's sensing range is set as Irs=60, unless otherwise specified. Figure 5, Figure 6 and Figure 7 illustrate the WSN win probability (Pwsn), the escape probability (Pintru) and the network detection probability (Pdet) of an intruder that adopts the linear, pinball and flood-fill algorithms in random WSNs with varying node densities λ. All results plotted here are the average of 500 simulation runs under the same network settings. In each simulation run, we use two random variables, *x* and *y*, to generate the coordinates for each sensor in the FoI. In other words, 500 different network topologies within the considered node density range are generated and tested for statistical analysis in this section.

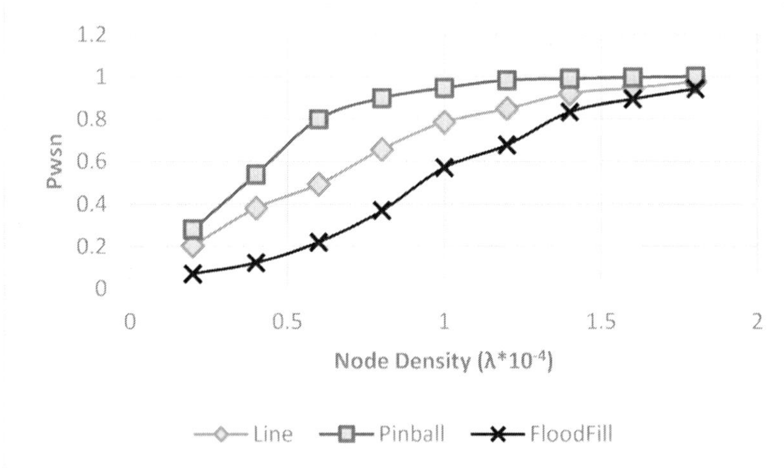

Figure 5. The WSN win probability (Pwsn) of an intruder that adopts the linear, pinball and flood-fill algorithms in a WSN with varying node densities λ.

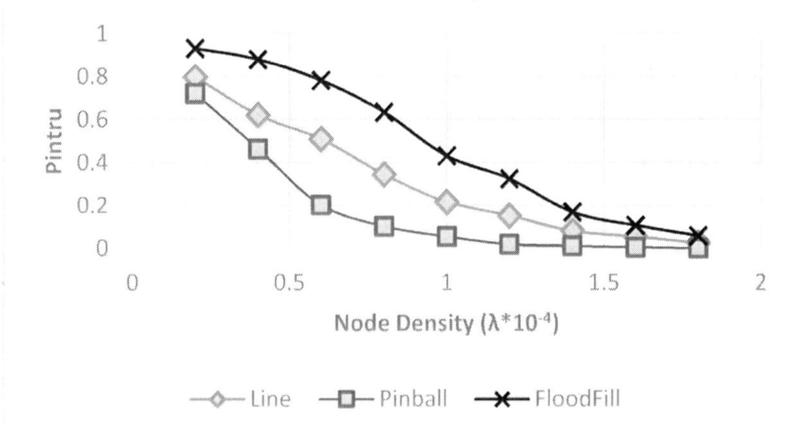

Figure 6. The escape probability (Pintru) of an intruder that adopts the linear, pinball and flood-fill algorithms in a WSN with varying node densities λ.

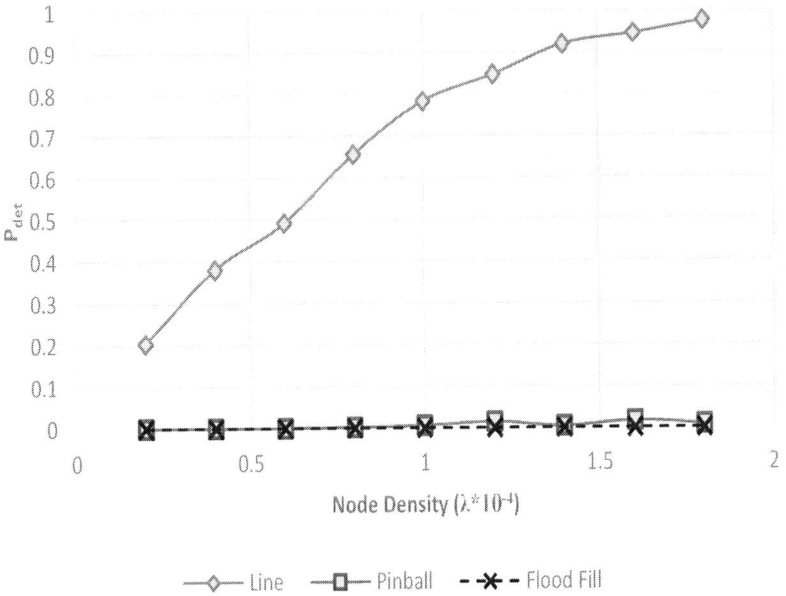

Figure 7. The detection probability Pdet of an intruder that adopts the linear, pinball and flood-fill algorithms in a WSN with varying node densities λ.

As Figure 5 and Figure 6 illustrate, the WSN win probability (Pwsn) increases and the intruder's escape probability (Pintru) decreases as the node density λ increases. This is because increased node density leads to higher connected coverage in the network field with a reduced safe area for the intruder to find a successful escape path. Second, there exist significant differences when an intruder traverses the same WSN field using different intrusion algorithms. Among the three considered algorithms, the flood-fill algorithm performs the best, while the pinball algorithm performs the worst. This is caused by the different design and implementation of detection avoidance strategies on the intruder side. To be specific, the pinball intruder simply avoids nearby sensors without taking into consideration the destination when adjusting its intrusion path. It then frequently moves to an area or position that is further away from the destination and results in the worst escape probability. This observation coincides with the results in a related work [16,30], "for an intruder, following a sine-curve intrusion path can be more beneficial than following a straight-line path as the probability of being detected can be substantially decreased, however, with a side effect of reducing intrusion progress towards the destination to some extent". Namely, a linear intruder moves directly toward the destination without avoiding nearby sensors, and hence, it has a higher probability of escaping the WSN as compared to the pinball intruder. On the other hand, the flood-fill intruder aims to reach its destination and takes into consideration the destination when avoiding nearby sensors during its traversal and, thus, leads to the best performance in escaping the WSN field among the three algorithms.

Figure 8 demonstrates the variances of the intruder's escape probability (Pintru) of an intruder that adopts the linear, pinball and flood-fill algorithms *versus* node densities λ. As the node density increases, the escape probability (Pintru) of a pinball intruder gets closer to "0" most quickly while the flood-fill intruder gets the highest probability to escape the sensor field. This is caused by the different intelligent strategies applied in the intruder's intrusion strategies. The results also suggest that there is a saturation point of the node density, after which deploying more sensors in the field of interest does not significantly decrease the intruder escape probability. The saturation point differs when the intruder takes different intrusion strategies.

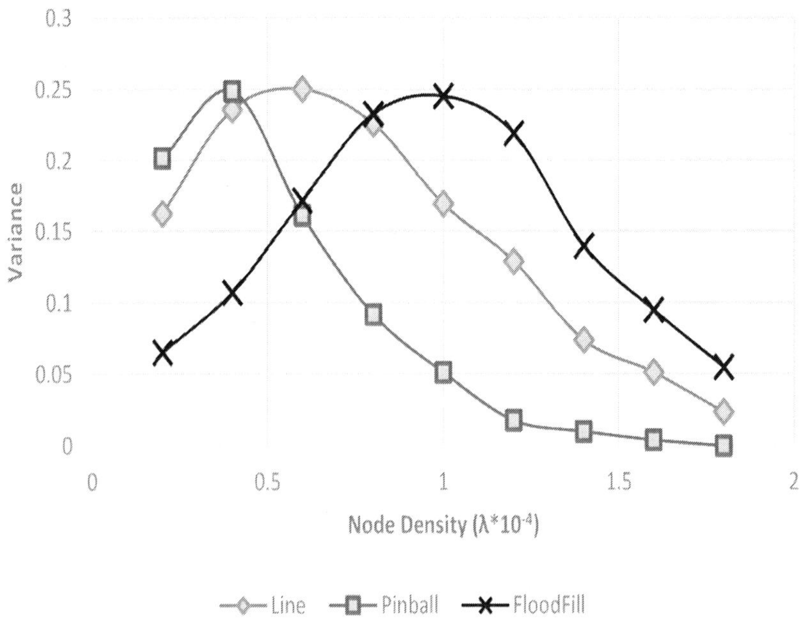

Figure 8. The variances of the intruder's escape probability (Pintru) of an intruder that adopts the linear, pinball and flood-fill algorithms in a WSN with varying node densities λ.

It should be noted that the sensor detection avoidance strategy adopted by the pinball intruder may not be able to help improve its escape probability; however, it does help in reducing the detection probability (Pdet) to a significant extent. As illustrated in Figure 7, the detection probability of the considered WSN in detecting the intelligent pinball intruder and the flood-fill intruder approaches zero, while the detection probability of a linear intruder keeps increasing as the node density increases. The results confirm the necessity of integrating intruder's intelligence in the WSN research for intruder detection for different applications.

4.2. Impact of Sensing Range rs

In this section, we examine the impact of sensing range rs on the WSN win probability (Pwsn) and the intruder escape probability (Pintru). Again, we fix the network parameters as N=25, rc=100 m, L=500 m, A=5002 square meters and vary the the sensing range rs from 25 to 75 m. Figure 9 and Figure 10 illustrate the WSN win probability (Pwsn) and the escape probability (Pintru) of an intruder that adopts the linear, pinball and flood-fill algorithms in random WSNs with varying sensing range rs. All results plotted here are the average of 500 simulation runs under the same network settings.

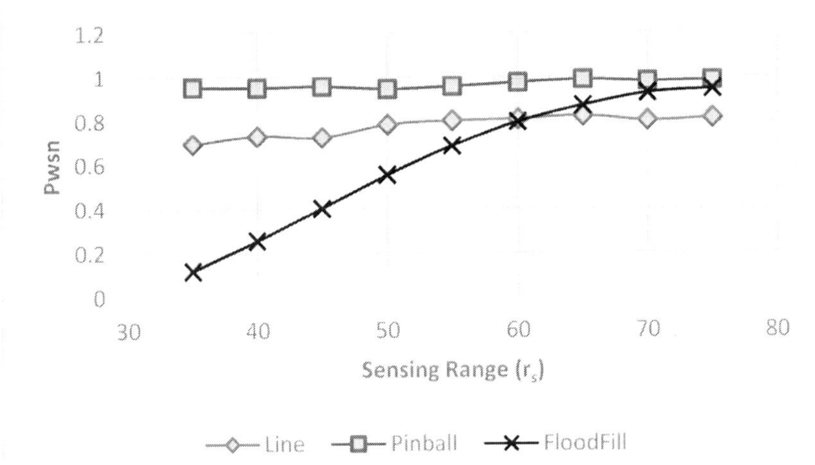

Figure 9. The WSN win probability (Pwsn) of an intruder that adopts the linear, pinball and flood-fill algorithms in a WSN with varying sensing range rs.

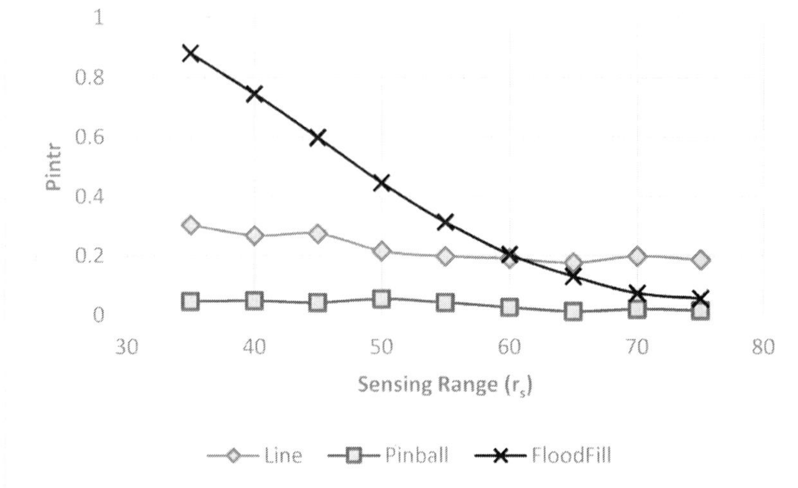

Figure 10. The escape probability (Pintru) of an intruder that adopts the linear, pinball and flood-fill algorithms in a WSN with varying sensing range rs.

It is observed in Figure 9 and Figure 10 that, as the sensing range rs increases, the WSN win probability (Pwsn) increases, and the intruder's escape probability (Pintru) decreases for all three considered intruders. This is because the network sensing coverage increases as the increase of the sensing range rs, which makes it more difficult for the intruders to find a safe path to escape the WSN and reach their destination. Second, the WSN win probability (Pwsn) in detecting and preventing the pinball intruder stays the highest, as indicated in Figure 9, and the pinball intruder performs the worst in escaping the WSN, as shown in Figure 10. This is because the pinball algorithm only avoids nearby sensors for detection avoidance without trying to make progress toward the destination. In addition, there exists a critical sensing range rs=60 m, below which the WSN is shown to have the worst probability in preventing and detecting the flood-fill intruder. This is due to the best artificial intelligence strategies applied by the flood-fill intruder, including sensor detection, detection avoidance, map building, updating and backtracking, as described inSection 3.3. On the other hand, when the sensing range rs exceeds 60 m, the escape probability of the flood-fill intruder drops below the linear intruder and converges to the pinball intruder. This is caused by the high sensing coverage of the WSN when the sensing range exceeds 60 m, where the flood-fill intruder has to spend most of the time in avoiding nearby sensors instead of making progress toward the destination and, thus, gradually degrades to a pinball intruder.

The results in this section indicate that intelligent intruders may not always outperform the linear intruders when the network is well covered with a high sensing range. More specifically, there exists a critical sensing range, below which intelligent intruders have a higher probability of successfully traversing the WSN and reaching its destination and above which linear intruders outperform the intelligent intruders in terms of having a higher probability of reaching its destination.

4.3. Impact of Communication Range *rc*

To detect an intruder, a WSN should be well connected, so that detection can be reported to the base station. Namely, the network connectivity impacts the detection and prevention probability of a WSN and the escape probability of an intruder. The sensor's communication range rc determines the network connectivity of a WSN. In order to examine the impact of communication range rc on the WSN win probability (Pwsn) and the intruder's escape probability (Pintru), we fix the network parameters as N=25, rs=50 m, L=500 m, A=5002 m2 and vary the the communication range rc from 25 to 250 m. Each result plotted here is the average of 500 simulation runs under the same network settings.

Figure 11 and Figure 12 depict the WSN win probability (Pwsn) and the escape probability (Pintru) of an intruder in traversing a WSN with varying communication ranges rc, taking into consideration the three considered intrusion algorithms. In the two figures, we have the following observations. First, the WSN win probability increases quickly in preventing and detecting the linear intruder, while that for the pinball and flood-fill intruders remains nearly constant as the communication range rc increases. This is because the network's coverage remains the same with a constant number of deployed sensors *N* and sensing range rs. The same sensing coverage poses the same challenge for pinball and flood-fill intruders to detect and avoid sensors in their traversing. Namely, increased communication range has no contribution to the sensing coverage of the WSN. Thus, the WSN win probability of detecting and preventing pinball and flood-fill intruders keeps constant at the increase of the communication range rc. This also explains the nearly constant escape probability of the pinball and flood-fill intruder, as shown in Figure 12.

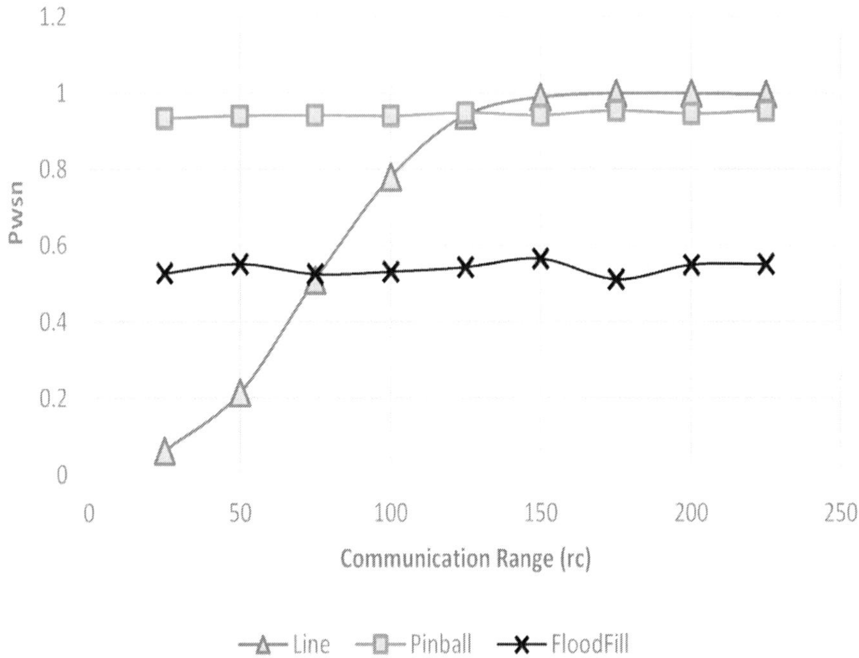

Figure 11. The WSN win probability (Pwsn) of a WSN in detecting and preventing an intruder that adopts the linear, pinball and flood-fill algorithms in a WSN with varying communication range rc.

On the other hand, it is observed that the WSN win probability of detecting and preventing the linear intruders increases, and the escape probability of the linear intruder drops with the increase of the communication range. This is because an increased communication range significantly contributes to the network connectivity and the connected coverage of a WSN. With increased communication range, more sensors that were initially isolated get connected to report the detection of the linear intruder to the base station. In other words, when the communication range is low, there exists a fraction of sensors that may be able detect the linear intruder within its sensing range; however, they may not able to report the detection to the base station for successful intruder detection. Hence, as the communication range increases, the probability that a linear intruder gets caught by a connected sensor increases, and its escape probability decreases accordingly.

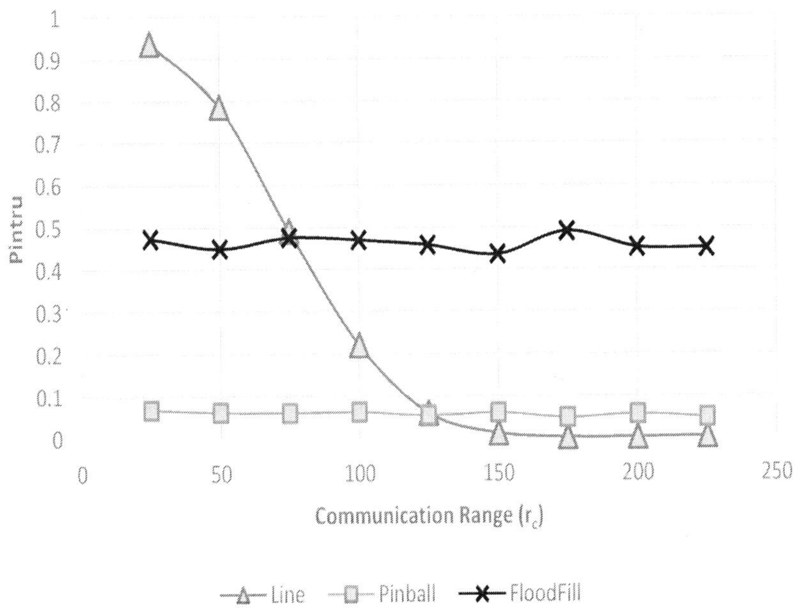

Figure 12. The escape probability (Pintru) of an intruder that adopts the linear, pinball and flood-fill algorithms in a WSN with varying communication range rc.

Moreover, we observe that there exist two critical communication ranges rc1=60 and rc2=120. Specifically, when the communication range is below rc1, *i.e.*, *rc*<*rc*1, the linear intruder outperforms the other two intelligent counterparts in terms of escape probability under the same network settings. Second, when the communication is above rc2, *i.e.*, rc>rc2, both pinball and flood-fill intruders outperform the linear intruder, while the flood-fill intruder excels. Third, when the communication range is between the two critical ranges, *i.e.*, *rc*1<*rc*<*rc*2, the flood-fill algorithm outperforms the linear algorithm, while the pinball algorithm performs the worst. The results indicate that intruder's intelligence in detecting and avoiding nearby sensors has a significant impact on its escape probability, so as for the network connectivity.

4.4. Coverage, Connectivity, Connected Coverage versus Intruder Detection

From the above discussions, it is apparent that the general network quality of service (QoS), including sensing coverage, connectivity and connected coverage, has a significant impact on the detection probability of a WSN and the escape probability of an intruder. Therefore, it is important to examine the interplay between the general network QoS and the detection probability in a random WSN in Section 2.3.

Figure 13 illustrates the probability of coverage, connectivity, connected coverage and the detection probability of a random WSN in capturing linear, pinball and flood-fill intruders with varying node densities. In this simulation, we use the simulator to generate random topologies with different numbers of sensors ranging from five to 45 in an area of 500×500 square meters. Sensors are identical with a sensing range of rs=50 m and a transmission range of rc=100 m. In each case, we test 500 samples, and the probabilities are computed according to the definitions in Section 2.3.

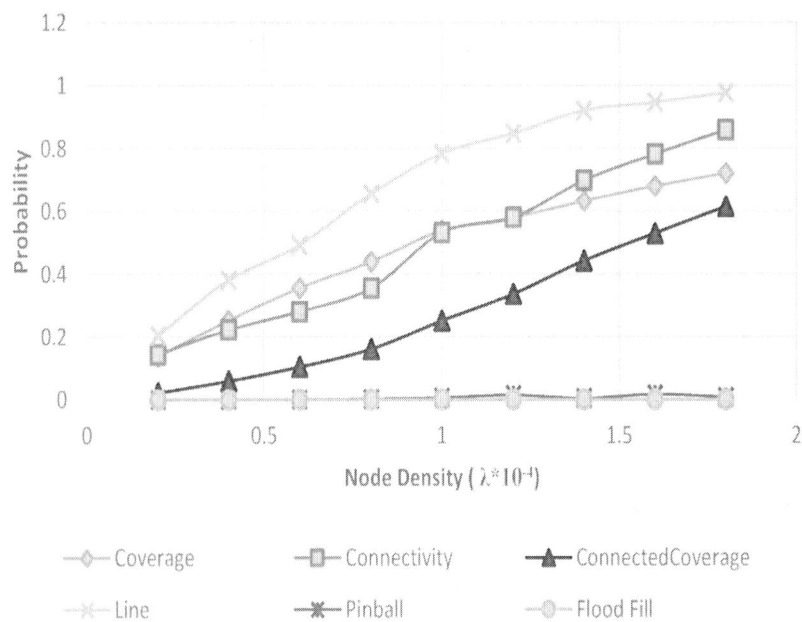

Figure 13. Probability of coverage, connectivity, connected coverage and the detection probabilities of a random WSN with varying node densities λ.

The simulation results in Figure 13 indicate that the coverage, the connectivity and the connected coverage all increase as the node density increases, and the probability of the connected coverage is always the lowest under the same network settings, as expected. Another observation is that the behaviors of both coverage and connectivity have similar tendencies over the node density and almost overlapped each other. This is because the communication range rc is set as twice the sensing range rs, *i.e.*, *rc*=2∗*rs* in the study, which is a critical condition that a complete coverage of a convex WSN implies connectivity among the set of working sensors [31]. Last, but most importantly, the results demonstrate the significant differences among the coverage, connectivity, connected coverage and the detection probability of a WSN. More specifically, the probability of detecting a linear intruder is always higher than the network coverage, connectivity and connected coverage, while that of detecting the intelligent pinball and flood-fill intruders is always lower than the network coverage, connectivity and connected coverage. The results support our claim that: (1) existing results on general QoS in a WSN, including coverage, connectivity and connected coverage, cannot be directly applied to the intruder detection applications; and (2) intruder's intelligence plays an important role in the detection probability of a WSN and requires a separate treatment in WSN research.

5. CONCLUSIONS

This work investigates the impact of intruder's intelligence on the intrusion detection problem of a WSN under various circumstances for the first time. Two AI-enabled algorithms, pinball and flood-fill, are proposed and integrated into a WSN simulator for intrusion detection analysis. Simulation results demonstrate a significant impact of intruder's intelligence on the intrusion detection probability of a WSN under various circumstances. In addition, network parameters, including node density, sensing range and communication range, have a crucial impact on the effectiveness of the intruder's intrusion algorithms. It is therefore imperative to consider intruder's intelligence in the design and deployment of WSNs for intrusion detection tasks. In the future, we are to consider more advanced path-planning strategies and study their impact on the intrusion detection problem in WSNs for various applications, aiming to provide practical insights into the real-life WSN design and implementation. The primary contribution of our work lies in the fact that it expands the knowledge of WSN research, leads to new research directions, and provides foundations for research in the field of

WSNs for real-life intruder detection. We plan to investigate additional network factors, such as access delays, collisions, repetitions, routing, *etc.*, on the detection capability of a WSN, taking into consideration advanced environmental learning and path planning algorithms.

AUTHOR CONTRIBUTIONS

Y. W. conceived and directed the project; The remaining authors are students who all substantially contributed to the implementation of the project and the writing sections of this paper.

REFERENCES

1. Yang, H.; Sikdar, B. A protocol for tracking mobile targets using sensor networks. In Proceedings of the First IEEE International Workshop on Sensor Network Protocols and Applications, Anchorage, AK, USA, 11 May 2003; pp. 71–81.
2. Yick, J.; Mukherjee, B.; Ghosal, D. Wireless sensor network survey. *Comput. Netw.* **2008**, *52*, 2292–2330.
3. Bokareva, T.; Hu, W.; Kanhere, S.; Ristic, B.; Gordon, N.; Bessell, T.; Rutten, M.; Jha, S. Wireless sensor networks for battlefield surveillance. In Proceedings of the Land Warfare Conference, Brisbane, Australia, 24-27 October 2006; pp. 1–8.
4. Hamdi, M.; Boudriga, N.; Obaidat, M.S. WHOMoVeS: An optimized broadband sensor network for military vehicle tracking. *Int. J. Commun. Syst.* **2008**, *21*, 277–300.
5. Severino, R.; Alves, M. Engineering a search and rescue application with a wireless sensor network-based localization mechanism. In Proceedings of the IEEE International Symposium on a World of Wireless, Mobile and Multimedia Networks, WoWMoM 2007, Espoo, Finland, 18–21 June 2007; pp. 1–4.
6. Sharp, C.; Schaffert, S.; Woo, A.; Sastry, N.; Karlof, C.; Sastry, S.; Culler, D. Design and implementation of a sensor network system for vehicle tracking and autonomous interception. In Proceedings of the Second European Workshop on Wireless

Sensor Networks, Istanbul, Turkey, 31 January–2 February 2005; pp. 93–107.

7. Tsai, H.W.; Chu, C.P.; Chen, T.S. Mobile object tracking in wireless sensor networks. *Comput. Commun.* **2007**, *30*, 1811–1825.

8. Bhatti, S.; Xu, J. Survey of target tracking protocols using wireless sensor network. In Proceedings of the Fifth International Conference on Wireless and Mobile Communications, ICWMC'09, Cannes, France, 23–29 August 2009; pp. 110–115.

9. Dyo, V.; Ellwood, S.A.; Macdonald, D.W.; Markham, A.; Mascolo, C.; Pásztor, B.; Scellato, S.; Trigoni, N.; Wohlers, R.; Yousef, K. Evolution and sustainability of a wildlife monitoring sensor network. In Proceedings of the 8th ACM Conference on Embedded Networked Sensor Systems, Zurich, Switzerland, 3–5 November 2010; pp. 127–140.

10. Lazos, L.; Poovendran, R.; Ritcey, J.A. Analytic evaluation of target detection in heterogeneous wireless sensor networks. *ACM Trans. Sens. Netw.* **2009**, *5*, 1–18.

11. Gui, C.; Mohapatra, P. Power conservation and quality of surveillance in target tracking sensor networks. In Proceedings of the 10th Annual International Conference on Mobile Computing and Networking, Philadelphia, PA, USA, 26 September–1 October 2004; pp. 129–143.

12. Arora, A.; Dutta, P.; Bapat, S.; Kulathumani, V.; Zhang, H.; Naik, V.; Mittal, V.; Cao, H.; Demirbas, M.; Gouda, M.; *et al.* A line in the sand: A wireless sensor network for target detection, classification, and tracking. *Comput. Netw.* **2004**, *46*, 605–634.

13. Lazos, L.; Poovendran, R.; Ritcey, J.A. Probabilistic detection of mobile targets in heterogeneous sensor networks. In Proceedings of the 6th International Conference on Information Processing in Sensor Networks, Cambridge, MA, USA, 25–27 April 2007; pp. 519–528.

14. Agah, A.; Das, S.K.; Basu, K.; Asadi, M. Intrusion detection in sensor networks: A non-cooperative game approach. In Proceedings of the Third IEEE International Symposium on Network Computing and Applications, (NCA 2004), Cambridge, MA, USA, 30 August–1 September 2004; pp. 343–346.

15. Wang, Y.; Wang, X.; Xie, B.; Wang, D.; Agrawal, D.P. Intrusion detection in homogeneous and heterogeneous wireless sensor networks. *IEEE Trans. Mob. Comput.* **2008**, *7*, 698–711.

16. Wang, Y.; Leow, Y.K.; Yin, J. Is straight-line path always the best for intrusion detection in wireless sensor networks. In Proceedings of the 2009 15th International Conference on Parallel and Distributed Systems (ICPADS), Shenzhen, China, 8–11 December 2009; pp. 564–571.

17. Hart, P.E.; Nilsson, N.J.; Raphael, B. A formal basis for the heuristic determination of minimum cost paths. *IEEE Trans. Syst. Sci. Cybern.* **1968**, *4*, 100–107.

18. Rao, N.S.V. An algorithmic framework for navigation in unknown terrains. *IEEE Comput.* **1989**, *22*, 37–43.

19. Cao, Q.; Yan, T.; Stankovic, J.; Abdelzaher, T. Analysis of target detection performance for wireless sensor networks. In *Distributed Computing in Sensor Systems*; Springer: Berlin, Heidelberg, 2005; pp. 276–292.

20. Wang, Y.; Fu, W.; Agrawal, D.P. Gaussian versus uniform distribution for intrusion detection in wireless sensor networks. *IEEE Trans. Parallel Distrib. Syst.* **2013**, *24*, 342–355.

21. Camp, T.; Boleng, J.; Davies, V. A survey of mobility models for ad hoc network research. *Wirel. Commun. Mob. Comput.* **2002**, *2*, 483–502.

22. Liu, B.; Brass, P.; Dousse, O.; Nain, P.; Towsley, D. Mobility improves coverage of sensor networks. In Proceedings of the 6th ACM International Symposium on Mobile Ad Hoc Networking and Computing, Chicago, IL, USA, 25–28 May 2005; pp. 300–308.

23. Keung, Y.; Li, B.; Zhang, Q. The intrusion detection in mobile sensor network. In Proceedings of the Eleventh ACM International Symposium on Mobile Ad Hoc Networking and Computing, Chicago, IL, USA, 20–24 September 2010; pp. 11–20.

24. Morris, P. *Introduction to Game Theory*; Springer Science & Business Media: New York, NY, USA, 1994.

25. Picker, R.C. *An Introduction to Game Theory and the Law*; Law School, University of Chicago: Chicago, IL, USA, 1994.

26. Cutnell, J.D.; Johnson, K.W. *Physics*; John Wiley & Sons: Hoboken, NJ, USA, 2009.

27. Kinetic Theory. Available online: http://physics.bu.edu/duffy/py105/Kinetictheory.html(accessed on 18 April 2015).

28. Unity3D. Available online: http://unity3d.com/unity (accessed on 28 March 2015).

29. Blackman, S. *Beginning 3D Game Development with Unity: All-in-One, Multi-Platform Game Development*; Apress: New York, NY, USA, 2011.

30. Wang, Y.; Leow, Y.K.; Yin, J. A novel sine-curve mobility model for intrusion detection in wireless sensor networks. *Wirel. Commun. Mob. Comput.* **2013**, *13*, 1555–1570.

31. Zhang, H.; Hou, J.C. Maintaining sensing coverage and connectivity in large sensor networks. *Ad Hoc Sens. Wirel. Netw.* **2005**, *1*, 89–124.

5

CHAPTER

INEFFICIENCY OF IDS STATIC ANOMALY DETECTORS IN REAL-WORLD NETWORKS

Edward Guillen [1,*], Jeisson Sánchez [1] and Rafael Paez [2]

[1]*Telecommunication Engineering Department, Nueva Granada Military University, Bogotá 110911, Colombia*

[2]*Engineering Systems Department, Xaverian University, Bogotá 110911, Colombia*

ABSTRACT

A wide range of IDS implementations with anomaly detection modules have been deployed. In general, those modules depend on intrusion knowledge databases, such as Knowledge Discovery Dataset (KDD99), Center for Applied Internet Data Analysis (CAIDA) or Community Resource for Archiving Wireless Data at Dartmouth (CRAWDAD), among others. Once the database is analyzed and a machine learning method is employed to generate detectors, some classes of new detectors are created. Thereafter, detectors are supposed to be deployed in real network environments in order to achieve detection with good results for false positives and detection rates. Since the traffic behavior is quite different according to the user's network activities over available services, restrictions and applications, it is supposed that behavioral-based detectors are not well suited to all kind of networks. This paper presents the differences of detection results between some network scenarios by applying traditional detectors that were calculated with artificial neural networks. The same detector is deployed in different scenarios to measure the efficiency or inefficiency of static training detectors.

Keywords: NIDS; Knowledge database; Artificial neural networks; Anomaly detection; Information security; Intelligent detection

1. INTRODUCTION

Nowadays, network security systems require new techniques or methodologies to detect and avoid threats from intruders. An intruder tries to find the way to enter and explore a system with the maximum possible access [1]. Intrusion detection systems (IDS) are designed to recognize intrusion attempts in order to block attacks or produce alerts to be analyzed by an intelligent instance. According to the detection method, IDS are categorized into anomaly detection and misuse detection [2,3,4]. Although this classification is not recent, in general, the same categorization is accepted to classify IDS. For example, in 2000, Stefan Axelsson presented an IDS taxonomy to classify some research approaches, as can be seen in Figure 1 [5], among many other taxonomies that have been proposed.

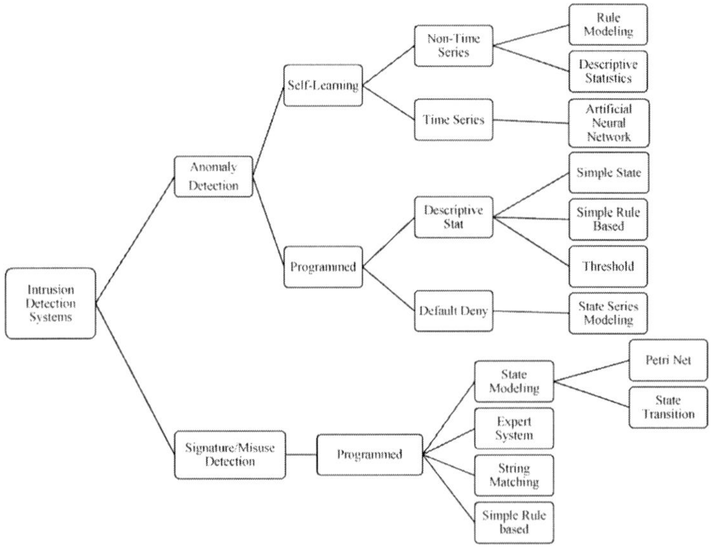

Figure 1. Intrusion detection system taxonomy.

In 2012, Liao *et al.* worked in the IDS taxonomy based on the Computer Emergency Response Team (CERT) statistics report of the increment of the amount of intrusions year-by-year [6]. They classified the intrusion detection approaches into five subcategories: statistics based, pattern based, rule based, state based and heuristic based. Finally, they concluded that the pattern-based approach is effective at identifying unknown and hidden attacks.

In recent years, anomaly detection IDS have been the source of great interest because of their capabilities for zero-day attack detection and self-learning. Anomaly detection is composed of a set of processes to identify differences between normal activities by comparing observed events with behavioral deviations in a network. The IDS analysis scheme can build profiles according to sèlected features from knowledge databases [7]. Those profiles are created by selecting, analyzing and ordering the behavioral characteristics of the computer network, such as connections, virtual ports, user profiles, among others, over a defined time period in normal operation [8].

According to the data source and connectivity properties, IDS are classified into two types, network intrusion detection systems (NIDS) and host intrusion detection systems (HIDS) [3,9]. Although many hybrid approaches have been proposed, commercial network security implementations have deployed NIDS because they are more efficient against malware attacks than HIDS [10]. An NIDS has a sensor that is activated in promiscuous mode to capture all data traffic in a network and stores the attack patterns in a database [11].

For many years, IDS have been widely deployed in secure network infrastructures as the first line of defense against security threats and intruders. As early as 1985, Denning and Neumann [12] suggested a basic model of IDS that included system design and activity profiles. Nowadays, new threats are born within every hour, and the time between attack deployment and detection is uncertain. Most of these attacks are Internet-based events that are triggered by activity from inside or even outside of the computer network.

For some approaches, attacks are classified into four categories: denial of services, remote to local (R2L), user to root (U2R) and probes [13,14]. Tang and Cao in 2009 proposed a new approach to discover novel attacks, which aims at machine learning implementation to demonstrate the high performance against common attacks, with detectors obtained with artificial neural networks (ANN) [15]. The portion of analyzed attacks can be seen in Figure 2.

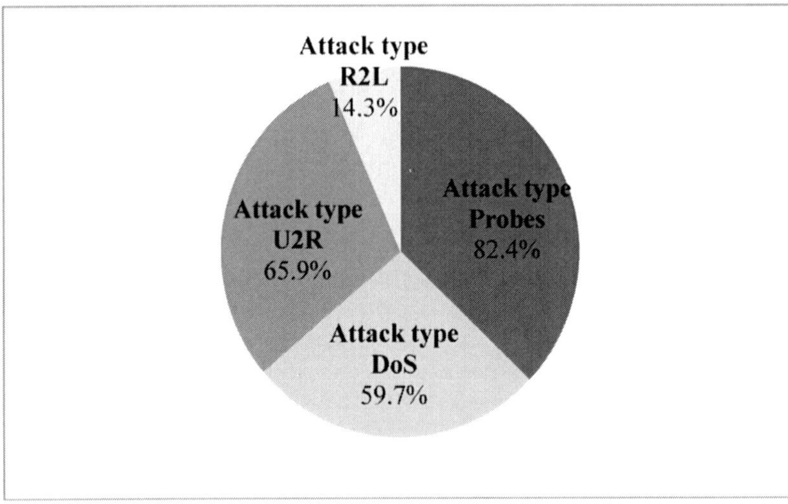

Figure 2. The portion of analyzed attacks with the ANN approach [15].

In 2003, Lazarevic *et al.* evaluated anomaly detection techniques in NIDS with DARPA datasets to analyze the unsolved problems for IDS design and the complexity of deploying machine learning techniques with real network data [16]. They concluded that with the DARPA dataset, it is possible to achieve an effectiveness of up to 74% to detect attacks in multiple connections and a detection rate of 56% in a single connection, which is obviously not as useful today. Subsequently, Zhao *et al.* in 2010 conducted an analysis to design IDS based on data mining methods in order to identify the advantages and disadvantages of using hybrid systems with misuse detection and anomaly detection techniques. They concluded that the combination of intrusion detection engines is efficient to detect known and unknown threats, but the design of an accurate system is more complex [1].

Another important issue is the selection of the relevant features, as Olusola *et al.* identified in 2010 [17]. They evaluated the relevance of feature selection for IDS design along with data mining and machine learning methods. With most of these approaches, when the proposals are implemented in real network scenarios, the results had failed for false positive rates or even detection results.

Most of the anomaly detection approaches have deployed similar steps:

(1)

Acquire or use knowledge databases for traffic behavior in network scenarios, such as KDD99, CAIDA or CRAWDAD, among others, with samples of normal and under attack behavior.

(2)

Select the best representative features.

(3)

Reduce the search space by diminishing redundant information.

(4)

Apply a machine learning method to generate detectors.

Detectors must be applied in network scenarios in order to detect threats for real time traffic, but, when they are applied in real scenarios, the results for false positives and the detection rates are not predictable. This is in part because the behavior of a network depends on conditions, such as applications, servers or even telecommunication architectures, and the network where the IDS is installed does not have the same behavior as that in which the detector was trained. The main goal of this paper is to show the statistical differences of the performance between the same detectors in dissimilar network scenarios.

2. MATERIALS AND METHODS

The applied method began by acquiring the traffic information for real scenarios to then select the correct features and to filter them to reduce the search space. ANN is the machine learning method deployed to generate detectors. The system was trained based on a real network scenario, and the obtained ANN was tested for four different network scenarios with a dissimilar network behavior. Insider attacks were deployed to calculate the performance for detection and false positive rates.

2.1. Features Selection

The features are acquired with the Spleen application [18], and the structure of the variables are similar to KDD99 [19]. It is important to make clear that neither the database nor the same number of features of KDD99 were used, just its structure. The dataset is acquired from normal traffic and under attack samples and finally labeled by the application. The data is captured from the network traffic samples during peak hours.

Principal component analysis (PCA) was the method selected to extract the attributes, because it is a useful technique for very large-dimensional datasets compared to other analysis tools that are limited to low-dimensional datasets [20]. The relevant advantage of PCA for anomaly detection is its capacity to identify high and low values of the features with high accuracy [21]. In this work, PCA is employed for the feature selection phase, in order to reduce the dimensionality in the feature space. The method has been employed in previous approaches for feature selection for IDSs, specifically with KDD, NSL-KDD and CAIDA, among others [22,23,24]. In the work of Kuchimanchi, *et al.* [24], they employed the critical eigenvalue test. The test recommends using the principal components whose eigenvalues exceed the threshold $\tau_e = d^{0.6}/15$, where d is the dimension of the dataset before the feature selection process. With our dataset, the threshold is $\tau_e = 0.7136$. The rest of the features are assumed to contain redundancy and noise. In previous works, the significant features of KDD were calculated for 19 of the original 42, but we had to calculate the relevant features again, because our dataset is different from KDD, as was stated before.

With the selected features, it is necessary to learn the search space with a machine learning technique. Many machine learning approaches, such as genetic algorithms (GA), support vector machines (SVM), artificial immune systems (AIS), decision trees or ANN, among others, have been applied to anomaly detection, and although it is possible to find differences regarding the detection results between those methods, their effectiveness is not so different, so the machine learning technique employed in this work is ANN [25], because it is a well-known Machine Learning (ML) method with proven performance for anomaly detection and there are many approaches to compare with our results [2,5,9,10,21,26].

The basic attributes are analyzed in different network scenarios as unusual TCP flags, the number of out of sequence packets and the average of the payload size [27]. The number of connections and the percentage of connections are statistical features based on the host checking the number of packets with the optimal connection during the three-way hand-shake process and synchronization. Other features are based on the behavior change detector (BCD) as shown inTable 1. The advantage of BCD features for IDS is their capacity to detect anomaly changes in events during connection [28,29,30].

The features are shown in lines through an array of *m* trainings and *n* features. Datasets are generated in comma separated value (CSV) files, and they contain 52 features. The selected features are numeric and the non-selected features are represented as a null value with the "$" symbol. Null fields for the non-selected features are then simplified into a new variable. The connections structure is represented in the next matrix. The feature representation is based on the number of connections and the number of features.

$$\begin{matrix} F_{11} & F_{12} & \cdots & F_{1xn} \\ F_{21} & F_{22} & \cdots & F_{2xn} \\ \vdots & \vdots & & \vdots \\ F_{mx1} & F_{mx2} & \cdots & F_{mxn} \end{matrix}$$

The main variables are a combination of the original features stored in a new matrix that represents the network profiles. Network scenarios have different features and data traffic, according to frequent services, virtual ports, traffic requests, the number of users, among others.

2.2. Network Scenarios

Four network scenarios were selected for the deployed detectors. Tests were made during working hours and at the same time periods. The first scenario is a wireless network in a public segment. The second scenario is a wired network in a private environment, mostly with World Wide Web traffic. The third segment is a server farm with a secure configuration. The last scenario is a LAN in a militarized zone (MZ) with VoIP and streaming services.

Table 1. Behavior change detector features description.

Feature	Description
Unusual TCP flags	Boolean variable to check the connection when it has received packets with an unusual TCP flag configuration.
Number of out of sequence packets	Number of packets that arrive with delay and change the message's order (latency).
Average of the payload size in bytes	This is the average size of the real message without the header. Payload size is shown in an integer variable represented in bytes series. The result sizes shown depend on services requested and connections active.
Count of the connections from this client in the last connection	This feature has control of the connections from the specific host-client only in the last capture or data analysis. This feature is an integer variable.
Percentage of connections from the current client with the States S0 and S1	The S0 state is a configuration to check an initial Synchronization (SYN), but after, there are no reports of a server request. The S1 state is the configuration of the three-way hand-shake connection, but does not show more packets between the network traffic.
Percentage of connections from the current client to the current host	This is a feature shown in a double variable, because it represents a percentage of the connections from the current client that has the same host and request services.
Percentage of connections to the current host with State S0 and others	The percentage of connections that has attempted connecting with the server, but has not received answer. Then, the same sends another package with a new attempt to receive an answer.
Difference between the number of connections to the current host	Represents the connections rejected from the host. The host rejected difference is compared with the ACK package request that has this host.
Difference between the number of connections to the current service	Represents the connections rejected, but depends on the service requested. The service rejected difference is compared for the current service approved against requested services.
Unanswered host count	This feature is shown in an integer variable based on the number of connections unanswered by the host. It is based on the number of packages that have not arrived to the destination.
Unanswered service count	This feature is shown in an integer variable for the number of connections unanswered according to the services request. It is based on the number of packages that have not arrived to the destination.

2.2.1. Wireless Scenario

e architecture of the wireless network is presented in Figure 3. The most frequent identified services were e-mail, streaming, data and audio transmission through ports 80, 2869, 993 and 5222. There were 100,023 connections during the test time, which is equivalent to around 300 users. Datasets were collected in 51 buffers, and there were 58,679 closed connections.

2.2.2. Wired Scenario

The wired network has a structure with 20 hosts connected, including serial port connections with standard output devices. User's access is limited to web services such as corporate e-mail, database access and secure websites. The most frequent identified services were connected through ports: 80, 443, 13,000, 445, 16,881 and 2,011. The wired network architecture is shown inFigure 4. There were 35,047 connections. Datasets were collected in 17 buffers, and there were 27,465 closed connections with 3,534,549 packets.

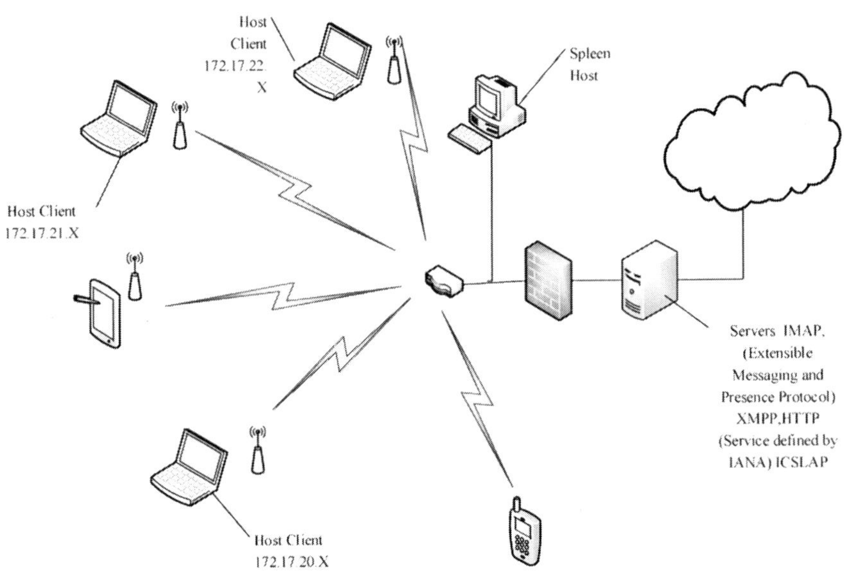

Figure 3. Architecture of the wireless network scenario.

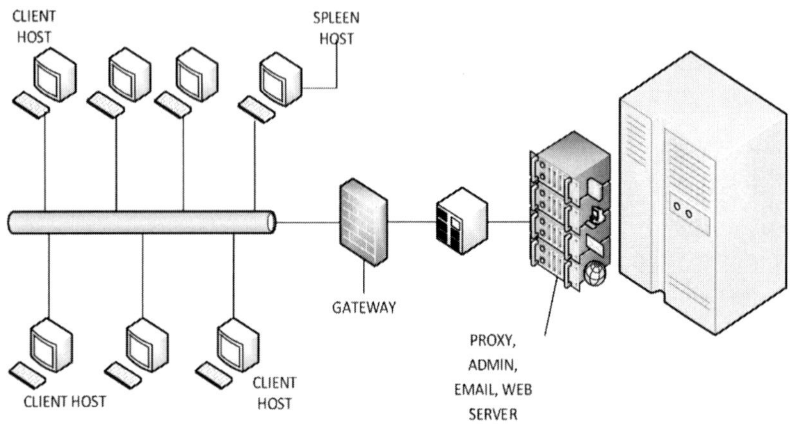

Figure 4. Architecture of the wired scenario.

2.2.3. Server Scenario

The server's network provides services, such as firewall, local DHCP, basic streaming, DNS and web servers, streaming and FTP, as can be seen in Figure 5. The identified services employed ports 88, 13,000, 445, 135, 49,155, 389 and 8,443. One of the main protocols for the analyzed traffic was Kerberos [31]. There were about 100,100 connections. Datasets were collect in 33 buffers, and there were 3,839 closed connections with 6,769,309 packets. Demilitarized Zone (DMZ) is composed by six servers, and a host with the tool to monitor the traffic is also included.

2.2.4. LAN MZ Scenario

The selected LAN is in an MZ, as in Figure 6. Each user has access to the intranet to update and share information across departments. The most frequent services were identified through ports 80, 443, 13,000, 445, and 5,678. Management traffic services are bigger in the intranet than over Internet connections. Some common services are remote replication agent connection (RRAC) with 5678 TCP/UDP protocols. Another frequent service is Windows-DS through port 445. The number of connections was approximately 111,000, with about 15 users during the test time. Datasets were collected in 21 buffers, and there were 5,505 closed connections with 16,818,686 packets.

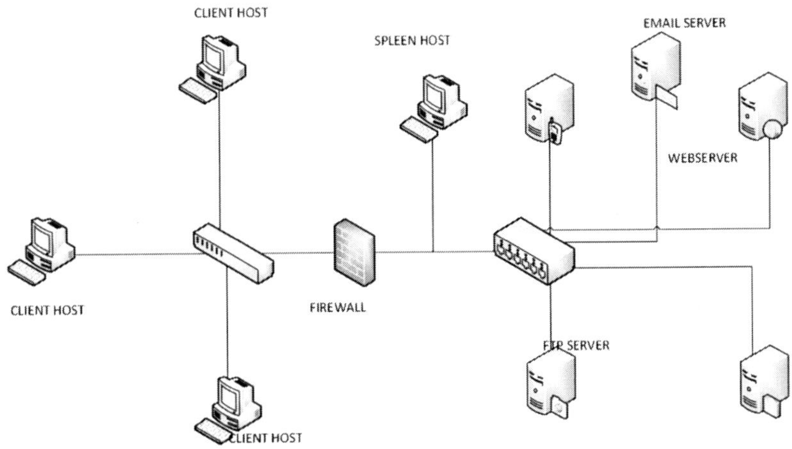

Figure 5. Architecture of the server scenario.

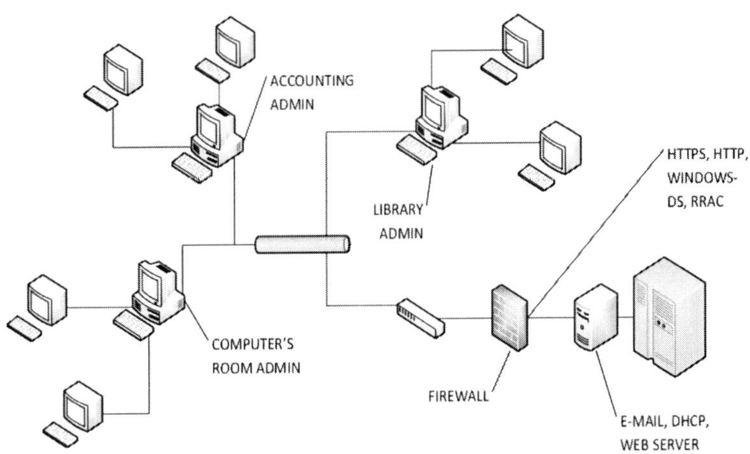

Figure 6. Architecture of the LAN militarized zone (MZ) scenario. RRAC, remote replication agent connection.

2.3. Artificial Neural Network as the Machine Learning Method

Variables that were selected with PCA from the original datasets according to characteristics and priority weights are employed in the training, validation and test stages [31]. The features applied to the ANN are composed of four BCD variables, and they are complemented with four variables from the traditional features [13,32,33]. Each feature represents an input to the neural network, based on the status flag of the main attributes. The first stage is to select the data and to load the matrix with eight input variables. The target is loaded to establish the output network. The percentage of the training, test and validation stages is configured according to the dataset samples. Fifty percent of the dataset samples was selected for the training stage, 25 percent for the testing stage and the remaining 25 percent for the validation stage. Then, a suitable neural network is designed by selecting the hidden neurons and the output layer based on the target.

A variable's status depends on its statistical value and its selection in each connection. The destination host error rate is a BCD variable that has two status flags, which are represented in bits. The input variable is normalized between those values that represent the true or false status of the error. The features with percentage values are normalized for the training. Normalization is implemented to improve the training time and to standardize the inputs in order to stabilize weights and biases. The normalization value has a range 0 to 1 to represent the high and low status. Weight and bias values are stored into a matrix; afterwards, they are tested in each network scenario.

The training was performed with the Levenberg–Marquardt (LM) standard back-propagation algorithm. LM is an iterative algorithm represented in Equation (1) [34]. The LM algorithm is one of the most efficient algorithms to combine the gradient descent method and the Gauss–Newton method for the training stage.

$$f(x) = \sum_{i=1}^{m} \left(y(x, t_i) - \varphi(t_i)\right)^2 \tag{1}$$

The function has m number of connections, where x is a vector of input variables and t is a scalar. φ is a scalar that includes the weights of the inputs of the training matrix. The LM algorithm is based on the Hessian matrix [34,35]. The Hessian matrix can be calculated with Equation (2) as a typical training feedforward network.

$$H = J^T J \tag{2}$$

where J is the Jacobian component of the principal matrix with input variables. The matrix has m rows that represent the number of connections and has n columns that represent the input variables. J implements a gradient vector for each function with e, which is the vector of network errors. The gradient vector is represented in Equation (3) [35].

$$g = J^T e \tag{3}$$

The selected features applied to the ANN are described as follows: The first input is the number of connections with the same service at the current connection in the past two seconds. The second feature is the percentage of connections that have synchronization status error. The third feature is the percentage of connections that have a reject status error. The last variable of the normal database for IDS is the count of connections having the same destination host. The BCD features are: the average of payload size in bytes, the count of connections from this client in the last connection, the percentage of connections from the current client to the current host and the percentage of connections to the current host with States S0 and others. The processing system and the power of the network is delayed for the training algorithm. The appropriate fitting configuration in this ANN is represented with ten hidden neurons for the input data. The ANN structure is shown in Figure 7, with eight inputs trained by the Levenberg–Marquardt algorithm and one output. The output variable acquires two values: possible attack or a normal connection. We create an ANN for each type of attack; that means that there are three developed detectors. The initial ANN was set to train for 320 epochs for the first set of detectors, 360 epochs for the second set and 290 for the third set.

Tests were reported for the connections captured with the software tool. Statistical events are extracted from services for the TCP requests, HTTP sessions and processing times, among others. String and decimal classes are processed to convert the values to binary representation based on the variable's status. The target is the last variable of the connections collected in a vector array. The first target is used to identify the attack type. The attacks are based on the probe category to test each scenario; Table 2 shows the attack types implemented during the training and the code.

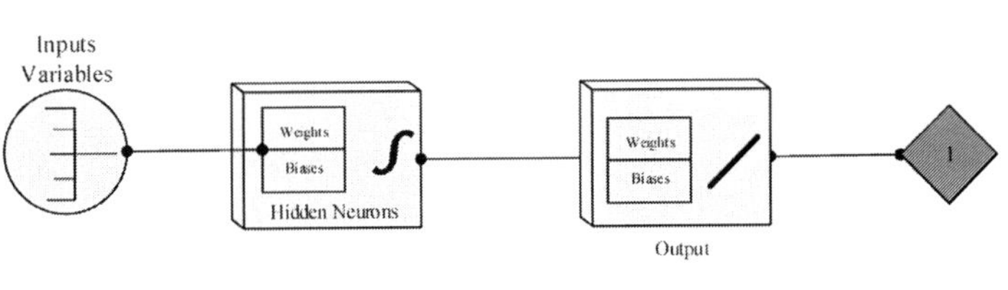

Figure 7. Artificial neural network structure for each type of attack.

Table 2. Attack types and their numerical representation.

Attack type	Numerical value
Normal	00
ExplorePorts probes	01
IpAgry probes	10
Nessus probes	11

Each attack has been used to test the efficiency in detection. Vulnerabilities are scanned to develop IDS detectors and to generate reports based on alerts for the incidents. The Nessus scan ports looking for intrusions in a system.

Analysis of the changes in the behavior in the network scenarios is based on the mean squared error (MSE). For each single detector, the MSE was calculated, and the final detection result is the mean of the three detectors.

The evaluation stage has additional tests of the training network. The main process is to analyze the weights and biases of training network, because these results are located in an array and modified in all of the scenarios to make the test. Inputs and targets are selected in this step to test the new network. Each scenario is tested, and its results are collected in statistics graphics.

3. DETECTION RESULTS

As was stated, detectors were acquired with lab traffic applied to an ANN at three stages, training validation and testing. Afterwards, those detectors were deployed in acquired databases in each single network scenario without retraining the ANN. Due to the nature of the ANN training process, the analysis was made in the same portion of the traffic scenarios, which is why there are results for scenarios for the training stage although, there was no training process; this is just to compare the results under the same conditions. The results can be seen in Figure 8.

MSE is the difference between targets and practical outputs; its ideal value is closer to zero, and it is related to the detection rate. The MSE training ANN represents the results of the detectors with the portion of the traffic database in the lab environment. These are the optimal results, because the lab data were employed to generate the ANN. The next results show the MSE of the network scenarios with the detectors of the lab data [36].

The best result for the performance test is the server network with an error of 0.116, and the worst performance was for the wireless network with 0.21719.

In order to determine if the detectors developed under the lab conditions can be used in real environments, due to the behavior for which they were trained being different from that for which they were set up, the traffic samples for each network scenario were employed to generate new detectors. The results for the detection with detectors created with ANN based on the same scenario in which they were deployed are called "MSE own training", and the results explained previously are called "MSE ext training". The results can be seen in Figure 9.

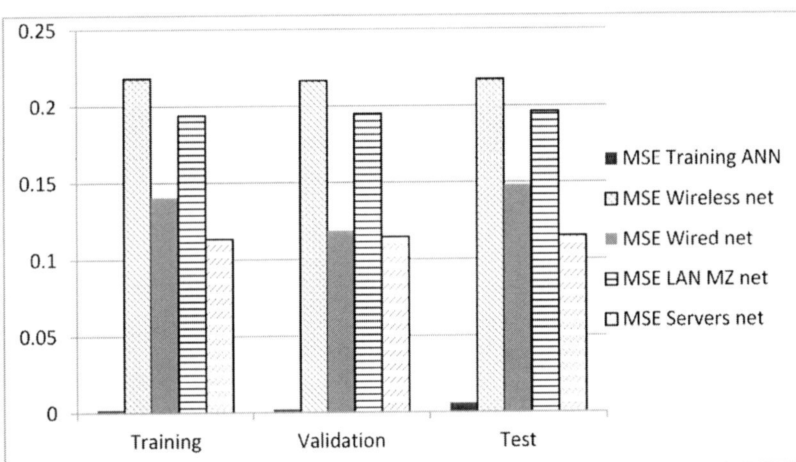

Figure 8. Detection results for the test stages of each network scenario to compare the detectors trained in the lab environment when applied in real-world networks.

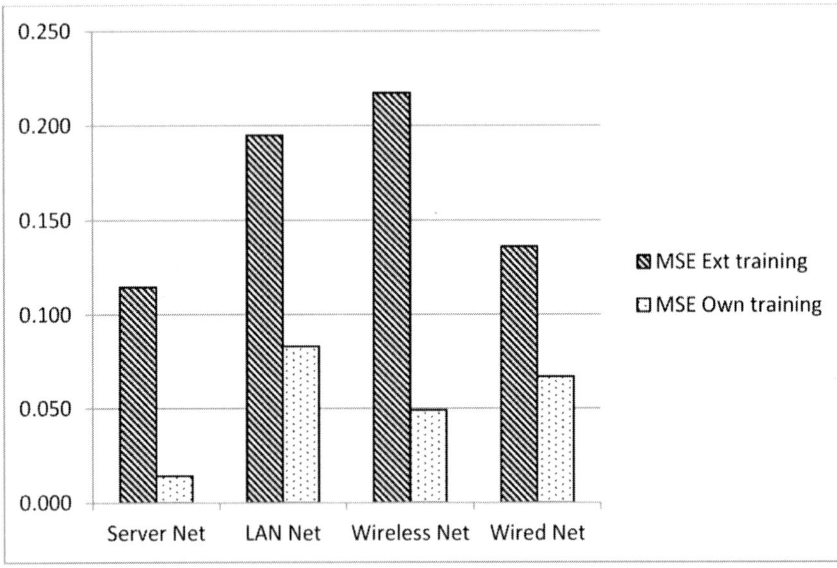

Figure 9. Statistics results for MSE external training and its own training network.

Detection is improved when the ANN is retrained, but in a real environment, this means that new data must be acquired each time a detector is installed.

4. DISCUSSION AND ANALYSIS

Internet-based attacks are changing dynamically from polymorphisms to mobile integrated attacks. As we increase web services and cloud dependency, the number of security holes also increases, which is posing a completely new threat in the near future. It is necessary to employ intelligent methods, and anomaly detection could provide the necessary detection availability. However, it turns out that most of the intelligent approaches employ similar general steps with different machine learning techniques. The main problem is not the learning method, as it is possible to see differences between them, but these differences are not really significant. It seems that the difficult point is to find a way to obtain the training data from realistic scenarios and to create a technique to retrain the system constantly, something similar to a biological immune system, not as an algorithm, but as a complete network solution. In fact, artificial immune systems and sub-applications have been presented as machine learning methods, but as was stated, this is just another interesting method.

With anomaly detection, the results show that an IDS detector that was developed in the context of a network's behavior is not useful in another network with dissimilar applications. The detector is well adapted in its own environment, but it needs to be retrained to achieve good detection results. The detection differences between the network where the ANN detectors were calculated and the tested scenarios are unacceptable in real environments, going from an error of 0.1% in the same network that was used for training, to almost 22% in a different scenario.

It would be useful to apply a methodology for transfer learning, also known as knowledge transfer. This is an emerging field in machine learning that tries to solve the problem of rebuilding the solution when the feature space and distribution have changed [37]. In fact, from the differences shown in this paper regarding the detection results in different network scenarios, it is clear that there will be a definition for the problem of knowledge transfer that could solve detection stability for IDS architectures in the near future.

Additionally, most approaches use old datasets, which is useful to probe machine learning methodologies, but is not helpful for new attack detection. This changes the accuracy of the system, because the old datasets were developed for simulation scenarios or with different network topologies. The parameters to be considered in Anomaly Detection (AD) IDS design are: network applications, security policies, memory capabilities to reinforce detectors, support of learning on the go, coordination between detectors for different behaviors and compatibility with auditing processes.

Although there are uncountable network user behaviors, it is possible to imagine a network classification according to its behavior, but in order to probe this statement, it is necessary to establish traffic behaviors that are not necessary related to topologies. For example, we calculated differences for detectors with two similar network topologies: a wired network and a LAN MZ network, but the variation of the detection error is near 10%, so a classification by Layer 1, 2 or 3 of the Open System Interconnection (OSI) model is not possible.

5. CONCLUSIONS

As expected for AD-based on behavior, detectors that were trained in a network environment are not suitable when installed in a network where the behavior is quite different. Those differences are not easy to model, because the user's behavior depends on variables, such as available ports, security policies for appliances, network architectures and even operating systems. What is normal in a network is not necessarily normal in another.

Nevertheless, the advantages of AD, such as the detection of zero-day attacks, obfuscated variations and insiders and their ability to reduce the search space compared with the growing rules of misuse detection, are motivations to develop a system capable of self-learning in the network in which the detector is set up.

ACKNOWLEDGMENTS

Edward Guillen thanks Jhordany Rodriguez for his work at "Grupo de Investigación en Seguridad y Sistemas de Comunicaciones" GISSIC on Spleen programming. This work was possible in part with the support of the Military University with funds of Project ING1199, and Colciencias young research program.

AUTHOR CONTRIBUTIONS

E.G author worked on the design of the tests, network scenarios, and analysis of results.

J. S author worked with the measurements of the scenarios and ML method.

R. P. worked on the architecture of the network scenarios

CONFLICTS OF INTEREST

The authors declare no conflict of interest.

REFERENCES

1. Zhao, D.; Xu, Q.; Feng, Z. Analysis and Design for Intrusion Detection System Based on Data Mining. In Proceedings of the 2010 Second International Workshop on Education Technology and Computer Science (ETCS), Wuhan, China, 6–7 March 2010; pp. 339–342.
2. Chen, C.-M.; Chen, Y.-L.; Lin, H.-C. An efficient network intrusion detection. *Comput. Commun.* **2010**, *33*, 477–484.
3. Hoque, M.S.; Mukit, M.A.; Bikas, M.A.N. An implementation of intrusion detection system using genetic algorithm. *Int. J. Network Secur. Appl.* **2012**, *4*, 109–120.
4. Kim, G.; Lee, S.; Kim, S. A novel hybrid intrusion detection method integrating anomaly detection with misuse detection. *Expert Syst. Appl.* **2014**, *41*, 1690–1700.
5. Axelsson, S. *Intrusion Detection Systems: A Survey and Taxonomy*; Technical Report: Chalmers University of Technology, Goteborg, Sweden; 14; March; 2000.
6. Liao, H.-J.; Richard Lin, C.-H.; Lin, Y.-C.; Tung, K.-Y. Intrusion detection system: A comprehensive review. *J. Netw. Comput. Appl.* **2013**, *36*, 16–24.
7. Cannady, J.; Harrell, J. A comparative analysis of current intrusion detection technologies. In Proceedings of the Fourth Technology for Information Security Conference, Houston, TX, USA, May 1996.
8. Scarfone, K.; Mell, P. Guide to intrusion detection and prevention systems (idps). *NIST Spec. Publ.* **2007**, *800*, 94.
9. Corchado, E.; Herrero, Á. Neural visualization of network traffic data for intrusion detection. *Appl. Soft Comput.* **2011**, *11*, 2042–2056.
10. Bhat, A.H.; Patra, S.; Jena, D. Machine Learning Approach for Intrusion Detection on Cloud Virtual Machines. *Int. J. Appl. Innov. Eng. Manage.* **2013**, *2*, 57–65.
11. Guillen, E.; Padilla, D.; Colorado, Y. Weaknesses and strengths analysis over network-based intrusion detection and prevention systems. In Proceedings on the IEEE Latin-American Conference

on Communications, 2009 (LATINCOM'09), Medellín, Colombia, 10–11 September 2009; pp. 1–5.

12. Denning, D.E.; Neumann, P.G. *Requirements and Model for Ides—A Real-Time Intrusion Detection Expert System*; SRI International Final Technical Report: Menlo Park, CA, USA; 28; February; 1985.

13. Kayacik, H.G.; Zincir-Heywood, A.N.; Heywood, M.I. Selecting features for intrusion detection: A feature relevance analysis on KDD 99 intrusion detection datasets. In Proceedings of the Third Annual Conference on Privacy, Security and Trust, New Brunswick, Canada, 12–14 October 2005.

14. Mukkamala, S.; Janoski, G.; Sung, A. Intrusion detection using neural networks and support vector machines. In Proceedings of the 2002 International Joint Conference on Neural Networks, 2002 (IJCNN'02.), Honolulu, HI, USA, 12–17 May 2002; pp. 1702–1707.

15. Tang, H.; Cao, Z. Machine Learning-based Intrusion Detection Algorithms. *J. Comput. Inf. Syst.* **2009**, *5*, 1825–1831.

16. Lazarevic, A.; Ertцz, L.; Kumar, V.; Ozgur, A.; Srivastava, J. A Comparative Study of Anomaly Detection Schemes in Network Intrusion Detection. In Proceedings of the Third SIAM International Conference on Data Mining, San Francisco, CA, USA, 1–3 May 2003; pp. 25–36.

17. Olusola, A.A.; Oladele, A.S.; Abosede, D.O. Analysis of KDD 99 intrusion detection dataset for selection of relevance features. In Proceedings of the World Congress on Engineering and Computer Science, San Francisco, CA, USA, 20–22 October 2010; pp. 20–22.

18. Rodriguez, J. GTS: GNU Triangulated Surface Library. Available online: http://gts.sourceforge.net/ (accessed on 13 April 2015).

19. Stolfo, S.J.; Fan, W.; Lee, W.; Prodromidis, A.; Chan, P.K. Cost-based modeling for fraud and intrusion detection: Results from the JAM project. In Proceedings of the DARPA Information Survivability Conference and Exposition, 2000 (DISCEX'00), Hilton Head, SC, USA, 25–27 January 2000; pp. 130–144.

20. Kim, B.-J.; Kim, I.K. *Machine Learning Approach to Realtime Intrusion Detection Systems. AI 2005: Advances in Artificial Intelligence*; Springer Berlin Heidelberg: Berlin, Germany, 2005; pp. 153–163.

21. Camacho, J.; Macia-Fernandez, G.; Diaz-Verdejo, J.; Garcia-Teodoro, P. Tackling the Big Data 4 vs for anomaly detection. In Proceedings of the 2014 IEEE Conference on Computer Communications Workshops (INFOCOM WKSHPS), Toronto, Canadá, 27 April–02 May 2014; pp. 500–505.

22. Eid, H.F.; Darwish, A.; Abraham, A. Principle components analysis and support vector machine based intrusion detection system. In Proceedings of the 2010 10th International Conference on Intelligent Systems Design and Applications (ISDA), Cairo, Egypt, 29 November–1 December 2010; pp. 363–367.

23. Chen, Y.; Li, Y.; Cheng, X.Q.; Guo, L. Survey and taxonomy of feature selection algorithms in intrusion detection system. In *Information Security and Cryptology*; Springer Berlin Heidelberg: Berlin, Germany, 2006; pp. 153–167.

24. Kuchimanchi, G.K.; Phoha, V.V.; Balagani, K.S.; Gaddam, S.R. Dimension reduction using feature extraction methods for Real-time misuse detection systems. In Proceedings of the Fifth Annual IEEE SMC on Information Assurance Workshop, West Point, NY, USA, 10–11 June 2004; pp. 195–202.

25. Govindarajan, M.; Chandrasekaran, R. Intrusion detection using neural based hybrid classification methods. *Comput. Netw.* **2011**, *55*, 1662–1671.

26. Amiri, F.; Rezaei Yousefi, M.; Lucas, C.; Shakery, A.; Yazdani, N. Mutual information based feature selection for intrusion detection systems. *J. Netw. Comput. Appl.* **2011**, *34*, 1184–1199.

27. Rangadurai Karthick, R.; Hattiwale, V.P.; Ravindran, B. Adaptive network intrusion detection system using a hybrid approach. In Proceedings of 2012 Fourth International Conference on Communication Systems and Networks (COMSNETS), Bangalore, India, 3–7 January 2012; pp. 1–7.

28. Guillén, E.; Rodriguez, J.; Páez, R. Evaluating Performance of an Anomaly Detection Module with Artificial Neural Network Implementation. *Int. J. Comput. Inf. Syst. Control Eng.* **2013**, *7*, 836–842.

29. Sommer, R.; Paxson, V. Outside the closed world: On using machine learning for network intrusion detection. In Proeedings of the 2010 IEEE Symposium on Security and Privacy (SP), Oakland, CA, USA, 16-19 May, 2010; pp. 305–316.

30. Wang, K.; Stolfo, S.J. Anomalous payload-based network intrusion detection. In Proceedings of the Recent Advances in Intrusion Detection, Sophia Antipolis, France, 15–17 September 2004; pp. 203–222.

31. Neuman, B.C.; Ts'o, T. Kerberos: An authentication service for computer networks. *IEEE Commun. Mag.* **1994**, *32*, 33–38.

32. Mahoney, M.V.; Chan, P.K. *PHAD: Packet header anomaly detection for identifying hostile network traffic*; Florida Institute of Technology Technical Report: Melbourne, FL. USA; April; 2001.

33. Sung, A.H.; Mukkamala, S. Identifying important features for intrusion detection using support vector machines and neural networks. In Proceedings of the 2003 Symposium on Applications and the Internet, Orlando, FL, USA, 27–31 January 2003; pp. 209–216.

34. Wilamowski, B.M.; Yu, H. Improved computation for Levenberg–Marquardt training. *IEEE Trans. Neural Netw.* **2010**, *21*, 930–937.

35. Yu, H.; Wilamowski, B.M. Levenberg-Marquardt Training. *Ind. Electron. Handb.* **2011**, *5*, 1–15.

36. Guillén, E.; Rodriguez, J.; Páez, R.; Rodriguez, A. Detection of non-content based attacks using GA with extended KDD features. In Proceedings of the World Congress on Engineering and Computer Science, San Francisco, CA, USA, 24–26 October 2012; pp. 30–35.

37. Pan, S.J.; Yang, Q. A survey on transfer learning. Knowledge and Data Engineering. *IEEE Trans.* **2010**, *22*, 1345–1359.

6

CHAPTER

AN ENTROPY-BASED NETWORK ANOMALY DETECTION METHOD

Przemysław Bereziński [1], Bartosz Jasiul [1,*] and Marcin Szpyrka [2]

[1]C4I Systems' Department, Military Communication Institute, ul. Warszawska 22a, 05-130 Zegrze, Poland

[2]Department of Applied Computer Science, AGH University of Science and Technology, al. Mickiewicza 30, 30-059 Krakow, Poland

ABSTRACT

Data mining is an interdisciplinary subfield of computer science involving methods at the intersection of artificial intelligence, machine learning and statistics. One of the data mining tasks is anomaly detection which is the analysis of large quantities of data to identify items, events or observations which do not conform to an expected pattern. Anomaly detection is applicable in a variety of domains, e.g., fraud detection, fault detection, system health monitoring but this article focuses on application of anomaly detection in the field of network intrusion detection. The main goal of the article is to prove that an entropy-based approach is suitable to detect modern botnet-like malware based on anomalous patterns in network. This aim is achieved by realization of the following points: (i) preparation of a concept of original entropy-based network anomaly detection method, (ii) implementation of the method, (iii) preparation of original dataset, (iv) evaluation of the method.

Keywords: Anomaly detection; Entropy; Malware detection

1. INTRODUCTION

The first anomaly detection method for intrusion detection was proposed almost 40 years ago [1]. Today, network anomaly detection is a very broad and heavily explored subject but the problem of finding a generic method for a wide range of network anomalies is still unsolved. Widely used intrusion detection systems are ineffective against a modern malicious software (malware). Such systems mostly make use of common signature-based (or misuse-based) technique. This approach is known for its shortcomings [2–5]. Signatures describe only illegal patterns in network traffic, so a prior knowledge is required [2]. Signature-based solutions do not cope with evasion techniques and not known yet attacks (0-days) [3]. Moreover, they are unable to detect a specific attack until a rule for the corresponding vulnerability is created, tested, released and deployed, which usually takes long time [4,5]. Therefore, a proper network anomaly detection as one of possible solutions to complement signature-based solutions is essential. Recently, entropy-based methods which rely on network feature distributions has been of a great interest [6–11]. It is crucial to check if entropy-based approach is efficient in detection of anomalous network activities caused by modern botnet-like malware [12]. Botnet is a group of infected hosts (bots) controlled by Command and Cotrol (C&C) servers operated by cyber-criminals. The number of such a malware as well as the level of its sophistication increases each year [13]. Damage from this type of malware can take many serious forms including loss of important data, reputation or money. Moreover, nowadays such malware is also used in a warfare to cunduct sabotega and espionage [14]. Entropy-based approach to detect anomalies caused by botnet-like malware in a local networks is not investigated area. Entropy-based methods proposed in the past e.g. [8,10,15] deals with a massive spreads of old types of worms (not botnet-like) or different types of Distributed Denial of Service (DDoS) attacks in a high-speed networks. In this article we propose an effective entropy based method for detection and categorization of network anomalies that indicate existence of the botnet-like malware in the local networks. This type of anomalies are often very small and hidden in a network traffic volume expressed by the number of flows, packets or bytes, so their detection with popular solutions and methods which rely mostly on a traffic volume changes, e.g., [16–19] is highly difficult.

The main goal of this article is to prove that entropy-based approach is suitable to detect modern botnet-like malware based on anomalous network patterns. The aim was achieved by realization the following points: (i) preparation of a concept of original entropy-based network anomaly detection method, (ii) implementation of the method, (iii) preparation of original dataset, (iv) evaluation of the method.

These steps are discussed in details in the further part of the article that is organized as follows:

- Section 2 reviews related work in the area of network anomaly detection.
- Section 3 introduces the definition of Shannon entropy and describes Renyi and Tsallis generalizations. Brief overview as well as comparison of entropy measures are provided.
- Section 4 presents the architecture of the proposed method. Detailed specification as well as results of implementation are given.
- Section 5 refers to the dataset developed in order to evaluate a performance of the proposed method.
- Section 6 presents results of verification of the method.
- Section 7 finishes this article providing conclusions and short summary. It also outlines further work.

2. RELATED WORK

This section reviews related work in the area of network anomaly detection. The section starts with a general overview of the latest advances in this broad subject. Then, more details on anomaly detection techniques that are closely related to the approach proposed in this article are presented and comments are provided.

2.1. General Overview of Network Anomaly Techniques

The problem of anomaly detection in network traffic has been extensively studied. There are many surveys, review articles, as well as books on this broad subject. A good number of research on anomaly detection techniques is found in several books, e.g. [20–23]. In surveys such as [24,25], authors discuss anomaly detection in general and cover the network intrusion detection domain only briefly. In several review papers [26–32] various network anomaly detection methods have been summarized. From aforementioned surveys one can find that the most effective methods of network anomaly detection are Principle Component Analysis [33–35], Wavelet analysis [36–38], Markovian models [39,40], Clustering [41–43], Histograms [44,45], Sketches [46,47], and Entropies [8,15,48].

2.2. Closely Related Work

In this paragraph a closer look at works strictly related to approach proposed in this article is taken. Analysis of detection methods based on summarizing feature distributions via entropy, histograms and sketches is provided. Special attention is devoted to the methods employing different forms of entropy. Some comments according noticed gaps are given. Section starts with the comparison of the feature distributions approach to the older but still more popular detection via counters.

2.2.1. Detection via Counters

In the past, anomalies were treated as deviations in the traffic volume. Simple counters like: number of flows, packets (total, forwarded, fragmented, discarded) and bytes (per packet, per second) were used. These counters can be derived from network devices via Simple Network Management Protocol (SNMP) [49] or NetFlow [50].

Barford *et al.* [17] presented wavelet analysis to distinguish between predictable and anomalous traffic volume changes using a very basic set of counters from NetFlow and SNMP data. They used rather advanced signal analysis technique combined with very simple metrics, *i.e.*, number of flows, packets and bytes. The authors reported some positive results in detection of high-volume anomalies like network failure, bandwidth flood and flash crowd.

Kim *et al.* [18] proposed a method where many different DDoS attacks [51,52] are described in terms of traffic patterns in a flow characteristics. In particular, the authors focused on counters like: number of flows, packets, bytes, the flow and packet sizes, average flow size and number of packets per flow. In the presented TCP SYN flood example the following pattern was applied: a large number of flows, yet small number of small packets and no constraints on the bandwidth and the total amount of packets. This pattern differs significantly from the one generated for an ICMP/UDP flooding attacks, where high bandwidth consumption and a large number of packets is involved. Although the authors reported some good results, they also mentioned that common legitimate peer-to-peer (P2P) traffic [53] may result in some false alarms in their approach.

A threshold-based detector measuring the deviation from a mean value present in a traffic collection algorithm for frequent collection of SNMP data was proposed by Lee *et al.* [54]. To assess the algorithm, the authors examined how it impacts detection of volume anomalies. Only some minor differences were reported in comparison to the original traffic collection algorithm.

Casas *et al.* [55] introduced an anomaly detection algorithm based on SNMP data which deals with abrupt and large traffic changes. The authors proposed a novel linear parsimonious model for anomaly-free network flows. This model makes it possible to treat the legitimate traffic as a nuisance parameter, to remove it from the detection problem and to detect the anomalies in the residuals. Authors reported that with this approach they slightly improved previously introduced approach based on PCA in terms of a false alarms.

Many commercial and open source solutions that relay on SNMP or NetFlow counters are available on the market, e.g., NFSen [16], NtopNg [19], Plixer Scrutinizer [56], Peassler PRTG [57], and Solarwinds Network Traffic Analyzer [58]. All of them provide more or less the same functionality, *i.e.*, browsing and filtering network data, raporting and alerting. Several commercial solutions like, e.g., Invea-Tech FlowMon [59] or AKMA Labs FlowMatrix [60] offer some advanced anomaly detection methods which mostly rely on predefined set of rules for detection of undesirable behavior patterns and some simple long-term network behavior profiles in terms of services, traffic volume and communication sides.

Concluding this subsection, we noticed that although there are many methods that rely on counters, their use is limited. The problem with a counter-based approach is that it is strictly connected with a traffic volume. Nowadays many anomalous network activities such as low-rate DDoS [61,62] stealth scanning or botnet-like worm propagation and communication do not result in substantial traffic volume change. Presented above counter-based methods handles well large and abrupt traffic changes such as bandwidth flooding attacks or flash crowds, but a large group of anomalies which do not cause changes of volume remains undetected. Moreover there is also some practical issue connected with counters reported by Brauckhoff *et al.* [63] who stated that packets sampling used by many routers to save resources when collecting data can influence a counter-based anomaly detection metrics, but does not significantly affect the distribution of traffic features.

2.2.2. Detection via Feature Distributions

Network anomaly detection via traffic feature distributions is becoming more and more popular. Several feature distributions, *i.e.*, header-based (addresses, ports, flags), volume-based (host or service specific percentage of flows, packets and bytes) and behavior-based (in/out connections for particular host) have been suggested in the past [8,15,64]. However, it is unclear which feature distributions perform best. Nychis in [8], based on his results of pairwise correlation reported dependencies between addresses and ports and recommended the use of volume-based and behavior-based feature distributions. In opposite, Tellenbach in [15] found no correlation among header-based features.

In this article, original results of feature correlation are presented and some interesting conclusions are given in Section 6.

Shannon Entropy

Entropy as the measure of uncertainty can be used to summarize feature distributions in a compact form, *i.e.*, single number. Many forms of entropy exist, but only a few have been applied to network anomaly detection. The most popular is the well-known Shannon entropy [65,66]. Application of Shannon measures like relative entropy and conditional entropy to conduct network anomaly detection were proposed by Lee and Xiang [67]. Also, Lakhina *et al.* [64] made use of Shannon entropy to sum up a feature distribution of network flows. By using unsupervised learning, the authors showed that anomalies can be successfully clustered. Wagner and Plattner [7] made use of the Kolmogorov Complexity (related to Shannon entropy) [68,69] in order to detect worms in network traffic. Their work mostly focuses on implementation aspects and scalability and does not propose any specific analysis techniques. The authors reported that their method is able to detect worm outbreaks and massive scanning activities in a near real time. Ranjan *et al.* [70] suggested another worm detection algorithm which measures Shannon entropy ratios for traffic feature pairs and issues an alarm on sudden changes. Gu *et al.* [71] made use of Shannon maximum entropy estimation to estimate the network baseline distribution and to give a multi-dimensional view of network traffic. The authors claim that with their approach they were able to distinguish anomalies that change the traffic either abruptly or slowly.

Generalized entropy

Besides Shannon entropy, some generalization of entropy have been recently introduced in the context of network anomaly detection. Einman in [6,72,73] reported some positive results of using T-entropy [74] for intrusion detection based on packet analysis. T-entropy can be estimated from a string complexity measure called T-complexity. String complexity is a minimum number of steps required to construct a given string. In contrast to entropy, where probabilities (estimated from frequencies) can be permuted, in a complexity-based approach, the order matters. A string is compressed with some algorithm and the output length is used to estimate the complexity. Finally, the complexity becomes an estimate for the entropy. Because in this approach sequence of events is crucial, it fits to fine-grinded methods of network data analysis like full packet or header packet inspection. However, this type of inspection is not scalable in the context of network speed. Some details about T-entropy are also presented in our paper [75]. A parameterized generalization of entropy have also been recently reported as very promising. The Shannon entropy assumes a tradeoff between contributions from the main mass of the distribution and the tail. With the parameterized Tsallis [76–78] or Renyi [79,80] entropy, one can control this tradeoff. In general, if the parameter denoted as α has a positive value, it exposes the main mass, if the value is negative – it refers to the tail. Ziviani *et al.* [81] investigated Tsallis entropy in the context of the best value ofα parameter in DoS attacks detection. They found that α-value around 0.9 is the best for detecting such attacks. Shafiq *et al.* [82] did the same for port scan anomalies caused by malware. He reported that for scan anomalies α-value around 0.5 is the best choice. A comparative study of the use of the Shannon, Renyi and Tsallis entropy for attribute selecting to obtain an optimal attribute subset, which increases the detection capability of decision tree and k-means classifiers was presented by Lima *et al.* [83]. The experimental results demonstrate that the performance of the models built with smaller subsets of attributes is comparable and sometimes better than that associated with the complete set of attributes for DoS and scan attack categories. The authors found, that for the DoS category, Renyi entropy with α-value around 0.5 and Tsallis entropy withα-value around 1.2 are the best for decision tree classifier. We believe, the proper choice of the α-value depends either on the anomaly or the legitimate traffic used as a baseline, or for both, since none of the authors mentioned above reported similar results. Thus, such goals like finding the proper value of parameter for entropy in order to improve detection of particular group of anomalies remains unachieved. Some authors, e.g., Tellenbach *et al.* [9,15,84] employed a set of α-values in their methods. The authors proposed the Traffic Entropy Telescope prototype based on Tsallis entropy capable to detect a broad spectrum of anomalies in a backbone traffic including fast-spreading worms (not that common nowadays), scans and different form of DoS/DDoS attacks. Although Tsallis entropy seems to be more popular than Renyi entropy in the context of network anomaly detection the latter was also successfully applied in detection of different anomalies. An example is the work by Yang *et al.* [10] who employed Renyi entropy to early detection of low-rate DDoS attacks and Kopylova *et al.* [11] who reported positive results of using Renyi conditional entropy in detection of selected worms. We believe that with parameterized entropy some limitations of Shannon entropy caused by small descriptive capability [9] which results in a little ability to detect typical small or low-rate anomalies can be overcome. Moreover, we think that with some properly chosen spectrum of α-values this detection will be accurate in terms of low false alarms and high detection rate. In this article we present original results of our research on the most suitable set of α-values as well as original results of research on the most suitable entropy type.

Others Techniques

Apart from entropy, some other feature distributions summarization techniques are successfully used in the context of network anomaly detection [85], namely sketches and histograms. Soule *et al.*[45] proposed a flow classification method based on modeling network flow histograms using Dirichlet Mixture Processes for random distributions. The authors validated their model against three synthetic test cases and achieved almost 100% classification accuracy. In [46], Stoecklin *et al.*introduced a two-layered sketch anomaly detection technique. The first layer models typical values of different feature components (e.g., typical number of flows connecting to a specific port) and the second layer evaluates the differences between observed feature distribution and the corresponding model. The authors claim that the main strength of their method is the construction of fine-grained models that capture the details of feature distributions, instead of summarizing it into an entropy value. A more general approach was presented by Kind *et al.* [18]. In their method histogram-based baselines were constructed from selected essential network traffic features distributions like addresses and ports. This work was augmented by Brauckhoff *et al.* in [47] who applied association rule mining, in order to identify flows representing anomalous network traffic. The main problem with non-entropic feature distributions summarization techniques is a proper tuning [9]. The performance of detection depends to a great extent on the accuracy of a bin size. This may be difficult to manage while network traffic changes.

3. ENTROPY

This chapter introduces theoretic fundamentals of entropy. It starts with a brief overview of Shannon entropy. Next, the parameterized generalizations are presented. Finally a comparison of entropy measures is provided.

3.1. Shannon Entropy

Definition of entropy as a measure of disorder comes from thermodynamic and was proposed in the early 1850s by Clausius [86]. In 1948 Shannon [65] adopted entropy to information theory. In information theory, entropy is a measure of the uncertainty associated with a random variable The more random the variable, the bigger the entropy and in contrast, the greater certainty of the variable, the smaller the entropy. For a probability distribution $p(X = x_i)$ of a discrete random variable X, the Shannon entropy is defined as:

$$H_s(X) = \sum_{i=1}^{n} p(x_i) \log_a \frac{1}{p(x_i)} \tag{1}$$

X is the feature that can take values $\{x_1...x_n\}$ and $p(x_i)$ is the probability mass function of outcome x_i. The entropy of X can be also interpreted as the expected value of $\log_a \frac{1}{p(X)}$ where X is drown according to probability mass function $p(x)$. Depending on the base of the logarithm, different units can be used: bits ($a = 2$), nats ($a = e$) or hurtleys ($a = 10$). For the purpose of network anomaly detection, sampled probabilities estimated from a number of occurrences of x_i in a time window t are typically used. The value of entropy depends on randomness (it attains maximum when probability $p(x_i)$ for every x_i is equal) but also on the value of n. In order to measure randomness only, normalized forms have to be employed. For example, an entropy value can be divided by n or by maximum entropy defined as $\log_a(n)$. Some important properties of Shannon entropy are listed below:

- Nonnegativity $\forall p(xi) \in [0,1] Hs(X) \geq 0$;
- Symmetry $H_s(p(x_1), p(x_2), ...) = H_s(p(x_2), p(x_1), ...)$;
- Maximality $Hs(p(x1),...,p(xn)) \leq Hs(1n,...,1n) = loga(n)$;

- Additivity $H_s(X, Y) = H_s(X) + H_s(Y)$ if X and Y are independent variables.

Much more properties of Shannon entropy can be found in [87,88].

If not only the degree of uncertainty is important but also the extent of changes between assumed and observed distributions, denoted as q and p respectively, a relative entropy, also known as the Kullback-Leibler divergence [89] can be used:

$$D_{KL}(p||q) = \sum_{i=1}^{n} p(i) \log_a \frac{p(i)}{q(i)} \tag{2}$$

This definition is not symmetric, $D_{KL}(p//q) \neq D_{KL}(q//p)$ unless $p = q$.

To measure how much uncertainty is eliminated in X by observing Y the conditional entropy (or equivocation) [90] may be employed:

$$H_S(X|Y) = \sum_{i=1}^{m} \sum_{j=1}^{n} p(x_i, y_j) \log_a p(x_i|y_j) \tag{3}$$

3.2. Parameterized Entropy

The Shannon entropy assumes a tradeoff between contributions from the main mass of the distribution and the tail [91]. To control this tradeoff, two parameterized Shannon entropy generalizations were proposed, by Renyi (1970s) [79] and Tsallis (late 1980s) [76] respectively. If the parameter denoted as α (or q) has a positive value, it exposes the main mass (the concentration of events that occur often), if the value is negative – it refers to the tail (the dispersion caused by seldom events).

Both parameterized entropies (Renyi and Tsallis) derive from the Kolmogorov-Nagumo generalization of an average [92,93]:

$$\langle X \rangle_\phi = \phi^{-1} \left(\sum_{i=1}^{n} p(x_i)\phi(x_i) \right), \tag{4}$$

where ϕ is a function which satisfies the postulate of additivity (only affine or exponential functions satisfy this) and ϕ^{-1} is the inverse function. Due to affine transformations $\phi(x_i) \to \gamma(x_i) = a\phi(x_i) + b$ (where *a* and *b* are numbers), the inverse function $\phi(x_i)$ is expressed $\gamma^{-1}(x_i) = \phi^{-1}(\frac{x_i - b}{a})$.

Renyi proposed the following function ϕ:

$$\phi(x_i) = 2^{(1-\alpha)x_i} \tag{5}$$

Renyi entropy can be obtained from the Shannon entropy with the following transformations [93]:

$$H_{R\alpha}(X) = \phi^{-1}\left(\sum_{i=1}^{n} p(x_i)\phi(-\log_2 p(x_i))\right) \tag{6}$$

Given $\phi(x_i) = 2^{(1-\alpha)x_i}$ and $\phi^{-1}(x_i) = \frac{1}{(1-\alpha)} \log_2 x_i$

$$\begin{aligned} H_{R\alpha}(X) &= \frac{1}{1-\alpha} \log_2 \left(\sum_{i=1}^{n} p(x_i) 2^{-(1-\alpha)\log_2 p(x_i)}\right) \\ &= \frac{1}{1-\alpha} \log_2 \left(\sum_{i=1}^{n} p(x_i) 2^{\log_2 p(x_i)^{(\alpha-1)}}\right) \\ &= \frac{1}{1-\alpha} \log_2 \left(\sum_{i=1}^{n} p(x_i) p(x_i)^{(\alpha-1)}\right) \\ &= \frac{1}{1-\alpha} \log_2 \left(\sum_{i=1}^{n} p(x_i)^{\alpha}\right) \end{aligned} \tag{7}$$

After transformation, a well-known form of Renyi entropy is obtained:

$$H_{R\alpha}(X) = \frac{1}{1-\alpha} \log_a \left(\sum_{i=1}^{n} p(x_i)^{\alpha}\right) \tag{8}$$

The Renyi entropy satisfies the same postulates as the Shannon entropy and there are the following relation between these two:

$$H_{R\alpha_1}(X) \geq H_S(X) \geq H_{R\alpha_2}(X) \quad \text{where } \alpha_1 < 1 \text{ and } \alpha_2 > 1 \tag{9}$$

$$\lim_{\alpha \to 1} \frac{1}{1-\alpha} \log_a \left(\sum_{i=1}^{n} p(x_i)^{\alpha}\right) = H_s(X) = \sum_{i=1}^{n} p(x_i) \log_a \frac{1}{p(x_i)} \tag{10}$$

Tsallis proposed the following function ϕ:

$$\phi(x_i) = \frac{2^{(1-\alpha)x_i} - 1}{1 - \alpha} \quad (11)$$

After transformation, a well-known form of Tsallis entropy is as follows:

$$H_{T\alpha}(X) = \frac{1}{1-\alpha}\left(\sum_{i=1}^{n} p(x_i)^{\alpha} - 1\right) \quad (12)$$

As one can see this entropy is non logarithmic. There are the following relation between the Shannon and the Tsallis entropy:

$$H_{T\alpha_1}(X) \geq H_S(X) \geq H_{T\alpha_2}(X), \quad \text{where } \alpha_1 < 1 \text{ and } \alpha_2 > 1 \quad (13)$$

$$\lim_{\alpha \to 1} \frac{1}{1-\alpha}\left(\sum_{i=1}^{n} p(x_i)^{\alpha} - 1\right) = \log 2 H_s(X) = \log 2 \sum_{i=1}^{n} p(x_i) \log_a \frac{1}{p(x_i)} \quad (14)$$

Moreover, Tsallis entropy is non-extensive *i.e.*, it satisfies only pseudo-additivity criteria. For an independent discrete random variables *X*,*Y*:

$$H_{T\alpha}(X,Y) = H_{T\alpha}(X) + H_{T\alpha}(Y) + (1-\alpha)H_{T\alpha}(X) + H_{T\alpha}(Y). \quad (15)$$

It means that:

$$H_{T\alpha}(X,Y) > H_{T\alpha}(X) + H_{T\alpha}(Y) \text{ for } \alpha \in (-\infty, 1)$$

and

$$H_{T\alpha}(X,Y) < H_{T\alpha}(X) + H_{T\alpha}(Y) \text{ for } \alpha \in (1, \infty)$$

To summarize parameterized (Renyi and Tsallis) entropies – both of them:

- expose concentration for $\alpha > 1$ and dispersion for $\alpha < 1$,

- converge to Shannon entropy for $\alpha \to 1$,

3.3. Comparison

In order to understand, compare and successfully apply parameterized entropies in our approach some experiments were conducted.

Firstly, a comparison of Shannon, Renyi and Tsallis entropy of a bi-nominal probability distributions was performed. Then we compared calculated entropies for an uniform distribution to check how they depends on number of equal probabilities and α-values. Next, the impact of rare and frequent events on the value of entropy for different α-values was examined.

3.3.1. Binominal Distribution

Shannon, Renyi and Tsallis entropy for a bi-nominal probability distribution where the probability of success is p, and the probability of failure is $1 - p$ is depicted in Figure 1, Figure 2and Figure 3 respectively.

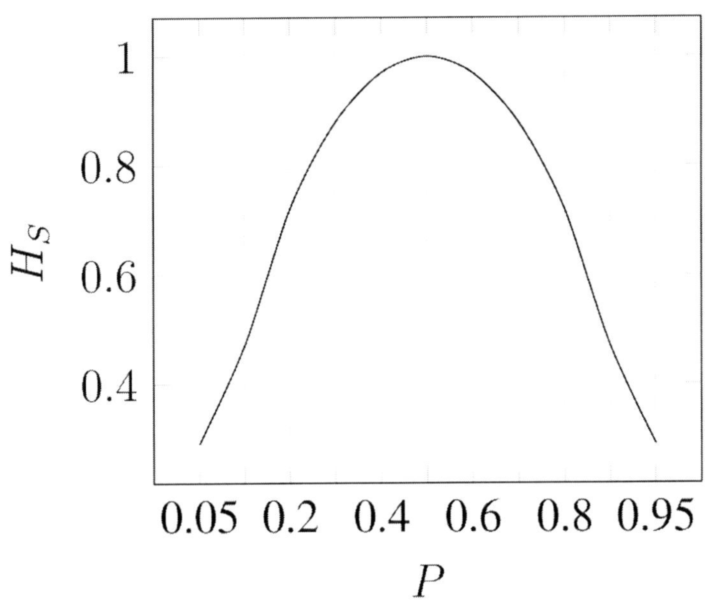

Figure 1. Shannon entropy.

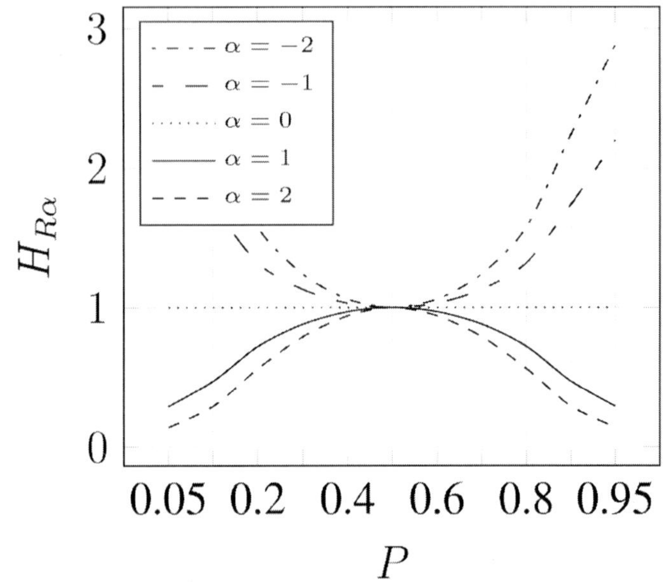

Figure 2. Renyi entropy of several α-values.

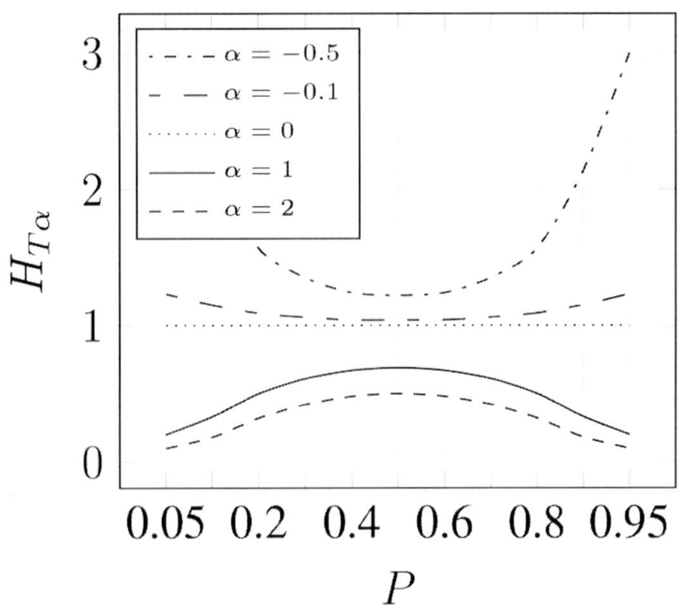

Figure 3. Tsallis entropy of several α-values.

As one can see both Renyi and Tsallis converge to the Shannon entropy for $\alpha \rightarrow 1$. (Note: According to Equation (14) Tsallis needs to be multiplied by $\frac{1}{\log 2}$ to get the similar to Shannon curve for $\alpha \rightarrow 1$). Tsallis entropy is much more sensitive than Renyi for negative α-values and less sensitive for positive α-values. Moreover, Tsallis maximum entropy changes for different α-values, while Renyi is always equal to 1.

3.3.2. Uniform Distribution

Shannon, Renyi and Tsallis entropy for a uniform probability distribution is depicted in Figure 4. In this distribution maximum entropy (case when probabilities are equal) is calculated for different n representing number of equal probabilities.

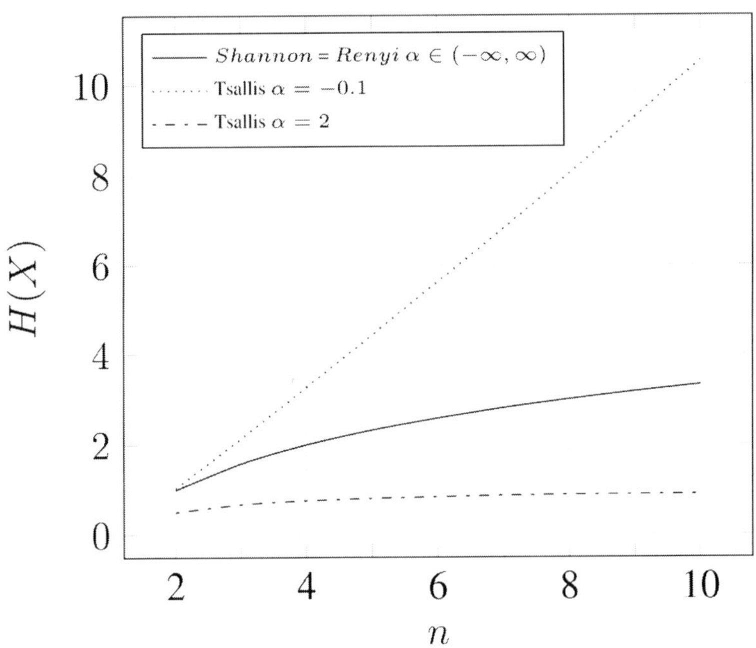

Figure 4. Shannon, Renyi and Tsallis entropy for an uniform distribution.

As one can see in contrast to Shannon and Renyi entropy, value of Tsallis entropy depends not only on n but also on value of α.

3.3.3. Impact of Frequent and Rare Events

Example 1. *Let's assume a discrete random variable X = ip addresses observed in network within last 1 min. X = {"10.1.0.1", "10.1.0.2", "10.1.0.3", "10.1.0.4", "10.1.0.5"}. Suppose the following number of occurrences for the subsequent ip addresses Freq = {96, 1, 1, 1, 1}. Based on frequencies let's estimate the following probability distribution of X (see Table 1).*

Table 1. Probability distribution of *X*.

X	"10.1.0.1"	"10.1.0.2"	"10.1.0.3"	"10.1.0.4"	"10.1.0.5"
$p(X = x)$	0.96	0.01	0.01	0.01	0.01

Let's examine what is the impact of a frequent event p(X="10.1.0.1") = 0.96 and rare event p(X="10.1.0.2") = 0.01 on the Renyi and Tsallis entropy when $\alpha = -2$ and $\alpha = 2$ are used. In order to measure the impact of these events, we can check results of exponential expression $p(x_i)^\alpha$ existing in both Renyi and Tsallis formulas in Equation (8), Equation (12). The results are presented in Table 2.

Table 2. Impact of frequent and rare events on the value of parameterized entropy.

$p(x_i)$ \ α	-2	2
0.96	1.08	0.92
0.01	10000	0.0001

As one can see the impact of frequent events (expressed by $p(x_i) = 0.96$) on the entropy is greater than impact of rare events (expressed by $p(x_i) = 0.01$) when positive α-values are used and in opposite the impact of rare events is greater than frequent events when negative α-values are used.

4. ANODE—ENTROPY-BASED NETWORK ANOMALY DETECTOR

This chapter is focused on the proposed method and its implementation named *Anode*. Firstly, an operating principle is presented. Then, results of implementation are given.

In order to verify if entropy-based approach is suitable to detect modern botnet-like malware based on anomalous network patterns the entropy-based network anomaly detector named *Anode*has been proposed. Operating principle of *Anode* is presented in Figure 5.

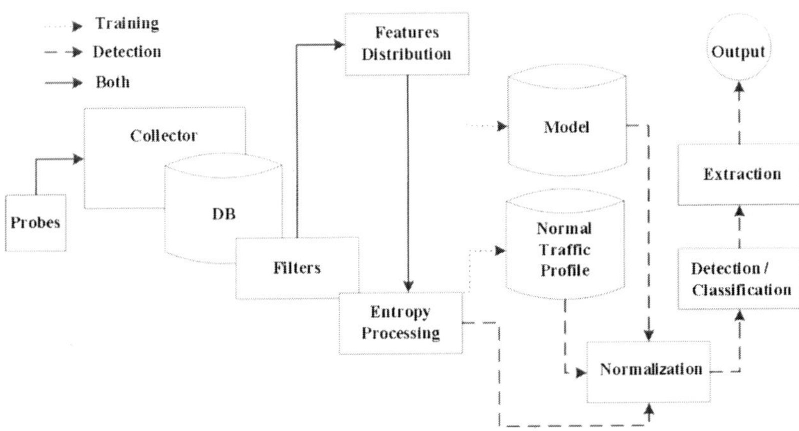

Figure 5. *Anode*—the architecture.

4.1. Architecture

The architecture of *Anode* is presented in Figure 5.

Anode analyzes network data captured by NetFlow probes. Typical probes like routers or dedicated probes, e.g., *Softlowd* [94] connected to TAPs [95] or SPAN ports [95] on switches are assumed. Flows are analyzed within fixed time intervals (every 5 min by default). Bidirectional flows [96] are used since, according to some works (e.g. [8]), unidirectional flows may entail biased results. Collected flows are recorded in the relational database and then analyzed. In order to limit the area of search for anomalies, filters per direction, protocol and subnet are provided. Next, depends on the mode, Tsallis or Renyi entropy of positive and negative α-values is calculated for traffic feature distributions presented in Table 3. (Note: the Shannon version of our method use internally Renyi entropy with α set to 1).

Table 3. Selected traffic feature distributions.

Feature	Probability mass function
src(dst)address(port)	$\frac{number\ of\ x_i\ as\ src(dst)address(port)}{total\ number\ of\ src(dst)addresses(ports)}$
flows duration	$\frac{number\ of\ flows\ with\ x_i\ as\ duration}{total\ number\ of\ flows}$
packets, bytes	$\frac{number\ of\ pkts(bytes)\ with\ x_i\ as\ src(dst)\ addr(port)}{total\ number\ of\ pkts(bytes)}$
in(out)-degree	$\frac{number\ of\ hosts\ with\ x_i\ as\ in(out)-degree}{total\ number\ of\ hosts}$

There are two phases in our approach: training and detection. In the training phase profile of legitimate traffic is built and model for classification is prepared. In the detection phase current observation are compared with the model. Initially, during the training phase, a dynamic profile is built using *min* and *max* entropy values within a sliding time window for every ⟨feature, α⟩ pair. Thus, we can reflect traffic changes during the day but in the same time a margin for some minor differences, e.g., small delays between the profile and current traffic is provided. A way of building a profile based on entropy values is presented in Figure 6.

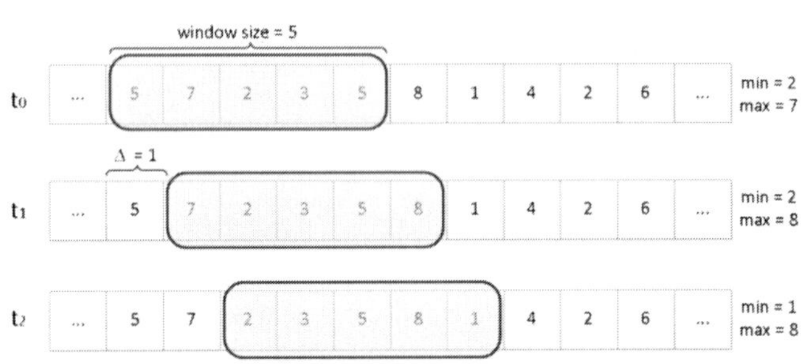

Figure 6. A way of building a profile.

In the detection phase, the observed entropy is compared with the *min* and *max* values stored in the profile according to the following rule:

$$r_\alpha(x_i) = \frac{H_\alpha(x_i) - k * \min_\alpha}{k * (\max_a - \min_\alpha)}, \qquad k \in \langle 1..2 \rangle \tag{16}$$

With the use of this rule, anomaly threshold is defined. Values $r_\alpha(x_i) < 0$ or $r_\alpha(x_i) > 1$ indicate abnormal concentration or dispersion. These abnormal dispersion or concentration for different feature distributions are characteristic for anomalies. For example, during a port scan, a high dispersion in port numbers and high concentration in addresses should be observed. Detection is based on the relative value of entropy with respect to the distance between *min* and *max*. Coefficient *k* in the formula determines a margin for *min* and *max* boundaries and may be used for tuning purposes. A high value of *k*, e.g., $k = 2$, limits the number of false alarms (alarms where no anomaly has taken placed) while a low value ($k = 1$) increases the detection rate (the percentage of anomalies correctly detected). Some other approaches to thresholding based on standard deviation – *mean* ± 2*sdev*, median absolute deviation – *median* ± 2*mad* [97] has been also taken into consideration but empirical results proved that proposed rule is the best choice. The detection is based on the results from all feature distributions presented in Table 3. Classification is based on popular classifiers (decision trees, Bayes nets [98], rules and functions) employed in Weka [99]. Extraction of anomaly details is also assumed – related ports and addresses are obtained by looking into the top contributors to the entropy value.

4.2. Implementation

A proof of concept implementation of *Anode* has been developed in Microsoft.NET environment in C# language. Currently it allows to detect anomalies in an off-line mode. All experiments presented in this article has been conducted with this implementation. Our software produces Weka *arff* files based on entropy calculations for each network feature. Recorded NetFlow data (e.g. whole day traffic) has to be captured and labeled in advance. Classification performance is evaluated with Weka (ten-fold cross-validation mode) based on provided *arff* files.

Currently *Anode* is also a component of the anomaly detection and security event data correlation system developed in SECOR project [100]. A final implementation in SECOR has been developed in JAVA WSO2 (http://wso2.com) environment. This implementation allows on-line detection and classification an anomalies based on NetFlow reports coming from probes deployed in network. SECOR is not limited to network anomaly detection, e.g., PRONTO module [101,102] developed by another team of the project detects obfuscated malware at infected hosts.

5. DATASET

This chapter presents the dataset developed to evaluate proposed method. This dataset is based on a real legitimate traffic and synthetic anomalies. It consist of labeled flows which are stored in the relational database. Chapter starts with the origin of the idea. Next, details concerning legitimate and anomalous traffic are presented.

5.1. Origin of the Idea

One of the main problem in network anomaly detection is the lack of realistic and publicly available datasets for evaluation purposes. The most valuable are real network traces but because of privacy issues they are rarely published even though some anonimization techniques exists. Another problem with real traces is a proper labeling, which in many cases have to be done manually. Alternative approach are synthetic datasets. To build such dataset a deep domain knowledge and appropriate methods and tools are required in order to get a realistic data. Most authors do not disclose self-crafted traces used for evaluation of their methods. Real traffic traces can be found in some publicly available repositories like Internet Traffic Archive [103], LBNL/ICSI Enterprise Tracing [104], SimpleWeb [105], Caida [106], MOME [107], WITS [108], UMASS [109]. Unfortunately, these traces are usually old, often unlabeled and they are not dedicated to anomaly detection. Lack of contemporary anomalies, e.g., traces of botnet activity in available datasets question thier timeliness. According to recent reports provided by cyber security organizations [13,110–112] botnets are one of the most sophisticated and popular types of cybercrime today. So anomalies connected with botnet-like malware should be included in contemporary datasets and researches should address this anomalies in their methods. The number of datasets containing modern malware traces is limited. Worth mentioning are ISOT [113] and CTU-13 [114]. The first one is a mixture of malicious and non-malicious datasets. Regrettably only one host in this dataset is infected with botnet-like malware. The second dataset which has just been made public is much richer and consist of traces of serveral bots, namely Neris, Rbot, Sogou, Murlo, Menti. Unfortunately, as this dataset has appeared recentlym, we had no chance to use it in our studies. Interesting flow-based traffic dataset has been recently made publicly available by Sperotto *et al.*[115]. This set is based on data collected from a real honeypot (monitored trap) featuring HTTP, SSH and FTP services. The authors gathered about 14 million malicious flows but most of them referred to activity of web and network scanners. Some details about particular anomalies in this dataset are also presented in our research [116]. Instead of tracking anomalies caused by modern malware some authors still make use of very old and criticized DARPA [117] data set and their modified versions, namely, KDD99 [118] and NSL-KDD [119] to evaluate their methods. Besides strong criticism by McHugh [120], Mahoney *et al.* [121] or Thomas [122] for being unrealistic and not balanced, nowadays DARPA dataset are simply out of date in the context of network services and attacks. According to Brauckhoff *et al.* [123], a realistic simulation of legitimate traffic is largely an unsolved problem today and one of the solution is combining generated anomalies with real, legitimate traffic traces. In [123] and then in [124], Brauckhoff *et al.* introduced the FLAME tool for injection of hand-crafted anomalies into a given background traffic trace. This tool is freely available but the current distribution does not include any models reflecting anomalies. Another interesting concept was introduced by Shiravi *et al.* [125]. Authors proposed to describe network traffic (not only flows) by a set of so-called α and β profiles which can subsequently be used to generate a synthetic dataset. The α-profiles consist of actions which should be executed to generate a given event in the network (such as attack) while in β-profiles certain entities (packet sizes, number of packets per flow) are represented by a statistical model. Regrettably, this tool is not freely available.

All things considered—the effort to build own dataset was taken due to:

- limited availability of such datasets;
- the lack of proper labeling in shared datasets;
- the fact that most of available datasets are obsolete in terms of legitimate traffic and anomalies;
- the absence of realistic data in synthetic datasets;
- small number of dataset with flows (conversion from packets is needed, labels are lost);
- incompleteness of data (narrow range of anomalies, lack of anomalies related to botnet-like malware);

5.2. Legitimate Traffic

Firstly, one-week legitimate traffic from a medium size network connected to the Internet was captured. This was accomplished using open source software—*Softflowd* [94] and *NfDump* [16]. Because daily profile of each working day in this traffic is similar (except some minor differences on Monday morning and Friday afternoon) one-day profiling approach was chosen. From the whole traffic it was enough to extract two days (Tuesday, Wednesday) in order to build the dataset. The first day is reserved for a training (only legitimate traffic) and the second day for a detection (legitimate traffic + injected anomalies). The profile expressed by the number of flows of this 2-day traffic (before any injection of anomalies) is depicted in Figure 7.

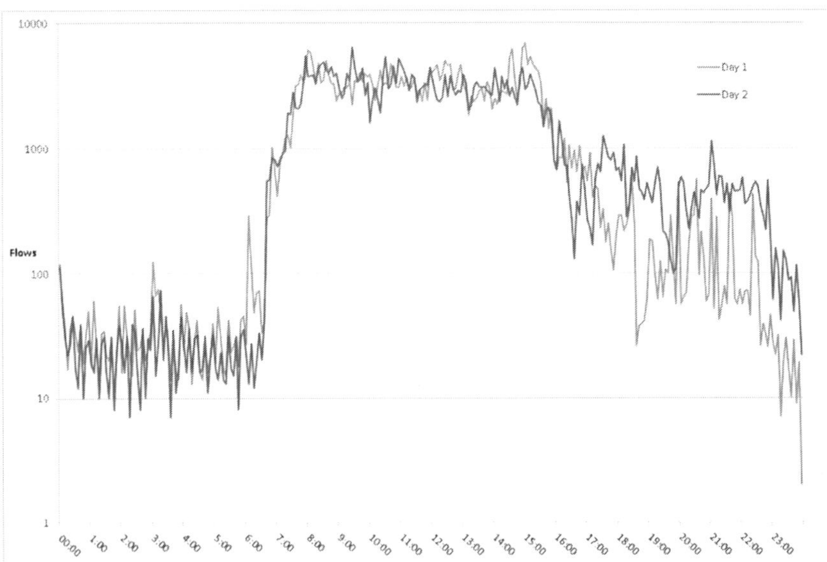

Figure 7. Legitimate traffic profile by number of flows.

We can see time t on x axis (5 min fixed time window) and the number of flows on y (log scale) axis. Working day starts around 7 am. and finishes around 4 pm. The volume of the traffic expressed by the number of flows for both days is similar.

In the next step implementation of different scenarios of malicious network activities has been prepared. Synthetic anomalies typical for botnet-like network behavior were generated and then injected into the legitimate traffic. To produce synthetic anomaly traces a dedicated tool in Python language was developed. More details about the tool and the generation process can be found in our research [126].

5.3. Scenario 1

In this scenario a small and slow *ssh brute force, port scan, ssh network scan* and *TCP SYN flood DDoS* anomalies in different variants were generated. These anomalies do not form any realistic traces of malware but detection and proper classification of such set of anomalies is crucial because they are typical for network behavior of botnet-like malware. Main characteristics of generated anomalies are presented in Table 4.

Table 4. Characteristics of anomalies.

Type/kind	No. of flows	Duration [s]	No. of victims	No. of attackers
SSH brute force (bf)				
1	1K	300	1	1
2	1K	100	1	1
3	2K	300	1	1
TCP SYN flood DDoS (dd)				
1	2K	200	1	50
2	2K	200	1	250
3	3K	300	1	50
4	3K	300	1	250
5	4K	400	1	50
6	4K	400	1	250
SSH network scan (ns)				
1	6K	60	6K	1
2	6K	300	6K	1
3	8K	80	8K	1
4	8K	400	8K	1
Port scan (ps)				
1	1K	50	1	1
2	1K	100	1	1
3	2K	100	1	1
4	2K	200	1	1

Generated anomalies were mixed with the legitimate traffic from Day2 (Wednesday) in the way presented in Figure 8. Anomalies are not injected into the traffic from Day1 (Tuesday) as it is intended for the profile of a legitimate traffic. As one can see, each anomaly is injected every 15 min mainly during the working hours. After injection only a few anomalies are visible in the volume expressed by a number of flows as depicted in Figure 9.

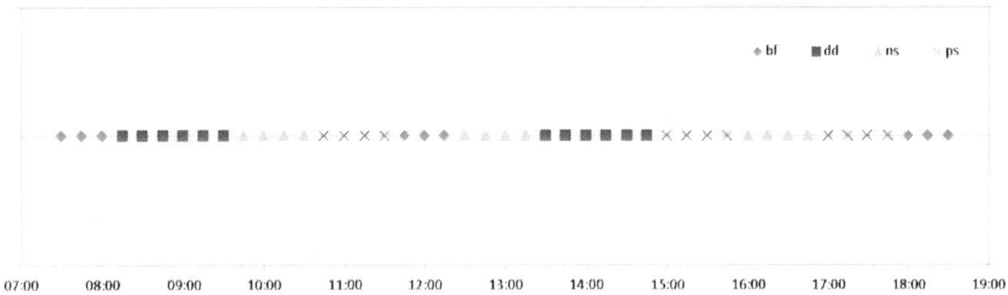

Figure 8. Distribution of anomalies in time.

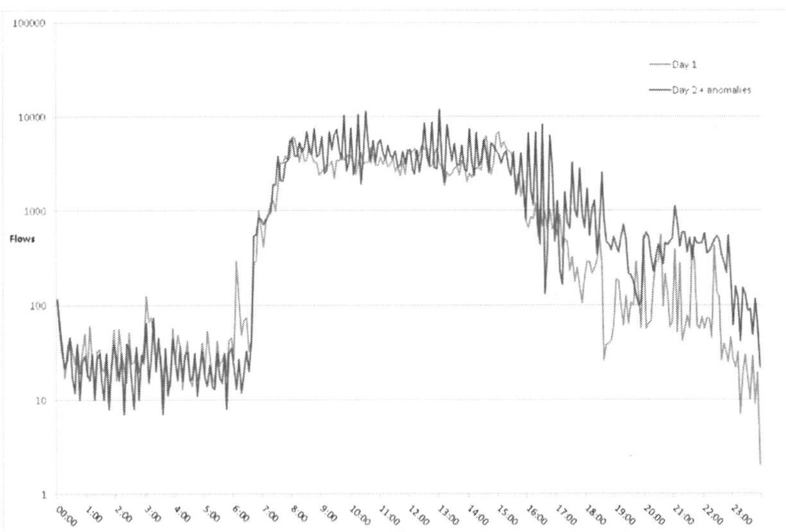

Figure 9. Legitimate and anomalous traffic by number of flows.

5.4. Scenario 2

In this scenario, we prepared much more realistic sequence of a modern botnet-like malware network behavior. The subsequent stages looks as follows:

1. One of the host in local network gets infected with a botnet-like malware. In order to propagate via network it starts scanning his neighbors. Malware is looking for hosts running Remote Desktop Protocol (RDP) services. RDP is a proprietary protocol developed by Microsoft, which provides a user with a graphical interface to connect to another computer over a network. RDP servers are built into Windows operating systems. By default, the server listens on TCP/UDP port 3389.
2. Hosts serving Remote Desktop services are attacked with a dictionary attack (similarly to the technique found in MORTO worm [127]).
3. After successful dictionary attack vulnerable machines are infected and become a member of botnet.
4. A peer-to-peer communication based on UDP transport protocol is established among infected hosts.
5. On C&C server command botnet members start a low rate Distributed Denial of Service attack called Slowrolis [128] on an external HTTP server. After a few min the server is blocked.

Main characteristics of generated anomalies are presented in Table 5.

Table 5. Characteristics of anomalies.

Type	No. of flows	Duration [s]	No. of victims	No. of attackers
Network scan (ns)	252	200	252	1
RDP brute force (bf)	720	550	53	1
Botnet p2p (p2p)	150	185	15	15
Slowrolis DDoS (dd)	1124	117	15	1

Anomalies generated for the scenario were mixed with the legitimate traffic from Day2 (Wednesday) in the way presented in Figure 10.

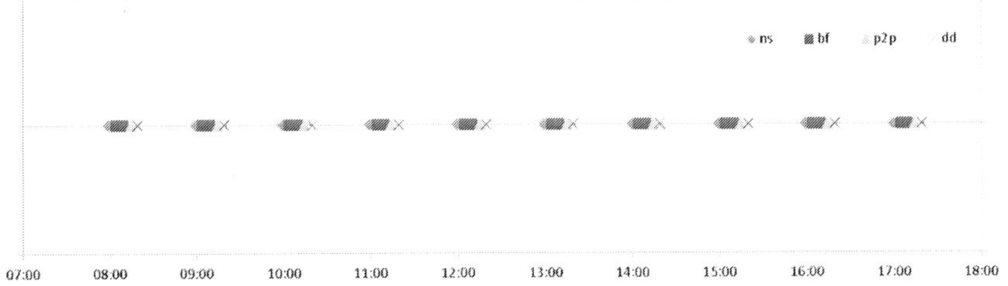

Figure 10. Distribution of anomalies in time.

One can see, the whole scenario which consists of four anomalies is injected every hour during the working time. Anomalies in this scenario are low and slow. They represent only o small fraction of total traffic so after injection none of them is visible in the volume expressed by a number of flows as depicted in Figure 11.

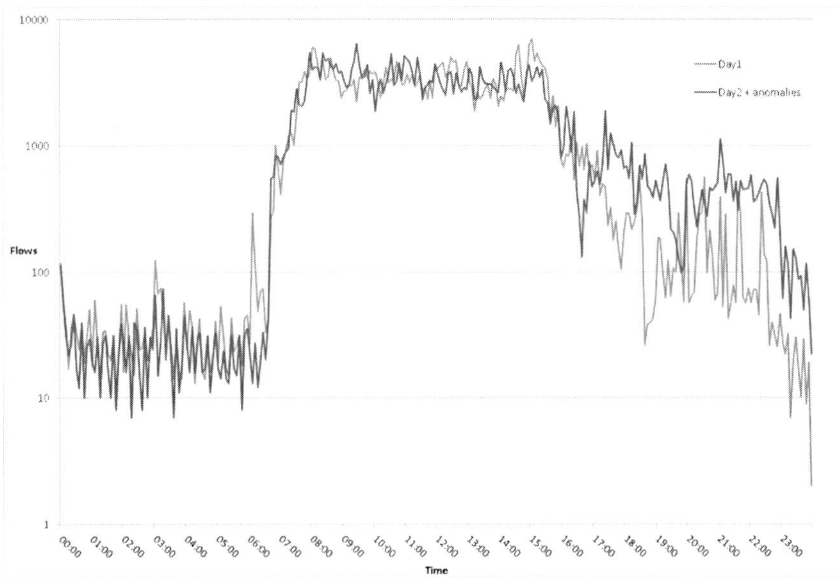

Figure 11. Legitimate and anomalous traffic by number of flows.

5.5. Scenario 3

In this scenario, we prepared another realistic sequence of a modern botnet-like malware network behavior. The subsequent stages looks as follows:

1. One of the local host which is infected with a modern botnet malware starts scanning his neighbors in order to propagate via network. It uses similar network propagation mechanism as it is employed in Stuxnet worm [129,130]. Malware is looking for hosts with open TCP and UDP ports reserved for Microsoft Remote Procedure Call (RPC). In Windows RPC is an interprocess communication mechanism that enables data exchange and invocation of functionality residing in a different process localy or via network. The list of ports used to initiate a connection

with RPC is as follows: UDP – 135, 137, 138, 445, TCP – 135, 139, 445, 593.

2. Hosts with an open RPC ports are attacked with a specially crafted RPC requests.
3. After successful attack, vulnerable machines are infected and become a member of botnet.
4. A direct communication to a single C&C server is established on each infected host.
5. On C&C server command botnet members start a DDoS amplification attack based on Network Time Protocol (NTP). This attack is targeted to an external server. Botnet members send packets with a forged source IP address (set to this used by the victim). Because the source IP address is forged the remote server replies and sends data to the victim. Moreover attack is amplified via NTP. Thus attackers send a small (234 bytes) packet "from" a forged source IP address with a command to get a list of interacting machines and NTP server sends a large (up to 200 times bigger) reply to the victim. As a result attackers turn small amount of bandwidth coming from a few machines into a significant traffic load hitting the victim. More details regarding NTP amplification in DDoS attacks can be found in [131].

Main characteristics of generated anomalies are presented in Table 6.

Table 6. Characteristics of anomalies.

Type	No. of flows	Duration [s]	No. of victims	No. of attackers
Block scan (bs)	1.5K	80	168	1
RPC attack (rpc)	650	200	90	1
Botnet C&C communication (c&c)	125	190	63	1
NTP DDoS (dd)	2.9K	580	1	63 (spoofed to 1)

Anomalies generated for the scenario were mixed with the legitimate traffic from Day2 (Wednesday) in the way presented in Figure 12.

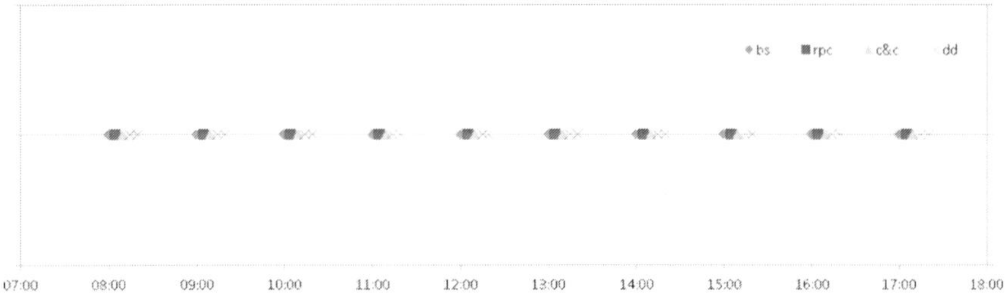

Figure 12. Distribution of anomalies in time.

As one can see, the whole scenario which consists of four anomalies is injected every hour during a working time. Similarly to Scenario 2 anomalies in this scenario are low and slow and they represent only a small fraction of total traffic. After injection none of them is visible in the volume expressed by a number of flows as depicted in Figure 13.

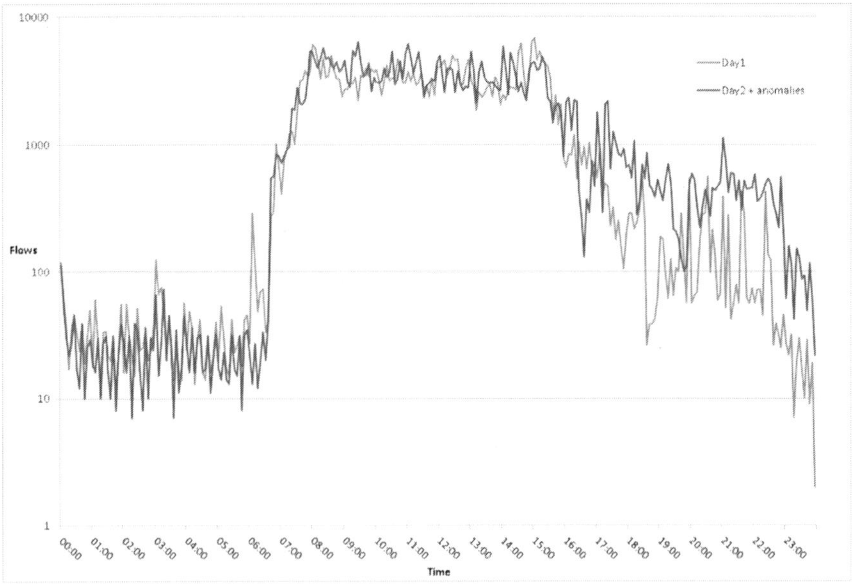

Figure 13. Legitimate and anomalous traffic by number of flows.

6. VERIFICATION OF THE APPROACH

This section presents verification of the proposed method. The aim of verification is to check if the proposed method is able to detect network anomalies and categorize them. Firstly, results of correlation tests performed in order to find the proper set of α-values and network features are presented. Next, the performance of the Tsallis, Renyi, Shannon and volume-based version of the method is evaluated. Finally conclusions are given.

6.1. Correlation

Firstly, correlation tests for various α-values and for various feature distributions were performed. This is important as strong correlation suggests that some results are closely related to each other and thus it may be sufficient to restrict the scope scope of α-values and network features without impairing validity of the method.

In the experiments Pearson and Spearman [132] correlation coefficients were used. For a sample of discrete random variables *X, Y* the formula for Pearson coefficient is defined as:

$$r_{X,Y} = \frac{\sum_{i=1}^{n}(X_i - \bar{X})(Y_i - \bar{Y})}{s_x s_y} \quad \text{where } \bar{X} = \frac{1}{n}\sum_{i=1}^{n} X_i \text{ and } s_x = \sqrt{\frac{1}{n-1}\sum_{i=1}^{n}(X_i - \bar{X})^2} \tag{17}$$

The formula for Spearman coefficient for a sample of discrete random variables *X, Y* is defined as:

$$r_{X,Y} = corr(RX, RY) \tag{18}$$

where *corr*—Pearson correlation coefficient for a sample, *RX*—ranks of X, *RY*—ranks of Y.

The results of correlation between entropy timeseries for different α-values are presented inTable 7. This table shows the pairwise Tsallis α correlation scores from range $\langle -1..1\rangle$ where scopes $|1 - 0.9|$, $|0.9 - 0.7|$, $|0.7 - 0.5|$, $|0.5 - 0|$ denote, respectively, strong, medium, weak, and no correlation. The sign determines if the correlation is positive (no sign) or negative (−). The presented values (see Table 7) are an average from 15 different feature distributions scores. Only results based on

Tsallis entropy are presented as these obtained for the Renyi entropy were similar.

Table 7. Results of linear and rank correlation of α.

		$\alpha=-3$	$\alpha=-2$	$\alpha=-1$	$\alpha=0$	$\alpha=1$	$\alpha=2$	$\alpha=3$
Pearson	$\alpha=-3$	1	0.99	0.96	0.66	0.12	−0.06	−0.09
	$\alpha=-2$	-	1	0.98	0.69	0.13	−0.06	−0.09
	$\alpha=-1$	-	-	1	0.75	0.16	−0.05	−0.08
	$\alpha=0$	-	-	-	1	0.44	0.18	0.12
	$\alpha=2$	-	-	-	-	-	1	0.97
	$\alpha=3$	-	-	-	-	-	-	1
Spearman	$\alpha=-3$	1	0.97	0.837	0.46	0.06	−0.09	−0.11
	$\alpha=-2$	-	1	0.94	0.57	0.1	−0.07	−0.1
	$\alpha=-1$	-	-	1	0.72	0.15	−0.06	−0.09
	$\alpha=0$	-	-	-	1	0.49	0.2	0.15
	$\alpha=2$	-	-	-	-	-	1	0.9
	$\alpha=3$	-	-	-	-	-	-	1

Table 8. Results of correlation of features for $\alpha = -3$.

Pearson	src ip	dst ip	src port	dst port	in-degree	out-degree
src ip	1	0.89	0.89	0.91	0.37	0.35
dst ip	-	1	0.98	0.89	0.27	0.55
src port	-	-	1	0.86	0.15	0.5
dst port	-	-	-	1	0.41	0.53
ind-egree	-	-	-	-	1	0.27
out-degree	-	-	-	-	-	1
Spearman	**src ip**	**dst ip**	**src port**	**dst port**	**in-degree**	**out-degree**
src ip	1	0.9	0.85	0.87	0.47	0.69
dst ip	-	1	0.96	0.89	0.43	0.83
src port	-	-	1	0.83	0.3	0.69
dst port	-	-	-	1	0.53	0.12
in-degree	-	-	-	-	1	0.48
out-degree	-	-	-	-	-	1

It should be noticed, that there is a strong positive linear (Pearson) and rank (Spearman) correlation for negative α-values and strong positive correlation between α-values which are higher than 1. For $\alpha = 0$ there is some small positive correlation with negative values. For $\alpha = 1$ (Shannon) there is a medium correlation with $\alpha = 2$ and $\alpha = 3$. These results suggest that it is sufficient to use α-values from range $\langle -2..2 \rangle$ to obtain different and distinctive sensitivity levels of entropy.

Results of pairwise correlation between Tsallis entropy timeseries of different feature distributions are presented in Table 8 and Table 9. The results obtained for the Renyi entropy are not presented as they closely reasemble these obtained for Tsallis.

Table 9. Results of correlation of features for $\alpha = 3$.

Pearson	src ip	dst ip	src port	dst port	in-degree	out-degree
src ip	1	−0.07	−0.34	−0.02	−0.07	0.44
dst ip	-	1	−0.29	0.05	0.08	−0.28
src port	-	-	1	−0.42	0.59	−0.04
dst port	-	-	-	1	−0.39	0.01
in-degree	-	-	-	-	1	0.03
out-degree	-	-	-	-	-	1
Spearman	**src ip**	**dst ip**	**src port**	**dst port**	**in-degree**	**out-degree**
src ip	1	0.03	−0.21	0.07	0.21	0.37
dst ip	-	1	−0.31	0.07	0.08	−0.35
src port	-	-	1	−0.55	0.64	0.23
dst port	-	-	-	1	0.52	0.76
in-degree	-	-	-	-	1	0.18
out-degree	-	-	-	-	-	1

The results for one positive and one negative value of α are presented because they differ significantly. Averaging (based on results from the whole range of α-values) would hide an essential property. It is noticeable that there is a strong positive correlation of addresses and ports for negative values of α but no correlation for positive α-values.

6.2. Performance Evaluation

Experiments were performed for Tsallis, Renyi and Shannon version of our method as well as traditional volume-based approach with flow, packet and byte counters. Final evaluation was performed with Weka [99]. Experiments were performed with the dataset presented in Section 5. Exemplary results of entropies for a selected feature distributions are presented below. Abnormally high dispersion in destination addresses distribution for network scan anomalies exposed by negative value of α parameters is depicted in Figure 14. One can see time t on x axis (5-minute time windows), result r on y axis and α-values on z axis. The r value corresponds to normalization applied in our method (Equation (16)). Values of r outside (0..1) threshold are considered as anomalous. Anomalies are marked with (A) on the time axis. Values of Shannon entropy are denoted as S. Abnormal concentration of flows duration for network scans is depicted in Figure 15. This concentration is typical for anomalies with a fixed data stream, *i.e.*, anomalies where all flows have similar size. Figure 16 shows ambiguous detection (no significant excess of 0–1 threshold) of port scan anomaly with volume-based approach using flow, packet and byte counters. While experimenting, we noticed that measurements for all feature distributions as a group work better than single ones or subsets. In our experiments, addresses, ports and duration feature distributions turned out to be the most deterministic, although we believe that the proper set of network features is specific for particular anomalies.

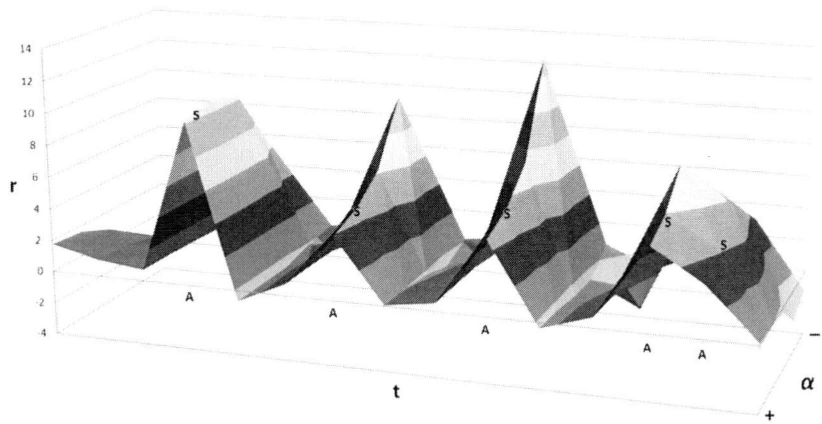

Figure 14. Abnormally high dispersion in destination addresses for network scan anomalies (Renyi/Shannon).

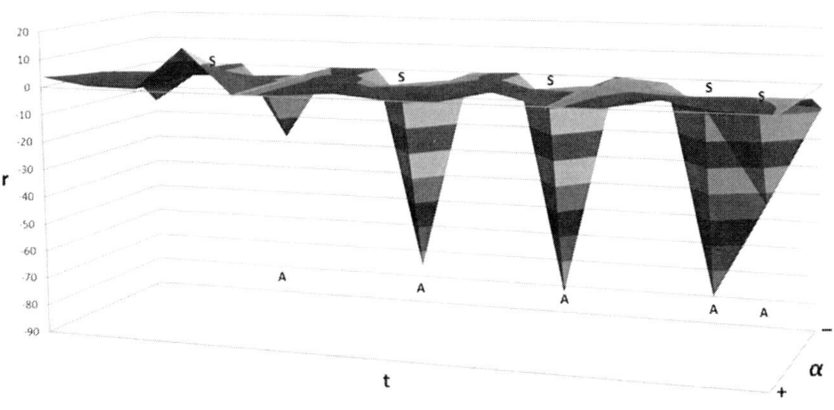

Figure 15. Abnormally high concentration in flows duration for network scan anomalies (Tsallis/Shannon).

Overall (whole data set, all feature distributions) multi-class classification was performed with Weka. We defined *n* classes – one for each anomaly type and one class for the legitimate traffic. In order to properly evaluate predictive performance 10-fold cross-validation method was used [99]. From the performance point of view, every classification attempt can produce one of four outcomes presented in Figure 17

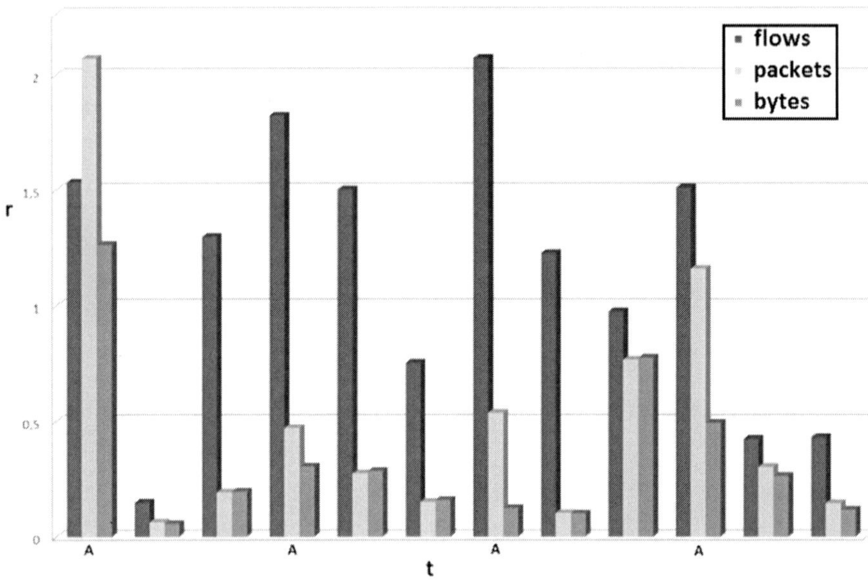

Figure 16. Ambiguous detection of port scan anomaly with a volume-based approach.

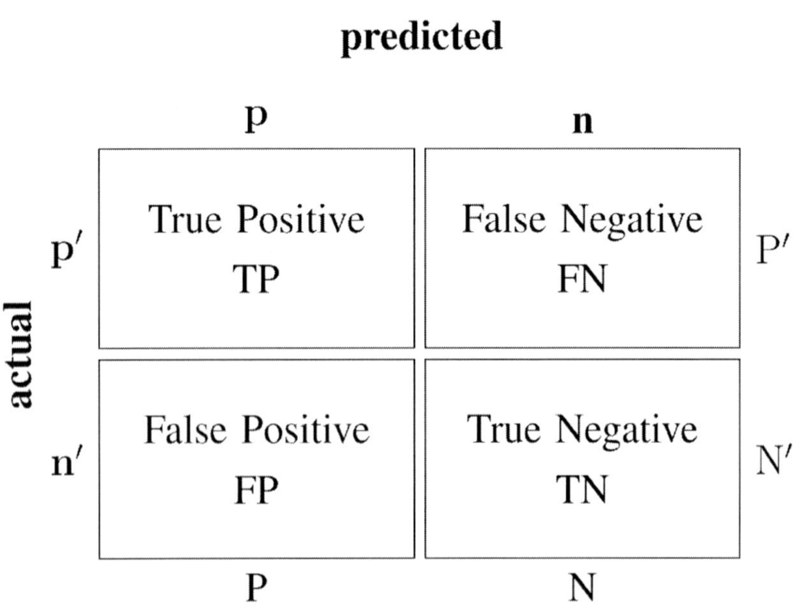

Figure 17. Possible results of classification.

An ideal classifier should not produce False Positive (FP) and False Negative (FN) statistical errors. To evaluate non-ideal classifiers, one could measure proportion of correct assessments to all assessments—Accuracy (ACC), the share of benign activities reported as anomalous—False Positive Rate (FPR) and the share of anomalies missed by the detector—False Negative Rate (FNR). Usage of Precision (proportion of correctly reported anomalies) and Recall (share of correctly reported anomalies compared to the total number of anomalies) is another option. Based on these measures some tools like Receiver Operating Characteristics (ROC) and Precision vs Recall (PR) are typically used [133,134]. Formulas for mentioned metrics as well as some additional measures which can be also used to evaluate the performance of classifier are presented in Table 10.

Table 10. Metrics used to evaluate performance of classification.

Name	Formula
True Positive Rate (TPR) eqv. with Recall, Sensitivity	$TPR = \frac{TP}{TP+FN}$
True Negative Rate (TNR) eqv. with Specificity	$TNR = \frac{TN}{FP+TN}$
Positive Predictive Value (PPV) eqv. with Precision	$PPV = \frac{TP}{TP+FP}$
Negative Predictive Value (NPV)	$NPV = \frac{TN}{TN+FN}$
False Positive Rate (FPR) eqv. with Fall-out	$FPR = \frac{FP}{FP+TN} = 1 - TNR$
False Discovery Rate (FDR)	$FDR = \frac{FP}{FP+TP} = 1 - PPV$
False Negative Rate (FNR)	$FNR = \frac{FN}{FN+TP}$
Accuracy (ACC)	$ACC = \frac{TP+TN}{TP+FN+FP+TN}$
F1 score – harmonic mean of Precision and Recall	$F1 = \frac{2TP}{2TP+FP+FN}$

In our approach we deal with multi-classification problem where more than two classes are utilized, instead of single binary classification (or detection) where only two classes, e.g., *anomalous*and *not anomalous* are used. We classify instances to be into one of many classes like *port scan, network scan, brute force, etc.* We use classifiers from Weka which transform internally multi-class problem into multiple binary class one. One of the possible way to handle it is One-vs-All classification [135]. The idea behind this method is:

1. Take n binary classifiers (one for each class);
2. For the ith classifier, let the positive examples be all the points in class i, and let the negative examples be all the points not in class i;

3. Let f_i be the ith classifier; Classify with the following rule:

$$f(x) = \arg\max_i f_i(x) \tag{19}$$

Averaged Accuracy and avaraged FPR results based on Scenario 1 are presented in the Table 11.

Table 11. Averaged performance of classification—Scenario 1.

		ZeroR	Bayes Network	Decision Tree J48	Random Forest	Simple Logistic
Accuracy	Tsallis	0.66	0.89	0.90	0.93	0.93
	Renyi	0.66	0.88	0.89	0.90	0.93
	Shannon	0.66	0.84	0.86	0.90	0.92
	volume-based	0.66	0.72	0.77	0.76	0.80
FPR	Tsallis	0.66	0.07	0.08	0.07	0.06
	Renyi	0.66	0.08	0.09	0.11	0.09
	Shannon	0.66	0.08	0.11	0.12	0.08
	volume-based	0.66	0.21	0.15	0.22	0.20

As one can see the results for several popular classifiers are presented. ZeroR is a trivial classifier which classifies the whole traffic as *not anomalous*. We included it here as a reference to other results as it is expected that other classifiers should perform better. Using weighted Accuracy and weighted FPR is the most popular way to measure the performance of multi-class classification but we also propose own measurement tool, namely weighted ROC curves which are presented later in this section. Evaluation results based on Scenario 2 and Scenario 3 are presented in the Table 12 and Table 13 respectively.

Table 12. Averaged performance of classification—Scenario 2.

		ZeroR	Bayes Network	Decision Tree J48	Random Forest	Simple Logistic
Accuracy	Tsallis	0.68	0.82	0.84	0.85	0.91
	Renyi	0.68	0.83	0.88	0.89	0.92
	Shannon	0.68	0.77	0.8	0.84	0.89
	volume-based	0.68	0.68	0.73	0.78	0.80
FPR	Tsallis	0.68	0.22	0.14	0.27	0.11
	Renyi	0.68	0.15	0.12	0.2	0.11
	Shannon	0.68	0.29	0.21	0.28	0.15
	volume-based	0.68	0.68	0.2	0.15	0.28

Table 13. Averaged performance of classification—Scenario 3.

		ZeroR	Bayes Network	Decision Tree J48	Random Forest	Simple Logistic
Accuracy	Tsallis	0.68	0.83	0.83	0.87	0.93
	Renyi	0.68	0.83	0.83	0.85	0.94
	Shannon	0.68	0.76	0.8	0.85	0.90
	volume-based	0.68	0.68	0.62	0.65	0.66
FPR	Tsallis	0.68	0.13	0.17	0.22	0.1
	Renyi	0.68	0.13	0.16	0.22	0.06
	Shannon	0.68	0.23	0.16	0.22	0.13
	volume-based	0.68	0.68	0.57	0.45	0.67

It is noticable that the best performance in each scenario was obtained by applying Simple Logistic. In Weka, SimpleLogistic is a classifier for building linear logistic regression models [136]. Logistic regression comes from the fact that linear regression [137] can also be used to perform classification problem. The idea of logistic regression is to make linear regression produce probabilities, thus instead of class prediction, there is a prediction of class probabilities. More details on SimpleLogistic can be found in [136,138]. If we look at the detailed results of SimpleLogistic (Renyi entropy case) for all scenarios Table 14 one can see that different classes are characterized by rather different performance of recognition. For example, models for *network scan*and *not anomalous* are very strong, whereas this for *p2p* is much weaker.

As was mentioned before ROC plots can be also used to evaluate a performance of a classifier. It presents more detailed characteristic of a classifier than ACC. The ROC curve is obtained for a classifier by plotting TPR an x-axis and FPR on y-axis. The Area Under a Curve (UAC) is a scalar measurement method connected with a ROC. While evaluating the classifier, the ROC plot considers all possible operating points (thresholds) in the classifier's prediction in order to identify the operating point at which the best performance is achieved. A ROC curve does nor directly present the optimal value instead it shows a tradeoff between TPR and FPR. Depending on the goals one can change the optimal operating point in order to limit FPR or to increase TPR. An examplary ROC for perfect (a), partially overlaped (b) and random (c) classifier is presented inFigure 18.

Table 14. Detailed performance of SimpleLogistic classifier (Renyi entropy case).

	TPR/FPR		
	Scenario1	Scenario2	Scenario3
brute force	0.78/0	1/0.01	–
network scan	0.92/0.02	0.9/0	–
port scan	0.92/0.01	–	–
block scan	–	–	0.9/0.01
DDoS	0.67/0.01	0.9/0	0.9/0.01
p2p	–	0.3/0.02	–
c&c	–	–	0.9/0.01
RPC exploitation	–	–	0.7/0.01
not anomalous	0.98/0.13	0.97/0.16	0.97/0.08

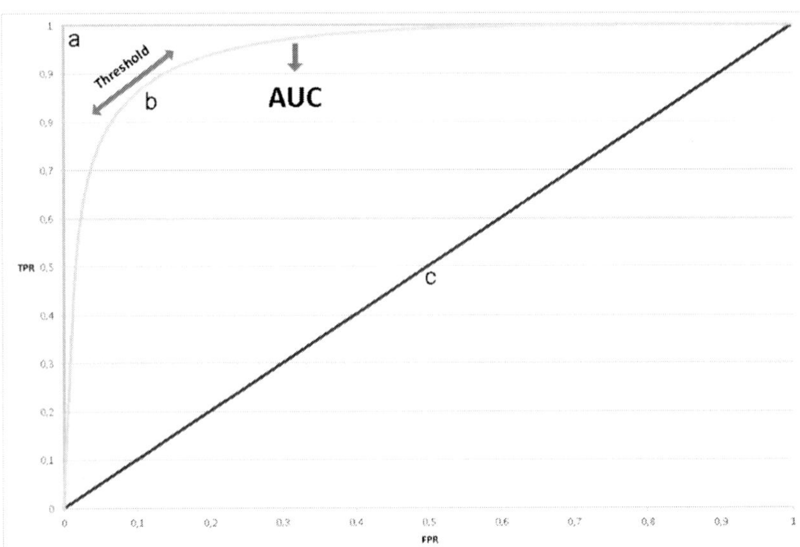

Figure 18. Examplary Receiver Operating Characteristics (ROC) curves.

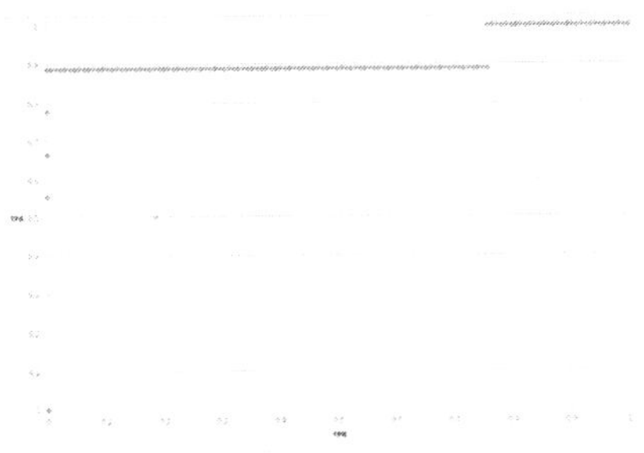

(a) brute force

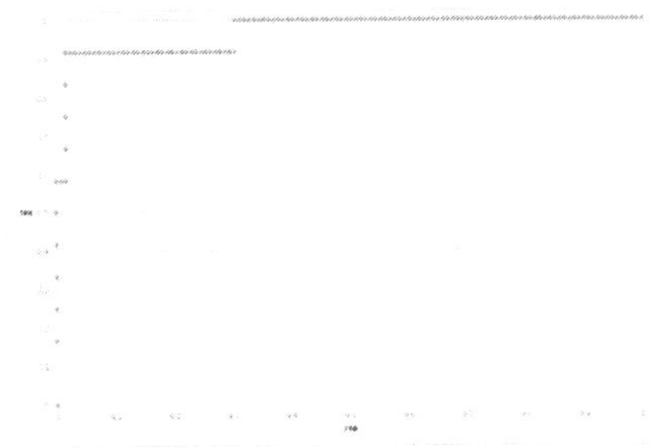

(b) network scan

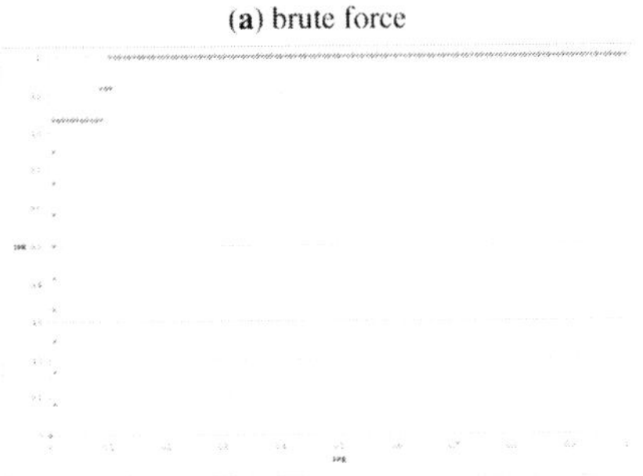

(c) ddos

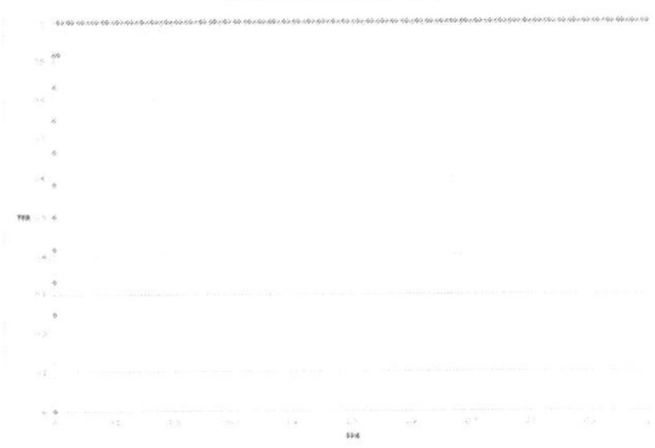

(d) port scan

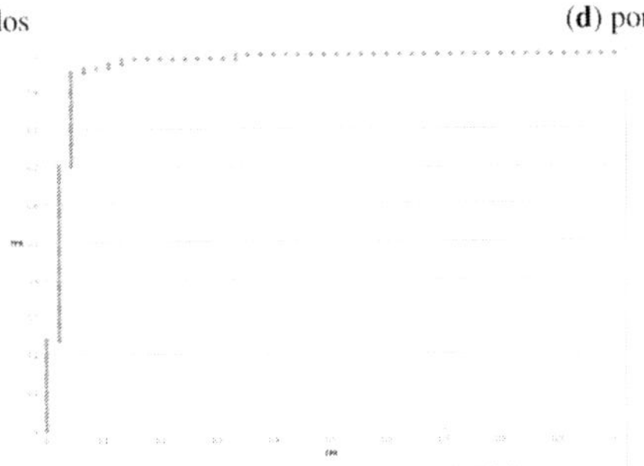

(e) not anomalous

Figure 19. ROC curves for SimpleLogistic classifier (Renyi) based on Scenario 1.

ROC is only applicable to the binary classification case. As in our approach more than two classes are considered we can analyze an individual ROC curves for each of the classes separately as presented in Figure 19. Based on such analysis we can find what is a performance of particular classifier for each class. This may be useful to find the best classifier for a specific anomaly but this is out of the scope of this article. In this work we are looking at classifiers which are (on average) the best for all classes. This is typically measured by weighted ACC and weighted

FPR, however these measures hide some important characteristics. Thus, we propose a method of calculating a multi-class ROC based on weighted results of binary ROC for each individual class. In Weka there is a feature to generate and save in files an individual ROC curves for each of the classes of multi-class classifier separately. Weka ROC file consists of operating points (threshold values) and confusion matrices containing relevant TP, FN, TN, FP values for binary classification of particular class. Our approach is to take ROC files generated by Weka (one file for each class in the dataset) and perform processing in order to average the results. The idea is to average the corresponding ROC for each class with respect to the number of class instances. As a result we received one weighted ROC based on all binary ROC results.

Weighted ROC curves for SimpleLogistic classifier for all scenarios are depicted in Figure 20, inFigure 21 and in Figure 22 respectively. It is noticeable that these for Tsallis and Renyi entropy are better than this for Shannon. ROC curves for volume-based shows that classifier based on this approach is really poor.

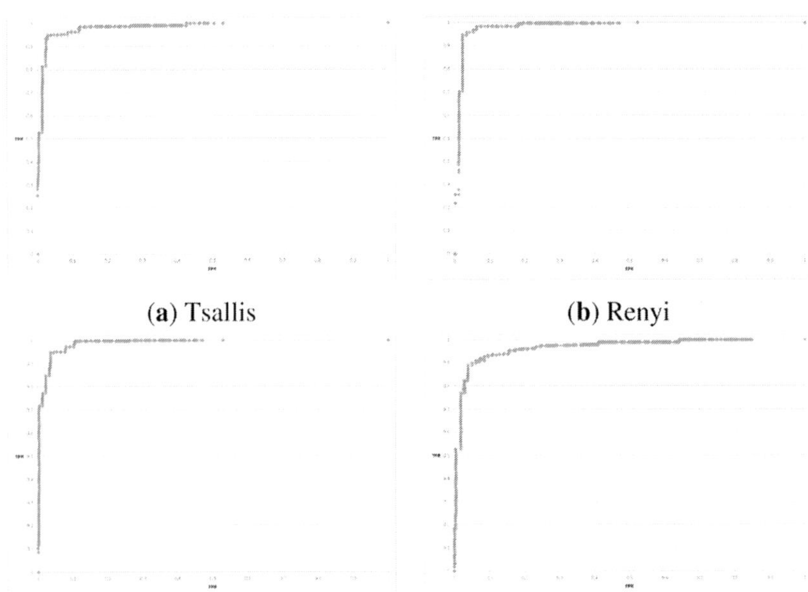

(a) Tsallis (b) Renyi

(c) Shannon (d) volume-based

Figure 20. Weighted ROC curves for SimpleLogistic classifier—Scenario 1.

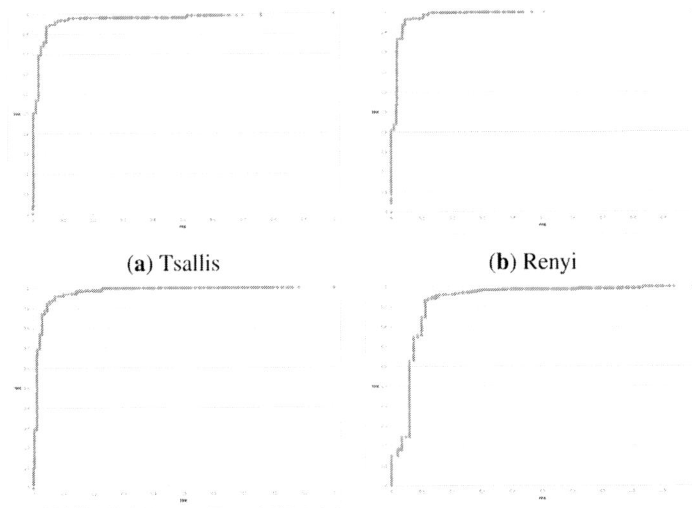

(**a**) Tsallis (**b**) Renyi

(**c**) Shannon (**d**) volume-based

Figure 21. Weighted ROC curves for SimpleLogistic classifier—Scenario 2.

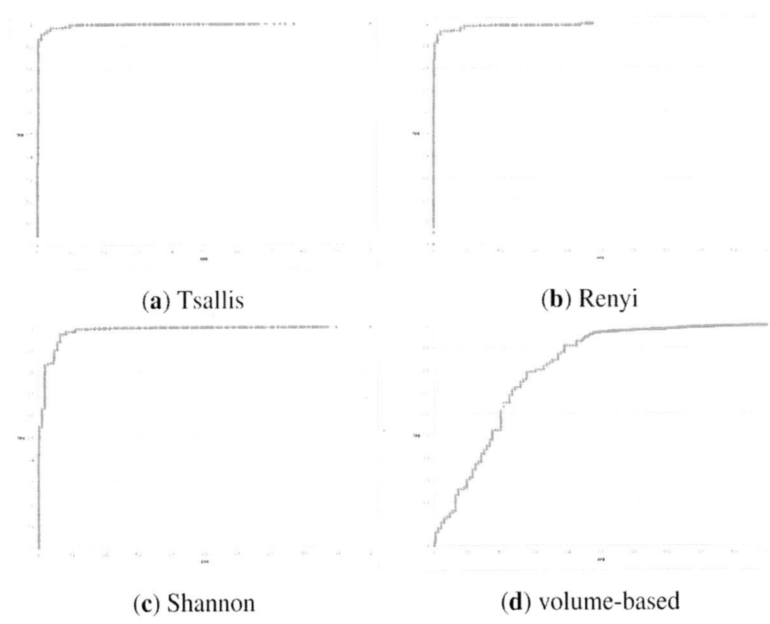

(**a**) Tsallis (**b**) Renyi

(**c**) Shannon (**d**) volume-based

Figure 22. Weighted ROC curves for SimpleLogistic classifier—Scenario 3.

7. SUMMARY

7.1. Conclusions

General conslusions for our studies is that it is possible to detect modern botnet-like malware based on anomalous patterns in network with entropy-based approach. Concluding particular results of our studies, we can observe that, based on our experiments:

- Tsallis and Renyi entropy performed best;
- Shannon entropy turned out to be worse both in Accuracy and False Positive Rate as well as weighted ROC curves;
- the volume-based approach performed poorly;
- using a broad spectrum of network traffic feature is essential to successfully detect and classify different types of anomalies; this was proved both by results of features correlation and good results of classification of different anomalies in tested scenarios;
- using α-values from a set $\{-2, -1, 0, 1, 2\}$ is a proper choice; it was proved by results of α-values correlation and good results of classification of different anomalies in tested scenarios; using a bigger set of α values is redundant; using one α-value is not enough to recognize different types of anomalies;
- the most suitable classifier (among popular classifiers employed in Weka) to our approach is the SimpleLogistic which relay on linear regression.

While we admit that our experiments were limited to few number of cases, we also believe that these cases were representative. Our dataset contains traces of network malicious activities which are typical for botnet-like malware propagation, communication and attacks performed by such a malware. Although, only one day legitimate traffic profile was built in our experiments, we have observed that this profile suits to each regular working day in the network we monitored so there was no need to prepare whole week profile. The weak performance of the Shannon entropy and poor performance of volume-based counters allows to question whether they are the right approach to detection of anomalies caused by botnet-like malware.

7.2. Further Work

Multiclass classification usually means classifying a data point into only one of the many (more than two) classes possible. It is much more advanced and sophisticated the simple detection where only two classes, e.g., *anomalous* and *not anomalous*, exist. However multiclass approach does not solve the problem when more than one class should be assign to one instance. For example instance may belong to *port scan* and *brute force* classes simultaneously because both anomalies appeared in the same time. With multi-label classification [139,140] one can classify a data point into more than one of the possible classes. In this work we do not cover multi-label problem, however this is one of the directions for a further work.

ACKNOWLEDGMENTS

This work has been partially supported by the Polish National Centre for Research and Development project no. PBS1/A3/14/2012 "Sensor Data Correlation Module for Attack Detection and Decision Support" and by the European Regional Development Fund the Innovative Economy Operational Programme, under the INSIGMA project no. 01.01.02-00-062/09 and under the project "Cyber Security Laboratory" no. 02.03.00-14-106/13.

AUTHOR CONTRIBUTIONS

All authors have contributed to the study and preparation of the article. They have read and approved the final manuscript.

CONFLICTS OF INTEREST

The authors declare no conflict of interest.

REFERENCES

1. Denning, D.E. An intrusion-detection model. *IEEE Trans. Softw. Eng.* **1987**, *13*, 222–232.
2. Li, Z.; Das, A.; Zhou, J. USAID: Unifying Signature-Based and Anomaly-Based Intrusion Detection. In *Advances in Knowledge Discovery and Data Mining*; Ho, T., Cheung, D., Liu, H., Eds.; Volume 3518, Lecture Notes in Computer Science; Springer: Berlin/Heidelberg, Germany, 2005; pp. 702–712.
3. Cheng, T.H.; Lin, Y.D.; Lai, Y.C.; Lin, P.C. Evasion Techniques: Sneaking through Your Intrusion Detection/Prevention Systems. *IEEE Commun. Surv. Tutor.* **2012**, *14*, 1011–1020.
4. Jasiul, B.; Śliwa, J.; Gleba, K.; Szpyrka, M. Identification of malware activities with rules. Proceedings of the 2014 Federated Conference on Computer Science and Information Systems (FedCSIS), Warsaw, Poland, 7–10 September 2014; Ganzha, M., Maciaszek, L., Paprzycki, M., Eds.; pp. 101–110.
5. Gascon, H.; Orfila, A.; Blasco, J. Analysis of update delays in signature-based network intrusion detection systems. *Comput. Secur.* **2011**, *30*, 613–624.
6. Eimann, R. Network Event Detection with Entropy Measures. Ph.D. Thesis, University of Auckland, Auckland, New Zealand, 2008.
7. Wagner, A.; Plattner, B. Entropy Based Worm and Anomaly Detection in Fast IP Networks. Proceedings of the 14th IEEE International Workshops on Enabling Technologies: Infrastructure for Collaborative Enterprise (WETICE'05), Linköping University, Linköping, Sweden, 13–15 June 2005; pp. 172–177.
8. Nychis, G.; Sekar, V.; Andersen, D.G.; Kim, H.; Zhang, H. An Empirical Evaluation of Entropy-based Traffic Anomaly Detection. Proceedings of the 8th ACM SIGCOMM Conference on Internet Measurement (IMC '08), Vouliagmeni, Greece, 20–22 October 2008; pp. 151–156.
9. Tellenbach, B. Detection, Classification and Visualization of Anomalies using Generalized Entropy Metrics. Ph.D. Thesis, ETH, Zürich, Switzerland, 2012; Ph.D Dissertation Nr. 20929.

10. Xiang, Y.; Li, K.; Zhou, W. Low-Rate DDoS Attacks Detection and Traceback by Using New Information Metrics. *IEEE Trans. Inf. Forensics Secur.* **2011**, *6*, 426–437.

11. Kopylova, Y.; Buell, D.A.; Huang, C.T.; Janies, J. Mutual information applied to anomaly detection. *J. Commun. Netw.* **2008**, *10*, 89–97.

12. *HP—The Bot Threat*, Available online: http:// www.bitpipe.com/detail/RES/1384218191_706.html accessed on 16 April 2015.

13. *Sophos—Security Threat Report 2014 Smarter, Shadier, Stealthier Malware*, Available online: https://cccure.training/ m/articles /view/Sophos-Security-Threat-Report-2014 accessed on 16 April 2015.

14. Scanlon, M.; Kechadi, M.T. The Case for a Collaborative Universal Peer-to-Peer Botnet Investigation Framework. Proceedings of the 9th International Conference on Cyber Warfare and Security (ICCWS 2014), Purdue University, West Lafayette, IN, USA, 24–25 March 2014; pp. 287–293.

15. Tellenbach, B.; Burkhart, M.; Sornette, D.; Maillart, T. Beyond Shannon: Characterizing Internet Traffic with Generalized Entropy Metrics. Proceedings of the 10th International Conference on Passive and Active Network Measurement (PAM'09), Seoul, Korea, 1–3 April 2009; pp. 239–248.

16. NfSen—Netflow Sensor. Available online: http:// nfsen.sourceforge.net accessed on 16 April 2015.

17. Barford, P.; Kline, J.; Plonka, D.; Ron, A. A Signal Analysis of Network Traffic Anomalies. Proceedings of the 2nd ACM SIGCOMM Workshop on Internet Measurement (IMW '02), Marseille, France, 6–8 November 2002; pp. 71–82.

18. Kim, M.S.; Kong, H.J.; Hong, S.C.; Chung, S.H.; Hong, J. A flow-based method for abnormal network traffic detection. Presented at IEEE/IFIP Network Operations and Management Symposium (NOMS 2004), Seoul, Korea, 19–23 April 2004; pp. 599–612.

19. NtopNg—High-Speed Web-based Traffic Analysis and Flow Collection. Available online: http://www.ntop.org accessed on 16 April 2015.

20. Witten, I.H.; Frank, E.; Hall, M.A. *Data Mining: Practical Machine Learning Tools and Techniques*, 3rd ed; Morgan Kaufmann Publishers Inc: San Francisco, CA, USA, 2011.

21. Bhattacharyya, D.K.; Kalita, J.K. *Network Anomaly Detection: A Machine Learning Perspective*; Chapman & Hall/CRC: Boca Raton, FL, USA, 2013.

22. Aggarwal, C. *Outlier Analysis*; Springer: New York, NY, USA, 2013.

23. Hastie, T.; Tibshirani, R.; Friedman, J. *The Elements of Statistical Learning: Data Mining, Inference and Prediction*, 2 ed; Springer: New York, NY, USA, 2009.

24. Chandola, V.; Banerjee, A.; Kumar, V. Anomaly Detection: A Survey. *ACM Comput. Surv.* **2009**, *41*, 15:1–15:58.

25. Hodge, V.; Austin, J. A Survey of Outlier Detection Methodologies. *Artif. Intell. Rev.* **2004**, *22*, 85–126.

26. Estevez-Tapiador, J.M.; Garcia-Teodoro, P.; Diaz-Verdejo, J.E. Anomaly Detection Methods in Wired Networks: A Survey and Taxonomy. *Comput. Commun.* **2004**, *27*, 1569–1584.

27. Patcha, A.; Park, J.M. An Overview of Anomaly Detection Techniques: Existing Solutions and Latest Technological Trends. *Comput. Netw.* **2007**, *51*, 3448–3470.

28. Callegari, C. Statistical approaches for network anomaly detection. Proceedings of the 4th International Conference on Internet Monitoring and Protection (ICIMP), Venice/Mestre, Italy, 24–28 May 2009.

29. Callado, A.; Kamienski, C.; Szabo, G.; Gero, B.; Kelner, J.; Fernandes, S.; Sadok, D. A Survey on Internet Traffic Identification. *IEEE Commun. Surv. Tutor.* **2009**, *11*, 37–52.

30. Garcia-Teodoro, P.; Diaz-Verdejo, J.; Macia-Fernandez, G.; Vazquez, E. Anomaly-based network intrusion detection: Techniques, systems and challenges. *Comput. Secur.* **2009**, *28*, 18–28.

31. Bhuyan, M.; Bhattacharyya, D.; Kalita, J. Network anomaly detection: methods, systems and tools. *IEEE Commun. Surv. Tutor.* **2013**, *16*, 1–34.

32. Sperotto, A.; Schaffrath, G.; Sadre, R.; Morariu, C.; Pras, A.; Stiller, B. An Overview of IP Flow-Based Intrusion Detection. *IEEE Commun. Surv. Tutor.* **2010**, *12*, 343–356.

33. Huang, L.; Nguyen, X.; Garofalakis, M.; Jordan, M.; Joseph, A.D.; Taft, N. *In-Network PCA and Anomaly Detection*; Technical Report UCB/EECS-2007-10; EECS Department, University of California: Berkeley, CA, USA, 2007.

34. Shyu, M.-L.; Chen, S.-C.; Sarinnapakorn, K.; Chang, L. A novel anomaly detection scheme based on principal component classifier. Proceedings of IEEE Foundations and New Directions of Data Mining Workshop, in conjunction with the Third IEEE International Conference on Data Mining (ICDM'03), Melbourne, FL, USA, 19–22 November 2003; pp. 171–179.

35. Lee, Y.J.; Yeh, Y.R.; Wang, Y.C.F. Anomaly Detection via Online Oversampling Principal Component Analysis. *IEEE Trans. Knowl. Data Eng.* **2013**, *25*, 1460–1470.

36. Lu, W.; Ghorbani, A.A. Network Anomaly Detection Based on Wavelet Analysis. *EURASIP J. Adv. Sig. Proc.* **2009**, *2009*.

37. Lu, W.; Tavallaee, M.; Ghorbani, A.A. Detecting Network Anomalies Using Different Wavelet Basis Functions. Proceedings of Sixth Annual Conference on Communication Networks and Services Research (CNSR 2008), Halifax, Nova Scotia, Canada, 5–8 May 2008; pp. 149–156.

38. Limthong, K.; Watanapongse, P.; Kensuke, F. A wavelet-based anomaly detection for outbound network traffic. Presented at 8th Asia-Pacific Symposium on Information and Telecommunication Technologies (APSITT), Kuching, Sarawak, Malaysia, 15–18 June 2010; pp. 1–6.

39. Ye, N.; Zhang, Y.; Borror, C.M. Robustness of the Markov-chain model for cyber-attack detection. *IEEE Trans. Reliab.* **2004**, *53*, 116–123.

40. Sha, W.; Zhu, Y.; Huang, T.; Qiu, M.; Zhu, Y.; Zhang, Q. A Multi-order Markov Chain Based Scheme for Anomaly Detection. Proceedings of IEEE 37th Annual Computer Software and Applications Conference, COMPSAC Workshops 2013, Kyoto, Japan, 22–26 July 2013; pp. 83–88.

41. Syarif, I.; Prugel-Bennett, A.; Wills, G. Unsupervised Clustering Approach for Network Anomaly Detection. In *Networked Digital Technologies*; Volume 293, Communications in Computer and Information Science; Springer: Berlin/Heidelberg, Germany, 2012; pp. 135–145.

42. Riad, A.; Elhenawy, I.; Hassan, A.; Awadallah, N. Visualize Network Anomaly Detection By Using K-Means Clustering Algorithm. *Int. J. Comput. Netw. Commun.* **2013**, *5*.

43. Bazan, J.; Szpyrka, M.; Szczur, A.; Dydo, L.; Wojtowicz, H. Classifiers for Behavioral Patterns Identification Induced from Huge Temporal Data. *Fundam. Inform.* **2015**. in press.

44. Kind, A.; Stoecklin, M.P.; Dimitropoulos, X. Histogram-based Traffic Anomaly Detection.*IEEE Trans. Netw. Serv. Manag.* **2009**, *6*, 110–121.

45. Soule, A.; Salamatia, K.; Taft, N.; Emilion, R.; Papagiannaki, K. Flow Classification by Histograms: Or How to Go on Safari in the Internet. Proceedings of the Joint International Conference on Measurement and Modeling of Computer Systems (SIGMETRICS-Performance 2004), Columbia University, New York, NY, USA, 12–16 June 2004; pp. 49–60.

46. Stoecklin, M.P.; Le Boudec, J.Y.; Kind, A. A Two-layered Anomaly Detection Technique Based on Multi-modal Flow Behavior Models. Proceedings of the 9th International Conference on Passive and Active Network Measurement (PAM'08), Cleveland, OH, USA, 29–30 April 2008; pp. 212–221.

47. Brauckhoff, D.; Dimitropoulos, X.; Wagner, A.; Salamatian, K. Anomaly Extraction in Backbone Networks Using Association Rules. Proceedings of the 9th ACM SIGCOMM Conference on Internet Measurement Conference (IMC '09), Chicago, IL, USA, 4–6 November 2009; pp. 28–34.

48. Iglesias, F.; Zseby, T. Entropy-Based Characterization of Internet Background Radiation.*Entropy* **2014**, *17*, 74–101.

49. Harrington, D.; Presuhn, R.; Wijnen, B. An Architecture for Describing Simple Network Management Protocol (SNMP) Management Frameworks. Available online: http://www.ietf.org/rfc/rfc3411.txt accessed on 16 April 2015.

50. Claise, B. Cisco Systems NetFlow Services Export Version 9. Available online: http://tools.ietf.org/html/rfc3954 accessed on 16 April 2015.

51. Kambourakis, G.; Kolias, C.; Gritzalis, S.; Park, J.H. DoS attacks exploiting signaling in {UMTS} and {IMS}. *Comput. Commun.* **2011**, *34*, 226–235.

52. Choi, K.; Chen, X.; Li, S.; Kim, M.; Chae, K.; Na, J. Intrusion Detection of NSM Based DoS Attacks Using Data Mining in Smart Grid. *Energies* **2012**, *5*, 4091–4109.

53. Liu, Y.; Xiong, N.; Park, J.; Yang, C.; Xu, K. Fair incentive mechanism with pyramidal structure for peer-to-peer networks. *IET Commun.* **2010**, *4*, 1–12.

54. Lee, D.C.; Park, B.; Kim, K.E.; Lee, J.J. Fast Traffic Anomalies Detection Using SNMP MIB Correlation Analysis. Proceedings of the 11th International Conference on Advanced Communication Technology (ICACT'09), Phoenix Park, Korea, 15–18 February 2009; 1, pp. 166–170.

55. Casas, P.; Fillatre, L.; Vaton, S.; Nikiforov, I. Volume Anomaly Detection in Data Networks: An Optimal Detection Algorithm vs. the PCA Approach. In *Traffic Management and Traffic Engineering for the Future Internet*; Valadas, R., Salvador, P., Eds.; Volume 5464, Lecture Notes in Computer Science; Springer: Berlin/Heidelberg, Germany, 2009; pp. 96–113.

56. Plixer Scrutinizer—Incydent Response System. Available online: http://www.plixer.comaccessed on 16 April 2015.

57. *Peassler PRTG—Network Monitor*, Available online: http:// www.paessler.com accessed on 16 April 2015.

58. *Solarwinds Network Traffic Analyzer*, Available online: http:// www.solarwinds.com accessed on 16 April 2015.

59. *Invea-Tech FlowMon*, Available online: https:// www. invea.com accessed on 16 April 2015.

60. *AKMA Labs FlowMatrix*, Available online: http:// www.akmalabs.com accessed on 16 April 2015.

61. Jingle, I.; Rajsingh, E. ColShield: An effective and collaborative protection shield for the detection and prevention of collaborative flooding of DDoS attacks in wireless mesh networks. *Human-centric Comput. Inf. Sci.* **2014**, *4*.

62. Zhou, W.; Jia, W.; Wen, S.; Xiang, Y.; Zhou, W. Detection and defense of application-layer {DDoS} attacks in backbone web traffic. *Future Gener. Comput. Syst.* **2014**, *38*, 36–46.

63. Brauckhoff, D.; Tellenbach, B.; Wagner, A.; May, M.; Lakhina, A. Impact of Packet Sampling on Anomaly Detection Metrics. Proceedings of the 6th ACM SIGCOMM Conference on Internet

Measurement (IMC '06), Rio de Janeiro, Brazil, 25–27 October 2006; pp. 159–164.

64. Lakhina, A.; Crovella, M.; Diot, C. Mining Anomalies Using Traffic Feature Distributions. Proceedings of the 2005 Conference on Applications, Technologies, Architectures, and Protocols for Computer Communications (SIGCOMM'05), Philadelphia, PA, USA, 22–26 August 2005; pp. 217–228.

65. Shannon, C. A Mathematical Theory of Communication. *Bell Syst. Tech. J.* **1948**, *27*, 379–423.

66. Baez, J.C.; Fritz, T.; Leinster, T. A Characterization of Entropy in Terms of Information Loss.*Entropy* **2011**, *13*, 1945–1957.

67. Lee, W.; Xiang, D. Information-theoretic measures for anomaly detection. Proceedings of 2001 IEEE Symposium on Security and Privacy, Oakland, CA, USA, 14–16 May 2001; pp. 130–143.

68. Grünwald, P.; Vitányi, P. Kolmogorov Complexity and Information Theory. With an Interpretation in Terms of Questions and Answers. *J. Logic Lang. Inf.* **2003**, *12*, 497–529.

69. Teixeira, A.; Matos, A.; Souto, A.; Antunes, L. Entropy Measures vs. Kolmogorov Complexity. *Entropy* **2011**, *13*, 595–611.

70. Ranjan, S.; Shah, S.; Nucci, A.; Munafo, M.; Cruz, R.; Muthukrishnan, S. DoWitcher: Effective Worm Detection and Containment in the Internet Core. Proceedings of 26th IEEE International Conference on Computer Communications (INFOCOM 2007), Anchorage, AL, USA, 6–12 May 2007; pp. 2541–2545.

71. Gu, Y.; McCallum, A.; Towsley, D. Detecting Anomalies in Network Traffic Using Maximum Entropy Estimation. Proceedings of the 5th ACM SIGCOMM Conference on Internet Measurement (IMC '05), Berkeley, CA, USA, 19–21 October 2005; pp. 32–32.

72. Speidel, U.; Eimann, R.; Brownlee, N. Detecting network events via T-entropy. Proceedings of 6th International Conference on Information, Communications Signal Processing, Singapore, Singapore, 10–13 December 2007; 2007; pp. 1–5.

73. Eimann, R.; Speidel, U.; Brownlee, J. A T-entropy Analysis of the Slammer Worm Outbreak. Proceedings of Asia-Pacific Network Operations and Management Symposium, Okinawa, Japan, 27–30 September 2005; pp. 434–445.

74. Titchener, M.R.; Nicolescu, R.; Staiger, L.; Gulliver, T.A.; Speidel, U. Deterministic Complexity and Entropy. *Fundam. Inform.* **2005**, *64*, 443–461.

75. Pawelec, J.; Bereziński, P.; Piotrowski, R.; Chamela, W. Entropy Measures For Internet Traffic Anomaly Detection. Proceedings of 16th International Conference on Computer Systems Aided Science, Industry and Transport (TransComp), hlcity, country, date 2012; pp. 309–318.

76. Tsallis, C. Possible generalization of Boltzmann-Gibbs statistics. *J. Stat. Phys.* **1988**, *52*, 479–487.

77. Tsallis, C. The Nonadditive Entropy Sq and Its Applications in Physics and Elsewhere: Some Remarks. *Entropy* **2011**, *13*, 1765–1804.

78. Prehl, J.; Essex, C.; Hoffmann, K.H. Tsallis Relative Entropy and Anomalous Diffusion.*Entropy* **2012**, *14*, 701–716.

79. Renyi, A. *Probability Theory*; Enlarged version of Wahrscheinlichkeitsrechnung, Valoszinusegszamitas and Calcul des probabilites. English translation by Laszlo Vekerdi; North-Holland: Amsterdam, The Netherlands, 1970.

80. Csiszár, I. Axiomatic Characterizations of Information Measures. *Entropy* **2008**, *10*, 261–273.

81. Ziviani, A.; Gomes, A.; Monsores, M.; Rodrigues, P. Network anomaly detection using nonextensive entropy. *IEEE Commun. Lett.* **2007**, *11*, 1034–1036.

82. Shafiq, M.Z.; Khayam, S.A.; Farooq, M. Improving Accuracy of Immune-inspired Malware Detectors by Using Intelligent Features. Proceedings of the 10th Annual Conference on Genetic and Evolutionary Computation (GECCO '08), Atlanta, GA, USA, 12–16 July 2008; pp. 119–126.

83. Lima, C.F.L.; de Assis, F.M.; de Souza, C.P. A Comparative Study of Use of Shannon, Rényi and Tsallis Entropy for Attribute Selecting in Network Intrusion Detection. Proceedings of the 13th Intl Conf. on Intelligent Data Engineering and Automated Learning (IDEAL'12), Natal, Brazil, 29–31 August 2012; pp. 492–501.

84. Tellenbach, B.; Burkhart, M.; Schatzmann, D.; Gugelmann, D.; Sornette, D. Accurate Network Anomaly Classification with Generalized Entropy Metrics. *Comput. Netw.* **2011**, *55*, 3485–3502.

85. Zhang, J.; Chen, X.; Xiang, Y.; Zhou, W.; Wu, J. Robust Network Traffic Classification.*IEEE/ACM Trans. Netw.* **2014**, *PP*, 1–1.

86. Clausius, R.; Hirst, T. *The Mechanical Theory of Heat: With its applications to the steam-engine and to the physical properties of bodies*; J. van Voorst: London, UK, 1867.

87. Karmeshu, J. *Entropy Measures, Maximum Entropy Principle and Emerging Applications*; Springer: New York, NY, USA, 2003.

88. Harremoes, P.; Topsoe, F. Maximum Entropy Fundamentals. *Entropy* **2001**, *3*, 191–226.

89. Kullback, S. *Information Theory and Statistics*; Wiley: New York, NY, USA, 1959.

90. Cover, T.; Thomas, J. *Elements of Information Theory*; Wiley: Hoboken, NJ, USA, 2006.

91. Maszczyk, T.; Duch, W. Comparison of Shannon, Renyi and Tsallis Entropy Used in Decision Trees. In *Artificial Intelligence and Soft Computing—ICAISC 2008*; Rutkowski, L., Tadeusiewicz, R., Zadeh, L., Zurada, J., Eds.; Volume 5097, Lecture Notes in Computer Science; Springer: Berlin/Heidelberg, Germany, 2008; pp. 643–651.

92. Marco, M. A step beyond Tsallis and Rényi entropies. *Phys. Lett. A* **2005**, *338*, 217–224.

93. Węgdrowska, E. *Miary entropii i dywergencji w analizie struktur*; Wydawnictwo Uniwersytetu Warminsko-Mazurskiego: Olsztyn, Poland, 2012.

94. Softflowd—Flow-based Network Traffic Analyser. Available online: http://code.google.com/p/softflowd/ accessed on 16 April 2015.

95. Gigamon—SPAN Port Or TAP? White Paper. Available online: https://www.netdescribe.com/downloads/span_port_or_tap_web.pdf accessed on 16 April 2015.

96. Trammell, B.; Wagner, A.; Claise, B. Flow Aggregation for the IP Flow Information Export (IPFIX) Protocol. Available online: http://tools.ietf.org/html/rfc7015 accessed on 16 April 2015.

97. Reimann, C.; Filzmoser, P.; Garrett, R.G. Background and threshold: critical comparison of methods of determination. *Sci. Total Environ.* **2005**, *346*, 1–16.

98. Szpyrka, M.; Jasiul, B.; Wrona, K.; Dziedzic, F. Telecommunications Networks Risk Assessment with Bayesian Networks. In *Computer Information Systems and Industrial Management*; Saeed, K., Chaki, R., Cortesi, A., Wierzchoń, S., Eds.; Volume 8104, Lecture Notes in Computer Science; Springer: Berlin/Heidelberg, Germany, 2013; pp. 277–288.

99. Hall, M.; Frank, E.; Holmes, G.; Pfahringer, B.; Reutemann, P.; Witten, I. The WEKA Data Mining Software: An Update. *SIGKDD Explor. Newslett.* **2009**, *11*, 10–18.

100. Jasiul, B.; Szpyrka, M.; Śliwa, J. Detection and Modeling of Cyber Attacks with Petri Nets.*Entropy* **2014**, *16*, 6602–6623.

101. Jasiul, B.; Szpyrka, M.; Śliwa, J. Malware Behavior Modeling with Colored Petri Nets. In*Computer Information Systems and Industrial Management*; Saeed, K., Snasel, V., Eds.; Volume 8838, Lecture Notes in Computer Science; Springer: Berlin/Heidelberg, Germany, 2014; pp. 667–679.

102. Jasiul, B.; Szpyrka, M.; Śliwa, J. Formal Specification of Malware Models in the Form of Colored Petri Nets. In *Computer Science and its Applications*; Park, J.J.J.H., Stojmenovic, I., Jeong, H.Y., Yi, G., Eds.; Volume 330, Lecture Notes in Electrical Engineering; Springer: Berlin/Heidelberg, Germany, 2015; pp. 475–482.

103. ACM Sigcomm Internet Traffic Archive. Available online: http://www.sigcomm.org/ITAaccessed on 16 April 2015.

104. Lawrence Berkeley National Laboratory/International Computer Science Institute Enterprise Tracing. Available online: http://www.icir.org/enterprise-tracing/ accessed on 16 April 2015.

105. SimpleWeb. Available online: http:// www.simpleweb. org/wiki/Traces accessed on 16 April 2015.

106. Center for Applied Internet Data Analysis (CAIDA). Available online: http:// www.caida.org/ data/ overview accessed on 16 April 2015.

107. Cluster of European Projects aimed at Monitoring and Measurement (MoMe). Available online: http://www.ist-mome.org/database/MeasurementData accessed on 16 April 2015.

108. Waikato Internet Traffic Storage (WITS). Available online: http:// wand.net.nz/wits accessed on 16 April 2015.

109. UMass Trace Repository (UMass). Available online: http://traces.cs.umass.edu accessed on 16 April 2015.

110. Verizon Data Breach Investigations Report. Available online: http://www.verizonenterprise.com/DBIR/2014/(accessed accessed on 16 April 2015.

111. *Symantec Internet Security Threat Report*, Available online: http://www.symantec.com/security_response/publications/threatreport.jsp accessed on 16 April 2015.

112. *CERT Poland Raport*, Availableonline: http:// www.cert.pl/PDF/Report_CP_2013.pdf accessed on 16 April 2015.

113. Saad, S.; Traore, I.; Ghorbani, A.A.; Sayed, B.; Zhao, D.; Lu, W.; Felix, J.; Hakimian, P. Detecting P2P botnets through network behavior analysis and machine learning. Proceedings of 2011 Ninth Annual International Conference on Privacy, Security and Trust (PST), Montreal, QC, Canada, 19–21 July 2011; pp. 174–180.

114. García, S.; Grill, M.; Stiborek, J.; Zunino, A. An Empirical Comparison of Botnet Detection Methods. *Comput. Secur.* **2014**, *45*, 100–123.

115. Sperotto, A.; Sadre, R.; Vliet, F.; Pras, A. A Labeled Data Set for Flow-Based Intrusion Detection. Proceedings of the 9th IEEE International Workshop on IP Operations and Management (IPOM '09), Venice, Italy, 29–30 October 2009; Springer: Berlin/Heidelberg, Germany, 2009; pp. 39–50.

116. Bereziński, P.; Pawelec, J.; Małowidzki, M.; Piotrowski, R. Entropy-Based Internet Traffic Anomaly Detection: A Case Study. Proceedings of the Ninth International Conference on Dependability and Complex Systems DepCoS-RELCOMEX, Brunów, Poland, 30 June – 4 July 2014; Zamojski, W., Mazurkiewicz, J., Sugier, J., Walkowiak, T., Kacprzyk, J., Eds.; Springer: Cham, Switzerland, 2014; 286, pp. 47–58.

117. Haines, J.; Lippmann, R.; Fried, D.; Zissman, M.; Tran, E.; Boswell, S. *1999 DARPA Intrusion Detection Evaluation: Design and Procedures*; Technical Report 1062; MIT Lincoln Laboratory: Lexington, MA, USA, 2001. Available online: https://www.ll.mit.edu/mission/communications/cyber/CSTcorpora/files/TR-1062.pdf accessed on 16 April 2015.

118. The Third International Knowledge Discovery and Data Mining Tools (KDD) Cup 1999 Data. Available online: http://kdd.ics.uci.edu/databases/kddcup99/kddcup99.html accessed on 16 April 2015.

119. Tavallaee, M.; Bagheri, E.; Lu, W.; Ghorbani, A.A. A Detailed Analysis of the KDD CUP 99 Data Set. Proceedings of the 2nd IEEE Intl Conference on Computational Intelligence for Security and Defense Applications, Ottawa, ON, Canada, 8–10 July 2009; pp. 53–58.

120. McHugh, J. Testing Intrusion Detection Systems: A Critique of the 1998 and 1999 DARPA Intrusion Detection System Evaluations As Performed by Lincoln Laboratory. *ACM Trans. Inf. Syst. Secur.* **2000**, *3*, 262–294.

121. Mahoney, M.V.; Chan, P.K. An Analysis of the 1999 DARPA/Lincoln Laboratory Evaluation Data for Network Anomaly Detection. In *Recent Advances in Intrusion Detection*; Vigna, G., Kruegel, C., Jonsson, E., Eds.; Volume 2820, Lecture Notes in Computer Science; Springer: Berlin/Heidelberg, Germany, 2003; pp. 220–237.

122. Thomas, C.; Sharma, V.; Balakrishnan, N. Usefulness of DARPA dataset for intrusion detection system evaluation. *SPIE Proc.* **2008**.

123. Brauckhoff, D.; Wagner, A.; May, M. FLAME: A Flow-level Anomaly Modeling Engine. Proceedings of the Conference on Cyber Security Experimentation and Test (CSET'08), San Jose, CA, USA, 28 July 2008; pp. 1–6.

124. Brauckhoff, D. Network traffic anomaly detection and evaluation. Ph.D. Thesis, ETH Zürich, Switzerland, 2010; PhD Dissertation Nr. 18835.

125. Shiravi, A.; Shiravi, H.; Tavallaee, M.; Ghorbani, A.A. Toward Developing a Systematic Approach to Generate Benchmark Datasets for Intrusion Detection. *Comput. Secur.* **2012**, *31*, 357–374.

126. Bereziński, P.; Szpyrka, M.; Jasiul, B.; Mazur, M. Network Anomaly Detection Using Parameterized Entropy. In *Computer Information Systems and Industrial Management*; Saeed, K., Snasel, V., Eds.; Volume 8838, Lecture Notes in Computer Science; Springer: Berlin/Heidelberg, Germany, 2014; pp. 465–478.

127. Tomer, B. *Morto Post Mortem: Dissecting a Worm*, Available online: http://blog.imperva.com/2011/09/morto-post-mortem-a-worm-deep-dive.html accessed on 16 April 2015.

128. Damon, E.; Dale, J.; Laron, E.; Mache, J.; Land, N.; Weiss, R. Hands-on Denial of Service Lab Exercises Using SlowLoris and RUDY. Proceedings of the 2012 Information Security Curriculum Development Conference (InfoSecCD '12), Kennesaw, GA, USA, 12–13 October 2012; pp. 21–29.

129. Bencsáth, B.; Pék, G.; Buttyán, L.; Félegyházi, M. The Cousins of Stuxnet: Duqu, Flame, and Gauss. *Future Internet* **2012**, *4*, 971–1003.

130. Denning, D.E. Stuxnet: What Has Changed? *Future Internet* **2012**, *4*, 672–687.

131. Kührer, M.; Hupperich, T.; Rossow, C.; Holz, T. Exit from Hell? Reducing the Impact of Amplification DDoS Attacks. Proceedings of the 23rd USENIX Security Symposium, San Diego, CA, USA, 20–22 August 2014.

132. Hauke, J.; Kossowski, T. Comparison of Values of Pearson's and Spearman's Correlation Coefficients on the Same Sets of Data. *Quaest. Geogr.* **2011**, *30*, 87–93.

133. Davis, J.; Goadrich, M. The Relationship Between Precision-Recall and ROC Curves. Proceedings of the 23rd International Conference on Machine Learning (ICML'06), Pittsburgh, PA, USA, 25–29 June 2006; pp. 233–240.

134. Wu, Y.; Cai, S.; Yang, S.; Zheng, F.; Xiang, N. Classification of Knee Joint Vibration Signals Using Bivariate Feature Distribution Estimation and Maximal Posterior Probability Decision Criterion. *Entropy* **2013**, *15*, 1375–1387.

135. Rifkin, R. *MIT—Multiclass Classification*, Available online: http://www.mit.edu/~9.520/spring09/Classes/multiclass.pdf accessed on 16 April 2015.

136. Sumner, M.; Frank, E.; Hall, M. Speeding up Logistic Model Tree Induction. Proceedings of 9th European Conference on Principles and Practice of Knowledge Discovery in Databases, Porto, Portugal, 3–7 October 2005; pp. 675–683.

137. Seber, G.; Lee, A. *Linear Regression Analysis*; Wiley Series in Probability and Statistics; Wiley: Hoboken, NJ, USA, 2012.

138. Landwehr, N.; Hall, M.; Frank, E. Logistic Model Trees. *Mach. Learn.* **2005**, *59*, 161–205.

139. Madjarov, G.; Kocev, D.; Gjorgjevikj, D.; Deroski, S. An Extensive Experimental Comparison of Methods for Multi-label Learning. *Pattern Recogn.* **2012**, *45*, 3084–3104.

140. *MEKA: A Multi-label Extension to WEKA*, Available online: http: // meka.sourceforge.net/accessed on 16 April 2015.

7

CHAPTER

ANOMALY DETECTION BASED ON SENSOR DATA IN PETROLEUM INDUSTRY APPLICATIONS

Luis Martí [1,*], Nayat Sanchez-Pi [2], José Manuel Molina [3] and Ana Cristina Bicharra Garcia [4]

[1]*Department of Electrical Engineering, Pontifícia Universidade Católica do Rio de Janeiro, Rio de Janeiro 22451-900, Brazil*

[2]*Instituto de Lógica, Filosofia e Teoria da Ciência (ILTC), Niterói 24020-042, Brazil*

[3]*Department of Informatics, Universidad Carlos III de Madrid, Colmenarejo, Madrid 28270, Spain*

[4]*ADDLabs, Universidade Federal Fluminense, Niterói 24210-340, Brazil*

ABSTRACT

Anomaly detection is the problem of finding patterns in data that do not conform to an a priori expected behavior. This is related to the problem in which some samples are distant, in terms of a given metric, from the rest of the dataset, where these anomalous samples are indicated as outliers. Anomaly detection has recently attracted the attention of the research community, because of its relevance in real-world applications, like intrusion detection, fraud detection, fault detection and system health monitoring, among many others. Anomalies themselves can have a positive or negative nature, depending on their context and interpretation. However, in either case, it is important for decision makers to be able to detect them in order to take appropriate actions. The petroleum industry is one of the application contexts where these problems are present. The correct detection of such types of unusual information empowers the decision maker with the capacity to act on the system in order to correctly avoid, correct or react to the situations associated with them. In that application context, heavy extraction machines for pumping and generation operations, like turbomachines, are intensively monitored by hundreds of sensors each that send measurements with a high frequency for damage prevention. In this paper, we propose a combination of yet another segmentation algorithm (YASA), a novel fast and high quality segmentation algorithm, with a one-class support vector machine approach for efficient anomaly detection in turbomachines. The proposal is meant for dealing with the aforementioned task and to cope with the lack of labeled training data. As a result, we perform a series of empirical studies comparing our approach to other methods applied to benchmark problems and a real-life application related to oil platform turbomachinery anomaly detection.

Keywords: Anomaly detection; Big data; Time-series segmentation; Outlier detection; Oil industry applications

1. INTRODUCTION

The petroleum industry has evolved into a highly-supervised industry, where operational security and safety are present and foundational values. In the particular context of modern offshore oil platforms, almost all of the installed equipment include sensors for monitoring their behavior and remote-controlled actuators to act upon them in order to regulate the operational profile, to avoid undesired events and to prevent possible catastrophic failures. Oil plant automation physically protects plant integrity. However, it acts by reacting to anomalous conditions. Extracting information in an on-line fashion from raw data generated by the sensors is not a simple task when turbomachinery—a key class of equipment—is involved.

The term, turbomachine, applies to any device that extracts energy or imports energy from a continuously-moving stream of fluid, either liquid or gas [1]. Elaborating further, a turbomachine is a power or head generating machine, which employs the dynamic action of a rotating element, the rotor. The action of the rotor changes the energy level of the continuously-flowing fluid through the machine. Turbines, compressors and fans are all members of this family of machines. In contrast to positive displacement machines, especially of the reciprocating type, which are low-speed machines based on the mechanical and volumetric efficiency considerations, the majority of turbomachines run at comparatively higher speeds without any mechanical problems and with volumetric efficiency close to the ideal (100%). This application context calls for the application of anomaly detection methods [2] that grant and supervise the effective and safe usage of the machinery involved.

Anomalies themselves can have a positive or negative nature, depending on their context and interpretation. The importance of anomaly detection is a consequence of the fact that anomalies in data translate to significant actionable information in a wide variety of application domains. The correct detection of such types of unusual information empowers the decision maker with the capacity to act on the system in order to adequately react, avoid or correct the situations associated with them.

Anomaly detection has seen extensive study and use in a wide variety of applications, such as fraud and intrusion detection [3], fault detection in safety critical systems [4], finance [5] or industrial systems [6], among many others (see [2] for a survey).

In the case of industrial anomaly detection, units suffer damage due to continuous intensive use. Those damages need to be detected as early as possible to prevent further escalation and losses. Data in this domain are referred to as sensor data, because these are recorded using different sensors and collected for analysis. Hence, it can be said that, in this context, anomaly detection techniques monitor the performance of industrial components, such as motors, turbines, oil flow in pipelines or other mechanical components, and detect defects that might occur due to wear and tear or other unexpected circumstances. Data in this domain have a temporal aspect, and time series analysis is also used in some works, like [7].

The problem debated in this paper was prompted by the complexity and requirements of the task of the early detection of behaviors that could potentially lead to turbomachine or platform failures in the application context of interest. One additional characteristic of this problem is that these machines have different operational profiles. For example, they are used at different intensities or throttle depending on the active platform operational profile. Therefore, in order to correctly detect future anomalies, it is essential to segment the dataset available in order to automatically discover the operational regime of the machine in the recent past. This segmentation algorithm would allow one to discriminate the changes of the operational profile from anomalies and faults, as manual changes are not logged, and sometimes, those modifications take place without human supervision.

Furthermore, in this particular case, it can be argued that we are also facing a Big Data problem [8]. Each machine has from 150 to 300 sensors that submit information to the data hub every 5 s. Since oil platforms have between six to 20 of these machines, a conservative estimate provided by the partner yielded that, on average, 43,200,000 measurements are collected on a daily basis. Furthermore, as the industry partner already exploits more than 70 platforms, a conservative estimate is that every 5 s, more than 100,000 sensor measurements should be processed by the central data hub. Hence, the dataset available for processing has more than 1×10^{12} measurements per year. This characteristic imposes extra requirements on the low computational complexities of the algorithms and methods to be applied, as well as on the supporting computational engine.

In order to deal with such an amount of noisy data, time series segmentation is identified as a necessary technique to be used as a preprocessing step for time series analysis. This step must be able to identify blocks of homogeneous data that can be analyzed in a separate fashion. However, the massive amount of data to be processed in an on-line fashion poses a challenge to current time series segmentation methods. Consequently, we proposed a novel segmentation algorithm that was able to correctly identify those blocks of data at a viable computational cost.

Due to the lack of labeled data for the training and validation of models, we propose a solution for the detection of anomalies in turbomachinery that relies on using a one-class support vector machine (SVM) [9]. The one-class SVM learns a region that contains the training data instances (a boundary). Kernels, such as radial basis functions (RBF) [10], linear, Fourier, etc. [11], can be used to learn complex regions. For each test instance, the basic technique determines if the test instance falls within the learned region. If a test instance falls within the learned region, it is declared as normal; else it is declared as anomalous. We combine this technique with a time series segmentation to prune noisy, unreliable and inconsistent data.

Therefore, the novelty of our approach is the combination of a fast and high-quality segmentation algorithm with a one-class support vector machine approach for efficient anomaly detection.

The remainder of this paper is organized as follows. In the next section, we discuss some related work. Subsequently, we describe our proposal in detail. After that, we present a case study for offshore oil platform turbomachinery. This case study is devised to compare our approach with alternatives methods of anomalies or outlier detection. In the final section of the paper, some conclusive remarks and directions for future work are put forward.

2. FOUNDATIONS

The present work addresses the problem of anomaly detection by combining a one-class SVM classifier that has previously been used with success for anomaly detection with a novel and fast segmentation algorithm specially devised for this problem. In this section, we present the theoretical pillars supporting the proposal.

2.1. Anomaly Detection

Fault and damage prevention is known as the problem of finding patterns in data that do not conform to an expected behavior [2]. Unexpected patterns are often referred to as anomalies, outliers or faults, depending on the application domain. In broad terms, anomalies are patterns in data that do not conform to a well-defined normal behavior [12]. There are also extensive surveys of anomaly detection techniques.

Anomaly detection techniques have been proposed in the literature, based on distribution, distance, density, clustering and classification. Their applications vary depending on the user, the problem domains and even the dataset. In many cases, the anomaly detection is related to outlier detection. In statistics, outliers are data instances that deviate from a given sample in which they occur. Grubbs in [13] defined them as follows: an outlying observation, or "outlier", is one that appears to deviate markedly from other members of the sample in which it occurs.

Anomaly detection techniques can be summarized by grouping them into a sets of similar approaches:

- Distribution-based approaches: A given statistical distribution is used to model the data points [7]. Then, points that deviate from the model are flagged as anomalies or outliers. These approaches are unsuitable for moderately high-dimensional datasets and require prior knowledge of the data distribution. They are also called parametric and non-parametric statistical modeling.
- Depth-based approaches: This computes the different layers of convex hulls and flag objects in the outer layer as anomalies or

outliers [14]. It avoids the requirement of fitting a distribution to the data, but has a high computational complexity.

- Clustering approaches: Many clustering algorithms can detect anomalies or outliers as elements that do not belong, or that are near, to any cluster [15,16].
- Distance-based approaches: Distance-based anomalies or outlier detection marks how distant an element is from a subset of the elements closest to it. It has been pointed out [17] that these methods cannot cope with datasets having both dense and sparse regions, an issue denominated the multi-density problem.
- Density-based approaches: Density-based anomalies or outlier detection have been proposed to overcome the multi-density problem by means of the local outlier factor (LOF). LOF measures the degree of outlierness for each dataset element and depends on the local density of its neighborhood. This approach fails to deal correctly with another important issue: the multi-granularity problem.The local correlation integral (LOCI) method, and its outlier metric, the multi-granularity deviation factor (MDEF), were proposed with the purpose of correctly dealing with multi-density and multi-granularity [18].
- Spectral decomposition: Spectral decomposition is used to embed the data in lower dimensional subspace in which the data instances can be discriminated easily Many techniques based on principal component analysis (PCA) have emerged [19]. Some of them decompose space into normal, anomaly and noise subspaces. The anomalies can be then detected in the anomaly subspace [20].
- Classification approaches: In this case, the problem is posed as the identification of which categories to which an observation belongs. It operates in two phases: first, it learns a model based on subset observations (training set), and second, it infers a class for new observations (testing set) based on the learned model. This method operates under the assumption that a classifier distinguishes between normal and anomalous classes that can be learned in the given feature space. Based on the labels available for the training phase, anomaly detection techniques based on classification can be grouped into two broad categories: multi-class [21] and one-class anomaly detection techniques [22].

2.2. Time Series Segmentation

In the problem of finding frequent patterns, the primary purpose of time series segmentation is dimensionality reduction. For the anomaly detection problem in turbomachines, it is necessary to segment the dataset available in order to automatically discover how the operational regime of the machine in the recent past was. There is a vast amount of work that has been done in time series segmentation, but let us state a segmentation definition and describe the available segmentation method classification, before starting to cite them.

In general terms, a time series can be expressed as a set of time-ordered possible infinite measurements [23], $\mathcal{S}$, that consists of pairs $\langle s_i, t_i \rangle$ of sensor measurements, s_i, and time instants, t_i, such that,

$$\mathcal{S} = \{\langle s_0, t_0 \rangle, \langle s_1, t_1 \rangle, \ldots \langle s_i, t_i \rangle, \ldots\}, i \in \mathbb{N}^+; \forall t_i, t_j : t_i < t_j \text{ if } i < j \quad (1)$$

Sensor measurements s_i take values on a set that depends on the particular characteristics of the sensor.

In practice, time series frequently have a simpler definition as: measurements that are usually obtained at equal time intervals between them. This type of time series is known as a regular time series. In this case, the explicit reference to time can be dropped and exchanged for an order reference index, leading to a simpler expression:

$$\mathcal{S} = \{s_0, s_1, \ldots s_i, \ldots\}, i \in \mathbb{N}^+ \quad (2)$$

The use of regular time series is so pervasive that the remainder of this paper will deal only with them. Henceforth, the term, time series, will be used to refer to a regular time series.

Depending on the application, the goal of the segmentation is to locate stable periods of time, to identify change points or to simply compress the original time series into a more compact representation. Although in many real-life applications, a lot of variables must be simultaneously tracked and monitored, most of the segmentation algorithms are used for the analysis of only one time-variant variable.

A segmentation algorithm can be represented as a function $\Theta(\cdot)$ that creates K segments of time series, such that,

$$\Theta : \mathcal{S} \rightarrow \langle \mathcal{S}_1, \mathcal{S}_2, \ldots, \mathcal{S}_K \rangle \quad (3)$$

where $\langle \mathcal{S}_1, \mathcal{S}_2, \ldots, \mathcal{S}_k \rangle$ exhibit the properties: (i) S=UKi=1Si, or, in other words, that $\mathcal{S}$ can be reconstructed from the segmentation without data loss; and (ii) $\mathcal{S}_i \cap \mathcal{S}_j = \emptyset, \forall i, j = 1, \ldots, K$ and $i \neq j$, which implies that each segment is disjoint with regard to the rest.

There is a vast literature about segmentation methods for different applications. Basically, there are mainly three categories of time series segmentation algorithms using dynamic programming. Firstly, there are sliding windows [24,25], top-down [26] and bottom-up [27] strategies.

The sliding windows method is a purely implicit segmentation technique. It consists of a segment that is grown until it exceeds some error bound. This process is repeated with the next data point not included in the newly approximated segment. However, like all implicit methods, it is extremely slow and not useful for real-time applications; its complexity is $O(Ln\mathcal{S})$, where $n\mathcal{S}$ is the number of elements of $\mathcal{S}$ $(n\mathcal{S} = |\mathcal{S}|)$ and $L = n\mathcal{S}/K$ is the average segment length.

Top-down methods are those where the time series is recursively partitioned until some stopping criteria is met. This method is faster than the sliding window method above, but it is still slow; the complexity is $O(n^2K)$. Additionally, the bottom-up starts from the finest possible approximation, and segments are merged until some stopping criteria is met.

Later, during the process of approximating a time series with straight lines, there are at least two ways of finding the approximating line: linear interpolation and linear regression [28]. Linear interpolation tends to closely align the endpoint of consecutive segments, giving the piecewise approximation a "smooth" look. In contrast, piecewise linear regression can produce a very disjointed look on some datasets. However, the quality of the approximating line, in terms of Euclidean distance, is generally better in the regression approach [29].

There are also more novel methods, for instance those using clustering for segmentation. The clustered segmentation problem is clearly related to the time series clustering problem [30], and there are also several definitions for time series [31,32]. One natural view of segmentation is the attempt to determine which components of a dataset naturally "belong together".

There exist two classes of algorithms for solving the clustered segmentation problem. The distance-based clustering of segmentations measures the distance between sequence segmentations. In our approach, we employ a standard clustering algorithm (e.g., k-means) on the pair-wise distance matrix. The second class of algorithms consists of two randomized algorithms that cluster sequences using segmentations as "centroids". In particular, we use the notion of a distance between a segmentation and a sequence, which is the error induced on the sequence when the segmentation is applied to it. The algorithms of the second class treat the clustered-segmentation problem as a model selection problem and then try to find the best model that describes the data.

There also methods considering multiple regression models. In [33], a segmented regression model is considered with one independent variable under the continuity constraints, and the asymptotic distributions of the estimated regression coefficients and change points are studied. In [34-36], some special cases of the model studied cited before are considered, and more details on the distributional properties of the estimators are provided. Bai [37–39] considered a multiple regression model with structural changes, a model without the continuity constraints at the change points, and studied the asymptotic properties of the estimators.

3. ALGORITHM PROPOSAL

As already hinted earlier, our proposal combines a fast segmentation algorithm with a support vector machine one-class classifier. The segmentation algorithm takes care of identifying relatively homogeneous parts of the time series in order to focus the attention of the classifier on the most relevant portion of the time series. Therefore, parts of the time series that remain in the past can be safely disregarded.

3.1. Problem Formalization

Nowadays, it is common that offshore oil platforms use equipment control automation to act upon perceived events. This equipment control automation includes sensors for monitoring equipment behavior and remotely-controlled valves. Plant automation physically protects plant integrity and acts by reacting to anomalous conditions. Equipment usage is automatically controlled by a priori limit values, usually provided by the equipment manufacturer, that establish an operational interval. Figure 1 presents a general operational workflow of an oil platform, detailing the main components and processes.

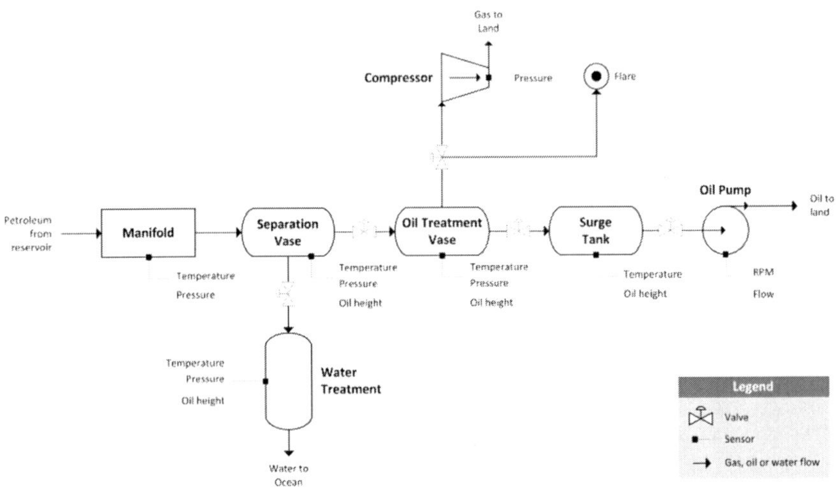

Figure 1. Oil platform process plant work-flow.

Assuming independence between turbomachines and that their sensors operate in a reliable and consistent mode, we can deal with each one separately. Although, in practice, different machines do affect each other, as they are interconnected, for the sake of simplicity, we will be dealing with one at a time.

Using this scheme, we can construct an abstract model of the problem. A given turbomachine, $\mathcal{M}$, is monitored by a set of m sensors $s^{(j)} \in \mathcal{M}$, with $j = 1, ..., m$. Each of these sensors are sampled at regular time intervals in order to produce the time series:

$$\mathcal{S}^{(j)}_{t_{\max};t_0} := \left\{ s^{(j)}_t \right\}, t_0 \leq t \leq t_{\max} \tag{4}$$

Using this representation and assuming that sensors are independent, the problem of interest can be expressed as a two-part problem: (i) to predict a future anomaly in a sensor; and (ii) to perform an action based on anomaly predictions (decision-making). This can be expressed more formally as:

Definition 1 (Sensor Anomaly Prediction)

Find a set of anomaly prediction functions, $A^{(j)}(\cdot)$*, Such That:*

$$A^{(j)}\left(S^{(j)}_{t,t-\Delta t}\middle|\widehat{S}^{(j)}_{t_{\max},t_0}\right)=\begin{cases}1\ \textit{predicted anomaly}\\ 0\ \textit{in other case}\end{cases}\tag{5}$$

that is constructed using a given reference (training) set of sensor data, $\widehat{S}^{(j)}_{t_{\max},t_0}$*, and determines if there will be a failure in the near future by processing a sample of current sensor data* $S^{(j)}_{t,t-\Delta t}$*, with* $t_{\max} < t-\Delta t < t$ *and, generally,* $\Delta t \ll t_{\max}-t_0$.

Using those functions, the second problem can be stated as:

Definition 2 (Machine Anomaly Alarm)

For each turbomachine $\mathcal{M}$*, obtain a machine alarm function:*

$$F_{\mathcal{M}}\left(a_t^{(1)},\ldots,a_t^{(m)}\middle|\,\boldsymbol{w}_{\mathcal{M}}\right)=\begin{cases}1\ \textit{alarm signal}\\ 0\ \textit{in other case}\end{cases}\tag{6}$$

Where $a_t^{(j)}=A^{(j)}\left(S^{(j)}_{t,t-\Delta t}\right)$ *and the weights vector,* $w_{\mathcal{M}}=\{w^{(1)},\ldots,w^{(m)}\}$*, represents the contribution, or relevance, of each sensor to an alarm firing decision.*

It must be noted that, although we have expressed these problems in a crisp (Boolean) form, they can be expressed in a continuous [0, 1] form suitable for the application of fuzzy logic or other forms of uncertainty reasoning methods. The discussion of those approaches and their application is out of the scope of this paper.

In order to synthesize adequate $A^{(j)}$ and $f\mathcal{M}$, it is necessary to identify the different operational modes of the the machine. Knowing the operational modes of the machine enables the creation of $A^{(j)}$ and $f\mathcal{M}$ functions, either explicitly or by means of a modeling or machine learning method, that correctly respond to each mode.

3.2. Segmentation Algorithm

In this section, we introduce a novel and fast algorithm for time series segmentation. Besides the obvious purpose of obtaining a segmentation method that produces low approximation errors, another set of guidelines were observed while devising the algorithm. They can be summarized as follows:

- Low computational cost: The application context calls for algorithms capable of handling large amounts of data and that scale properly as the those amounts are increased. Most current segmentation algorithms have such a computational complexity, that it impairs them from correctly tackling the problems of interest.
- Easy parametrization: One important drawback of current approaches is that their parameters may be hard to set by the end users. In our case, we have as the main parameter the significance test threshold, which is very easy to understand feature.

Relying on those principles, we propose yet another segmentation algorithm (YASA). YASA is presented in Figure 2 in schematic form. The algorithm is best understood when presented in recursive form. A call to the segmentation procedure first checks if the current level of recursion is acceptable. After that, it fits a linear regression to the time series data. If the regression passes the linearity statistical hypothesis test, then the current time series is returned as a unique segment.

If the regression does not model the data correctly, this means that it is necessary to partition the time series into at least two parts that should be further segmented. The last part of YASA is dedicated to this task. It locates the time instant, t_s, where the regression had the largest error residuals. It also guarantees that that time instant does not create an excessively short time series chunk. Once an adequate time instant is located, it is used as a split point to carry out the segmentation of the parts of the time series located on both sides of it.

function SEGMENTDATA($\mathcal{S}^{(j)}_{t_{\max},t_0}, \rho_{\min}, l_{\max}, s_{\min}, l$)
Parameters:
▷ $\mathcal{S}^{(j)}_{t_{\max},t_0}$, time series data of sensor j corresponding to time interval $[t_0, t_{\max}]$.
▷ $\rho_{\min} \in [0, 1]$, minimum significance for statistical hypothesis test of linearity.
▷ $l_{\max} > 0$, maximum levels of recursive calls.
▷ $s_{\min} > 0$, minimum segment length.
Returns:
▷ $\Phi := \{\phi_1, \ldots, \phi_m\}$, data segments.
  if $l = l_{\max}$ **then**
    return $\Phi = \left\{\mathcal{S}^{(j)}_{t_{\max},t_0}\right\}$
  end if
  Perform linear regression, $\{m, b\} \leftarrow$ LINEARREGRESSION($\mathcal{S}^{(j)}_{t_{\max},t_0}$).
  if LINEARITYTEST($\mathcal{S}^{(j)}_{t_{\max},t_0}, m, b$) $> \rho_{\min}$ **then**
    return $\Phi = \left\{\mathcal{S}^{(j)}_{t_{\max},t_0}\right\}$.
  end if
  Calculate residual errors, $\{e_0, \ldots, e_{\max}\} =$ RESIDUALS($\mathcal{S}^{(j)}_{t_{\max},t_0}, m, b$).
  $t_s \leftarrow t_0$.
  while $\max(\{e_0, \ldots, e_{\max}\}) > 0$ **and** $t_s \notin (t_0 + s_{\min}, t_{\max} - s_{\min})$ **do**
    Determine split point, $t_s = \arg\max_t \{e_t\}$.
  end while
  if $t_s \in (t_0 + s_{\min}, t_{\max} - s_{\min})$ **then**
    $\Phi_{\text{left}} =$ SEGMENTDATA($\mathcal{S}^{(j)}_{t_s,t_0}, \rho_{\min}, l_{\max}, s_{\min}, l+1$).
    $\Phi_{\text{right}} =$ SEGMENTDATA($\mathcal{S}^{(j)}_{t_{\max},t_s}, \rho_{\min}, l_{\max}, s_{\min}, l+1$).
    return $\Phi = \Phi_{\text{left}} \cup \Phi_{\text{right}}$.
  end if
  return $\Phi = \left\{\mathcal{S}^{(j)}_{t_{\max},t_0}\right\}$.
end function

Figure 2. Pseudocode of yet another segmentation algorithm (YASA).

3.3. One-Class Support Vector Machine

The problem, as it is posed, implies determining whether (new) sensor data belong to a specific class, determined by the training data, or not.

To cope with this problem, one-class classification problems (and solutions) are introduced. By just providing the normal training data, an algorithm creates a (representational) model of this data. If newly encountered data is too different, according to some measurement from this model, it is labeled as out-of-class.

Support vector machines (SVMs) can be used for the problem described above. SVMs are supervised learning models with associated learning algorithms that analyze data and recognize patterns. SVMs have been successfully used for classification and regression analysis. Given a set of training examples, each marked as belonging to one of many categories, an SVM training algorithm builds a model that assigns new examples into one category or the other, making it a non-probabilistic binary linear classifier. An SVM model is a representation of the examples as points in space, mapped so that the examples of the separate categories are divided by a clear gap that is as wide as possible. More precisely, a support vector machine constructs a hyperplane or set of hyperplanes in a high- or infinite-dimensional space, which can be used for classification, regression or other tasks. Intuitively, a good separation is achieved by the hyperplane that has the largest distance to the nearest training data point of any class (the so-called functional margin), since, in general, the larger the margin, the lower the generalization error of the classifier.

In order to understand one-class SVMs, it is convenient to first examine the traditional two-class support vector machine. Consider a (possibly infinite) dataset,

$$\Psi = \{\langle \boldsymbol{x}_1, y_1 \rangle, \langle \boldsymbol{x}_2, y_2 \rangle, \ldots, \langle \boldsymbol{x}_i, y_i \rangle, \ldots\} \quad (7)$$

where $\boldsymbol{x}_i \in \mathbb{R}^n$ is a given data point and $y_i \in \{1, 1\}$ is the i-th output pattern, indicating the class membership.

SVMs can create a non-linear decision boundary by projecting the data through a non-linear function $\varphi()$ to a space with a higher dimension. This implies that data points, which cannot be separated by a linear threshold in their original (input) space, are converted to a feature space $\mathcal{F}$, where there is a hyperplane that separates the data points of one class from another. When that hyperplane is projected back to the original space, it has the shape of a non-linear curve. This hyperplane is represented by the equation,

$$\boldsymbol{w}^T \boldsymbol{x} + \boldsymbol{b} = 0, \text{ with } \boldsymbol{w} \in \mathcal{F}, \ \boldsymbol{b} \in \mathbb{R}^n \quad (8)$$

The hyperplane that is constructed determines the border between classes. All of the data points for the class "– 1" are on one side, and all of the data points for class "1" are on the other. The distance from the closest point from each class to the hyperplane is equal; thus, the constructed hyperplane searches for the maximal margin between the classes.

Slack variables, ξ_i, are introduced to allow some data points to lie within the margin in order to prevent the SVM classifier from over-fitting the noisy data (or creating a soft margin). Constant $C > 0$ determines the trade-off between maximizing the margin and the number of training data points within that margin (and, thus, training errors). Posed as an optimization problem, the adjustment of an SVM has as the objective to minimize the problem,

$$\begin{aligned} &\text{minimize} \quad f(\boldsymbol{w}, \boldsymbol{b}, \boldsymbol{xi}) = \tfrac{\|w\|^2}{2} + C\textstyle\sum_{i=1}^{n} \xi_i, \\ &\text{subject to} \quad y_i\left(\boldsymbol{w}^T\phi(x_i) + b\right) \geq 1 - \xi_i, \qquad \forall i = 1, \ldots, n; \\ &\qquad\qquad\quad \xi_i \geq 0. \end{aligned} \tag{9}$$

Solving Equation (9) using quadratic programming, the decision function (classification) rule,$c(\mathbf{x})$, for a data point $\mathbf{x}$, becomes:

$$c(\boldsymbol{x}) = \operatorname{sign}\left(\sum_{i=1}^{n} \alpha_i y_i K(\boldsymbol{x}, \boldsymbol{x}_i) + b\right) \tag{10}$$

Here, the $\alpha_i > 0$ are the Lagrange multipliers that weight the decision function and, thus, the "support" machine; hence, the name support vector machine. Since SVMs are generally considered to be sparse, there will be relatively few Lagrange multipliers with a non-zero value. Function $K(\mathbf{x},\mathbf{x}_i)$ is known as the kernel function. Popular choices for the kernel function are linear, polynomial and sigmoidal. However, the most popular choice by far, provided that there is not enough *a priori*knowledge about the problem, is the Gaussian radial basis function:

$$K(\boldsymbol{x}, \boldsymbol{x}') = \exp\left(-\frac{\|\boldsymbol{x} - \boldsymbol{x}'\|^2}{2\sigma^2}\right) \tag{11}$$

where $\sigma \in \mathbb{R}$, is the kernel parameter and $\|\cdot\|$ is the dissimilarity measure. This is derived from the fact that this kernel function is able to model a non-linear decision boundary with relatively simple mathematical tools. Furthermore, Gaussian kernels are universal kernels. This means that their use with appropriate regularization guarantees a globally optimal predictor, which minimizes both the estimation and approximation errors of a classifier.

One-class classification-based anomaly detection techniques assume that all training instances have only the same class label. Then, a machine learning algorithm is used to construct a discriminative boundary around the normal instances using a one-class classification algorithm. Any test instance that does not fall within the learned boundary is declared as an anomaly. Support vector machines (SVMs) have been applied to anomaly detection in the one-class setting. One-class SVMs find a hyperplane in feature space, which has the maximal margin to the origin, and a preset fraction of the training examples lays beyond it.

The support vector method for novelty detection [40] essentially separates all of the data points from the origin (in feature space $\mathcal{F}$) and maximizes the distance from this hyperplane to the origin. This results in a binary function that captures regions in the input space where the probability density of the data lives. Thus, the function returns "+1" in a reduced region (capturing the training data points) and "−1" elsewhere.

The quadratic programming minimization problem is slightly different from that previously stated, but the similarity is evident,

$$\begin{aligned} \text{minimize} \quad & f(\boldsymbol{w}, \boldsymbol{x}_i, \rho) = \tfrac{1}{2}\|\boldsymbol{w}\|^2 + \tfrac{1}{\nu n}\textstyle\sum_{i=1}^{n} \xi_i - \rho\,, \\ \text{subject to} \quad & \boldsymbol{w} \cdot \phi(\boldsymbol{x}_i) \geq \rho - \xi_i\,, \\ & \xi_i \geq 0\,, \\ & \forall i = 1, \ldots, n\,. \end{aligned} \tag{12}$$

Applying the Lagrange techniques and using a kernel function for the dot-product calculations, the decision function becomes:

$$c(\boldsymbol{x}) = \operatorname{sign}\left((\boldsymbol{w} \cdot \phi(\boldsymbol{x}_i)) - \rho\right) = \operatorname{sign}\left(\sum_{i=1}^{n} K(\boldsymbol{x}, \boldsymbol{x}_i) - \rho\right) \tag{13}$$

This method thus creates a classification hyperplane characterized by w and ρ, which has maximal distance from the origin in feature space $\mathcal{F}$ and separates all of the data points from the origin. Another method is to create a circumscribing hypersphere around the data in feature space.

In this paper, we have applied this approach combined with an evolutionary algorithm [41] for optimizing the maximal margin, as well as other SVM parameters, with respect to outlier detection accuracy.

4. ANOMALY DETECTION IN OFFSHORE OIL EXTRACTION TURBOMACHINES

In order to validate our approach, it was necessary to perform two comparative and validation experiments: one that focused on the segmentation algorithm and its performance compared with other state-of-the-art alternatives and other that had to do with the anomaly detection method as a whole. This section of the paper describes these experiments and their outcome.

4.1. Comparative Experiments for Time Series Segmentation

YASA is currently being applied with success to the problem of segmenting turbomachine sensor data of a major petroleum extraction and processing conglomerate of Brazil. In this section, we present a part of the experimental comparison involving some of the current state-of-the-art methods and our proposal, which was carried out in order to validate the suitability of our approach. Readers must be warned that the results presented here had to be transformed in order to preserve the sensitive details of the data.

For these experiments, we selected a dataset from sensors of the measurements taken with a five-minute frequency obtained during the first half of the year 2012 (from 1 January 2012, 00:00, to 30 June 2012, 23:59) from more than 250 sensors connected to an operational turbomachine. An initial analysis of the data yields that there are different profiles or patterns that are shared by different sensors. This is somewhat expected, because sensors with similar purposes or supervising similar physical properties should have similar reading characteristics.

Figure 3 displays the four prototypical example time series profiles found in the dataset. First, in Figure 3a, we have smooth and homogeneous time series that are generally associated with slow-changing and stable physical properties. Second, in Figure 3b, we found fast-changing, unstable sensor readings that could be a result of sensor noise, sensor malfunction or unstable physical quantity. There is a third class of time series, such as the one presented in Figure 3c, which exhibits a clear change in operating profile, attributable either to different operational regimes of the machine or the overall extraction/processing process. Finally, there is a class of sensors that are extremely unstable that contradict the *a priori* working principles of the machine itself. It must be noted that, in each case, we have marked with a color transition the moment in which the machine transitioned from "on" to "off" states and *vice versa*.

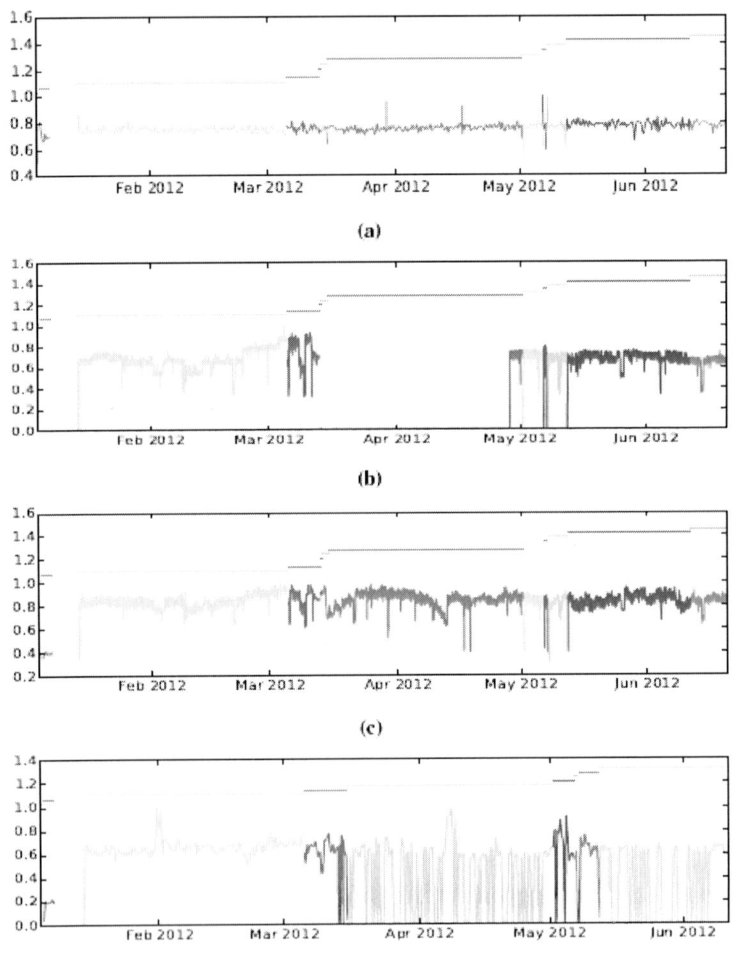

Figure 3. A sample of the four main types of time series contained in the dataset. We have marked with color changes the moments in which the machine was switched on/off. (**a**) Homogeneous time series; (**b**) unstable/noisy time series; (**c**) multi-modal series; (**d**) highly unstable time series, probably caused by faulty sensors.

Using this dataset, we carried out a study comparing four of the main segmentation algorithms and our proposal. In particular, we compare bottom-up [27], top-down [42], adaptive top-down [26] and sliding window and bottom-up algorithms [29].

The need for comparing the performance of the algorithms when confronted with the different sensor data prompts the use of statistical tools. These tools are used in order to reach a valid judgment regarding the quality of the solutions; to compare different algorithms with each other and their computational resource requirements.

Box plots [43] are one such representation and have been repeatedly applied in our context. However, box plots allow a visual comparison of the results, and in principle, some conclusions could be deduced out of them.

Figure 4 shows the quality of the results in terms of the mean squared error obtained from the segmentation produced by each algorithm in the form of box plots. We have grouped the results according to the class of sensor data for the sake of a more valuable presentation of the results. The main conclusion to be extracted from this initial set of results is that our proposal was able to achieve a similar performance, and, in some cases, a better performance, when compared with the other methods.

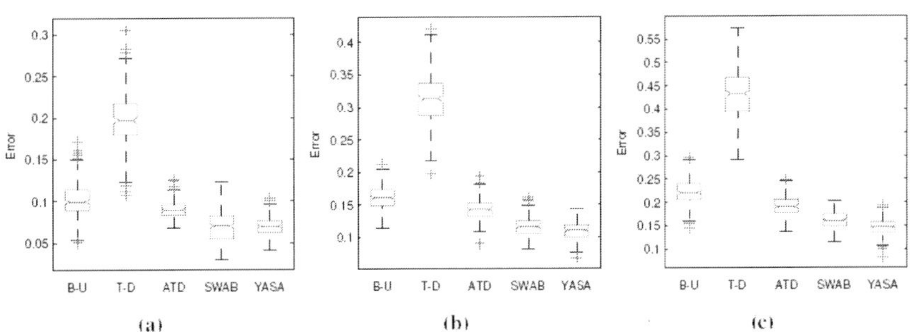

Figure 4. Box plots of the root mean squared errors yielded by the bottom-up (B-U), top-down (T-D), adaptive top-down (ATD), sliding window and bottom-up (SWAB) and our proposal (YASA). Data have been transformed for sensitivity reasons. (**a**) Errors for homogeneous series; (**b**) errors for multi-modal series; (**c**) errors for noisy series.

The statistical validity of the judgment of the results calls for the application of statistical hypothesis tests. It has been previously remarked by different authors that the Mann-Whitney-Wilcoxon U-test [44] is particularly suited for experiments of this class. This test is commonly used as a non-parametric method for testing the equality of population medians. In our case, we performed pair-wise tests on the significance of the difference of the indicator values yielded by the execution of the algorithms. A significance level, α, of 0.05 was used for all tests.

Table 1 contains the results of the statistical analysis, which confirm the judgments put forward before.

Table 1. Results of the statistical hypothesis tests on segmentation errors. Cells marked in green (+) are cases where a statistically-significant difference was observed. Red cells (—) denote cases where the results of both algorithms were statistically homogeneous.

	Top-Down	Bottom-Up	Adaptive T-D	SWAB	YASA
			Homogeneous series		
Top-Down	·	+	—	—	—
Bottom-Up		·	+	+	+
Adaptive Top-Down			·	+	—
Sliding Window and Bottom-up				·	—
YASA					·
			Multi-modal series		
Top-Down	·	+	—	—	—
Bottom-Up		·	+	+	+
Adaptive Top-Down			·	+	—
Sliding Window and Bottom-up				·	—
YASA					·
			Noisy series		
Top-Down	·	—	+	—	—
Bottom-Up		·	+	+	+
Adaptive Top-Down			·	+	—
Sliding Window and Bottom-up				·	—
YASA					·
			All data		
Top-Down	·	—	+	—	—
Bottom-Up		·	+	+	+
Adaptive Top-Down			·	+	—
Sliding Window and Bottom-up				·	—
YASA					·

Comparing performance is clearly not enough, as one of the leitmotifs of this work is to provide a good and fast segmentation algorithm. That is why we carry out a similar study as the previous one, this time focusing on the amount of CPU time required by each algorithm. Figure 5summarizes this analysis. It is visible how our approach required less computation to carry out the task. Table 2 allows one to assert this analysis with the help of statistical hypothesis tests, as explained in the previous analysis.

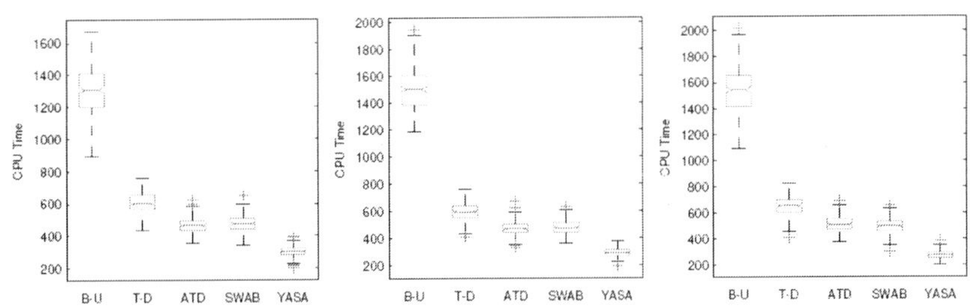

(a) (b) (c)

Figure 5. Box plots of the CPU time needed by the B-U, T-D, ATD, SWAB and our proposal (YASA). Data have been transformed for sensitivity reasons. (**a**) Errors for homogeneous series; (**b**) errors for multi-modal series; (**c**) errors for noisy series.

4.2. Comparative Experiments for Anomaly Prediction

In order to experimentally study and validate our approach, we carried out a study involving a real-world test case. In this case, we dealt with a dataset of measurements taken with a five-minute frequency obtained during the first half of the year 2012 from 64 sensors connected to an operational turbomachine. An initial analysis of the data yields that there are different profiles or patterns that are shared by different sensors. This is somewhat expected, as sensors with similar purposes or supervising similar physical properties should have similar reading characteristics.

Table 2. Results of the statistical hypothesis tests on the CPU time required to perform the segmentation. Green cells (+) mark cases where the results of both algorithms were statistically different. Cells marked in red (–) are cases where no statistically-significant difference was observed.

	Top-Down	Bottom-Up	Adaptive T-D	SWAB	YASA
Homogeneous series					
Top-Down	·	+	+	+	+
Bottom-Up		·	+	+	+
Adaptive Top-Down			·	–	+
Sliding Window and Bottom-up				·	+
YASA					·
Multi-modal series					
Top-Down	·	+	+	+	+
Bottom-Up		·	+	+	+
Adaptive Top-Down			·	–	+
Sliding Window and Bottom-up				·	+
YASA					·
Noisy series					
Top-Down	·	+	+	+	+
Bottom-Up		·	+	+	+
Adaptive Top-Down			·	–	+
Sliding Window and Bottom-up				·	–
YASA					·
All data					
Top-Down	·	+	+	+	+
Bottom-Up		·	+	+	+
Adaptive Top-Down			·	–	+
Sliding Window and Bottom-up				·	+
YASA					·

There are at least three time series profiles in the dataset. On the one hand, we have smooth homogeneous time series that are generally associated with slow-changing physical properties. Secondly, we found fast changing/unstable sensor readings that could be a result of sensor noise or unstable physical quantity. There is a third class of time series, which exhibit a clear change in operating profile attributable to different operational regimes of the machine or the overall extraction/processing process.

In order to provide a valid ground for comparison, we tested the method currently used by the platform operator, which is based on statistical confidence intervals [45], a one-class support vector machine-based classifier, as described earlier in this work, and our proposal. Problem data were transformed to detect an anomaly based on consecutive sensor measurements in one hour.

The approach in current use was not (and cannot be) fully disclosed, as it is business sensitive information. However, in broad terms, for each sensor, this method receives a sample data chunk, which has been selected by an expert as a valid one. It filters out outlier elements and computes the confidence intervals at a predefined percent of the resulting dataset. A possible failure is detected when a given set of sensor measurements are consistently outside such an interval.

We carried out this task by creating an experimental dataset, which contains 20 anomaly instances extracted from each of the 64 time series and 20 regular or non-anomalous situations.

Figure 6 shows the quality of the results in terms of the Kappa statistic [46] obtained from each algorithm in the form of box plots. We have grouped the results according to the class of sensor data for the sake of a more valuable presentation of results.

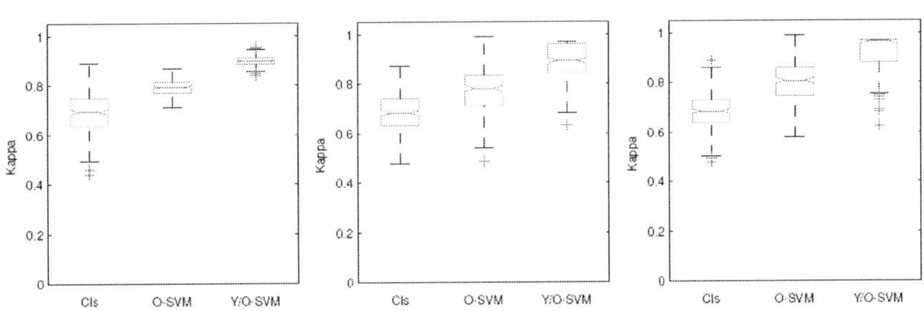

(a) (b) (c)

Figure 6. Box plots of the Kappa statistic yielded by each class of dataset. (**a**) Errors for homogeneous series; (**b**) errors for multi-modal series; (**c**) errors for noisy series.

Table 3. Results of the McNemar statistical hypothesis tests. Green cells (+) denote cases where the algorithm in the row statistically was better than the one in the row. Cells marked in red (—) are cases where the method in the column yielded statistically better results when compared to the method in the row. Finally, cells in blue (~) denote cases where results from both methods were statistically indistinguishable.

	Y + OSVM	OSVM	CIs
Homogeneous series			
YASA + One-class SVM (Y + OSVM)	·	~	+
One-class SVM (OSVM)		·	—
Confidence intervals (CIs)			·
Multi-modal series			
YASA + One-class SVM (Y + OSVM)	·	+	+
One-class SVM (OSVM)		·	~
Confidence intervals (CIs)			·
Noisy series			
YASA + One-class SVM (Y + OSVM)	·	+	+
One-class SVM (OSVM)		·	~
Confidence intervals (CIs)			·
All data			
YASA + One-class SVM (Y + OSVM)	·	+	+
One-class SVM (O-SVM)		·	+
Confidence intervals (CIs)			·

The statistical validity of the judgment of the results calls for the application of statistical hypothesis tests [47]. The McNemar test [48] is particularly suited for the assessment of classification problem results, like the ones addressed here. This test is a normal approximation used on paired nominal data. It is applied to 2 × 2 contingency tables with a dichotomous trait, with matched pairs of subjects, to determine whether the row and column marginal frequencies are equal. In our case, we applied the test to the confusion matrices performing pair-wise tests on the significance of the difference of the indicator values yielded by the executions of the algorithms. A significance level, α, of 0.05 was used for all tests.

Table 3 contains the results of the statistical analysis, which confirm the judgments put forward before. In particular, it is notable that the combination of YASA and a one-class SVM was able to outperform the other two approaches in all problem instances, with the exception of the homogeneous series. In this case, it produced similar results to the "plain" SVM and outperformed the confidence interval approach. This makes a certain sense, as in homogeneous data, there is relatively little need for segmentation, and it can be hypothesized that our approach tends to perform similarly to just using an SVM. It is also interesting that, in the homogeneous time series dataset, confidence intervals yielded better results than SVM. This can be a fact also derived from the nature of the data, which can be better captured through this technique.

In any case, in the more complicated problems, the ability of the methodology put forward earlier in this work to detect those anomalies is clear.

5. CONCLUSIONS

This work describes a comprehensive approach to anomaly detection in the context of the oil industry. Specifically, we have dealt with the problem of detecting anomalies in turbomachines used in offshore oil platforms relying on sensor data streams (time series). This problems posed some challenges derived from the amount of data that must be processed.

In order to cope with these problem characteristics, we proposed a novel segmentation algorithms, which we called YASA, and coupled it with a one-class support vector machine. YASA is a fast segmentation algorithm that has the additional feature of being easily parametrized. YASA takes care of identifying homogeneous sections of the sensor time series. Those sections are then fed to a one-class SVM. This one-class SVN creates a model of valid sensor signals. Consequently, this model is used to detect sensor measurements that do not conform with it and, hence, represent anomalous situations.

The methods being put forward have been assessed with some of the alternatives in a real-case scenario with the purpose of studying its validity, viability and performance. In particular, we have compared our method with the approach currently used by our industry partner, as well as the straightforward use of one-class SVMs. These methods were applied to a reduced problem that consisted of the supervision of a single turbomachine. The outcome of this experiment shows that the combination of YASA and one-class SVM was able to outperform the other approaches. Similarly, it is notable that YASA exhibited a smaller computational footprint than its alternative segmentation algorithms.

It is important to underline that an important feature of YASA has to do with simple parametrization and usability. Most other methods require having an *a priori* number of segments (or number or recursion levels) as the input. This implies a severe drawback, as knowing the amount of segments in a time series is almost the same problem as segmenting it. Therefore, an incorrect setting of those parameters would certainly have a negative bias on the outcome of the method. On the other hand, YASA uses a statistical hypothesis test as the criterion. This has the important consequence that setting the algorithm parameters becomes quite simple and intuitive. Furthermore, this scheme should add or reduce the number of segments accordingly.

An automatic supervision system, whose essential element is the method described in this paper, is currently deployed by a major petroleum industry conglomerate of Brazil. In this sense, our approach was able to outperform the current approach used in the production system, as well as the traditional formulation of a one-class support vector machine (SVM).

Further work on this topic is called for and is currently being carried out. An important direction is the formal understanding of the computational complexity of the proposal and, particularly, of YASA. The use of a statistical hypothesis test as the stop criterion for the algorithm complicated the straightforward deduction of the complexity. It is also important to propose methods for combining anomaly evidence from different sensors at onetime. We are currently working on detecting situations when, in a given period of time, different sensors report slightly anomalous measurements. In this cases, separate sensor deviations are not important enough to represent an anomaly, but all of them combined could be used to deduce a near-future anomaly.

We also intend to extend the context of application to other Big Data and/or related application contexts. More specifically, we are applying YASA and one-class SVMs to the problem of automatic activity recognition based on smart phone sensors. We also intend to extrapolate these results to data fusion applications for aerial and maritime vehicle tracking.

ACKNOWLEDGMENTS

This work was partially funded by the Brazilian National Council for Scientific and Technological Development projects CNPq BJT 407851/2012-7 and CNPq PVE 314017/2013-5 and projects MINECO TEC 2012-37832-C02-01, CICYT TEC 2011-28626-C02-02.

AUTHOR CONTRIBUTIONS

Luis Martí and Nayat Sanchez-Pi proposed the ideas that resulted in this study with the continuous and fruitful interaction with Ana Cristina Bicharra Garcia and José Manuel Molina. Ana Cristina Bicharra Garcia provided the test scenario data and baseline methods. Luis Martí, Nayat Sanchez-Pi and José Manuel Molina surveyed the state of the art. Luis Martí and Nayat Sanchez-Pi prepared the manuscript with constant feedback from the other authors. All authors revised and approved the final manuscript.

CONFLICTS OF INTEREST

The authors declare no conflict of interest.

REFERENCES

1. Logan, E., Jr. *Handbook of Turbomachinery*, 2nd ed.; Marcel Dekker: New York, NY, USA, 2003.
2. Chandola, V.; Banerjee, A.; Kumar, V. Anomaly detection: A survey. *ACM Comput. Surv. (CSUR)* **2009**, 41.
3. Eskin, E.; Arnold, A.; Prerau, M.; Portnoy, L.; Stolfo, S. A geometric framework for unsupervised anomaly detection. In *Applications of Data Mining in Computer Security*; Springer: New York, NY, USA, 2002; pp. 77–101.
4. King, S.; King, D.; Astley, K.; Tarassenko, L.; Hayton, P.; Utete, S. The use of novelty detection techniques for monitoring high-integrity plant. Proceedings of the 2002 International Conference on Control Applications, Glasgow, UK, 18–20 September 2002; Volume 1, pp. 221–226.

5. Borrajo, M.L.; Baruque, B.; Corchado, E.; Bajo, J.; Corchado, J.M. Hybrid neural intelligent system to predict business failure in small-to-medium-size enterprises. *Int. J. Neural Syst.* **2011**, *21*, 277–296.

6. Woźniak, M.; Graña, M.; Corchado, E. A survey of multiple classifier systems as hybrid systems. *Inform. Fusion* **2014**, *16*, 3–17.

7. Keogh, E.; Lonardi, S.; Chiu, B.C. Finding surprising patterns in a time series database in linear time and space. Proceedings of the Eighth ACM SIGKDD International Conference on Knowledge Discovery and Data Mining, Edmonton, AB, Canada, 23–26 July 2002; pp. 550–556.

8. Bizer, C.; Boncz, P.; Brodie, M.L.; Erling, O. The meaningful use of Big Data: Four perspectives—Four challenges. *SIGMOD Rec.* **2012**, *40*, 56–60.

9. Ratsch, G.; Mika, S.; Scholkopf, B.; Muller, K. Constructing boosting algorithms from SVMs: An application to one-class classification. *IEEE Trans. Pattern Anal. Mach. Intell* **2002**, *24*, 1184–1199.

10. Buhmann, M.D. *Radial Basis Functions: Theory and Implementations*; Cambridge University Press: Cambridge, UK, 2003; Volume 5.

11. Rüping, S. SVM Kernels for Time Series Analysis; *Technical Report, SFB 475: Komplexitätsreduktion in Multivariaten Datenstrukturen*; Universität Dortmund: Dortmund, Germany, 2001.

12. Patcha, A.; Park, J.M. An overview of anomaly detection techniques: Existing solutions and latest technological trends. *Comput. Netw.* **2007**, *51*, 3448–3470.

13. Grubbs, F.E. Procedures for detecting outlying observations in samples. *Technometrics* **1969**,*11*, 1–21.

14. Johnson, T.; Kwok, I.; Ng, R.T. Fast Computation of 2-Dimensional Depth Contours. Proceedings of the ACM KDD Conference, New York, NY, USA, 27–31 August 1998; pp. 224–228.

15. Jiang, M.F.; Tseng, S.S.; Su, C.M. Two-phase clustering process for outliers detection. *Pattern Recognit. Lett.* **2001**, *22*, 691–700.

16. Barbará, D.; Li, Y.; Couto, J.; Lin, J.L.; Jajodia, S. Bootstrapping a data mining intrusion detection system. Proceedings of the 2003 ACM Symposium on Applied Computing, Melbourne, FL, USA, 9–12 March 1998; pp. 421–425.

17. Breunig, M.M.; Kriegel, H.P.; Ng, R.T.; Sander, J. LOF: Identifying density-based local outliers. Proceedings of the 2000 ACM SIGMOD International Conference on Management of Data, Dallas, TX, USA, 16–18 May 2000; ACM: New York, NY, USA, 2000; pp. 93–104.

18. Papadimitriou, S.; Kitagawa, H.; Gibbons, P.; Faloutsos, C. LOCI: Fast outlier detection using the local correlation integral. Proceedings of the 19th International Conference on Data Engineering (ICDE'03), Bangalore, India, 5–8 March 2003; IEEE Press: Piscataway, NJ, USA, 2003; pp. 315–326.

19. Ringberg, H.; Soule, A.; Rexford, J.; Diot, C. Sensitivity of PCA for traffic anomaly detection. In *ACM SIGMETRICS Performance Evaluation Review*; ACM: New York, NY, USA, 2007; Volume 35, pp. 109–120.

20. Fujimaki, R.; Yairi, T.; Machida, K. An approach to spacecraft anomaly detection problem using kernel feature space. Proceedings of the Eleventh ACM SIGKDD International Conference on Knowledge Discovery in Data Mining, Chicago, IL, USA, 21–24 August 2005; pp. 401–410.

21. Barbara, D.; Wu, N.; Jajodia, S. Detecting novel network intrusions using bayes estimators. In Proceedings of the First SIAM Conference on Data Mining, Chicago, IL, USA, 5–7 April 2001.

22. Roth, V. *Outlier Detection with One-class Kernel Fisher Discriminants*; NIPS: Vancouver, BC, Canada, 2004.

23. Bouchard, D. *Automated Time Series Segmentation for Human Motion Analysis*; Center for Human Modeling and Simulation, University of Pennsylvania: Pensilvania, PA, USA, 2006.

24. Bingham, E.; Gionis, A.; Haiminen, N.; Hiisilä, H.; Mannila, H.; Terzi, E. *Segmentation and Dimensionality Reduction*; SDM, SIAM: Bethesda, MD, USA, 2006.

25. Terzi, E.; Tsaparas, P. *Efficient Algorithms for Sequence Segmentation*; SDM, SIAM: Bethesda, MD, USA, 2006.

26. Lemire, D. *A Better Alternative to Piecewise Linear Time Series Segmentation*; SDM, SIAM: Bethesda, MD, USA, 2007.

27. Hunter, J.; McIntosh, N. Knowledge-based event detection in complex time series data. In*Artificial Intelligence in Medicine*; Springer: Berlin/Heidelberg, Germany, 1999; pp. 271–280.

28. Shatkay, H.; Zdonik, S.B. Approximate queries and representations for large data sequences. Proceedings of the Twelfth International Conference on Data Engineering, New Orleans, LA, USA, 26 February– 1 March 1996; pp. 536–545.

29. Keogh, E.; Chu, S.; Hart, D.; Pazzani, M. Segmenting time series: A survey and novel approach. *Data Min. Time Ser. Databases* **2004**, *57*, 1–22.

30. Vlachos, M.; Lin, J.; Keogh, E.; Gunopulos, D. A wavelet-based anytime algorithm for k-means clustering of time series. Proceedings of the Workshop on Clustering High Dimensionality Data and Its Applications, San Francisco, CA, USA, 5 May 2003.

31. Bollobás, B.; Das, G.; Gunopulos, D.; Mannila, H. Time-series similarity problems and well-separated geometric sets. Proceedings of the Thirteenth Annual Symposium on Computational Geometry, Nice, France, 4–6 June 1997; pp. 454–456.

32. Faloutsos, C.; Ranganathan, M.; Manolopoulos, Y. *Fast Subsequence Matching in Time-Series Databases*; ACM: New York, NY, USA, 1994; Volume 23.

33. Feder, P.I. On asymptotic distribution theory in segmented regression problems-identified case. *Ann. Stat.* **1975**, *3*, 49–83.

34. Hinkley, D.V. Inference about the intersection in two-phase regression. *Biometrika* **1969**, *56*, 495–504.

35. Hinkley, D.V. Inference in two-phase regression. *J. Am. Stat. Assoc.* **1971**, *66*, 736–743.

36. Hušková, M. Estimators in the location model with gradual changes. *Comment. Math. Univ. Carolin.* **1998**, *39*, 147–157.

37. Bai, J. Estimation of a change point in multiple regression models. *Rev. Econ. Stat.* **1997**, *79*, 551–563.

38. Bai, J.; Perron, P. Estimating and testing linear models with multiple structural changes.*Econometrica* **1998**, *66*, 47–78.

39. Bai, J.; Perron, P. Computation and analysis of multiple structural change models. *J. Appl. Econ.* **2003**, *18*, 1–22.

40. Schölkopf, B.; Williamson, R.C.; Smola, A.J.; Shawe-Taylor, J.; Platt, J.C. Support Vector Method for Novelty Detection. *NIPS* **1999**, *12*, 582–588.

41. Martí, L. Scalable Multi-Objective Optimization. Ph.D. Thesis, Departmento de InformÃątica, Universidad Carlos III de Madrid, Colmenarejo, Spain, 2011.

42. Duda, R.O.; Hart, P.E. *Pattern Classification and Scene Analysis*; Wiley: New York, NY, USA, 1973; Volume 3.

43. Chambers, J.; Cleveland, W.; Kleiner, B.; Tukey, P. *Graphical Methods for Data Analysis*; Wadsworth: Belmont, MA, USA, 1983.

44. Mann, H.B.; Whitney, D.R. On a test of whether one of two random variables is stochastically larger than the other. *Ann. Math. Stat.* **1947**, *18*, 50–60.

45. Neyman, J. On the Problem of Confidence Intervals. *Ann. Math. Stat.* **1935**, *6*, 111–116.

46. Di Eugenio, B.; Glass, M. The Kappa Statistic: A Second Look. *Comput. Linguist* **2004**, *30*, 95–101.

47. Salzberg, S.L. On Comparing Classifiers: Pitfalls to Avoid and a Recommended Approach.*DataMin. Knowl. Discov.* **1997**, *1*, 317–328.

48. McNemar, Q. Note on the sampling error of the difference between correlated proportions or percentages. *Psychometrika* **1947**, *12*, 153–157.

8

CHAPTER

AN INTRUSION DETECTION SYSTEM FOR THE PROTECTION OF RAILWAY ASSETS USING FIBER BRAGG GRATING SENSORS

Angelo Catalano, Francesco Antonio Bruno, Marco Pisco, Antonello Cutolo and Andrea Cusano

Optoelectronic Division-Department of Engineering, University of Sannio, Corso Garibaldi 107, Benevento 82100, Italy

ABSTRACT

We demonstrate the ability of Fiber Bragg Gratings (FBGs) sensors to protect large areas from unauthorized activities in railway scenarios such as stations or tunnels. We report on the technological strategy adopted to protect a specific depot, representative of a common scenario for security applications in the railway environment. One of the concerns in the protection of a railway area centers on the presence of rail-tracks, which cannot be obstructed with physical barriers. We propose an integrated optical fiber system composed of FBG strain sensors that can detect human intrusion for protection of the perimeter combined with FBG accelerometer sensors for protection of rail-track access. Several trials were carried out in indoor and outdoor environments. The results demonstrate that FBG strain sensors bonded under a ribbed rubber mat enable the detection of intruder break-in via the pressure induced on the mat, whereas the FBG accelerometers installed under the rails enable the detection of intruders walking close to the railroad tracks via the acoustic surface waves generated by footsteps. Based on a single enabling technology, this integrated system represents a valuable intrusion detection system for railway security and could be integrated with other sensing functionalities in the railway field using fiber optic technology.

Keywords: Intrusion detection; Optical fiber; Sensors; Fiber Bragg Grating; security; Railway

1. INTRODUCTION

To meet the ever-increasing demand for improved security, worldwide research on intrusion detection sensing systems has grown significantly. In particular, intrusion-sensing systems are becoming much more attractive to the transport sector in which increased protection for passengers, assets, and infrastructure is greatly needed. The usage and implementation of intrusion detection systems in railway scenarios would allow monitoring and protection of railway tunnels, level crossings, train depots, and other similar areas featuring railway scenarios. In these cases, intrusion detection systems could be used to protect properties from theft or vandalization, leading to significant cost savings.

Conventional technologies for intrusion detection systems that are installed to complement human guards (and video cameras systems) typically involve microwave sensors, electric field sensors, ported coaxial cables, and infrared sensors [1]. Among these, the electronics-based technologies, even if well assessed, are inefficient and unsuitable for railway scenarios because they can be adversely affected by the electromagnetic interferences that are inevitably associated with the train transit. An additional difficulty lies in the increased complexity required to multiplex a large number of sensors, which affects the efficiency of their use for large-area protection. Infrared (or photoelectric) sensors instead are sensitive to dust and weather conditions, and their operation is also limited to straight-line detection.

In contrast to these conventional technologies, optical fiber sensors can be considered as a valid option due to the intrinsic advantages associated with their use. Optical fibers sensors offer immunity to electromagnetic interference as well as high sensitivity, compactness, remote sensing ability, and stability in harsh environments. Furthermore, the optical fiber plays the dual role of sensor and communication medium, which strongly reduces the complexity of the telemetry systems.

Among the fiber optic sensors, Fiber Bragg Grating (FBGs) sensors also offer high multiplexing capability, versatility, and simplicity of use, allowing the deployment of a cost-effective interrogation strategy. Additionally, FBGs have been employed previously for perimeter security systems. In particular, Rao *et al.* demonstrated an optical fiber fence based on FBGs [2]. Successively, Wu *et al.* reported an FBG-based fiber-optic fence and developed a method based on the autocorrelation characteristics of the signals to improve the system performances by reducing the number of nuisance alarms [3]. Nevertheless, even if sensorized fences have demonstrated their effectiveness in protecting a perimeter [4], the use of sensing fences in a railway scenario is not an attractive strategy. In fact, fences represent a physical barrier that inhibits personnel passage (even when it should be allowed) and obstructs the rail tracks and thus the transit of trains.

Alternatively, Allwood *et al.* [5,6] investigated the possibility of using FBGs as acoustic emission receivers for in-ground intrusion detection systems. Laboratory trials showed that an FBG sensor embedded within a thick concrete slab can be used effectively as an in-ground acoustic sensor to detect the acoustic emissions associated with a human walking on a concrete surface. Similarly, Zhang *et al.* demonstrated a FBG seismic sensor in a cantilever configuration for military vehicle detection [7]. These reports follow previous and promising experimental studies carried out with conventional technologies in which the intruder is detected by measuring the seismic vibrations or acoustic signals produced by contact between the foot and the ground/floor [8–10]. In this paper, we report on the development of an intrusion detection system based on FBGs that is well suited for protecting railway areas from unauthorized access. Specifically, this method combines the advantages of solutions involving the sensorization of a perimeter with the advantages of solutions that exploit the propagation of the vibrations induced by intruder activities. Therefore, to protect railway areas, we propose the use of a hybrid solution composed of a sensorized mat for ground perimeter protection and an accelerometer sensing system for protection of rail tracks. Most of the railways scenarios that must be protected share a common feature, namely, the presence of access zones (for passengers, operators, *etc.*) interleaved by rail tracks (for train transit) that cannot be practically obstructed with physical barriers. As an example, we refer to a specific case, *i.e.*, the Service Area of Ente Autonomo Volturno Railway in Naples (Italy). As shown inFigure 1, the entry of the service area displays regular ground on which a sensing mat could be installed and also the presence of rail tracks, which should be covered by the accelerometer sensing system.

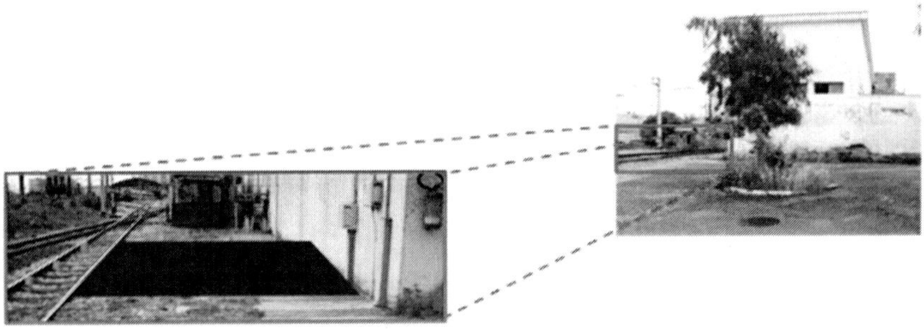

Figure 1. Ponticelli service area (Ente Autonomo Volturno-ex Circumvesuviana-Railway-Naples, Italy).

In the following section, we briefly describe the principle of operation of the proposed sensing system. In the successive sections, we describe the methodology and the experimental results for indoor lab experimental activities carried out for the development of an FBG sensorized mat and outdoor experimental activities used for the development of a fiber-optic accelerometer sensing system.

2. PRINCIPLE OF OPERATION

2.1. Sensorized Mat

The intrusion detection system for walkable access to a protected site is composed of a mat sensorized with FBG strain sensors, as schematized in Figure 2a. An intruder walking on the mat represents a load on the upper surface of the mat. The applied pressure leads to a deformation of the mat, according to its elastic properties, and an FBG bonded on the lower surface of the mat senses the strain associated with the load by converting the strain into a Bragg wavelength shift. By deploying a net of properly spaced FBGs under the mat, detection of a human walking on the mat can be achieved by monitoring the respective Bragg wavelengths.

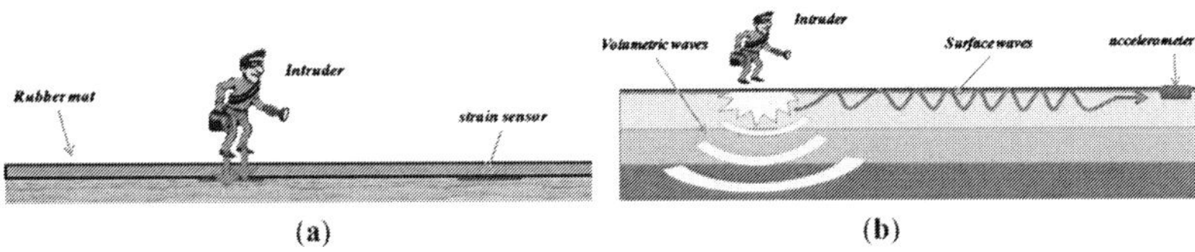

Figure 2. (**a**) Operational principle of the sensorized mat and (**b**) of the accelerometer sensing system.

2.2. Accelerometer Sensing System under the Rail Track

The fiber-optic sensing system for rail track access protection is composed of two accelerometers based on FBG technology, one for each rail track. An intruder moving on the ground represents a vibration source. The seismic/acoustic surface waves propagate omni-directionally in the ground. Because the surface wave couples to the rail tracks, FBG accelerometers installed under the rail tracks are able to detect the acoustic waves generated by the footsteps of a human. Thus, a person passing through a perimeter that must be protected via the rail tracks can be detected by monitoring the Bragg wavelength shifts of the FBG-based accelerometers (see Figure 2b).

3. METHODOLOGY

In this section, we report on the methodology of the experimental tests, which are divided according to strain and acceleration measurement trials.

3.1. Strain Measurement Trials

Preliminary lab activities were performed to characterize the elastic response of the sensorized mat in the presence of applied static loads and to determine the performance in terms of the sensitivity curve, response times, and required number of sensors per area unit.

To maximize the strain induced by the applied load, we selected rubber as the mat material due to its low Young modulus (10–100 MPa [11]). The mat thickness was as thin as 3 mm, and it was also patterned with ridges with a 1-mm depth on the lower side.

The "ribbed" mat allows for optical fiber placement and easy FBG sensor installation. Additionally, the possibility of damage or breakage of the optical fiber is minimized because the optical fiber is not exposed directly to the floor surface but is protected by the ribs of the mat.

Once the material and geometry of the mat were identified, a 1570-nm FBG was glued onto the lower surface of the ribbed rubber mat using cyanoacrylate. The FBG wavelength shifts are detected using a commercial FBG interrogator (Micron Optics Interrogator-SM125).

To characterize the elastic response of the sensorized mat, a sequence of cast iron discs (10 kg-10 kg-20 kg-20 kg) was applied on the mat one-by-one, with time intervals of five minutes corresponding to the FBG sensor. With the same time steps, all of the discs were singularly removed to recover the initial condition. During the tests, to assure uniformity of the applied pressure on the mat surface, an iron plate with a circular base, a diameter of 10 cm, and a thickness of 1 cm was positioned between the mat and the plates corresponding to the measured point. The size of the iron plate was selected such that its area was comparable with the area covered by a sole of a foot.

A similar analysis was performed by applying a static load at different distances from the FBG to retrieve the influence zone of each sensor, *i.e.*, the sensing area for a single FBG.

Based on the results of the performed characterizations, we deployed the FBG sensors in a network and verified the ability of the sensing system to detect an intruder walking on the mat.

Finally, we investigated the possibility of improving the performances of the sensorized mat by increasing the size of the sensing area for a single FBG (detection zone) through the use of a "rigid" plate superimposed on the rubber mat.

3.2. Acceleration Measurement Trials

Several trials were performed at the Maddaloni-Marcianise freight station in Italy to investigate the ability of the proposed sensing system to detect the presence of an intruder walking close to the rail tracks. The two accelerometers used in the fiber-optic sensing system for rail track access protection are both one-axis commercial accelerometers (os7100, Micron Optics, Atlanta, GA, USA) based on FBG technology. These accelerometers feature a flat responsivity (from DC to 300 Hz) of ~16 pm/g and a resonance frequency of ~700 Hz.

The accelerometers were positioned under the tracks according to the perimeter to be protected using proper packaging with the axis of measurement perpendicular to the ground plane, as shown in Figure 3. The packages were designed for installation without damage to the rail track (*i.e.*, without drilling and welding to the rail tracks) and obviously without removal of the rail tracks [12]. For interrogation of the system, we used a Smart Scan Fibre Interrogator (Smart Fibres Limited, Bracknell, UK) set to acquire the wavelength samples with a frequency of 2.5 kHz placed in a control room located at a far distance (400 m) from the measurement point.

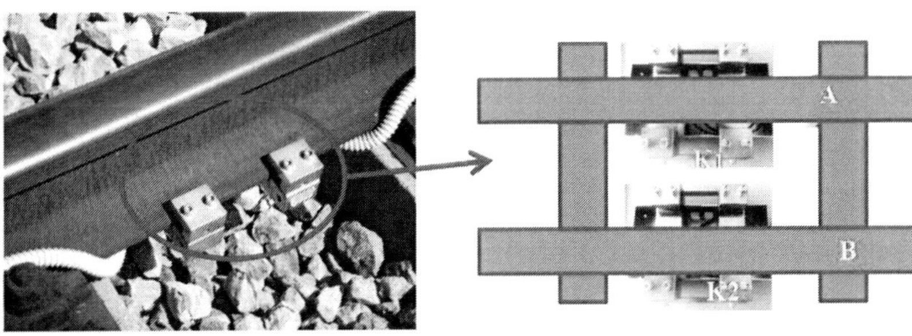

Figure 3. Packages containing the FBG accelerometer positioned under the rail track. Inset: Schematization of the rail track with the two FBG accelerometers fixed under the rails and labeled K1 and K2.

During the outdoor trials, an 80-kg male (the intruder) walks near the tracks, covering a total distance of 20 m. In particular, he begins by walking parallel to the rail tracks from a distance of 10 m from the sensors, subsequently walks up to the sensors, and walks away for an additional 10 m. We repeated these tests by changing the relative position between the intruder and the rails to investigate the influence zone of the accelerometer sensors.

4. EXPERIMENTAL RESULTS AND DISCUSSIONS

The following paragraphs report a selection of results that are representative of the performed tests and are divided according to strain and acceleration measurements.

4.1. Strain Measurements

The FBG response *versus* time is shown for different applied weights in Figure 4a. The figure clearly shows that the Bragg wavelength shift ($\Delta\lambda_B$) increases according to the positioning of each weight as it returns back to the initial position after the successive weight removal. The response times are as low as one second. In particular, for the FBG response shown in Figure 4a, the maximum value of the response time (which is evaluated as the time from 10% to 90% of the steady state values) is 0.6 s.

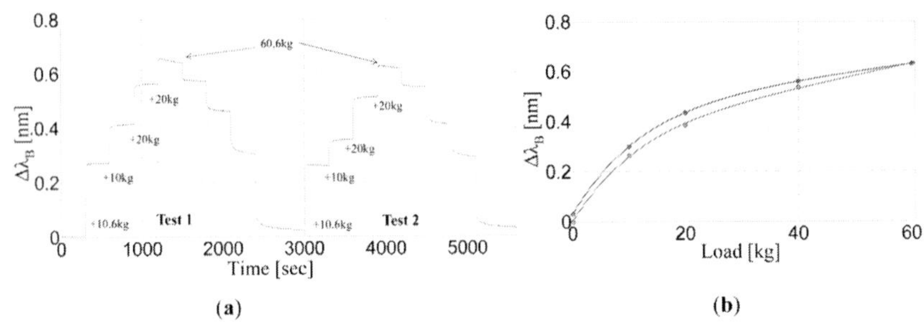

Figure 4. (**a**) Bragg wavelength shift *versus* time under the application of different weight plates; (**b**) Sensitivity curve: Ascent (Red) and the descent (Blue).

The observed wavelength shifts are repeatable with an error of up to 15% with respect to the steady-state wavelength value. Nevertheless, the Bragg wavelength does not completely recover to the initial value after 5 min from the removal of all weights. As evident in Figure 4b, indeed, the sensitivity curve presents a hysteretic behavior that can be attributed to the physical and mechanical properties of the natural rubber itself. The calculated value for the elastic hysteresis (the integral area between the upper and the lower curve) is approximately 1857 kg·pm, whereas the linear sensitivity, which is calculated in the limit of the zero-load condition, is approximately 33.2 pm/kg. Such sensitivity would allow the detection of a weight positioned on the FBG of as low as 3 kg (assuming a wavelength resolution of 1 pm). It is worth noting that intruder detection does not require such low resolution. However, in a practical situation, the intruder step could occur at a distance from the FBG, and therefore, it is of crucial importance to investigate the FBG response when the load is not applied directly to it.

To this end, we applied a 60-kg static load at difference distances from the FBG. Figure 5a shows the time response of the Bragg wavelength shift when the load is applied to the sensor, at distances of 7.5 cm and 10 cm. As shown in Figure 5a, the FBG still responds to applied loads that are not strictly positioned on it, but the amplitude of the wavelength shift obtained with the same weight decreases rapidly with distance from the FBG. Figure 5b shows the Bragg wavelength shift *versus*the distance from the FBG, and in the same plot (on the right *y*-axis), we also report the Bragg wavelength shift normalized to its maximum value. As highlighted by the exponential fitting, the wavelength shift strongly decays for increasing distances and reaches less than 10% of its initial value at a distance of 10 cm. In particular, the shift is as low as 5 pm when the weight is located 25 cm from the FBG. We used this value as a threshold to establish the limit of operation of a single FBG. Consequently, we estimated that the required number of sensors per area unit required to detect a walking human using a sensorized mat is four FBG units per square meter.

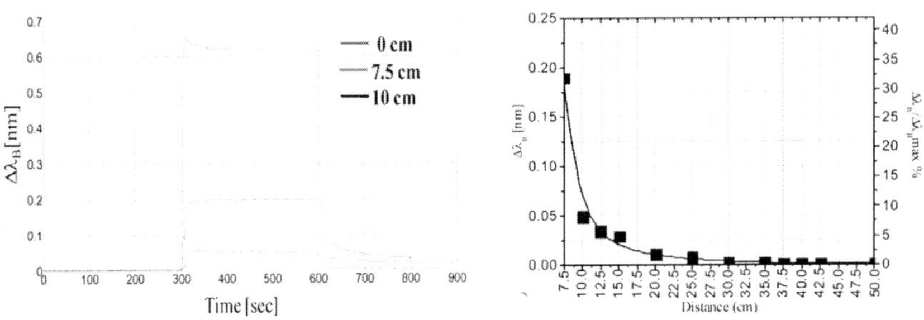

(a) (b)

Figure 5. (**a**) Time response of the Bragg wavelength shift at difference distances from the FBG; (**b**) Bragg wavelength shift*versus* distance from the FBG fitted with an exponential decay.

Based on these results, we fixed eight FBGs equally spaced in a square array configuration on the ribbed surface of a mat with an area of 1 × 2 m^2 and a thickness of 3 mm, as shown in Figure 6a.Figure 6b displays a picture of the mat. The placement of the FBGs in a regular array is carried out in such a manner that all of the surface area is covered, in terms of detection capability, by at least one FBG. The farthest point from the FBGs (located in the middle of the diagonal of the square with four FBGs at the vertices) is located at a distance of 35 cm at which a wavelength shift of approximately 2 pm is predicted (the interrogation system resolution is 1 pm).

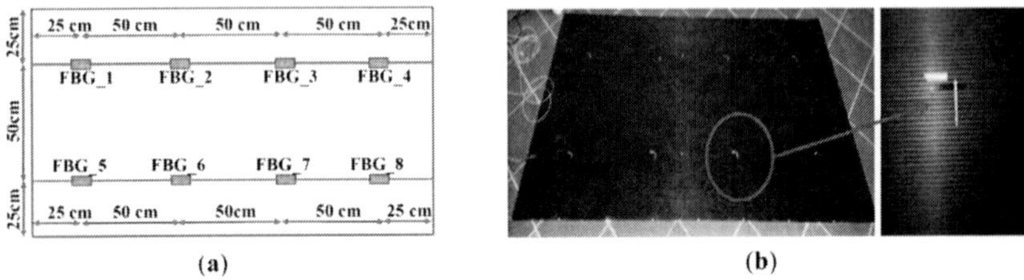

Figure 6. (**a**) Schematic of the sensorized rubber mat; (**b**) Picture of the sensorized mat (Inset: FBGs glued under the ribbed rubber mat).

We performed several walking tests on the mat and found that the ribbed rubber mat sensorized with FBGs is always able to detect a human walking on the mat and is thus suitable to reveal "intrusion" through the protected perimeter.

Figure 7a presents the wavelength shifts of all eight FBGs recorded during the walk of a 50-kg woman wearing sneakers and crossing all over the mat at the center (see Figure 7b,c). Even if all of the steps fall essentially at the center of the mat, *i.e.*, at the maximum distance from the FBGs, each step is easily detected by the nearest FBGs. Indeed, human footsteps can be clearly determined by observing the Bragg wavelength shifts, and each FBG response is characterized by a peak due to an intruder footstep. The maximum amplitudes of the wavelength shifts perceived by each FBG are approximately 20–50 pm, which are much higher (one order of magnitude) than the responses that we observed when we applied a 60-kg static load at a distance of 35 cm from the FBG.

Actually, the load induced by a walking intruder is generally different from the previously applied static loads. Indeed, the FBG response is primarily ruled by the resulting "pressure" applied, and thus, we can expect different responses with the same applied weight if different contact surfaces occur between the foot and the mat. Basically, the static load can be viewed as a worst-case scenario because all of the weight is uniformly distributed on the iron plate in this case. In contrast, when a human walks, the weight is concentrated first on the heel, next on the entire sole, and finally, on the toe of the foot.

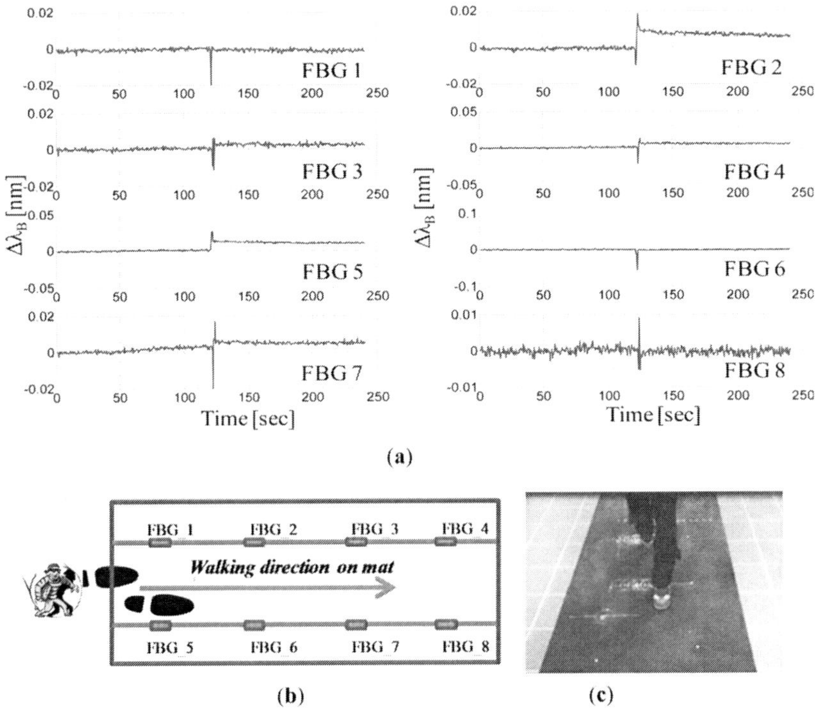

Figure 7. (**a**) Bragg wavelength shift *versus* time; (**b**) Schematic of the intruder's crossing pattern; (**c**) Photo of the walking test on the mat.

As confirmation of this circumstance, Figure 8 shows the wavelength shifts of all eight FBGs recorded during the walk of the same woman (weight of 50 kg and wearing sneakers) crossing all over the mat on the upper side (see Figure 8a,b). The nearest FBGs clearly respond to the footsteps with excursions of up to 500 pm and greater, but it is also interesting to note that the farthest FBGs (on the lower side) slightly respond to the walking woman. Wavelength shifts of approximately 1–5 pm can be observed for the FBGs numbered 6 and 7, even if they are located approximately 50 cm away from the steps. Additionally, it is worth noting that the peaks are not simultaneous, but they are slightly time shifted. Specifically, the maximum absolute wavelength shift for the FBG1 occurs at the 124 s, followed by the maximum shift for the FBG2 at the 124.5 s, for the FBG3 at the 125.5 s and for the FBG4 at the 126 s. By assuming that the wavelength shift achieves its maximum when the foot falls in the detection area of the corresponding sensor, it is possible thus to localize the intruder on the mat and to read out the crossing pattern of a single intruder as well as its speed of crossing. Of course, to this end, the data coming from all FBGs must be properly correlated and analyzed.

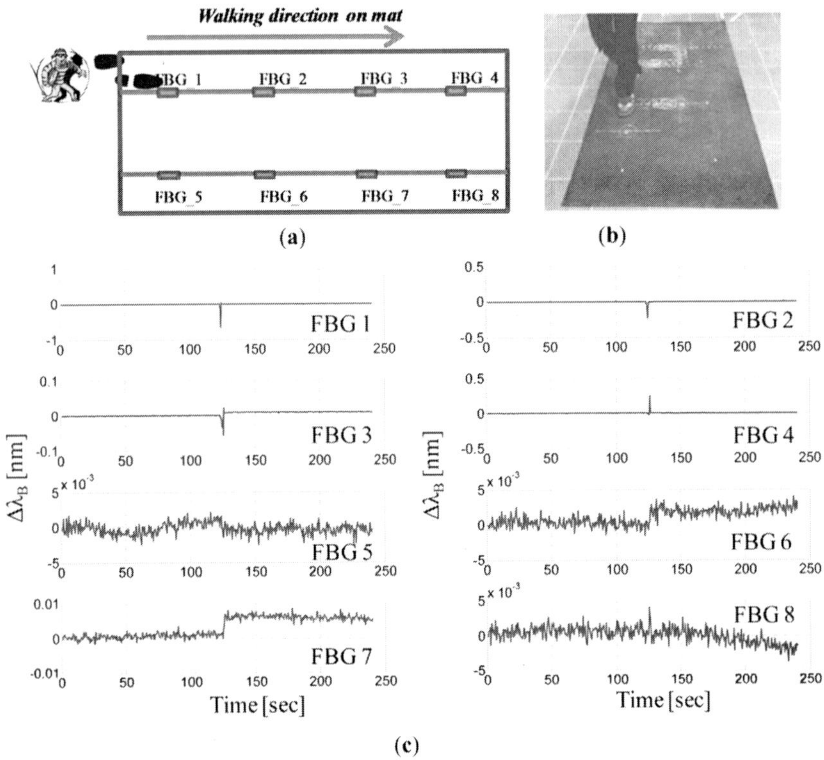

Figure 8. (**a**) Schematic of the intruder's crossing pattern; (**b**) Photo of the walking test on the mat; (**c**) Bragg wavelength shift *versus* time.

We performed also experimental tests on the sensorized mat in which multiple intruders are accessing to the protected perimeter. Figure 9a,b show respectively the schematic of the intruders' crossing pattern and a picture of the experimental test featured by three intruders which walk simultaneously over the mat along its short side. Figure 8c presents the wavelength shifts of all eight FBGs during the multiple access. All intruders footsteps are easily detected by the closest FBGs. The maximum amplitude of the wavelength shift of the FBGs ranges approximately from 25 up to 80 pm, mainly in dependence on the proximity of the foot with respect to the sensor (rather than the intruder weight). It can be also noted, by analyzing the peaks' time positions, that the peaks associated to the first raw of FBGs (FBG1-FBG4) are simultaneous (below 1 s) and precede approximately one second the successive peaks associated to the FBGs (FBG5-FBG8).

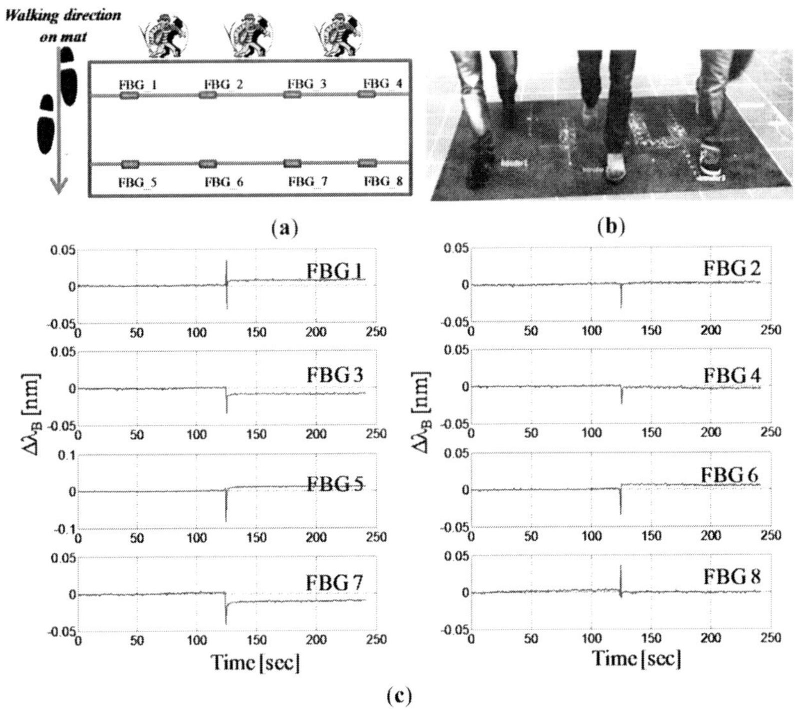

Figure 9. (**a**) Schematic of the intruder's crossing pattern; (**b**) Photo of the walking test on the mat; (**c**) Bragg wavelength shift *versus* time for the eight FBGs.

By taking advantage of the spatial distribution of the sensors or the simultaneity of different FBG responses, in principle, thus it is possible to infer the presence of multiple intruders. Obviously from the collective response of the FBGs is not trivial or always possible to retrieve the intruders number as well as their direction. However, it is worth remarking that the system demonstrated again to be able to reveal the presence of an intrusion.

Once the proper functioning of the sensing system is established for intrusion detection, we focused attention on the alarm generation by privileging some basic aspects specific to the proposed sensing system. Until this point, we recognized the FBG response using the Bragg wavelength shift created by intruder steps, but the Bragg wavelength shift cannot be considered as a valid observable signal. The effects of the elastic hysteresis as well as the daily thermal cycles (drifts) can affect the Bragg wavelength in a "slow" temporal regime. Therefore, to neglect these effects, a signal processing strategy must be adopted based on the comparison of the derivative of the Bragg wavelength with respect to a predetermined threshold. To exemplify this issue, Figure 10 shows an 80-kg man walking and crossing all over the mat at the center. We observe a slight drift in the wavelength response of FBG2 (still recovering from a previous test) as well as the partial recovery of the FBG7 after the step. In contrast, the derivative of the Bragg wavelength still highlights the same steps but neglects the slow terms (Figure 11).

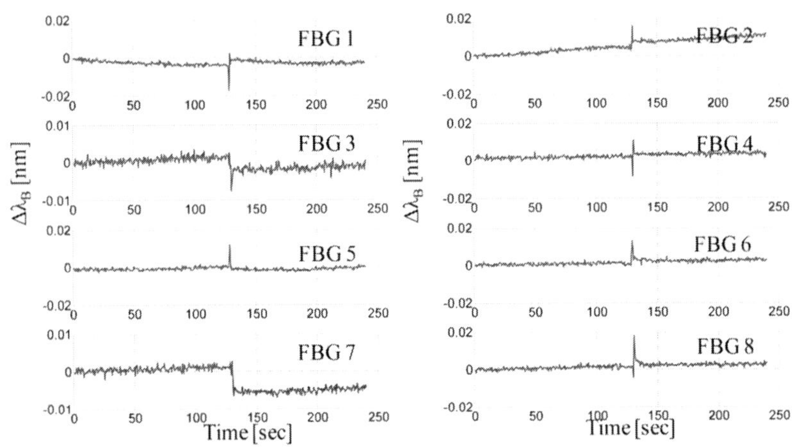

Figure 10. Bragg wavelength shift *versus* time for the eight FBGs.

These results essentially indicate that a smart data processing technique must be applied to judge (and assign) an alarm based not only on the wavelength shift but also on the derivative of the Bragg wavelength's shift. This caution is necessary in order to face specific effects, such as the elastic hysteresis and the daily thermal cycles, potentially affecting the behavior of the FBGs sensorized mat.

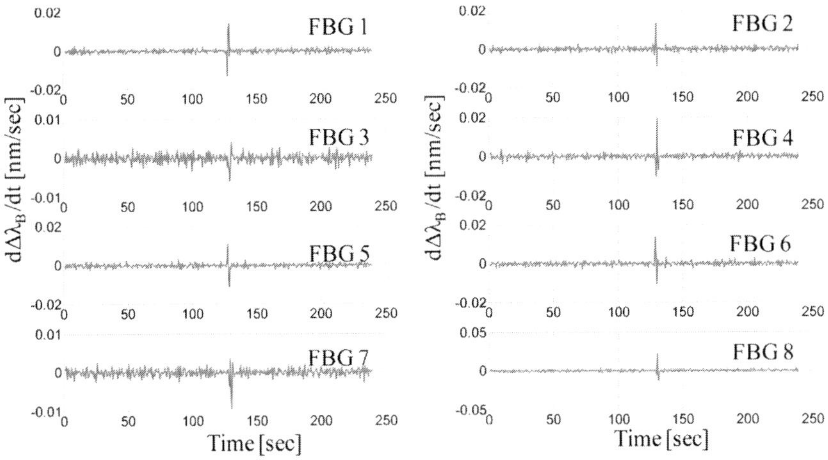

Figure 11. Derivative of the Bragg wavelength shift *versus* time for the eight FBGs.

Also the duration of the threshold exceedance can be efficiently used in order to reduce the possibility to have false alarms due to random noise. Nevertheless, in general, to reduce the possibility of false alarms, a more sophisticated signal processing strategy should be adopted to infer more detailed information on the intruder characteristics. Furthermore, dedicated studies on targets classifications are needed to improve the recognition capabilities (even if this is out the scopes of this framework mainly focused on the technological development and demonstration of the sensing system).

Finally, here we report on recent results obtained with the intent of optimizing the performance of the proposed sensing mat. Specifically, to decrease the number of FBGs per area unit, we investigated the possibility of increasing the detection zone of each FBG using an aluminum plate on the rubber mat. Thus, we simply superimposed an aluminum plate with an area of 1×1 m^2 and a thickness of 1.5 mm on the rubber mat (see Figure 12a) and reapplied the 60-kg static loads at difference distances from the FBG.

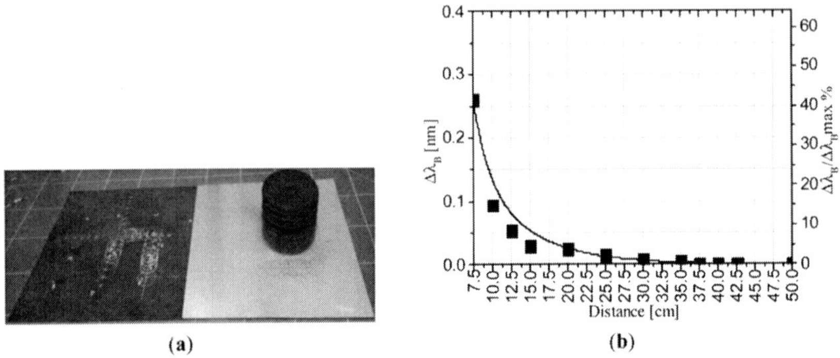

Figure 12. (**a**) Picture of the mat with aluminum plate; (**b**) Bragg wavelength shift *versus* the distance from the FBG fitted with an exponential decay.

Figure 12b shows the Bragg wavelength shift *versus* the distance from the FBG under test conditions. For the aluminum-covered mat, the amplitude of the wavelength shift decreases rapidly with positioning of the load at different distances from FBG. The wavelength shift indeed exponentially decays for increasing distances. Nevertheless, in this case, the decay is slightly slower because the wavelength shifts are greater for increasing distances. This result can be attributed to the rigidity of the plate, which distributes the load on a wider surface, improving the sensitivity of the FBG to loads located far away. Again, if we refer to the threshold of 5 pm to establish the limit of operation of a single FBG, we identify a separation length of approximately 33 cm, which implies a number of FBGs for the area unit of approximately 2.3 per square meter (instead of four FBG/m^2).

Although significant for large areas, the beneficial effect of the reduction in the number of FBGs for unit area should obviously be evaluated by taking into account the additional costs due to the use of a rigid plate and the relative installation costs.

4.2. Acceleration Measurements

Figure 13a,b display the Bragg wavelengths shifts of the two accelerometers (labeled K1 and K2, respectively) *versus* time when the intruder walks between the rails of the track (see Figure 13c). The arrows indicate the correspondence between the time and the distance from the sensors as retrieved with the support of a camera that recorded the walk. It is possible to note that the accelerometer response is characterized by peaks due to the intruder's footsteps. These peaks are quite clearly distinguishable up at to 5 m of distance from both sides.

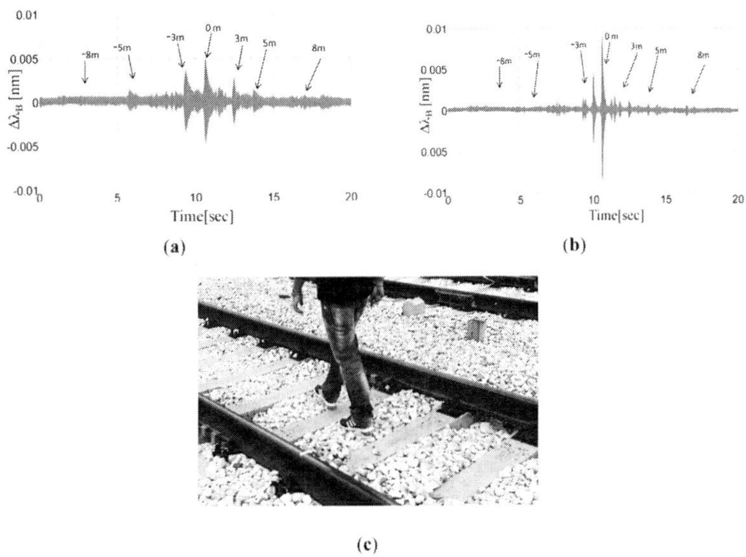

Figure 13. (**a**) Bragg wavelengths of the accelerometers *versus*time during the intruder's walk for the FBG labeled K1; (**b**) for the FBG labeled K2; and (**c**) the intruder's walk between the rails.

Overall, the amplitude of each peak is related to the distance of the intruder's step from the accelerometer. Nevertheless, differences in the response amplitudes of two identical accelerometers can be observed and are attributed to the structural non-uniformity of the ballast. The temporal separation between adjacent peaks is obviously related to the speed of the walking intruder (approximately 1 m/s) and the increasing amplitude of successive peaks is due to the intruder approach.

Figure 14 shows the Fast Fourier Transform of the FBG accelerometer responses. The signals are primarily featured by one fundamental harmonic component at approximately 750 Hz corresponding to the resonance frequency of the accelerometer, which means that the accelerometer response is essentially due to excitation of its resonance frequency.

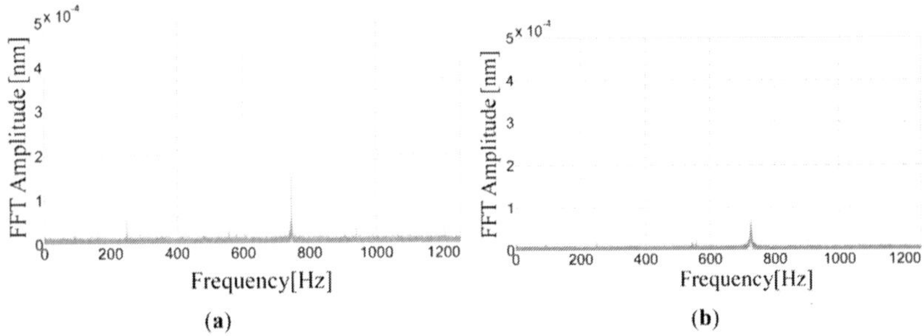

Figure 14. (**a**) FFT Amplitude of FBG accelerometers labeled K1; (**b**) FFT Amplitude of FBG accelerometers labeled K1.

We performed further intrusion tests through the rail track. Figure 15 shows the Bragg wavelength shift of the two accelerometers (labeled K1 and K2, respectively) *versus* time, when the intruder runs between the rails of the track. Peaks due to the footsteps can be clearly appreciated and no significant amplitude variations can be seen with respect to the walking intruder. The temporal separation of the peaks instead is reduced revealing a running speed of approximately 2.5–3 m/s.

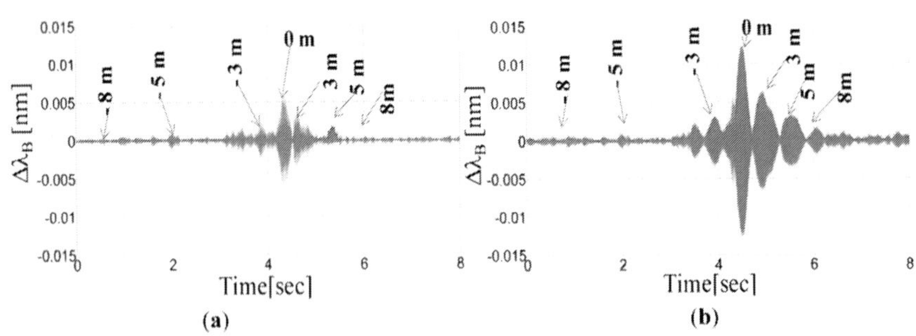

Figure 15. (**a**) Bragg wavelengths of the accelerometers *versus*time during the intruder's run between the rail-track for the FBG labeled K1; (**b**) for the FBG labeled K2.

Additionally, in Figure 16a, we show the response of the FBG accelerometers labeled K1 in the time domain when the intruder walks outside and parallel to the rail (side A) at a distance of 80 cm. In these experimental tests, human footsteps can be detected at up to three meters of distance, whereas for distances exceeding 80 cm, we found that the expected peaks are comparable with the noise floor.

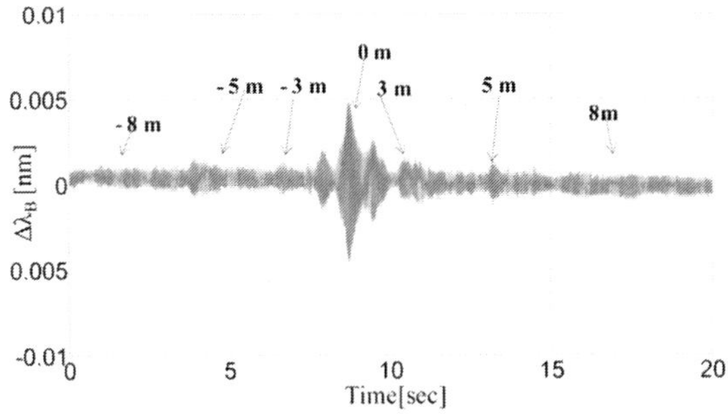

(a)

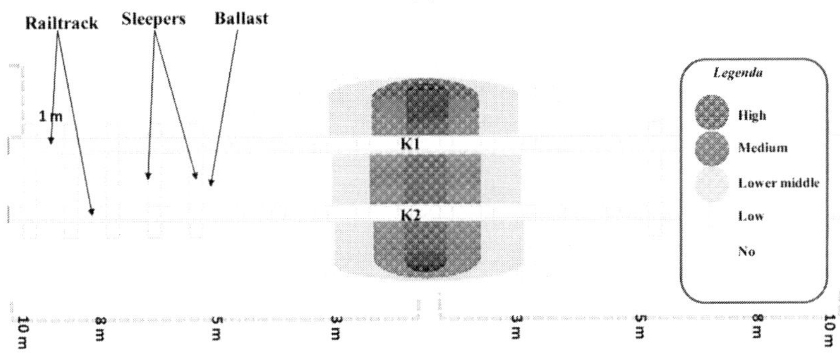

(b)

Figure 16. (**a**) Bragg wavelengths of the accelerometer K1 *vs.* time when the intruder walks outside and parallel at a distance of 80 cm from the rail (side A); (**b**) Schematics of the detection zone for FBG accelerometers sensing system.

Figure 16b illustrates the results of further and similar experimental tests using a colored representation. The schematics, although qualitative, illustrate the detection zone of the sensing system and its ability to reveal the presence of a man walking near the rail track access zone.

Finally, it is worth remarking that in this configuration, the proposed sensing system does not exploit "human signatures" to discriminate among different events [9], but the detection is generally associated with the intensity of the induced vibration. Nevertheless, the FBG accelerometers are able to detect a walking human and are thus suitable to reveal "intrusion" through the perimeter to be protected. Additionally, optimization margins still exist because the applied accelerometers and the package have been not optimized for this specific application.

5. DISCUSSION AND CONCLUSIONS

In this work, we demonstrated a technological solution based on FBG sensors suitable for protecting railway areas from unauthorized access. Using the same enabling technology, we designed and developed an optical fiber sensing system composed of a network of FBG strain sensors bonded on a ribbed mat combined with FBG accelerometers sensors installed directly on the rail tracks.

We carried out several experimental trials to characterize the elastic response of the sensorized mat and determine the performance in terms of the sensitivity curve, response times, and required number of sensors per area unit. The experimental results demonstrate that a network with four equally spaced FBGs per square meter enables the real-time detection of a human walking on the mat. Moreover, we demonstrated that optimization of the number of FBG per area unit is possible by covering the mat with a rigid plate that guarantees a wider distribution of the applied load.

Furthermore, we installed two FBG accelerometers in proper packages under the rail tracks at the Maddaloni-Marcianise freight station, where we performed several walking tests. The accelerometer sensors detected a walking human on the rail tracks, demonstrating their ability to detect unauthorized access through the rail tracks. An intruder was also detected at 5 m of distance from the installed sensors and approximately 0.8 m away from the railroad area.

During the performed tests, both subsystems demonstrated to be always able to detect a human walking through the protected perimeter, without exhibiting false negative. Additionally the experimental results indicated that the sensing system is able to provide further information on the intrusion such as the intruder speed and direction. The presence of multiple sensors, such as those installed on the mat, potentially enables also the localization of the intruder and the crossing pattern recognition.

We did not carry out dedicated studies on the sensing system's response to different moving targets. Nevertheless, in principle, we expect that also our sensing system could be subject to false positive as far as an interfering event induces an excitation on the sensors similar to the signals detected in presence of human walking.

In order to reduce the possibility of false alarms, high level signal processing strategies should be adopted also by exploiting and "fusing" data related to different spatial locations and time. Additionally (or alternatively), when the presence of false positive must be absolutely minimized, the proposed system could be used in combination with another intrusion detection system, such as a video camera system supported by automatic recognition algorithms. It is well known, indeed, that even if any intrusion detection system is subjected to its own false alarms, the combination of two systems with different technologies strongly improves the discrimination capability and reduces the false alarms [1].

In spite of the underlined potential limitations, the proposed FBG's integrated system offers a wide variety of features and benefits. Indeed, FBG sensors do not require electrical power, offer immunity to electromagnetic interferences, and high multiplexing capability allowing the deployment of a cost-effective interrogation strategy. Other basic components, constituting the integrated system, such as the rubber mat and the accelerometers packages, are low cost materials. Consequently, the startup, operation and maintenance costs of this integrated system are competitive or lower than other security methods.

Furthermore, the use of a technologically integrated solution paves the way for further functionalities integrated into the same platform for other possible security applications in the railway field. From the perspective of using a unique multifunctional technological platform, it is worth mentioning that FBG sensors have been widely used to perform smart diagnostics in such railway applications as switch monitoring, axle counting, weighing in motion, and wheel flat detection [12–15].

ACKNOWLEDGMENTS

The work is supported by the Italian Ministry of University and Research under the National Projects PON-SICURFER (Tecnologie innovative per la SICURezza della circolazione dei veicoli FERroviari) PON01_00142, CUP: B81C1100017000.

AUTHOR CONTRIBUTIONS

M. Pisco, A. Cutolo and A. Cusano conceived and designed the experiments; A. Catalano, F. Bruno and M. Pisco performed the experiments; A. Catalano, F. Bruno, M. Pisco and A. Cusano analyzed and interpreted the data; A. Catalano, F. Bruno, M. Pisco, A. Cusano wrote the paper.

REFERENCES

1. Division of Security Policy, Office of Nuclear Security and Incident Response. In *Intrusion Detection Systems and Subsystems*; Office of Nuclear Security and Incident Response: Washington, DC, USA; March; 2011.
2. Jiang, Q.; Rao, Y.; Zeng, D.H. A Fiber-optical Intrusion Alarm System Based on Quasi-distributed Fiber Bragg Grating Sensors. Proceedings of the Asia-Pacific Optical Fiber Sensors Conference, Chengdu, China, 7–9 November 2008; pp. 1–5.
3. Wu, H.; Rao, Y.; Tang, C.; Wu, Y.; Gong, Y. A novel FBG-based security fence enabling to detect extremely weak intrusion signals from nonequivalent sensor nodes. *Sens. Actuators A Phys.* **2011**, *167*, 548–555.
4. Maki, M.C.; Weese, J.K. Fiber optic fence sensor developments. *Aerosp. Electron. Syst. Mag. IEEE* **2004**, *19*, 8–13.
5. Allwood, G.; Hinckley, S.; Wild, G. Optical Fiber Bragg grating based intrusion detection systems for homeland security. Proceedings of the Sensors Applications Symposium (SAS), IEEE, Galveston, TX, USA, 19–21 February 2013; pp. 66–70.
6. Allwood, G.A.; Wild, G.; Hinckley, S. Fibre optic acoustic sensing for intrusion detection systems. In Proceedings of ACOUSTICS, Gold Coast, Australia, 2–4 November 2011.
7. Dorleus, J.; Zhang, Y.; Ning, J.; Koscica, T.; Li, H.; Cui, H.L. A Fiber Optic Seismic Sensor for Unattended Ground Sensing Applications. *ITEA J.* **2009**, *30*, 455–460.
8. Ekimov, A.; Sabatier, J.M. Vibration and sound signatures of human footsteps in buildings. *J. Acoust. Soc. Am.* **2006**, *120*, 762–768.
9. Sabatier, J.M.; Ekimov, A.E. A review of human signatures in urban environments using seismic and acoustic methods. Proceedings of the 2008 IEEE Conference on Technologies for

Homeland Security, Waltham, MA, USA, 12–13 May 2008; pp. 215–220.

10. Lan, J.; Lan, T.; Nahavandi, S. A Novel Application of a Microaccelerometer for Target Classification. *IEEE Sens. J.* **2004**, *4*, 519–524.

11. The Engineering Toolbox. Available online: http://www.engineeringtoolbox.com/young-modulus-d_417.html (accessed on 14 April 2014).

12. Cusano, A.; Laudati, A.; Iele, A.; Bruno, F.A.; Parente, G.; Giordano, M.; Mazzino, N.; Bocchetti, G. Smart Railways in Italy. Proceedings of the 3th Asia Pacific Workshop on Structural Health Monitoring APWSHM, Tokyo, Japan, 30 November–2 December 2010.

13. Laudati, A.; Mennella, F.; Esposito, M.; Cusano, A.; Cutolo, A.; Giordano, M.; Campopiano, S. Railway Monitoring by Fiber Bragg Grating Sensors. Proceedings of the Third European Workshop on Optical Fibre Sensors, Naples, Italy, 4–6 July 2007.

14. Laudati, A.; Lanza, G.; Cusano, A.; Cutolo, A.; Breglio, G.; Giordano, M.; Antonelli, A. Railway Monitoring and Train Tracking by Fiber Bragg Grating Sensors: A Case Study in Italy. Proceedings of the 4th European Workshop on Structural Health monitoring EWSHM, Krakow, Poland, 2–4 July 2008.

15. Wei, C.; Lai, C.; Liu, S.; Chung, W.H.; Ho, T.K.; Tam, H.; Ho, S.L.; McCusker, A.; Kam, J.; Lee, K.Y. A Fiber Bragg Grating Sensor System for Train Axle Counting. *Sens. J. IEEE* **2010**,*10*, 1905–1912.

9

CHAPTER

A PARTIALLY DISTRIBUTED INTRUSION DETECTION SYSTEM FOR WIRELESS SENSOR NETWORKS

Eung Jun Cho, Choong Seon Hong *, Sungwon Lee and Seokhee Jeon *

Department of Computer Engineering, Kyung Hee University, Gyeonggi-do 446-701, Korea

ABSTRACT

The increasing use of wireless sensor networks, which normally comprise several very small sensor nodes, makes their security an increasingly important issue. They can be practically and efficiently secured using intrusion detection systems. Conventional security mechanisms are not usually applicable due to the sensor nodes having limitations of computational power, memory capacity, and battery power. Therefore, specific security systems should be designed to function under constraints of energy or memory. A partially distributed intrusion detection system with low memory and power demands is proposed here. It employs a Bloom filter, which allows reduced signature code size. Multiple Bloom filters can be combined to reduce the signature code for each Bloom filter array. The mechanism could then cope with potential denial of service attacks, unlike many previous detection systems with Bloom filters. The mechanism was evaluated and validated through analysis and simulation.

Keywords: Bloom filter; Intrusion detection system; Low memory usage; Wireless sensor network; Security

1. INTRODUCTION

Wireless sensor networks (WSNs) are composed of several very small sensor nodes. They are generally designed to operate in non-infrastructure environments using inexpensive hardware. This can be achieved using IEEE 802.15.4 PHY/MAC [1] and the ZigBee [2] stack. Sensor nodes can be assigned IPv6 addresses using IPv6 over Low-power Wireless Personal Area Networks (6LoWPAN) [3]. An Internet of Things [4] can be achieved using WSNs. However, security vulnerabilities associated with the IP networks in the WSNs may result. The wide potential applicability of WSNs, including in critical infrastructure, makes their security a prominent concern.

Intrusion detection systems (IDSs) are practical and efficient security mechanisms. They can be classified into two categories by their method of attack detection: those which use attack signatures and those which use abnormal states. The latter type requires large amounts of memory to store the traffic states and high computation power to analyze traffic, making them unsuitable for use in sensor nodes. Signature-based IDSs require the storage of many attack signatures, which increases memory use. A behavior-based IDS needs strong processing power to analyze abnormal behavior. While conventional IP networks can employ various intrusion detection mechanisms, the high resource requirements make some systems less suited to wireless sensor nodes, and several researchers have sought to develop various systems compatible with WSNs [5]. Most such IDSs analyze anomalous behavior; signature-based IDSs for WSNs receive much less attention. Syed *et al.* [6] proposed an IDS based on Bloom filter arrays for implement on WSNs. Their approach significantly reduces the size of attack signatures. This paper analyzes the threats inherent to this previous work, proposes a partially distributed IDS mechanism to overcome these threats, and optimizes memory and energy usage.

This paper is organized as follows: Section 2 describes the basic concept of a Bloom filter. Section 3 describes the problems of the previous system and proposes a partially distributed IDS mechanism. Section 4 tests our proposal through mathematical analysis. Finally, concluding remarks are presented in Section 5.

2. RELATED WORK

2.1. Bloom Filter

Bloom filters can efficiently reduce the data structure size [7] by using multiple hash functions. A Bloom filter has a specific false positive rate based on the number of hash functions, the amount of input data, and the size of the Bloom filter array. The characteristics of Bloom filters and their applications are described in detail elsewhere [7]. The false positive rate can be controlled by optimizing the size of the Bloom filter array.

Figure 1 shows a basic example of Bloom filter operation. All the Bloom filter array spaces are initialized at 0 before they are used. During the Insert phase, input data points X_1 and X_2 are passed through multiple hash functions. The Bloom filter in Figure 1 has two hash functions and produces two results that indicate the specific positions of each input data point. In the figure, X_1indicates positions 2 and 10. Each bit of the corresponding positions is set to 1. X_2 indicates the positions 4 and 10. These processes occur whenever data are inserted into the Bloom filter array during the Insert phase. After the Insert phase, the Bloom filter arrays are implemented in the specific system to be used. During the Search Phase, data represented by Y_1 and Y_2 arrive at the system with the Bloom filters. Once the data are passed to the two hash functions used in the Insert phase, two results are derived. If the corresponding position bits are 1, the inserted data point matches the Bloom filter. Figure 1 shows that Y_1 derives positions 2 and 10, with both position bits already marked as 1. Therefore, we can say that the data Y_1 was inserted as input data during the Insert phase. However, some other data (such as Z_1 in Figure 1) might give a false positive result. When Z_1 passes through the hash functions it derives positions 2 and 4, both of which have a value of 1. Therefore, it may mistakenly be concluded that Z_1 was inserted during the Insert phase. The combination of the two data points causes Z_1 to match to the Bloom filter because the bit at position 2 is marked by X_1 and that at position 4 is marked by X_2. Therefore, a false positive occurs. If more data are inserted into the Bloom filter array, the false positive rate will increase. However, if more space is available for the array, the false positive rate will decrease.

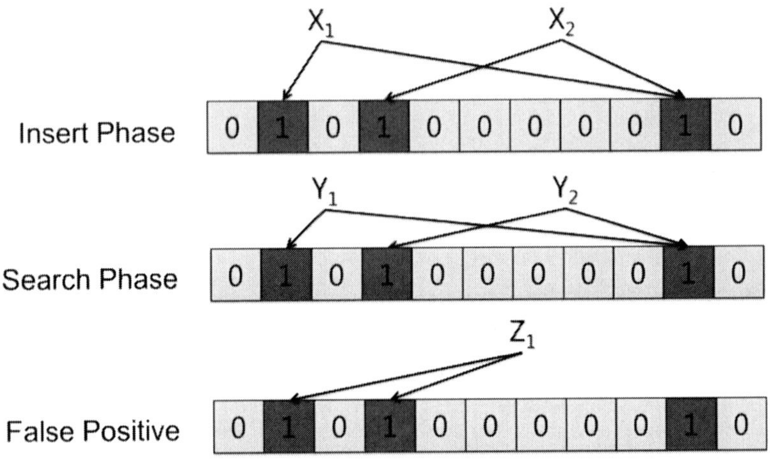

Figure 1. Simple operation of a Bloom filter.

Syed *et al.* [6] reported the expected false positive rate *fpr* to be calculated as follows:

$$fpr = \left(1 - \left(1 - \frac{1}{m}\right)^{kn}\right)^{k} \approx \left(1 - e^{-kn/m}\right)^{k}, \tag{1}$$

where *n* is the number of input data points, *m* the array size of the Bloom filter, and *k* the number of hash functions. Equation (2) can be derived for the simple case of two hash functions (*i.e.*, $k = 2$) [7]:

$$m \geq n \log_2 e \log_2 \left({}^{1}\!/_{fpr}\right) \approx 1.44n \log_2 \left({}^{1}\!/_{fpr}\right). \tag{2}$$

This equation allows the minimum memory requirements needed to achieve a specific *fpr* to be calculated for other given variables.

2.2. 6LoWPAN

6LoWAPN [3] is an Internet Engineering Task Force (IETF) working group that defines an encapsulation and header compression mechanism to assign IPv6 addresses to small devices using IEEE 802.15.4 [1], which supports low-rate wireless personal area networks. IEEE 802.15.4 has the capability to deliver packets of up to 127 bytes. However, many bytes are consumed by overhead in 6LoWPAN. At the application layer, only 33 bytes of free space is available in the worst case, meaning that data over 33 bytes should be segmented.

2.3. IDSs using Bloom Filters

Syed *et al.* [6] proposed an IDS for a WSN using a Bloom filter. In a WSN, the resource-constrained sensor nodes require mechanisms implemented in them to be resource-efficient. A sensor node uses much more energy when sending and receiving data than when performing complex calculations. Therefore, mechanisms for WSNs must be designed with reduced messaging overhead. Syed *et al.* [6] used Bloom filters to reduce the memory usage of IDSs based on signatures. The application of a complete set of SNORT [8] rules, including 13,339 attack patterns, uses about 252 KB of memory. However, using a Bloom filter in the IDS reduces memory use by 13 KB when there are two hash functions and *fpr* = 0.024.

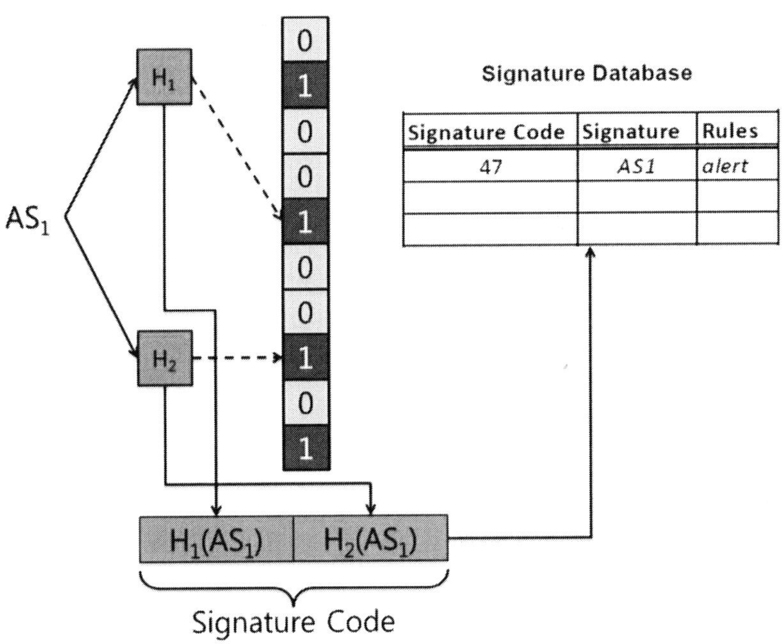

Figure 2. IDS operation using Bloom filters.

When a specific attack is detected, action needs to be taken against it. A correct response requires knowledge of the kind of attack. However, attacks cannot be identified using a Bloom filter array. To overcome this, Syed *et al.* [6] proposed generating a signature code that is then sent to the gateway (or sink) where the signature database resides (Figure 2). There are corresponding rules in the signature database that determine which action to take against a specific attack.

3. PROBLEM STATEMENT AND PROPOSAL

3.1. Problem Statement

Syed *et al.* [6] used a Bloom filter to reduce the signature size. When an attack is detected, the sensor node sends the signature code to the gateway to identify the attack. However, the attacker can instruct sensor nodes to send useless messages to the gateway because every Bloom filter has a certain *fpr*. Sensor nodes are usually deployed in an open area, and thus an attacker may be able to access them and extract information regarding the Bloom filter array. If an attacker can identify false positive messages to the Bloom filter array in the sensor nodes, he would be able to send repeated messages to several sensor nodes. The sensor nodes receiving such messages would check them and identify malicious messages. The sensor nodes would then send the signature code to the gateway. From the gateway's perspective, when many sensor nodes begin to send a signature code, it would not be identified as an attack signature code. This functions as a Denial of Service (DoS) attack on the gateway. In this situation, sensor nodes will exhaust their limited battery power.

3.2. Partially Distributed IDS Mechanisms

Our previous work proposed a distributed IDS mechanism to address the above problems [9]. However, the proposal had a limitation: relay nodes participate in an IDS on the network layer, causing the distributed IDS mechanism to operate on the network layer, which leads to the module not being able to detect fragmented attack signatures. To improve the distributed IDS and to address the problem described above, we extend our previous work and evaluate our new proposal in terms of power consumption, memory use, and detection rate.

The goals of this work are to develop a system that can:

- Detect fragmented attack packets;
- Use less memory and energy than the system of Syed *et al.* [6].

To solve the problem encountered by [9] and to enhance resource efficiency, we propose a partially distributed IDS using multiple Bloom filter arrays. The assumptions of our proposal are:

- The wireless sensor network works in an *ad hoc* manner;
- Multiple Bloom filter arrays are randomly deployed;
- Every node has two types of Bloom filter array.

3.2.1. Insert Phase for the Partially Distributed IDS

To construct a partially distributed IDS, we propose a classification method to distribute attack signatures among multiple Bloom filter arrays. As mentioned above, 6LoWPAN has 33 bytes of space for the application layer in a packet. Data over the 33 byte limit should be fragmented. This can cause problems, because if the attack signature is fragmented into several packets, the IDS working on the network layer will not be able to detect it. In SNORT V2.8 [8], the maximum length of an attack signature is 487 bytes; the average length is 20 bytes [6]. The string length distribution of SNORT V2.3.2 has been reported previously [10]. These statistics indicate that the average size of an attack signature using the SNORT rule sets will be less than 33 bytes, and hence these attack signatures do not need to be fragmented.

However, the fragmenting of attack signatures into several packets generally cannot be avoided due to their size. To detect fragmented attack signatures, multiple Bloom filter arrays are used in the application layer and the network layer.

During the Insert phase, two kinds of Bloom filter are made: one for the application layer to detect fragmented attack signatures and one for the network layer to detect unfragmented attack signatures. To detect fragmented attack signatures, data should be reassembled by the IDS. If fragmented packets are reassembled whenever the IDS checks them, processing power will be wasted. Moreover, the relay nodes should retain the fragmented packets until all its parts have arrived. This significantly increases the end-to-end delay. In this paper, we propose a multiple-layer IDS to efficiently detect the attack signatures. The IDS can detect fragmented attack signatures at the application layer and can detect unfragmented attack signatures at the network layer.

An application layer IDS does not need a new mechanism to make a Bloom filter array. Every sensor node has the same Bloom filter array, and these can detect all attack signatures that are more than 33 bytes long. However, at the network layer, the IDS uses a distributed IDS mechanism to reduce memory and energy use.

Attack signatures over 33 bytes are passed through hash functions and marked on the application-layer Bloom filter array. However, another mechanism is needed for the network layer to enhance the detection rate and to reduce the memory use of the IDS. WSNs generally work in an ad hoc manner with nodes acting as end points and intermediate nodes. In this case, intermediate nodes, which are also called relay nodes, can participate in intrusion detection. To distribute the attack signatures into several Bloom filter arrays, we use the priority feature of the SNORT rule set. Figure 3 shows a simple example of the Insert phase of a Bloom filter array in the network layer. In the figure, S_1, S_2, and S_3 represent signatures 1, 2, and 3, respectively.

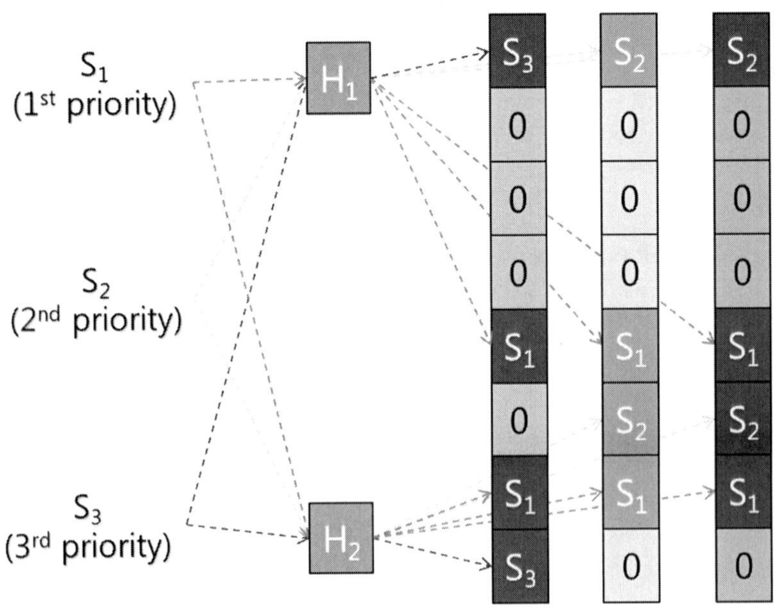

Figure 3. Simple example of the Insert phase of an IDS in the network layer.

In Figure 3, S1 has the highest priority, and S3 the lowest. Without the priority feature of SNORT, S_1, S_2, and S_3 would be stored in only one Bloom filter array, and would have the same detection rate. However, the SNORT rule prioritizes attack signatures, defining as first priority those attack signatures that can cause serious problems to the system, and as third priority attack signatures that are merely unusual traffic. As such, if a first-priority attack signature is missed, the system could be disabled. To prevent this, the detection rate of first-priority attack signatures must be increased. S_1, which has the highest priority, can be stored in every Bloom filter array, while S3 is stored in only one Bloom filter (Figure 3). Higher-priority signatures can be stored in more Bloom filters compared with those with lower priorities. This distribution mechanism increases the detection rate of the higher-priority signatures, without compromising the detection rates of lower-priority signatures. Algorithm 1 shows the process of creating the proposed Bloom filter arrays.

Algorithm 1. Insert phase of Bloom filter arrays.

```
for signature i = 1 : n do
Hash the signature i using two hash function
  if signature i is lower than 33 bytes then
if signature i has 1st priority then
       insert hashed signature i into all BF arrays
    else if signature i has 2nd priority then
       insert hashed signature i into half of BF arrays
    else
      insert hashed signature i into a BF array
    end if
  else
      insert hashed signature i into an application layer BF array
  end if
 end for
```

3.2.2. Operation of Partially Distributed IDS

A node can communicate directly with its neighboring nodes at a distance of one hop. Relay nodes are required for more distant nodes to communicate, because ad hoc networks have no infrastructure support for nodes. This means that a node is not only the end point of communication but also a relay node for the delivery of data packets. A packet may pass through many relay nodes to arrive at its destination node. When packets pass through relay nodes, the relay nodes can detect attack signatures in them using the IDS in the network layer. If the packet is fragmented, the attack signature will be divided into several packets, and relay nodes would not be able to detect attack signatures. At the receiver, the fragmented packet will be reassembled and the attack signature would be detectable at the application layer.

Figure 4 shows how relay nodes participate in this partially distributed IDS mechanism. At the relay node, only the network layer IDS can participate in intrusion detection. Figure 5 shows in detail the operation of the distributed IDS on the network layer: a packet *M1* is sent by the sender to the receiver, with two relay nodes aiding the delivery. When the packet arrives at a relay node, the node uses its own Bloom filter array in the network layer to check the packet. Figure 5 shows packet *M1* passing two relay nodes without matching; however, a match is found at the receiver, and an attack signature is detected. In our proposed system, relay nodes maintain databases of different combinations of attack signatures. This means that the node does not need to store all the attack signatures by itself. Based on Equation (2), our mechanism can reduce memory use compared with the previously described system [6].

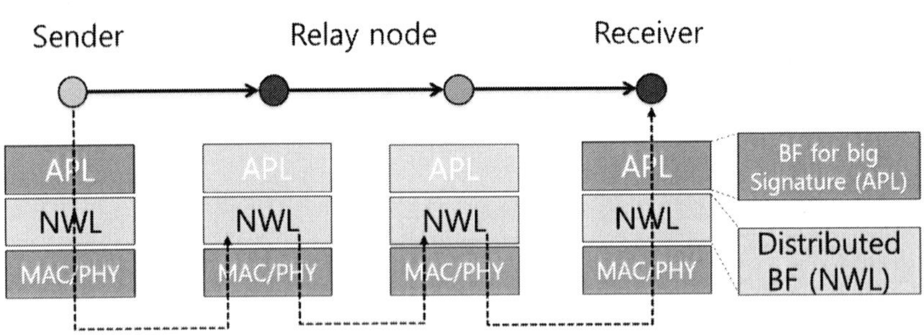

Figure 4. Example of the proposed IDS operation.

4. PERFORMANCE ANALYSIS

This section analyzes the energy and memory used by the proposed method, along with its detection rate. The energy and memory use are compared against those reported for the mechanism of Syed *et al.* [6].

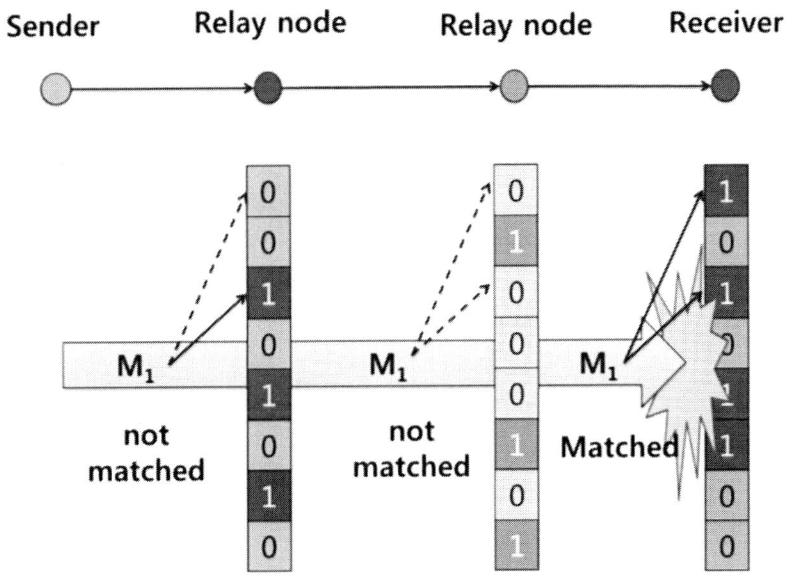

Figure 5. Operation of the distributed IDS on the network layer.

4.1. Memory Use

Section 2.1 states that the minimum memory requirements can be estimated for a specific *fpr*; *i.e.*, the memory required depends on the amount of input data. If the amount of input data decreases, the memory used by the Bloom filter arrays can be reduced. Therefore, a specific *fpr* can be obtained by reducing the size of the Bloom filter array. However, to achieve a similar *fpr* to that reported in the previous work [6], we need to adjust the *fpr* based on the number of distributed IDSs, because all data points have an independent *fpr* at each Bloom filter array. For the remaining*fpr* in the same level, the *fpr* value should be divided by the number of distributed IDSs when multiple Bloom filter arrays are implemented. The size of the Bloom filter array in the application layer also needs to be determined to give the total memory use. This leads to Equation (3) from the previous work [6], which computes the minimum memory required for the distributed IDS based on the number of Bloom filter arrays *j*:

$$m \geq 1.44\frac{n}{j}log_2\left(\frac{j}{fpr}\right) \tag{3}$$

Equation (3) can be used to calculate the memory requirements of the network layer IDS. Calculation of the total memory requirement must include the memory requirement of the application layer IDS. Equation (4) can be derived from Equation (3):

$$m \geq 1.44(1-k)nlog_2\frac{1}{fpr} + 1.44\frac{nk}{j}log_2\left(\frac{j}{fpr}\right) \tag{4}$$

where k is the ratio of attack signatures of less than 33 bytes, m the size of the Bloom filter array of a node, and n the total number of attack signatures. This equation can be modified to incorporate the priority-based distribution mechanism of Section 3.2.1, where a, b, and c are ratios of priority 1, 2, and 3 in SNORT, respectively:

$$m \geq 1.44(1-k)nlog_2\frac{1}{fpr} + 1.44nk\left(a+\frac{b}{2}+\frac{c}{j}\right)log_2\left(\frac{j}{fpr}\right) \tag{5}$$

To reduce the number of messages, the signature database and response policy need to be stored in sensor nodes. An attack signature can be compressed using hash functions; it can be reduced to 4 bytes if two hash functions are used and if there are fewer than 65,536 input data points [5]. A single byte can be used to express 256 kinds of policy; therefore, 5 bytes per attack signature is required to create the signature database. Assuming that Equation (3) is M, the total memory requirements, including the signature database, can be calculated as shown in Equation (6):

$$m \geq M + 40n\left\{(1-k) + \left(a+\frac{b}{2}+\frac{c}{j}\right)k\right\} \tag{6}$$

Calculations in this paper use the parameters of Syed *et al.* [6] to compare the two methods' memory and energy use. Syed *et al.* [6] had an *fpr* of 0.024 and used 13,312 attack signatures. SNORT can be used to determine the ratio of attack signatures that are of less than 33 bytes. An approximation of k = 0.92 can be obtained, and a, b, and c are set as 0.3, 0.48, and 0.22, respectively, according to the *classification.conf* file included in SNORT. Figure 6 compares the minimum memory requirements of the previous method [6] and of the proposed method according to the number of distributed Bloom filter arrays *j*.

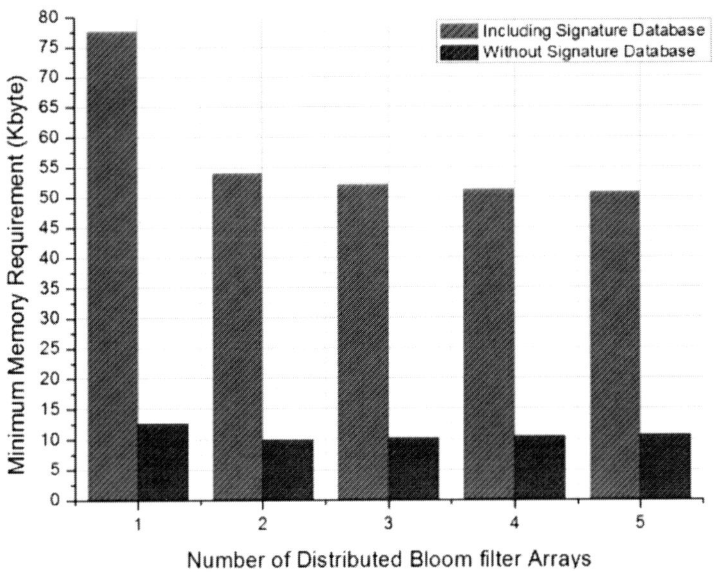

Figure 6. Minimum memory requirements according to the number of distributed Bloom filter arrays *j*.

When $j = 1$, the Bloom filter array is not distributed, and the two methods are equivalent. The figure shows that memory use can be reduced by 30% when two distributed Bloom filter arrays are used instead of one. Our method uses more memory space than the previous method [6] does, but as a tradeoff it allows the storage of the signature database on the sensor nodes. This design eliminates overhead messages that can allow potential DoS attacks. A memory saving of 10% compared with the previous method [6] can be achieved if the proposed method is implemented without a signature database.

Memory use by the proposed system was also compared with that of a completely distributed IDS [9]. The completely distributed system can be simulated by setting $k = 1$ in Equation (5), which represents that no attack signatures are to be fragmented. Our method uses more memory space than the completely distributed system. For example, when $k = 0.9$, our system uses 9.7 KB of memory to store the Bloom filter array *vs.* 9.4 KB used by the completely distributed system. Our proposed system uses two Bloom filter arrays for each layer, and all the sensor nodes have the same Bloom filter array in an application layer. Unfragmented attack signatures can be detected at an application layer, but this requires all unfragmented attack signatures to be inserted into a single Bloom filter array operated on the application layer. This increases the memory required by the proposed system compared with that used by the completely distributed IDS [9]. As such, there is a tradeoff between detection efficiency and memory use.

4.2. Energy Consumption

The specifications of CC2430 [11] and Hmote 2430 [12] sensor nodes are used to compare the energy consumption by our proposed method and by the previous system [6]. The Hmote 2430 (Hybus, Korea) uses CC2430 chips for its micro control unit (MCU) and transceiver. 6LoWPAN (named in the *Nanostack*) can be implemented on the Hmote 2430 using FreeRTOS [13]. The CC2430 chip uses 24.7 mA and 27 mA for sending and receiving, respectively [12]. When it uses the MCU at its highest speed, it uses 7.0 mA [12]. The amount of energy needed to transfer and receive specific packets can be calculated almost exactly for a given transfer rate. For example, the transfer of 1,024 Kbit at 128 kbps will take 8 s. The total energy consumption can be calculated from the required time and the rate of energy consumption. However, the exact running time of the hash function cannot be estimated; it can be measured using the Hmote 2430 node, which can also measure the data transfer. Running times of a simple integer hash function and a data transfer program are found to be 6 ms and 120 ms (average, range 87–187 ms), respectively. The average time for data transfer is used to calculate the energy consumption. Table 1 lists the symbols used in the following calculations of the expected energy consumption:

Table 1. Symbols used in energy consumption calculations.

Symbol	Description
c	Amount of energy consumption for running hash functions
s	Amount of energy consumption for signature code transfer
h	Average distance of packet delivered
p	Total number of packets
q	Number of attack packets

$$\text{Energy}_{conv} = (q + (p - q)fpr)\hbar s + pc \tag{7}$$

$$\text{Energy}_{prop} = phc \tag{8}$$

where c and s are constants (c = 0.03442 w and s = 0.000126 w, as measured during testing). Because data can be transferred and received simultaneously, the energy consumption by both processes is summed in calculating c. The previous IDS [6] checks each packet when it arrives at the destination; therefore, the hash function is run only once. However, whenever the sensor nodes detect a suspected attack signature (whether true or not), they must send 4 bytes of signature code to the signature database. This increases the energy consumption, and thus introduces a potential vulnerability to DoS attacks.

The total energy consumptions of the previous method [6] (Figure 7) and our proposed method (Figure 8) can be estimated using Equations (7) and (8), respectively.

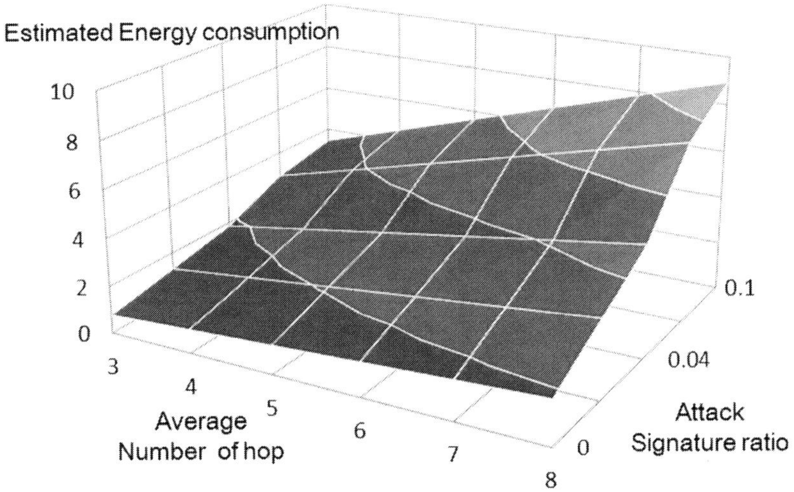

Figure 7. Estimated energy consumption of the previous method.

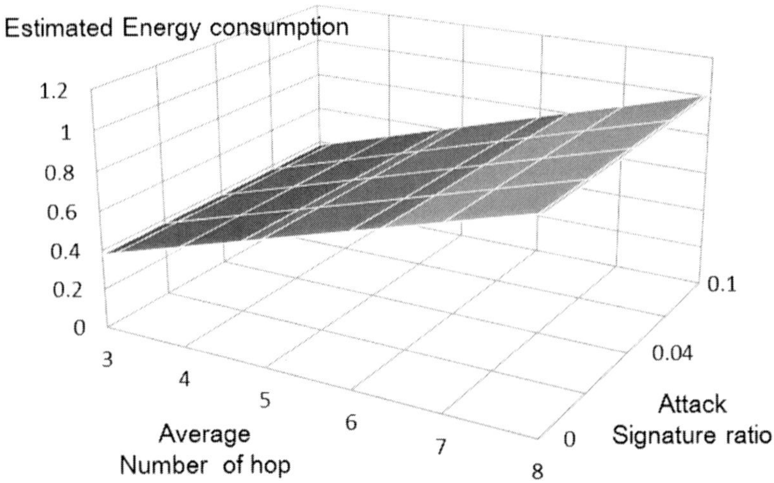

Figure 8. Estimated energy consumption of the proposed method.

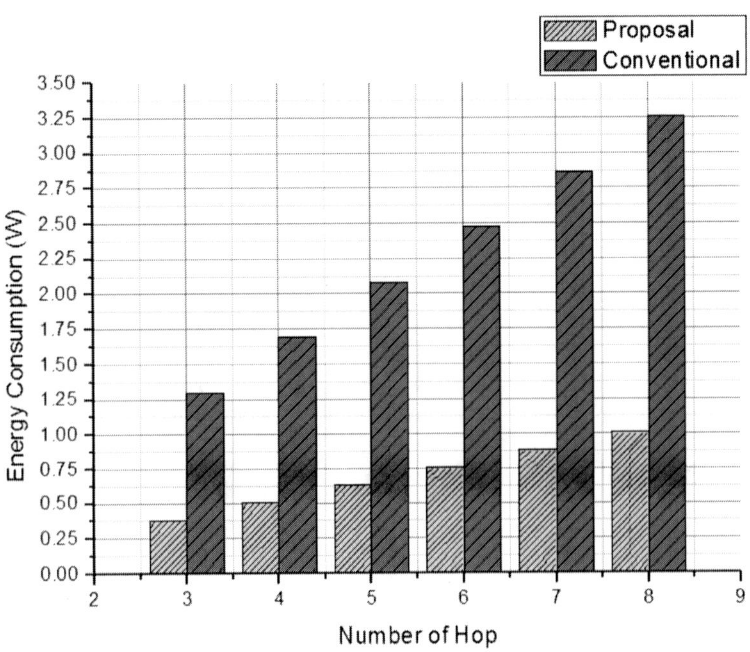

Figure 9. Estimated energy consumption.

Our method does not show increased energy consumption as the number of attack signatures increases. By comparison, the previous method [6] shows rapidly increasing energy consumption under similar conditions. Figure 9 compares the energy consumed by the two systems. Our proposal uses about 20% of the energy used by the other system, because it eliminates the overhead messages.

4.3. Detection Rate

There is no detection rate in signature-based IDS. If a system includes more attack signatures, more attacks can be detected, and if a system does not include a specific attack signature, it cannot detect that attack at all. However, our proposal does have a detection rate, despite it being a signature-based IDS. The proposed mechanism distributes attack signatures into several Bloom filter arrays. Several nodes help to deliver a packet as it is passed along a specific path. If all the relay nodes have the same Bloom filter array, the probability that attack packets can be detected is only $\left(a + \frac{b}{2} + \frac{c}{j}\right)$ in the worst case. If the hop distance to deliver the packet is longer, the detection probability increases.

The detection rate D of our proposal can be calculated probabilistically (Equation (9)) based on the number of Bloom filter arrays j, the average number of hops h, and the ratio of attack signatures shorter than 33 bytes k:

$$D = (1 - k) + \sum_{z=0}^{h-1} \left(1 - \frac{1}{j}\right)^{z} \frac{1}{j} \tag{9}$$

The detection rate of an application layer IDS is $(1 - k)$. An application layer IDS can detect all attacks that are stored in its application layer Bloom filter array owing to it not being a distributed system. At the network layer, the IDS has a distributed Bloom filter array, which cannot detect all kinds of attack signatures. Hence, the detection rate of a network layer IDS has to be calculated. The calculation of the detection rate at a specific hop number is a simple probability problem. For example, two probabilities should be considered for assessing detection of an attack signature on the second hop. The first is the undetected rate of an attack signature on the first hop (*i.e.*, $(1 - (1/j))$). For an attack signature to be detected on the second hop, it cannot have been detected on the first hop. The second probability is the detection rate of the attack signature on the second hop. The detection rate on a specific hop is $1/j$. The total detection rate for two-hop system is the product of these two probabilities. Equation (9) follows simply for the calculation of the total detection rate of a network layer IDS. Figure 10 shows detection rates obtained from Equation (9).

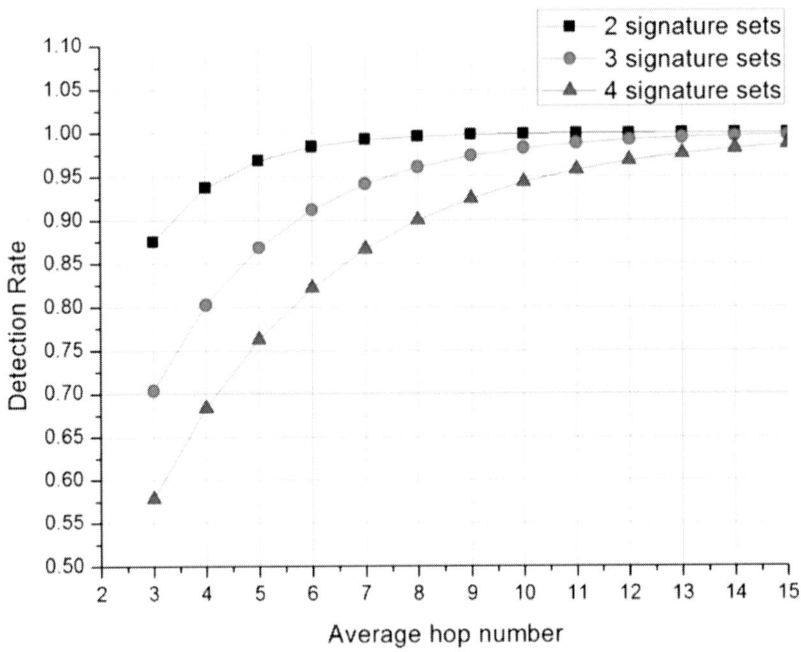

Figure 10. Detection rates when attack signatures are distributed.

Detection rates of around 95% are achieved by systems with averages of 4–10 hops. From a practical viewpoint, the highest efficiency is achieved using two Bloom filter arrays. However,Equation (9) cannot be applied to the priority-based distribution mechanism described in Section 3.2.1. If a, b, and c are the first, second, and third priority SNORT rules, respectively, then Equation (10) can be derived from (9):

$$D' = 1 - k + a + b\sum_{z=0}^{h-1}\left(1-\frac{1}{2}\right)^{z}\frac{1}{2} + c\sum_{z=0}^{h-1}\left(1-\frac{1}{j}\right)^{z}\frac{1}{j} \tag{10}$$

The detection rates shown in Figure 11 are calculated for *a*, *b*, and *c* being 0.3, 0.48, and 0.22, respectively, as obtained from the *classification.conf* file included in SNORT.

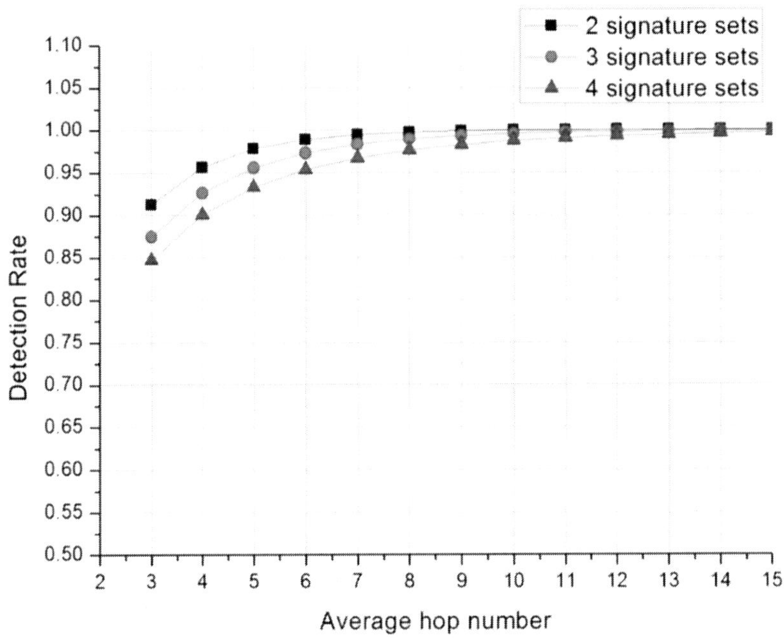

Figure 11. Detection rates when attack signatures are distributed by priority.

A comparison of Figures 10 and 11 shows that detection is better when a priority-based distribution mechanism is applied. An average hop distance of 6 leads to 95% detection rate being achieved with four Bloom filter arrays (Figure 11). When two Bloom filter arrays are used, over 98% can be achieved with a 6-hop distance. Similar 95% detection is achieved in the non-prioritized system using four Bloom filter arrays under similar conditions with an average hop distance of 10 (Figure 10).

The above results are based on calculations. In a network environment, the network topology also needs to be considered. To apply the network topology, C++ simulations that can measure detection rates are performed. We model the hexagonal direction space for each sensor node (Figure 12), and each sensor node has one distributed Bloom filter array.

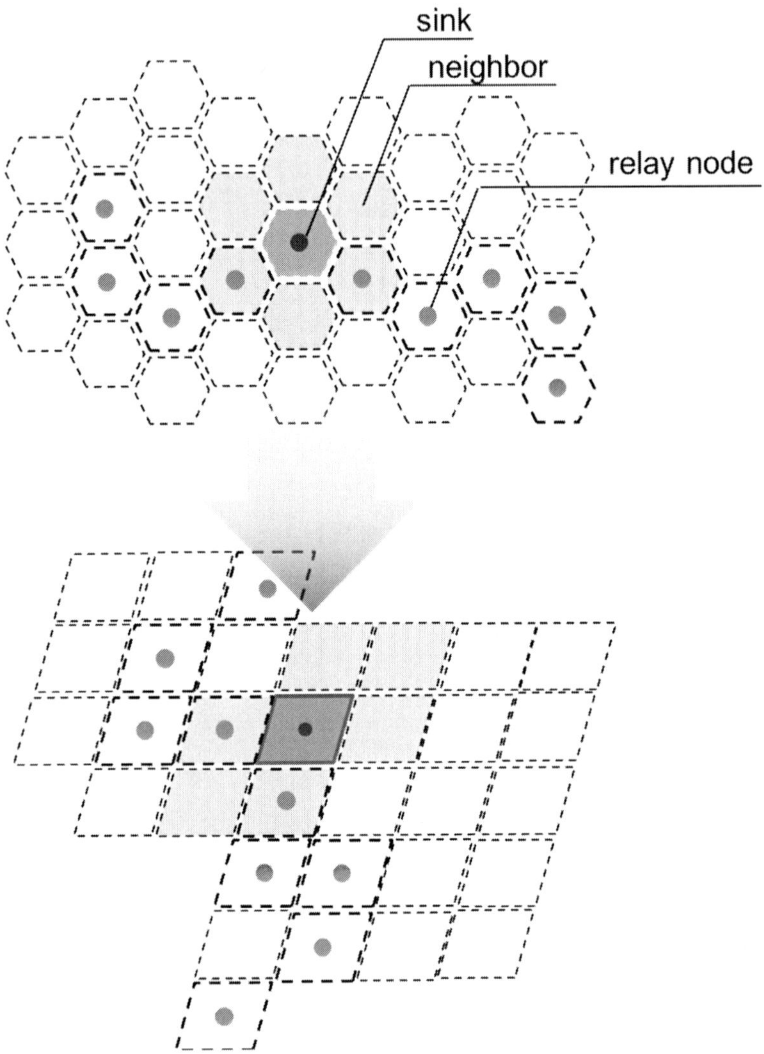

Figure 12. Simulation model and expression in C++.

The frequency of attack signature statistics from Ahnlab [14] are used to generate the attack signature codes used in the simulation (Table 2). The attack signatures are distributed into the three Bloom filter arrays based on our proposed method. The results show that the detection rate increases with increasing average hop distance (Figure 13).

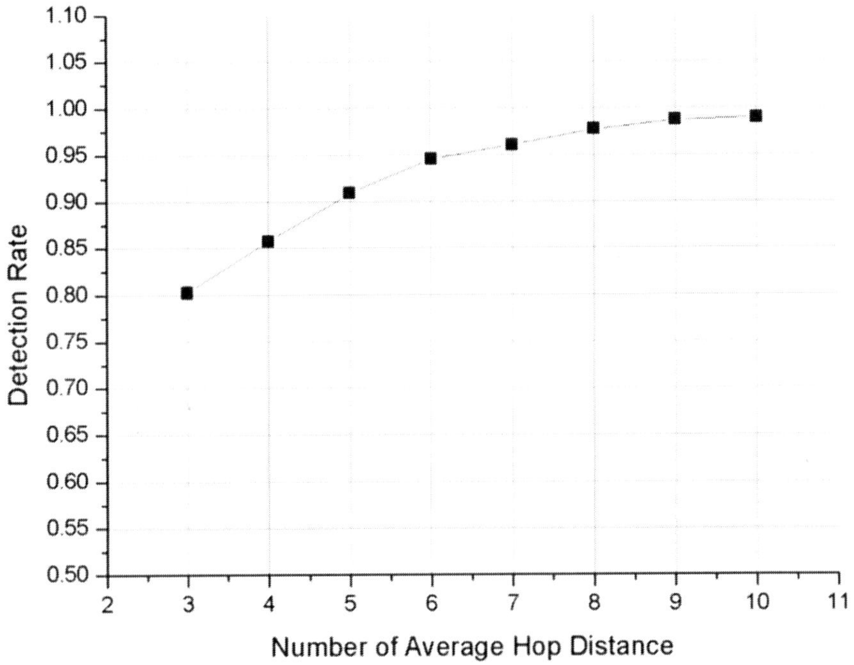

Figure 13. Simulated detection rates.

When compared with the analysis (Figure 11), the simulation (Figure 13) finds a lower detection rate. In the simulation, attack signatures are generated in set proportions (Table 2), and the analysis uses a slightly different distribution of attack signatures.

The simulation considers the real network topology shown in Figure 12, while the mathematical analysis cannot consider network topology. These factors resulted in the different detection rates shown in the two figures. However, in both cases, detection rates increased with increasing average hop distance. The analysis and the simulation both show that our proposed system works well when WSNs have larger hop distances.

Table 2. Attack signatures, their occurrence, and priority from Ahnlab.

Rank	Name	Percentage	Priority
1	Win-Trojan/downloader	10.4	3
2	Swf/Agent	9.2	2
3	Win-Trojan/Agent	9.1	1
4	Win-Adware/Korad	7.9	1
5	JS/Agent	7.4	2
6	Textimage/Autorun	7	1
7	Win-Trojan/Onlinegamehack	5.5	1
8	JS/Exploit	5	3
9	Html/Agent	4.9	2
10	JS/Iframe	4.6	3
11	Win32/Virut	4.3	2
12	Swf/Cve-2011-2110	4.1	1
13	Win32/Conflicker	3.6	2
14	Swf/Exploit	3	2
15	Win32/Autorun.worm	3	1
16	Win-Trojan/Startpage	2.6	3
17	Win-Trojan/Winsoft	2.3	1
18	Win32/Kido	2.3	1
19	Dropper/Malware	2.1	1
20	Win-Downloader/Korad	1.9	2

5. CONCLUSIONS

We propose here a partially distributed IDS for WSNs. Distributing attack signatures into several Bloom filter arrays can reduce memory and energy requirements. Our proposed method also eliminates overhead messages that can account for significant energy consumption. Analysis demonstrated that the method uses less energy and memory than reported for a previous system [6]. The proposed system can also prevent DoS attacks. Its multi-layer mechanism can detect fragmented attack signatures, whereas a completely distributed IDS [9] cannot. Specific requirements might depend on a system's purpose: some WSNs require very low memory use, others require high detection rates. The proposed system can control these factors based on specific requirements. To minimize memory use, more distributed Bloom filter arrays can be used; to maximize the detection rate, fewer Bloom filter arrays can be used. Our proposed method can add flexibility to the operation of an IDS in a WSN.

ACKNOWLEDGMENTS

This research was supported by the MSIP (Ministry of Science, ICT & Future Planning), Korea, under the C-ITRC (Convergence Information Technology Research Center) support program (NIPA-2013-H0301-13-3007) supervised by the NIPA (National IT Industry Promotion Agency).

REFERENCES

1. IEEE Standard for Information Technology-Telecommunications and Information Exchange between Systems—Local and Metropolitan Area Networks—Specific Requirements. Part 15.3: Wireless Medium Access Control (MAC) and Physical Layer (Phy) Specifications for High Rate Wireless Personal Area Networks (WPANs). Available online: http:// ieeexplore.ieee.org/xpl/mostRecentIssue.jsp?punumber=5284442 (accessed on 13 November 2013).
2. ZigBee Specification, Document 053474r13. Available online: http:// www.datasheetarchive.com/ZigBee+Specification,+Document+053474r13-datasheet.html (accessed on 13 November 2013).
3. IPv6 over Low-Power Wireless Personal Area Networks (6LoWPANs): Overview, Assumptions, Problem Statement, and Goals. Available online: http://www.rfc-base.org/rfc-4919.html (accessed on 13 November 2013).
4. Ashton, K. That "internet of things" thing. *RFID J.* **2009**, *22*, 97–114.
5. Farooqi, A.H.; Khan, F.A. A survey of intrusion detection systems in wireless sensor networks. *Int. J. Ad Hoc Ubiquitous Comput.* **2012**, *9*, 69–83.
6. Amin, S.O.; Siddiqui, M.S.; Hong, C.S.; Lee, S. Implementing signature based IDS in IP-based sensor networks with the help of signature-codes. *IEICE Trans. Commun.* **2010**, *93*, 389–391.
7. Broder, A.; Mitzenmacher, M. Network applications of bloom filters: A survey. *Internet Math.* **2004**, *1*, 485–509.
8. Snort. Available online: http://www.snort.org/ (accessed on 15 July 2013).

9. Cho, E.J.; Hong, C.S.; Choi, D. Distributed IDS for Efficient Resource Management in Wireless Sensor Network. Proceedings of the 13th Asia-Pacific Network Operations and Management Symposium, Taipei, Taiwan, 21–23 September 2011; pp. 1–5.

10. Song, H.; Sproull, T.; Attig, M.; Lockwood, J. Snort Offloader: A Reconfigurable Hardware NIDS Filter. Proceedings of 15th International Conference on Field Programmable Logic and Applications (FPL), Tampere, Finland, 24–26 August 2005; pp. 493–498.

11. CC2430. Available online: http://www.ti.com/product/cc2430 (accessed on 15 July 2013).

12. Hmote 2430. Available online: http://edu. hybus.net/eng/goods/goods_detail.asp?idx=88&ctg_code=02-07&intPageSize=12&schword=&page=1&goods_company=&sort = (accessed on 15 July 2013).

13. FreeRTOS™. Available online: http://www.freertos.org/ (accessed on 15 July 2013).

14. AnhLab. Available online: http:// www.ahnlab.com/kr /site/securitycenter/asec/ asecView.do? groupCode=VNI001 &web NewsInfoUnionVo. seq=18399 (accessed on 15 July 2013).

10
CHAPTER

A DISTRIBUTED SIGNATURE DETECTION METHOD FOR DETECTING INTRUSIONS IN SENSOR SYSTEMS

Ilkyu Kim [1], Doohwan Oh [1], Myung Kuk Yoon [1], Kyueun Yi [2] and Won Woo Ro [1,*]

[1]*School of Electrical and Electronic Engineering, Yonsei University, Seoul 120-749, Korea*

[2]*Software Platform R&D Laboratory, LG Electronics Inc., Seoul 137-130, Korea*

ABSTRACT

Sensor nodes in wireless sensor networks are easily exposed to open and unprotected regions. A security solution is strongly recommended to prevent networks against malicious attacks. Although many intrusion detection systems have been developed, most systems are difficult to implement for the sensor nodes owing to limited computation resources. To address this problem, we develop a novel distributed network intrusion detection system based on the Wu–Manber algorithm. In the proposed system, the algorithm is divided into two steps; the first step is dedicated to a sensor node, and the second step is assigned to a base station. In addition, the first step is modified to achieve efficient performance under limited computation resources. We conduct evaluations with random string sets and actual intrusion signatures to show the performance improvement of the proposed method. The proposed method achieves a speedup factor of 25.96 and reduces 43.94% of packet transmissions to the base station compared with the previously proposed method. The system achieves efficient utilization of the sensor nodes and provides a structural basis of cooperative systems among the sensors.

Keywords: Network intrusion detection system; Multiple pattern matching; Distributed computing; Wu-Manber; Snort

1. INTRODUCTION

Sensor nodes are widely used in various applications such as air pollution monitoring, forest fire detection, and anti-theft system. [1]. The advances in the technology of micro-scale electronic devices have enabled the development of tiny sensors that are inexpensive, consume low power, and multifunctional [2]. In addition, the improvement of the wireless communications technology has provided an untethered data communication protocol over a short distance. These technologies enable a number of sensor nodes to perceive and collect data from the external environment. Wireless sensor networks (WSNs) are utilized for various monitoring work including the long-term monitoring of harsh environments; thus the nodes should be sustained for a long time with a limited battery and respond well to external changes [3,4].

However, the WSN is vulnerable to many malicious attacks called network intrusions. This is because the sensor nodes utilize wireless communications and are deployed in open environments such as mountainous and urban terrains. There is a possibility of obtaining physical access to the sensor networks and intercepting the data from the networks [5]. At worst, the intrusions could be extremely dangerous because the WSN that monitors chemical gases or battlefields could be malfunctioning [6].

Managing a WSN is demanding work because of network intrusions, especially denial-of-service (DoS) attacks [6]. Intrusion detection systems can be easily made ineffective because the attacks contain messages that are similar to regular client requests. Many DoS attacks exist in each network layer, and resources are rapidly exhausted, disrupted, or even destructed by these simple and repeated attacks [6]. Furthermore, networks are easily exposed to the attacks because the networks normally deal with too many nodes to be controlled independently, and each node has restricted hardware resources to prevent the attacks [7,8]. Consequently, each compromised sensor node might accidentally deliver harmful data to the central server when the node is compromised by malicious patterns. To prevent attacks, efficient security solutions for the sensor nodes are needed to maintain the reliability of the networks.

Network intrusion detection system (NIDS) has been proposed to prevent the sensor networks from network-based malicious attacks. Each attack is analyzed as one of the many malicious signatures (patterns) and summarized by pattern data groups. From the pattern groups, the system avoids damage from the same or similar attacks. Using a pattern-matching algorithm that uses the intrusion pattern sets, the system can analyze incoming packets and filter out malicious attacks [1,3,9]. However, few studies on pattern-matching algorithms for sensor nodes have been conducted because most sensor nodes have constrained resources for low power.

In this paper, we propose a novel security solution for sensor networks by modifying the traditional Wu–Manber (WM) pattern-matching algorithm. Because the sensor node has limited performance, memory size, and power, a full implementation of a general pattern-matching algorithm on each node is difficult. To solve this issue, the algorithm is divided into two major steps: a shifting step and an exact pattern-matching step. The two steps are allocated respectively to the sensor node and the base station according to the demands of memory allocation and computing power. The modified shifting step is optimized for limited resources and is executed by the sensor node. The base station in the cluster-based structure is authorized to execute exact matching, which is difficult to process on the sensor node. Transmitted packets with searched results for each sensor node are processed by the base station. By answering each node with the result, cooperative pattern matching can be achieved.

We represent a framework between the sensor node and base station that can perform distributed intrusion detection with the WM algorithm. We conduct evaluations of the framework and analyze the results. The results show that the framework achieves a performance improvement for both the sensor node and the base station. The results allow the base station to process a large number of sensor nodes more efficiently.

The rest of this paper is organized as follows. First, we introduce background information about the various methods of detecting network intrusions in sensor nodes and related work in Section 2. In Section 3, the framework for network intrusion detection is introduced. Then, we explain the proposed algorithm in Section 4, which is a cooperative WM algorithm to develop the resources of both the sensor node and the base station. We evaluate the performance of the work in Section 5. Finally, conclusions with plans for future work are discussed in Section 6.

2. BACKGROUND

This section introduces an NIDS that is developed to detect or prevent various network intrusions. The WM pattern-matching algorithms used to detect intrusion signatures are also introduced.

2.1. Network Intrusion Detection System

Network intrusions refer to malicious attacks such as attempting DoS attacks, intercepting packet payloads, and cracking target nodes. These intrusions are detected and prevented by a security technology called intrusion detection [10]. NIDS is a complete system equipped with the intrusion detection technology. The system consists of all devices and information about the networks, such as host, routers, and monitoring results [1].

Detecting intrusions such as DoS is difficult to implement because most intrusions pretend that they are general packets. Moreover, many intrusions have polynomial characteristics and are not easily found by comparison with specific patterns. The implementation of an NIDS is difficult because the detection algorithm should not disturb its own intended flow of sensing work.

The intrusion detection systems are classified into misuse detection and anomaly detection systems [3,11]. A misuse detection system uses pattern-matching algorithms with predefined patterns called intrusion signatures. Most of the signatures were obtained by an empirical method. In other words, the signatures are created by obtaining the common context of payloads that are revealed as attacks. Firmly constructed databases of these signatures can prevent network devices from the same attacks again. However, this algorithm is unsuitable for the detection of newly introduced or polymorphic intrusions because only known patterns can be detected. A heuristic matching method that allows wild-card characters is used to supplement misuse detection [12].

Implementing a misuse detection system in sensor nodes has been studied in several previous works. Because the nodes have limited resources, many researchers introduced outlier detection systems that deploy additional distributed monitoring nodes containing larger resources than the others [8,13]. The outlier nodes only conduct intrusion detection work, and deliver the detection result to the base station and other sensor nodes. Amin *et al.* proposed a robust intrusion detection system (RIDES) that unified detection schemes, including the signature-based detecting system and anomaly detecting system [14]. The algorithm converted a packet's payloads to signature codes based on Bloom filters. Baig introduced five phases for detecting intrusions, including pattern recognition and feedback of the results [4].

An anomaly detection system recognizes normal activities in the networks. Comparing received packets with these activities, malicious intruders can be detected by the system. The system can find deliberately modified or unknown signatures that are difficult to detect by misuse detection systems. However, it is still difficult and time-consuming to determine a profile of the normal activities [7]. The profile is determined by input data, output results, data types, and labels. Stochastic approaches are generally used to set the profile [15].

Anomaly detection systems have also been regarded as one of the many intrusion detection systems. Distributed intrusion detection systems (IDSs) that have a systematic anomaly-detecting process were developed [16,17]. Similar to outlier systems, additional agents such as gateways are dedicated to execute the intrusion detection schemes. An intrusion alert function based on anomaly detection was also introduced [11]. The system can validate signals among the sensor networks using these functions. In addition, packet traffic can be a criterion for detecting an anomaly in networks. A matching algorithm, which regards observed packet traffics as specified patterns, was also proposed [15,18].

Snort is one of the well-known IDSs based on a hybrid algorithm that uses both misuse detection and anomaly-based inspection [19]. Snort has rule sets that define malicious attacks. Each rule contains information about a protocol, port number, and context of the packet. The rule sets support regular expressions that contain wild-card characters, and the sets require the algorithm to perform both signature and heuristic matching. Many researchers have conducted studies to accelerate and optimize the rule set finding mechanisms such as pattern-matching algorithms [9,20,21]. However, these efforts are still difficult to implement in sensor networks because the schemes should be modified for the constrained resources of the sensor node.

2.2. Multiple Pattern Matching Algorithm

A string-matching algorithm is a process of searching string subsets in a specific sentence called a text. The algorithm is used for finding words in a web page or a textbook, DNA pattern recognition, and network intrusion detection. This classical algorithm has issues of both memory efficiency and performance.

The WM algorithm is a powerful pattern-matching algorithm that can detect multiple patterns simultaneously [22]. This algorithm is one of the classical multiple pattern matching algorithms improved from the Boyer–Moore algorithm [23]. In addition, the WM algorithm is a shift-or algorithm using a hash table and prefix table that seeks a substring of the text to determine the shift amount. The substring, normally called a block, has two or three sequential characters [22]. These characters form the criterion for the shift amount. Referring to the hash- (*i.e.*, the shift) table indexes, the algorithm obtains the shift amount from the table entries. Zero-shifting entries mean that the substring is a suffix of the pattern sets and have a chance to be matched with the patterns. The prefix table gives additional information about prefix subsets of the patterns to match all characters. In this way, the algorithm can skip two or more characters in the text. The skipping method enables the algorithm to find multiple patterns at once and increases the searching speed. Snort uses a modified version of Wu–Manber [24].

Figure 1(a) shows a simple example for finding patterns using the WM algorithm. Let us first assume that there are only two patterns to search: "UNIVERSITY" and "LONDON". The WM algorithm first constructs the shift and hash tables from the patterns before it starts the actual matching operation. Because the shortest pattern "LONDON" has six characters, the minimum length *m* is set as 6. To make an appropriate shift table among *m* characters, the pattern "UNIVERSITY" is also considered as the first six letters "UNIVER." Assuming that the block size *B*is 2, we can make the shift table based on the two patterns. For example, the subsets "ER" and "ON" are zero-shifting entries and "VE" and "DO" indicate the shift value as 1. The pointer of the text string is continuously shifted by the entries of the shift table until the pointer reaches the end of the text string.

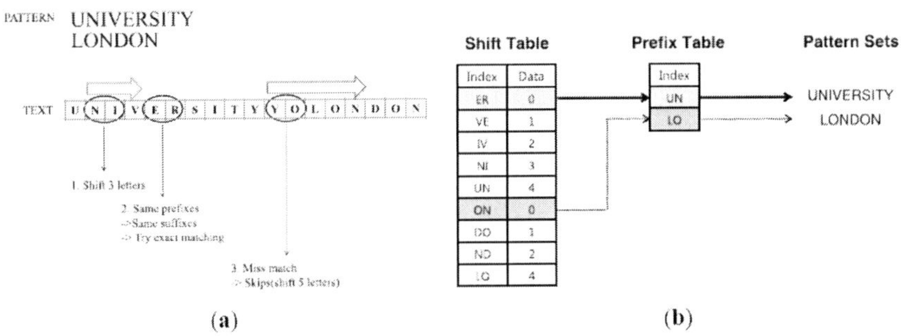

Figure 1. Shifting examples using the WM algorithm. (**a**) The shifting processes; (**b**) The two tables of WM.

Figure 1(b) shows both the suffix and prefix tables established by the two patterns in Figure 1(a). The algorithm first looks at block "NI" of the text, and the shift table indicates the algorithm shifts three characters. Then, the shift value of the next block "ER" is zero. In this case, the algorithm returns to $m - B = 4$ characters and takes another block of that position called the prefix block. The prefix block "UN" is also matched with the prefix table. Therefore, the algorithm starts to compare the text with the entire pattern and finds that the string matches one of the given patterns. The other case is shift-table mismatching. When mismatching occurs, the shift table indicates a full shift that can be derived by m and B as $m - B + 1$ characters. In this figure, the block should be shifted to five characters. Then, the block (*i.e.*, "YO") also leads to shift five characters. For the next case, the pointer indicates "DO" and eventually finds out the pattern "LONDON".

The patterns are always detected, although the algorithm skips two or more characters. For example, the third case (*i.e.*, "YO") in the Figure 1(a) leads to shift five characters. For the next case, the pointer indicates "DO" and eventually finds out the pattern "LONDON". Because the amount of the full shift is restricted by m, the pointer never misses the directly followed patterns. However, the algorithm improperly finds short-sized pattern sets for the same reason.

3. SENSOR NODE-BASED NIDS FRAMEWORKS

In this section, we introduce an NIDS framework modified for small-sized sensor nodes. This section first introduces the computation offloading method from a resource-constrained sensor node to a resource-rich base station. This section also describes MinWM (Minimized Wu–Manber algorithm) optimized for each device. MinWM uses a process dividing scheme and makes two nodes to manage the shift table and prefix table independently. Packet transmission management among the network is also discussed briefly where sensor nodes determine whether a packet is a malicious attack or not.

3.1. Networked Sensor Platform

The main objective of the node is to deliver gathered sensing information such as light, temperature, radio frequency, and vibration to central hosts called base stations. The base station creates valuable information from the gathered data. In this way, we can apply a cluster-based sensor system to observe large-scale natural phenomena and develop unmanned management systems of specific regions (e.g., industrial management and urban air-pollution observation).

The sensor nodes are low-power and low-performance devices because they are not connected with external wires and operate on internal battery power. Generally, a node has 64 KB memory and a micro-controller below 16 MHz frequency. Therefore, only light-weighted process that utilizes minimal resources can be implemented on the devices. Moreover, the detecting process should not disrupt the periodic sensing works (*i.e.*, the process should be terminated in a short time). Highly time and resource demanding process cannot be executed on the sensor nodes.

The framework based on MinWM is similar to other cooperative NIDS [8,14]. Both the nodes and the base stations take different jobs according to their hardware resources. The objective is to improve the overall performance of the NIDS and to decrease unnecessary network transmission. As we mentioned, the sensor node should not perform entire signature matching. Instead, the pattern matching algorithm should be modified to reduce resource usage. The strategy of MinWM is to divide the WM algorithm into table-matching and actual-matching steps. This approach allows the node to implement WM-based detection systems and utilizes the base station to boost the throughput of the entire detection process.

Figure 2 shows an example of the system model based on the multiple networked sensors. Each node is assigned to certain regions and gathers external sensing information for predefined purposes. For a certain time period, the nodes have transmitted the data to the assigned base station for summarization of the sensing works. Meanwhile, the base station of a particular region is responsible for collecting data and managing sensors in the same region. The packet from each base station to a top monitoring server represents the summarized sensing data of their own regions. Because of this cluster-based structure, the general analysis at the top monitoring server is simplified by these base stations.

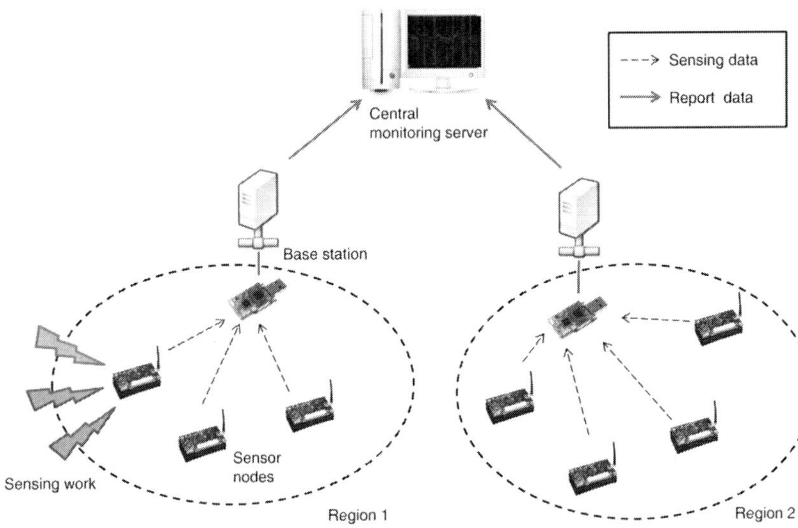

Figure 2. The system model of the networked sensor platform.

The intrusion detection systems based on the Snort signature-set checks additional information of incoming packets such as port numbers and protocol types besides the payloads. In other words, the system only inspects the payload of an incoming packet when the packet comes through a specific port number and protocol type corresponding to the signatures. The packet's payload is checked by both the shift table and the prefix table before transmitting the sensing data. The result of the inspection is inserted into the original payload. The base station is responsible for the remaining detection work (*i.e.*, the exact matching). Using the additional data from the sensor node, the attack attempts can be quickly determined by the base station, which has more computing resources than the sensor nodes. The sensor nodes and base stations notify other nodes of an intrusion if the packet is revealed as a malicious attack. Each sensor node has the same algorithm for consistent intrusion detection. Figure 3 shows how the general WM steps are divided and performed by the sensor nodes and the base stations.

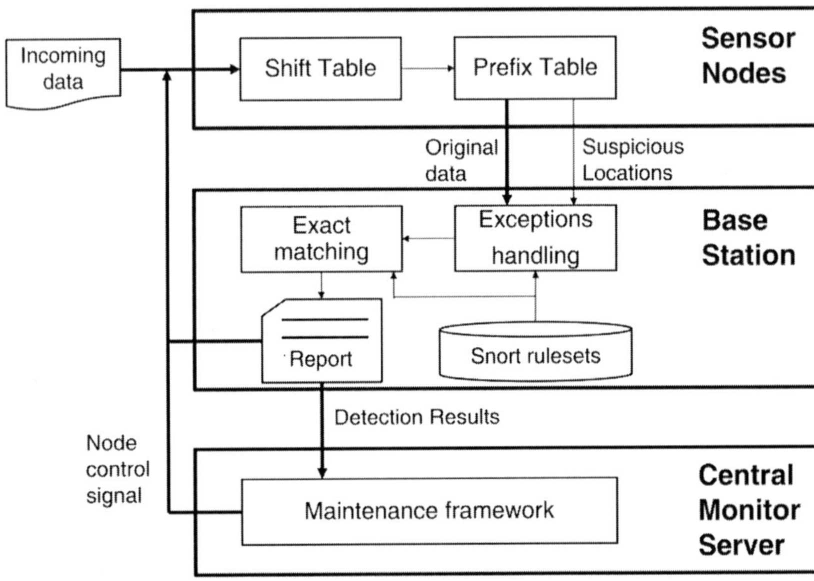

Figure 3. The division of processes of the distributedWM algorithm.

To process the work efficiently, MinWM is based on a sensing work provided by TinyOS's library. The overall process of the system is shown in Figure 3. The sensor nodes transmit the packet that contains the original data and locations of suspicious attacks. The base station operates the actual matching schemes using the location data set by each node. The result is also transmitted to the sensor nodes that suspect attacks. The informing step is a simple broadcasting step; however, other traceback mechanisms can be applied to improve network safety [25,26].

3.2. Intrusion Detection Schemes

The sensor node checks the existence of intrusions within the time period. Comparing substrings of the payload with shift-table entries, the node can examine substrings with high speed. We focus on the DoS rules among the Snort signatures because being exposed to DoS attacks can lead to a dangerous situation for the WSNs [6]. The table that was created by the content fields of the rules contains information about the amount of shifts. The skipped characters are irrelevant to the matching suffixes [27]. The shifting also indicates that suffix matching may exist at the shifting point. The algorithm searches the prefix table only if the shift table indicates a zero-valued entry. This skipping method helps the sensor node to finish searching the context in time despite its limited resources.

The prefix table represents the string's prefix portions of the NIDS content source. The prefix table rechecks a suspicious payload that indicates zero entries. In general, the exact-matching step occurs when the signature satisfies the conditions of the two tables. The second table can reduce incidences of warning alert messages and increases the matching accuracy notably.

The sensor node does not contain entire signatures owing to two reasons. The first reason is that the exact-matching step requires a large portion of the WM algorithm's execution time. The substrings are compared with all characters in the signatures that have the same suffixes and prefixes. Considering the extremely constrained computation power, this process is too slow to be executed while maintaining the periodic sensing process. Secondly, the sensor node does not have sufficient space to keep entire signatures. A low-end sensor node is known to be unsuitable to deal with general patterns without modifying the signatures [28]. Instead of processing all signatures on the sensor node, we mark the location of a suspicious string as a bookmark and pass it to be processed by the base station. Only one byte in size is sufficient to represent a bookmark in the packet because the general packet size is less than 128 bytes. The bookmark can also represent both suffix and prefix information because the block size and minimum length of the signatures are defined in advance.

The base station receives packets that contain the inserted location information (*i.e.*, the bookmarks) from multiple nodes. Using the bookmarks, MinWM checks suspicious signatures marked by the sensor nodes to determine whether the packets are actual attacks or not. The suffix and prefix information substrings are sent to the base station in the form of bookmarks. This approach reduces the time to find matching candidates. In addition, MinWM also skips the step where the suffix and prefix tables are compared, which is already executed on the sensor nodes. As a result, the MinWM framework can achieve higher throughput than processing the entire WM algorithm at the base station. A more powerful aspect is that MinWM can even skip the whole-detection steps if the payload checked by the node does not contain any bookmarks. Therefore, reducing the load of the base station helps in processing a large number of sensor nodes efficiently. While the prefix and suffix tables are simply utilized for each sensor node, the base station only focuses on complete signatures. In this way, both the sensor nodes and the base stations can achieve the objectives of memory efficiency and performance.

3.3. Packet Transmission Management

The detection results of the packet are sent to the sensor nodes that previously transmitted the packet. Considering the broadcast capabilities of the sensor nodes, a traceback for the network intrusion is emphasized. The sensor nodes that transmit the intrusions are distinguished and managed by the intrusion system according to the policy of the system. Traceback mechanisms have been studied by other researchers [25,26]. A small portion of trace information is inserted into the node, and the system is prepared to trace the information using the bloom filter, although a simple traceback mechanism is assumed in the MinWM framework.

Figure 4 shows the message format of MinWM. This is the format of a TinyOS 2.x message and ZigBee protocol [19]. The format mainly consists of five categories: AM packet, header, packet payload, footer, and metadata. The AM packet represents the category of the packet and its destination nodes. The header field contains the overall information about a packet, such as the source address, length, and packet groups. The footer field has cyclic-redundancy-checking (CRC) parity data to verify the contents of the packet. The metadata field contains additional information for the networks. The "dest addr" in the AM packet contains the address of the node that should receive the packet. For example, the address "FF FF" indicates a broadcasting mode, which means that the packet is transmitted to all nearby nodes.

Figure 5 indicates the overall message transmissions to conduct pattern matching between the sensor nodes and the base station. The payload data is transmitted by the encapsulated packet. Although the general WM system needs only the data field "string" in the packet payload to process the sensing data, additional fields that occupy small payload sizes are added. As we discussed in Sections 2.2 and 3.2, the sensor node compares the string field with the suffix and prefix tables. If a suspicious substring is detected, the position of the suffix is written on the checker array, and the total number of intrusion candidates is written on the counter field. The base station examines the partial substrings of the packet's payload using the bookmark data. The size of the packet is sufficient enough to contain the two additional fields because the ZigBee protocol provides a bandwidth of up to 20 KBps [2]. In addition, the data is compatible with other systems because the system uses general packet structures with minor conversions.

AM Packet	
Packet	dest addr
00	FF FF

Header			
link addr	Length	group	Handler
00 02	50	00	06

Packet Payload(up to 28 bytes)					
src id	node id	counter	mode	string[]	checker[]
00 01	00 02	00	00	00 ...	00 ...

Footer
CRC
ex ab

Metadata			
strength	ack	time	...
...	...	...	...

Figure 4. The packet format for the wireless sensor network.

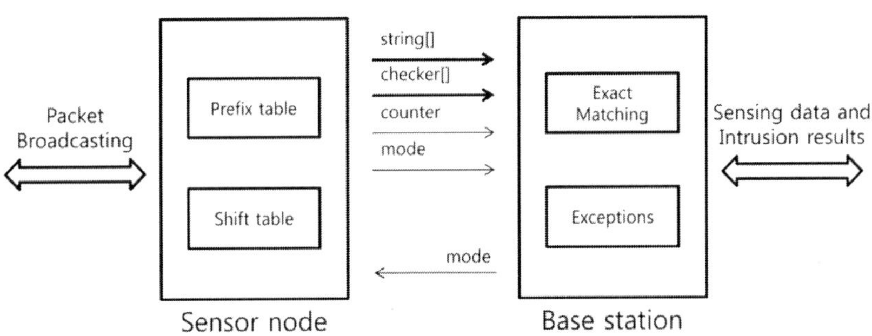

Figure 5. The packet messages between sensor nodes and a base station.

Distributed sensor nodes and the centralized base station notify each other of the classification of the transmitted packet. In other words, the packet of the sensor nodes contains additional information about checking status, including warnings of the intrusions. The packet of the base station has the results of intrusion detection and actual alerts of intrusions. An additional field "mode" makes each node recognize the status of incoming packets. After each detection step is finished, the status is determined and written at the one-byte field data. The field is also used for the network management methodology consisting of two or more sensor nodes. According to the network policy, each node and base station can notify each other of the current detection status of the packet. Because the field represents a total of 256 different states, the field can be used for the MinWM framework with a large number of sensors.

4. MODIFIED TABLES OF THE WU–MANBER ALGORITHM

Each sensor node commonly has two tables created by substrings of intrusion signatures. However, the tables based on the original WM algorithm cannot be used owing to two limitations: the structure of Snort signatures and restricted resources of the sensor nodes. In this section, we discuss the problems and novel solutions for the sensor nodes and the base station. We first minimize the shift and prefix tables to allocate them into the memory of the sensor node. Each entry of the tables is classified by single characters to reduce the required memory size. In addition, we prepare an additional scheme to deal with specific patterns that are difficult to implement.

4.1. One-Character Classification

Snort has recommended using the WM algorithm to find intrusions because it has an advantage in memory efficiency as compared with other pattern-matching algorithms [19]. However, the memory requirements of the algorithm are still too large to reside in the memory of the sensor node. Generally, the suffix and prefix tables of the WM algorithm use combinations of multiple characters to allocate the addresses of each entry. The address is derived from arithmetic equations of the characters as a block. The optimal B is known to be either $B = 2$ or $B = 3$ [22]. The system requires an additional one byte of data for every entry to represent a total of $C = 256$ different expressions. Although we set $B = 2$, the shift table requires the memory size to be $C^B \times 1 = 64$ KB. Considering that almost all sensor nodes have a memory size of less than 64 KB, the table cannot be allocated without modification.

Instead of using multiple character combinations, we propose tables based on single characters, i.e., $B = 1$. In this case, the required memory size of each table is $C^B \times 1$ = 256 bytes, which is significantly smaller than the memory size using multiple character combinations. However, the reduction of block size can cause significant performance degradation because the shift amount is also decreased by the block entries. A smaller table size contains a smaller resolution for detection clues. In other words, the suffix table has only 256 combinations of shifting information if the table consists of single character entries. As a result, the shift entry is forced to have smaller shifting amount. Still, this table-based approach shows better throughput than other algorithms based on single-character comparison owing to the skip method.

The prefix table can contain many more entries than the shift table can. The prefix table requires 256^2 = 65536 = 64 KB memory size at maximum if all two-character combinations appear among the signatures. However, allocation of the maximum memory size is not always necessary. The required memory size strictly depends on the number of signatures. As we mentioned in Section 2.2, MinWM examines the prefix table only if the suffix table indicates a zero shift. In addition, the prefix table can be represented by linked lists of prefix substrings indicated by a pointer of the suffix entry. In this case, the memory requirements of the prefix tables depend on the number of prefix characters in the signatures. In contrast to the original WM algorithm, MinWM on the sensor nodes does not make a copy of the matching candidates. MinWM simply records the positions of matching in the payload context to reduce the size of the packet and provide efficient control for the exact matching executed on the base station.

The performance and memory requirements heavily depend on the number of signatures. Therefore, a small number of packets are used to achieve high throughput. DoS signatures are suited for this scheme because the number of rules is less than 100. Considering overlapped signatures in the rules, this structure can allow the sensor node to provide a partial intrusion detection scheme with minuscule resource consumption.

4.2. Short String Exceptions

The content fields of each rule are considered as the signatures. Because the length of the fields is variable, generation of signature sets for all rules is difficult. Strings less than two characters long significantly reduce the performance of the WM-based algorithm because the maximum shifting value depends on m and B (*i.e.*, $m - B + 1$). Only one signature that has one character prevents shifting by more than one character.

To solve the problem, MinWM uses the structure of the Snort rules. In fact, the content fields shorter than two-character strings provide additional position information to clarify the ambiguous strings. Moreover, the position indicates either the exact or near position of the first letter in the string. Instead of inserting the short signatures into the two tables, we make exceptions for the signatures. The additional step is prepared to account for the exceptions before the algorithm executes the exact-matching step. In the additional step, the algorithm verifies the exceptions at the string locations specified by the rules. MinWM simply checks bytes in the location described in the exceptions and does not execute the whole string-finding algorithm for the short patterns. Consequently, MinWM requires almost no additional resource and execution time. In addition, the signature sets without short patterns create small-sized prefix tables and a shift table with the large shifts.

5. EVALUATIONS

In this section, we only consider networks that consist of a single sensor node and a base station because MinWM only considers implementing the distributed WM algorithm among two nodes. Although the evaluations are conducted with two nodes, MinWM can be expanded to multiple-node-based networks owing to the simplicity of the system. However, the networked system should control the overall traffic transmitted by the nodes. Traffic management is already discussed in Section 3.3. We first explain the environment of the sensor nodes and then discuss the results in detail.

5.1. Experimental Environments

We conduct evaluations using a Kmote device, which is a typical low-end sensor node. The device has an 8 MHz MSP430 microcontroller and a CC2420 radio chip that is compatible with other IEEE 802.15.4 (*i.e.*, ZigBee) based devices. The microcontroller has 10 KB RAM and 48 KB flash memory. If the size of each entry is set to 1 byte, the shift table requires only 256 bytes, and the table is sufficiently allocated in the device. The size of the prefix table depends on the number of signatures in a node. Considering the number of DoS signatures in Snort, the flash memory size sufficiently contains the prefix table.

In general, the misuse detection systems consider payload contents in target packets as strings. This is due to that most malicious rules are defined in a form of strings and traditional string matching algorithms can be effectively utilized to detect malicious data. Implementing a misuse detection system in sensor nodes also applies this approach [4,14,18]. In fact, the MinWM framework also detects intrusion signatures on the strings, which represent the payloads of incoming packets.

The MinWM framework uses a rule-based intrusion detection scheme, and Snort v2.9 DoS rule sets are used for the target signatures. A total of 77 rules are selected and contained in the sensor nodes to detect specific attacks. Generally, one rule in Snort consists of one or more string sets. The rule also has information about the distances between two sets. MinWM considers each string set as a single pattern. If one or more patterns are matched, the locations are recorded in the bookmarks and inserted into the sending packet. From the packet, the original context and the added bookmark can be delivered to the base station. Because the base station knows the locations of the suspicious strings, pattern sets that contain wildcard characters are quickly determined by checking the distances of the matching patterns. Strings below two characters are considered as exceptions, as described in Section 4.2, and are processed by the base station before exact matching.

The base station processes not only the exceptions but also other regular expressions that are not easily implemented on the sensor nodes. Specific signatures in Snort are written in a Perl-compatible regular expression syntax (PCRE) [29]. The signatures can be searched by the base station because the base station has the resources to load the PCRE library. A queue structure is prepared to receive multiple packets, and the structure helps the base station to use any parallelization techniques such as multi-threaded computing.

5.2. Performance Improvement of the Distributed Detection System

The time complexity of the detection scheme is derived by the original author of the WM algorithm. The throughput of the algorithm is dependent on B, the total length of the text N, and m[22]. MinWM needs time to construct the shift and prefix tables; however, we do not consider this in this evaluation because the tables are predefined and loaded in the memory. Including the time to compute hash functions $O(B)$, the complexity can be given by $O(BN/m)$ [22]. RIDES, which uses bloom filters to find signature codes, is presented for comparison with the proposed algorithm. RIDES represents a complexity of $O(N + \epsilon)$, where ϵ is the number of patterns [14]. As we mentioned in Section 4.1, the minimized block size $B = 1$ reduces the load to compute hash functions and increases the overall throughput. Considering another parameter set with $m = 3$, the algorithm theoretically shows better throughput than RIDES.

Simple attack emulations are conducted on the sensor nodes as shown in Figure 6. A target node periodically sends the current temperature to the base station; the time interval is set as one second in this evaluation, but it can be changed. We artificially generate attack signals that contain DDoS signatures and insert them into the sensor node through wireless networks. A sensor node that receives these signatures can detect them and make an alert signal. In the figure, only a certain part of payload in the alert signal is presented: counter, suspicious data, and checker referred in Figure 4. After the alert signal is sent to the base station, the node stops sensing the current temperature and waits for response from the base station. The base station verifies the suspicious data on the alert signal and then reports the result by sending the response signal. Under this emulation environment, we evaluate performance of the proposed approach.

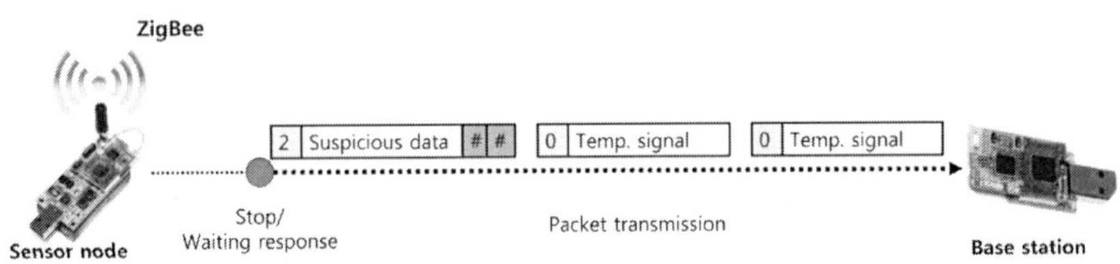

Figure 6. An intrusion emulation on the proposed sensor network.

Table 1 indicates the elapsed time and power consumption of the two algorithms in the sensor node. We have evaluated each test for 1,000 times and the average is represented in the table. We find that MinWM detects DoS intrusions more efficiently than RIDES because of the structural advantages of the approach. To find the number of intrusions, MinWM uses shifting techniques that can skip one or more characters, while RIDES uses hash techniques derived by the Rabin–Karp algorithm [30]. RIDES is known to be suitable for finding large numbers of patterns because the algorithm simplifies the exact-matching steps instead of applying the character-shifting schemes. In Table 1, the searching speed of RIDES remains constant while the searching speed of MinWM decreases according to the number of the bookmarks.

Table 1. Required resources to examine a single packet.

	MinWM		RIDES		
# of Bookmarks	Time (ms)	Power (μWs)	Time (ms)	Power (μWs)	Speedup Ratio
0	0.204	1.51	39.533	128.08	193.79
5	0.417	3.08	39.547	128.13	94.84
10	1.106	8.16	39.436	127.77	35.66
15	1.248	9.21	39.562	128.18	31.70
20	1.408	10.39	39.550	128.14	25.96

The power consumption in Table 1 is evaluated from the measured time and the power consumption of the sensor node [31]. The sensor node that integrates MinWM consumes 1.51 $\mu Ws$to detect any DoS attacks on a single packet when the number of bookmarks is zero. On the other hand, when using RIDES to detect DoS attacks, the sensor node requires 128.08 μWs energy. As a result, RIDES consumes up to 126.57 μWs more energy for inspecting a single packet compared with MinWM.

Using a simple probabilistic approach, we evaluate the performance of MinWM. Setting Σ to be the number of alphabets, a matching probability of only one pattern that equals the probability of zero shifting is simply derived as $(1/\Sigma^B)$. In addition, no pattern is matched with a substring of the text if actual shifting would occur. From the derivation, the non-zero shifting probability equals $(1 - 1/\Sigma^B)^\epsilon$. This equation shows that the performance is strongly related to the number of patterns to be detected. Figure 7 reveals the relationship between the signature size and the non-zero probability. In the proposed approach, each signature only requires one additional byte in the prefix table. Although the memory is sufficient to contain all signatures in Snort, the general WM algorithm restricts the appropriate number of patterns. Only 500 signatures drop the non-zero probability below 20% and definitely decrease the throughput of the algorithm. However, MinWM is still considered a reasonable method because the DoS attack signatures are limited in number and overlap with each other. Moreover, the problems of detecting a large number of patterns are solved by the distributed processing of multiple sensor nodes.

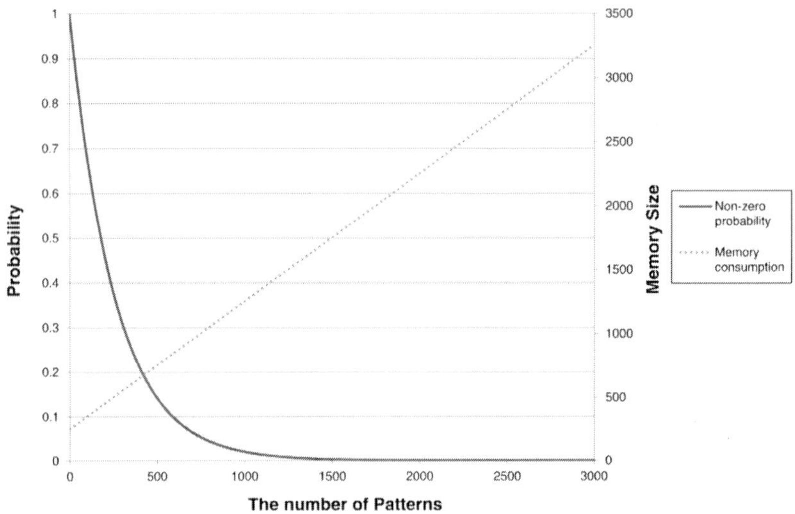

Figure 7. The non-zero probability and required memory occupation for the patterns.

To verify the effect of the bookmarks, we have performed simple evaluations. A number of strings are prepared and inserted into the process of the sensor node. As a result, the strings contain information about the location of suspicious substrings (the bookmarks). The actual matching step is executed using the bookmarks, and the throughput of the base station is calculated by measuring the processing time. To show the improvement, we measured the throughput of the general WM algorithm with the same strings. The evaluations are conducted on an identical machine equipped with an AMD Phenom II X4 955 processor running at 3.2 GHz and equipped with 4 GB of DDR3 RAM. The source patterns are string sets that are generated randomly with a length of 50. The number of patterns is varied to observe the performance of processing incessant data inflow. The throughput of two methods is calculated by the processing time and total string sizes.

Figure 8 shows the average throughput of the two pattern sets. In MinWM, the suffix and prefix matching steps are skipped by the bookmarks. MinWM only performs the entire pattern comparison using the pre-written bookmarks. By comparing the results, MinWM shows faster detection time of suspicious strings than the general WM algorithm. The figure indicates that MinWM is on average 4.76 times faster. The faster detection helps the base station to gather sensing information more efficiently. The improved detecting performance also helps to manage more sensor nodes. Considering that many sensor nodes are typically utilized for large-scale sensing activities, higher density sensing environments can possibly be provided by the increased capacity.

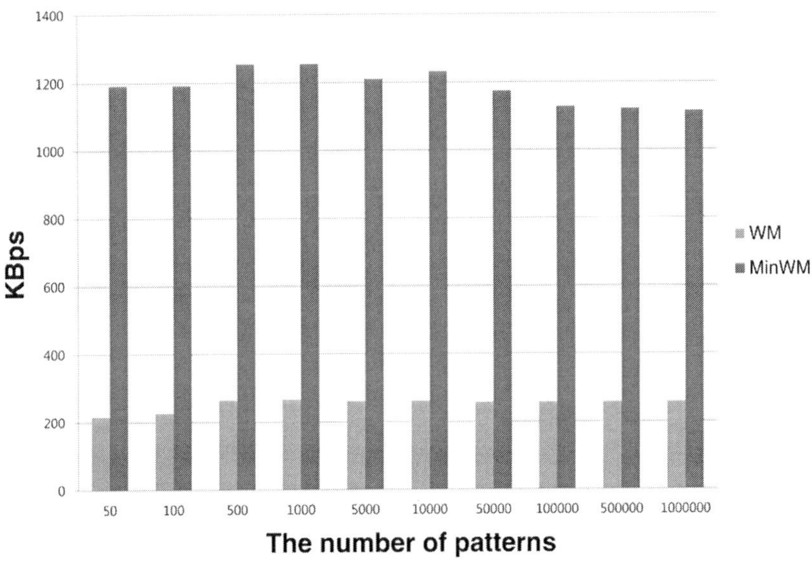

Figure 8. The average throughput of the two pattern sets in the base station.

The performance improvement is caused by the skipping schemes of the MinWM framework. The entire suffix- and prefix-matching steps are skipped in the base station. Although the exact-matching step takes a large portion of the execution time, reducing the amount of memory access to shift characters decreases the execution time. Furthermore, large numbers of payloads are considered as regular sensing activities without detection by the base station. Table 2 lists the average number of patterns that are examined by the exact-matching step. Only 2.55% of the patterns is alerted by the sensor node, and the rest is regarded as safe. Compared with the RIDES approach that we selected, fewer packets are examined by the base station, although the rates for RIDES depend on the types of hash functions. The results in the Table 2 indicate that MinWM can reduce the incidence of entire matching execution. From the analyses, the MinWM framework executes intrusion detection tasks more efficiently and has the capability to protect large numbers of sensor nodes from malicious DoS attacks.

Table 2. The number of alerted patterns that require actual matching.

Patterns	50	100	500	1000	5000	10,000	50,000	100,000	500,000	1,000,000
					MinWM					
Average Counts	1.16	2.69	12.93	24.70	124.43	253.43	1275.40	2527.52	12680.77	25375.59
Rates (%)	2.3200	2.6900	2.5860	2.4700	2.4886	2.5343	2.5508	2.5275	2.5362	2.5376
					RIDES					
Average Counts	2.64	5.16	25.63	50.33	251.27	506.09	2513.65	5040.52	25194.83	50345.80
Rates (%)	5.2800	5.1600	5.1260	5.0330	5.0254	5.0609	5.0273	5.0405	5.0390	5.0346

6. CONCLUSIONS

In this paper, the concept of a distributed WM algorithm called MinWM has been introduced to establish an NIDS for low-end sensor nodes. To solve the problem of constrained resources, the WM algorithm is divided into two parts; the sensor nodes execute smaller part and the base station executes the other. In addition, the sensor nodes use modified WM tables to reduce memory burden. MinWM outperforms the general WM and RIDES approaches in a number of evaluations. One possible explanation for these results is that the skipped shifting step occupies a large portion of the execution time. The base station is more efficient if it executes only the actual matching step. However, the evaluations were conducted for a limited range due to the restricted string pattern sets. MinWM may be required to design systematic evaluations with actually deployed multiple sensor nodes and activities. Nevertheless, the study is still valuable because the evaluations prove the efficiency of the proposed structures and provide the basis for distributed work to prevent malicious attacks. We expect that the MinWM framework can be implemented with the whole Snort signatures using a large scale distributed system with more nodes.

This study provides an example of implementing high resource demanding work such as multiple pattern-matching algorithms to constrained sensor devices. Making cooperative detection frameworks among the different sensor nodes is possible because MinWM is developed from a standard sensing framework. The MinWM framework can also be applied to any other compatible framework that consists of a large number of sensor nodes utilized for many practical fields. In addition, the automated intrusion defense agent can be implemented by enhancing the detection functions on the base station. To achieve these objectives, the study of effective communication frameworks among the sensors would be recommended to establish efficient network systems. This study provides a valuable resource for the future study of cooperative systems among a large number of sensor nodes and base stations.

ACKNOWLEDGMENTS

This research was supported by the MKE (The Ministry of Knowledge Economy) and NHN Corp., under IT/SW Creative research program supervised by the NIPA (National IT Industry Promotion Agency) (NIPA-2012-H0505-12-1011) and supported by the Industrial Strategic Technology Development Program (10041971, Development of Power Efficient High-Performance Multimedia Contents Service Technology using Context-Adapting Distributed Transcoding) funded by the Ministry of Knowledge Economy (MKE, Korea).

REFERENCES

1. Sun, B.; Osborne, L.; Xiao, Y.; Guizani, S. Intrusion detection techniques in mobile ad hoc and wireless sensor networks. *IEEE Wirel. Commun.* **2007**, *14*, 56–63.
2. Geer, D. Users make a Beeline for ZigBee sensor technology. *Computer* **2005**, *38*, 16–19.
3. Zhang, Y.; Lee, W.; Huang, Y.A. Intrusion detection techniques for mobile wireless networks. *Wirel. Netw.* **2003**, *9*, 545–556. Baig, Z. Pattern recognition for detecting distributed node exhaustion attacks in wireless sensor networks. *Comput. Commun.* **2011**, *34*, 468–484.
4. Xie, M.; Han, S.; Tian, B.; Parvin, S. Anomaly detection in wireless sensor networks: A survey. *J. Netw. Comput. Appl.* **2011**, *34*, 1302–1325.
5. Wood, A.; Stankovic, J. Denial of service in sensor networks. *Computer* **2002**, *35*, 54–62.
6. Chandola, V.; Banerjee, A.; Kumar, V. Anomaly detection: A survey. *ACM Comput. Surv.***2009**, *41*, 15:1–15:58.

7. Bahrepour, M.; Zhang, Y.; Meratnia, N.; Havinga, P. Use of Event Detection Approaches for Outlier Detection in Wireless Sensor Networks. Proceedings of 2009 5th International Conference on the Intelligent Sensors, Sensor Networks and Information Processing (ISSNIP), Melbourne, Australia, 7– 10 December 2009; pp. 439–444.

8. Coit, C.; Staniford, S.; McAlerney, J. Towards Faster String Matching for Intrusion Detection or Exceeding the Speed of Snort. Proceedings of the DARPA Information Survivability Conference Exposition II (DISCEX 2001), Anaheim, CA, USA, 12–14 June 2001; Volume 1, pp. 367–373.

9. Denning, D. An intrusion-detection model. *IEEE Trans. Softw. Eng.* **1987**, *SE-13*, 222–232.

10. Shaikh, R.A.; Jameel, H.; D'uriol, B.J.; Lee, H.; Lee, S.; Song, Y.J. Intrusion-aware alert validation algorithm for cooperative distributed intrusion detection schemes of wireless sensor networks. *Sensors* **2009**, *9*, 5989–6007.

11. Szor, P. *The Art of Computer Virus Research and Defense*; Addison-Wesley Professional: Indianapolis: Indiana, USA, 2005.

12. Cheng, S.T.; Li, S.-Y.; Chen, C.M. Distributed Detection in Wireless Sensor Networks. Proceedings of Seventh IEEE/ACIS International Conference on the Computer and Information Science (ICIS 08), Portland, OR, USA, 14– 16 May 2008; pp. 401–406.

13. Amin, S.O.; Siddiqui, M.S.; Hong, C.S.; Lee, S. RIDES: Robust intrusion detection system for IP-based ubiquitous sensor networks. *Sensors* **2009**, *9*, 3447–3468.

14. Wang, Q. Packet traffic: A good data source for wireless sensor network modeling and anomaly detection. *IEEE Netw.* **2011**, *25*, 15–21.

15. Martynov, D.; Roman, J.; Vaidya, S.; Fu, H. Design and Implementation of an Intrusion Detection System for Wireless Sensor Networks. Proceedings of 2007 IEEE International Conference on the Electro/Information Technology, Chicago, IL, USA, 17– 20 May 2007; pp. 507–512.

16. Amin, S.; Young, Y.J.; Siddiqui, M.; Hong, C.S. A Novel Intrusion Detection Framework for IP-Based Sensor Networks. Proceedings of International Conference on the Information

Networking (ICOIN 2009), Chiang Mai, Thailand, 20– 23 January 2009; pp. 1–3.

17. Wang, Q.; Zhang, T. Detecting Anomaly Node Behavior in Wireless Sensor Networks. Proceedings of 21st International Conference on the Advanced Information Networking and Applications Workshops (AINAW 2007), Niagara Falls, Canada, 21– 23 May 2007; Volume 1, pp. 451–456.

18. Norton, M.; Roelker, D. *Snort 2.0: Hi-Performance Multi-Rule Inspection Engine*; Sourcefire Network Security Inc.: Columbia, MD, USA, 2004.

19. Zaidi, A.; Agoulmine, N.; Kenaza, T. Piecewise Classification of Attack Patterns for Efficient Network Intrusion Detection. Proceedings of the 2010 International Conference on the Security and Cryptography (SECRYPT), Athens, Greece, 26– 28 July 2010; pp. 1–5.

20. Choi, Y.H.; Jung, M.Y.; Seo, S.W. A fast pattern matching algorithm with multi-byte search unit for high-speed network security. *Comput. Commun.* **2011**, *34*, 1750–1763.

21. Wu, S.; Manber, U. *A Fast Algorithm for Multi-Pattern Searching*; TR-94-17; University of Arizona: Tucson, AZ, USA, 1994.

22. Boyer, R.S.; Moore, J.S. A fast string searching algorithm. *ACM Commun.* **1977**, *20*, 762–772.

23. Antonatos, S.; Polychronakis, M.; Akritidis, P.; Anagnostakis, K.; Markatos, E. Piranha: Fast and Memory-Efficient Pattern Matching for Intrusion Detection. Proceedings of 20th IFIP International Information Security Conference (SEC), Chiba, Japan, 30 May– 1 June 2005; pp. 393–408.

24. Sy, D.; Bao, L. CAPTRA: Coordinated Packet Traceback. Proceedings of The Fifth International Conference on the Information Processing in Sensor Networks (IPSN 2006), Nashville, TN, USA, 19– 21 April 2006; pp. 152–159.

25. Kim, I.Y.; Kim, K.C. A Resource-Efficient IP Traceback Technique for Mobile Ad-hoc Networks Based on Time-Tagged Bloom Filter. Proceedings of Third International Conference on the Convergence and Hybrid Information Technology (ICCIT '08), Busan, Korea, 11– 13 November 2008; Volume 2, pp. 549–554.

26. Roesch, M. Snort-Lightweight Intrusion Detection for Networks. In *Proceedings of the 13th USENIX conference on System Administration*; Seattle, WA, USA, 1999; pp. 229–238.

27. Zoumboulakis, M.; Roussos, G. Efficient Pattern Detection in Extremely Resource-Constrained Devices. Proceedings of 6th Annual IEEE Communications Society Conference on the Sensor, Mesh and Ad Hoc Communications and Networks (SECON 2009), Rome, Italy, 22– 26 June 2009; pp. 1–9.

28. PCRE: Perl Compatible Regular Expression. Available online: http:// www.pcre.org/(accessed on 30 November 2012).

29. Karp, R.M.; Rabin, M.O. Efficient randomized pattern-matching algorithms. *IBM J. Res. Dev.* **1987**, *31*, 249–260.

30. Polastre, J.; Szewczyk, R.; Culler, D. Telos: Enabling Ultra-low Power Wireless Research. Proceedings of Fourth International Symposium on the Information Processing in Sensor Networks (IPSN 2005), Los Angeles, CA, USA, 25– 27 April 2005; pp. 364–369.

11 CHAPTER

INTRUSION DETECTION OF NSM BASED DOS ATTACKS USING DATA MINING IN SMART GRID

Kyung Choi [1], Xinyi Chen [1], Shi Li [1], Mihui Kim [2], Kijoon Chae [1,*] and JungChan Na [3]

[1]*Department of Computer Science and Engineering, Ewha Womans University, Seoul 120-750, Korea*

[2]*Department of Computer Engineering, Hankyong National University, Anseong 456-749, Korea*

[3]*Managed Security Research Team, Electronics and Telecommunications Research Institute, Daejeon 305-700, Korea*

ABSTRACT

In this paper, we analyze the Network and System Management (NSM) requirements and NSM data objects for the intrusion detection of power systems; NSM is an IEC 62351-7 standard. We analyze a SYN flood attack and a buffer overflow attack to cause the Denial of Service (DoS) attack described in NSM. After mounting the attack in our attack testbed, we collect a data set, which is based on attributes for the attack. We then run several data mining methods with the data set using the Waikato Environment for Knowledge Analysis (WEKA). In the results, we select the decision tree algorithms with high detection rates, and choose key attributes in high level components of the trees. When we run several data mining methods again with the data set of chosen key attributes, the detection rates of most data mining methods are higher than before. We prove that our selected attack attributes, and the proposed detection process, are efficient and suitable for intrusion detection in the smart grid environment.

Keywords: Denial of Service (DoS) attack; Intrusion detection; Network and System Management (NSM); Smart grid; Data mining

1. INTRODUCTION

The promotion and industrial development of smart grid technology is accelerating worldwide. However, service construction and research on intrusion detection, one of the most important security considerations in the smart grid, is lacking. Moreover, generality and security by applying standards is required.

The smart grid industry, which is a fusion between traditional industries and emerging industries continues to grow with other technologies. At this time, the security of data transmission and application of standard technology is an indispensable element. In addition, compared to the existing power grids, the smart grid environment is a new business platform fused with information and communication technology. Security problems in information technology still exist in smart grids, and without guarantee of security the impacts are more serious than in the existing information technology. Cyber vulnerabilities and violations are actually increasing, and causing cases of damage. In particular, various types of attacks including physical attacks continue to increase, and intrusion detection methods for this are needed.

IEC 62351-7 [1] is a developing standard in International Electrotechnical Commission (IEC) Technical Committee (TC) 57 on security that is focused on developing standardized Network and System Management (NSM) object definitions for monitoring and controlling the information infrastructure. What is needed is the promotion of generality, extendibility and security through NSM, so that these international standards are applied to the smart grid intrusion detection service.

In this paper, we analyze the security requirements of NSM data objects, which are defined by IEC 62351-7 for intrusion detection, and analyze detection of SYN flood attacks and buffer overflow attacks as a Denial of Service (DoS) attack. For this, we construct a smart grid environment, and select attributes for analysis of those attacks. We then collect data of each attribute actually used in the trial attack. Subsequently, we make a comparative analysis of the data mining algorithms, to detect the attack efficiency. We prove that our selected attack attributes and the proposed detection process are efficient. The overall detection rate is enhanced after selection of key attributes. The rest of this paper is organized as follows: Section 2 presents the network and system management. Section 3 presents the attack method. Section 4 illustrates the system environment, and presents the proposed modeling and detection process. Section 5analyzes the experimental results, to evaluate the effectiveness of our scheme. Finally, we conclude this paper in Section 6.

2. NETWORK AND SYSTEM MANAGEMENT

The IEC smart grid standardization roadmap is based on the recent work of IEC SG3. IEC 62351 [2] addresses power systems management and associated information exchange—data and communication security. The scope of IEC 62351-7 focuses on network and system management (NSM) of the information infrastructure. The goal of this standard is to provide a service related to security requirements, of confidentiality, integrity, availability, and non-repudiation. As a protocol approach, it provides a security service in terms of two aspects. First, it protects information, using encryption from the origin point to the target point, or a secure electronic communication system by means of a protected power distribution system. Second, it provides end-to-end security.

2.1. Denial of Service Attack

The NSM requirements in IEC 62351-7 deal with detecting resource exhaustion as a DoS attack, for example, a SYN flood attack and a buffer overflow attack.

2.1.1. SYN Flood Attack

A SYN flood is a form of DoS attack, in which an attacker sends a succession of SYN requests to a target's system, in an attempt to consume enough server resources to make the system unresponsive to legitimate traffic [3].

The passive intrusion detection system (IDS) can detect rapidly increasing SYN flooding, based upon time and/or bandwidth consumption. The NSM is required to detect resource exhaustion attacks [1]:

- Exceeding the maximum number of connection permitted over the network;
- Count of number of connections actually in place over the network;
- Exceeding the maximum number of connections which can be in use simultaneously;
- Count of the number of connections in use simultaneously;
- Exceeding minimum/maximum idle time;
- Actual idle time over a specified time period;
- Exceeding CPU load limits;
- Exceeding memory usage limits;
- Below low level battery power limits or too high rate of change.

2.1.2. Buffer Overflow Attack

A buffer overflow is an anomaly where a program, while writing data to a buffer, overruns the buffer's boundary and overwrites adjacent memory [4]. The passive IDS is not intrinsically able to determine whether a buffer overflow attack is underway. This is especially true for IEC 61850 [5] and IEC 60870-6 TASE.2 [6] where the application buffer size is negotiated at runtime. However, the application/communication stack could be aware of such overruns [1]. The NSM is required to detect buffer overflow attacks:

- Number of buffer over runs;
- Number of buffer under runs;
- Audit ability to detect which source caused the buffer overflow/underflow.

3. ATTACK METHOD

In recent smart grid attack trends, the false data injection attack [7] proposed in 2009 has taken center stage as a new type of attack, and relevant work to respond to this treat is being proposed continuously [8,9,10].

Other attack papers are as follows. Chen *et al.* [11] investigate the use of Petri nets for modeling coordinated cyber-physical attacks on the smart grid. Yuan *et al.* [12] propose a Smart Grids Distributed Intrusion Detection System (SGDIDS), by developing and deploying an intelligent module—the Analyzing Module (AM)—in the multiple layers of smart grids. Xie *et al.* [13] are the first ones attempting to formalize the economic impact of malicious data attacks on real-time market operations. Mohsenian-Rad and Leon-Garcia [14] propose a cost-efficient load protection strategy, which minimizes the cost of the load protection. Lu *et al.* [15] use experiments to quantitatively evaluate the impact of DoS attacks on a power substation network with a distributed network protocol (DNP3). They prove that long DNP3 packets are more vulnerable to DoS attacks than are short DNP3 packets, and that the performance of the power network does not degrade gradually with the increase of the DoS attack intensity. Kundur *et al.* [16] propose an impact analysis framework, based on a graph-theoretic dynamical systems approach, for modeling the cyber-physical interactions. Little research exists on the topic of DoS attacks on smart grids. In particular, research of a similar type to a SYN flood attack and a buffer overflow attack has not been conducted.

4. INTRUSION DETECTION

This section covers the system environment for our experiments, and the modeling and detection process to find an efficient detection rate.

4.1. System Environment

We try a SYN flood attack and a buffer overflow attack to cause a DoS attack on a smart grid environment, and experiment to find an efficient data mining mechanism for intrusion detection. The attack test bed is as shown in Figure 1. Our attack test bed consists of the substation and local area network. The substation originally divides into three levels: process level including the I/O devices, intelligent sensors and actuators, bay level including the protection and control IEDs, and station level including the substation computer, operators desk, and the interfaces with outside the substation [15,17,18]. However, we depict only two levels: bay level and station level because our attack experiments only need two levels. We use a personal computer (PC) that is similar to an intelligent electronic device (IED)—CPU: 550 MHz, Memory: 256 MB—that is a target, and transmit an attack message using a general object oriented substation event (GOOSE) [19] data format.

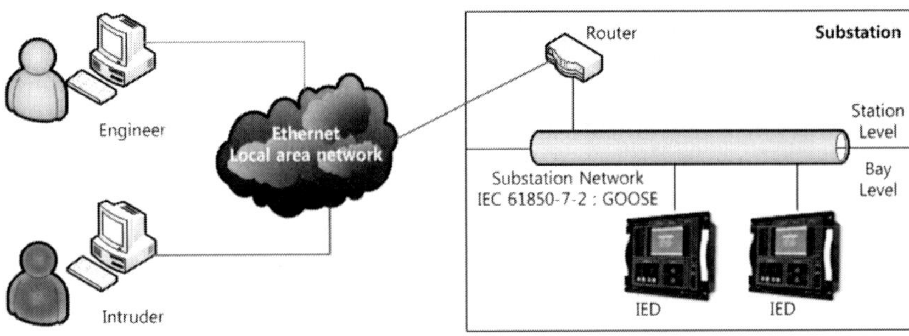

Figure 1. Attack test bed.

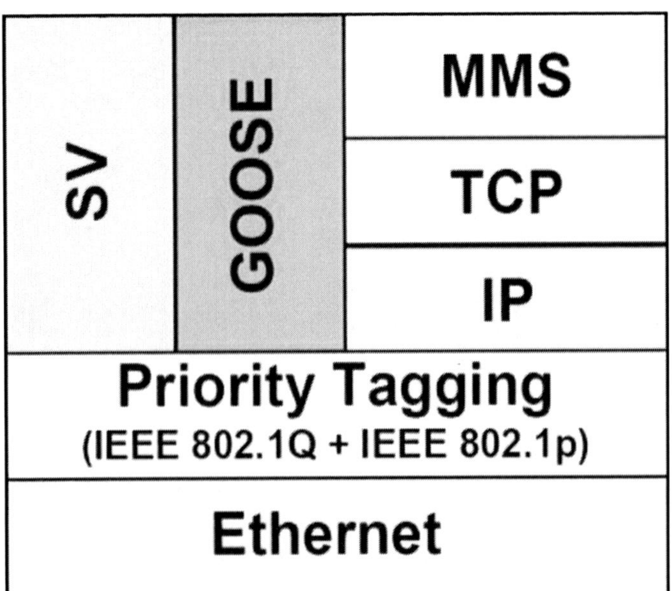

Figure 2. GOOSE communication stacks [20] (Copyright ABB).

An IED is a microprocessor-based controller of power system equipment. IEDs receive data from sensors and power equipment, and can issue control commands, such a tripping circuit breakers if they sense voltage, current, or frequency anomalies, or raise/lower voltage levels in order to maintain the desired level.

IEC 61850-7-2 [19] is a standard for communication between IEDs, and defines GOOSE communication stacks. GOOSE transmits trip commands and interlocking information with high priority frames, and ensures that these frames are handled with priority within all participating IEDs [20]. Figure 2 depicts a GOOSE communication stack.

An attacker tries a SYN flood attack and a buffer overflow attack using a GOOSE message through a router. We use a publish/subscribe communication model as a routing mechanism in this test system. The publish/subscribe communication model is designed for serving this special GOOSE communication requirements of the IEC 61850 standard. The publish/subscribe communication model is basically an added feature to the normal TCP/IP client/server model, any GOOSE message can be multicast by the sender (so called publisher) to the receiver(s) [so called subscriber(s)]. The main difference is that multicast group addresses are used instead of IP addresses [21]. The attacker tries a SYN flood attack and a buffer overflow attack by simultaneously sending a number of point to point GOOSE message through a router.

We analyze those attacks, and select data attributes for the use of data mining methods, and then collect data based on these attributes. Next, we run several data mining methods with collected data, using the Waikato Environment for Knowledge Analysis (WEKA) [22], and derive data mining methods showing the highest detection rate.

4.2. Modeling and Detection Process

We therefore implement a possible DoS attack in a smart grid environment, to experiment to find data mining methods with a better detection rate. Figure 3 depicts the experimental process.

4.2.1. Data Attribute Selection

We analyze attacks, and select data attributes for collection and detection. In this experiment, we analyze a SYN flood attack and a buffer overflow attack, and select data attributes for better detection of the SYN flood attack. First, we analyze the NSM requirements for each attack and select data attributes. After that, we monitor each attack with our monitoring tool during each attack experiment and select additional data attributes.

4.2.2. Attack Trial

We construct an attack test bed as shown in Figure 3, run a SYN flood attack and a buffer overflow attack, and then collect data related to data attributes.

4.2.3. Data Gathering

Before the attack attempts, we collect data related to data attributes in the normal status. After the attack attempts, we create a data set collected by the relevant data attributes.

4.2.4. Data Mining

The normal state data and attack state data are input into the WEKA program, all of the mining algorithms that are automatically selected are run, and the results are compared with the detection rate.

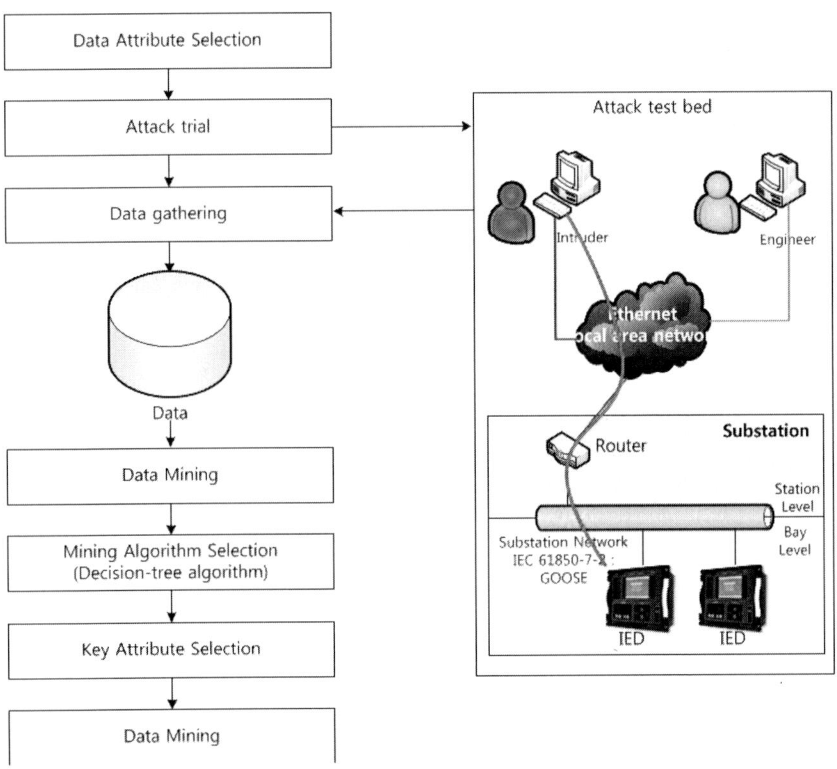

Figure 3. Experimental process.

4.2.5. Mining Algorithm Selection

After all mining algorithms in the previous step are compared and analyzed, decision tree algorithms with the best detection rate are selected.

4.2.6. Key Attribute Selection

Selected decision tree algorithms in the previous step show the decision tree with attributes as a result. We select key attributes in the top levels of the tree.

4.2.7. Data Mining

All mining algorithms are run with selected key attributes. After that, we compare and analyze between results, with key attributes, and results with all attributes.

5. EXPERIMENTAL RESULTS

In this section, the proposed experiments and the results of this experiment about two attacks show respectively depending on the process.

5.1. SYN Flood Attack

The SYN flood attack is a classic means of DoS attack. The SYN flood attack exploits the TCP's three-way handshake mechanism and its limitation in maintaining half-open connections. When a server receives a SYN request, it returns a SYN/ACK packet to the client. Until the SYN/ACK packet is acknowledged by the client, the connection remains in a half-open state for a period of up to the TCP connection timeout, which is typically set to 75 s. If a SYN request is spoofed, the victim server will never receive the final ACK packet to complete the three-way handshake. Flooding spoofed SYN requests can easily exhaust the victim server's backlog queue, causing all incoming SYN requests to be dropped [3].

5.1.1. Data Attribute Selection

Table 1 details the selected attributes after analysis of the SYN flood attack.

Table 1. SYN flood attack—attributes.

Attribute	Description
Traffic count	all count of packets during communication
Time of round trip (s)	the time that the traffic spent
Average packets/s	average count of packets per second
Average packets size	average packets size
Total transmission packets (bytes)	all count of bytes during communication
Average B/s	average count of byte per second
Average Mbit/s	average count of megabit per second
40–79 packets count	the count of packets which packet length is between 40 and 79
40–79 rate	average count of packets per ms (1 s = 10^3 ms); the packet length is between 40 and 79
40–79 percent	the percentage that the packet occupied : the packet length between 40 and 79
320–639 packets count	the count of packets which packet length is between 320 and 639
320–639 rate	average count of packets per ms; the packet length is between 320 and 639
320–639 percent	the percentage that the packet occupied : the packet length between 320 and 639
CPU percent	the usage of CPU when traffic stopped
Memory used (kB)	the memory used when traffic stopped
Buffer size (kB)	the buffer used when traffic stopped

5.1.2. Attack Trial and Data Gathering

The attacker tries 100 times to attack the victim IED. The attacker continually transmits a SYN packet to the victim IED. When the attack trial starts, the data relevant attributes are captured three times, once every minute, so a total of 300 data are collected. Normal data is also captured once every minute, so 300 normal data are captured. As a result, 300 normal state data and 300 attack state data are collected.

5.1.3. Data Mining

The 300 normal data and 300 attack data generated in the previous step are input into the WEKA, and then the available data mining algorithms are run to obtain the detection rate. The results are show in Table 2.

A total of 64 mining algorithms are performed and 30 algorithms including a tree. NBTree shows a 99.833% detection rate, followed by 11 algorithms that show a detection rate of 99.667%, four algorithms show 99.5%, three algorithms show 99.333%, one algorithm shows 98.833%, one algorithm shows 98%, one algorithm shows 96.833%, one algorithm shows 96.333%, two algorithms show 95.5%, thus 54 mining algorithms show a good detection rate. However, tree.SimpleCart and tree.BFTree show 54.833%, and eight algorithms including rules. ZeroR show the lowest detection rate of 50%. Figure 4 depicts all detection rates of the SYN flood attack.

Table 2. SYN flood attack—data mining results.

Detection rate	Mining algorithms
99.833%	bayes.BayesNet, bayes.NaiveBayesUpdateable, bayes.NaiveBayes, lazy.KStar, functions.SimpleLogistic, functions.RBFNetwork, functions.SMO, functions.Spegasos, lazy.LWL, lazy.IB1, lazy.IBk, meta.AdaBoostM1, meta.AttributeSelectedClassifier, rules.DTNB, meta.FilteredClassifier, meta.RandomCommitte, meta.RotationForest, meta.RandomSubSpace, meta.MultiBoostAB, meta.Bagging, rules.DecisionTable, tree.NBTree, tree.LADTree, tree.RandomForest, rules.Ridor, tree.DecisionSutmp, tree.ADTree (30)
99.667%	meta.OrdinalClassClassifier, tree.RandomTree, meta.nestedDataNearBalancedND, meta.nestedDichotomies.DataNearBalancedND, meta.ClassificationViaClustering, meta.END, rules.PART, meta.nestedDichotomies.ND, rules.Jrip, tree.J48graft, tree.J48 (11)
99.5%	misc.VFI, rules.ConjunctiveRule, misc.Decorate, meta.ThresholdSelector (4)
99.333%	meta.MultiClassClassifier, functions.Logistic, meta.Dagging (3)
98.833%	functions.VotedPerceptron (1)
98%	rules.NNge (1)
96.833%	tree.REPTree (1)
96.333%	misc.HyperPipes (1)
95.5%	meta.ClassificationViaRegression, rules.OneR (2)
54.833%	tree.BFTree, tree.SimpleCart (2)
50%	meta.CVParameterSelection, meta.MultiScheme, meta.RacedIncrementalLogitBoost, meta.Grading, meta.Stacking, meta.StackingC, meta.Vote, rules.ZeroR (8)

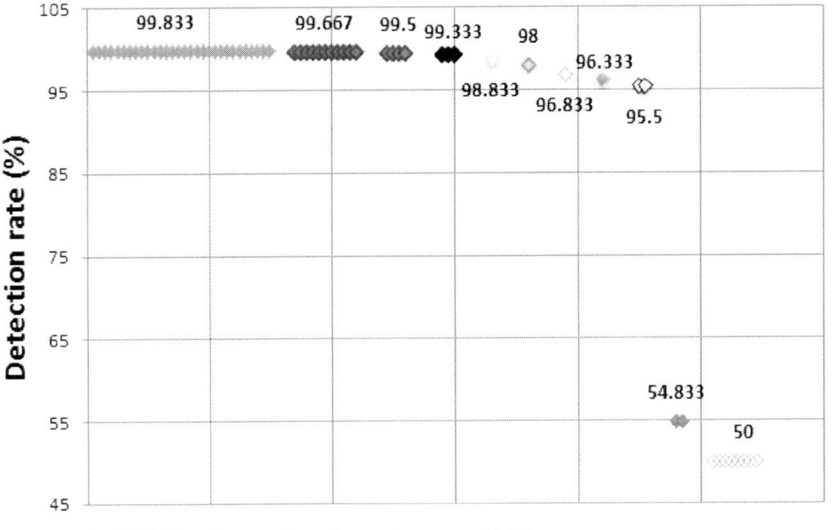

Figure 4. SYN flood attack—detection rate (all).

WEKA classifies the data mining algorithms as follows.

- Bayes: bayes classifier;
- Functions: neural network and support vector machines (SVM);
- Lazy: instance based classifier;
- Meta: combing algorithm;
- Misc: miscellaneous classifier including hyperpipes and voting feature intervals (VFI);
- Rules: rule-based classifier;
- Tree: decision tree classifier;

5.1.4. Mining Algorithm Selection and Key Attribute Selection

The Decision tree algorithms with the best detection rate in the above procedure are selected, and those algorithms show the decision tree as a result. Tree.ADTree and tree.LADTree are chosen.

An alternating decision tree (ADTree) [23] is a machine learning method for classification. It is a class for generating an alternating decision tree. The underlying learning algorithm for ADTrees is AdaBoost. LADTree [24] is a class for generating a multi-class decision tree, using LogitBoost strategy.

Traffic count, memory used, time of round trip (s), average packets size, average B/s, average packets/s are chosen as key attributes, as shown in Figure 5. When LADTree is performed, traffic count, average packets/s, memory used, 40–79 packets count, time of round trip (s), 320–639 percent, and average B/s are chosen as key attributes. Figure 6 depicts the results of LADTree.

5.1.5. Data Mining

All possible mining algorithms are performed with selected key attributes, using ADTree in the previous procedure. The results are as shown in Table 3. Three algorithms show a 100% detection rate, 29 algorithms show 99.833%, 10 algorithms show 99.667%, two algorithms show 99.5%, one algorithm shows 99.333%. The overall detection rate is better than before.

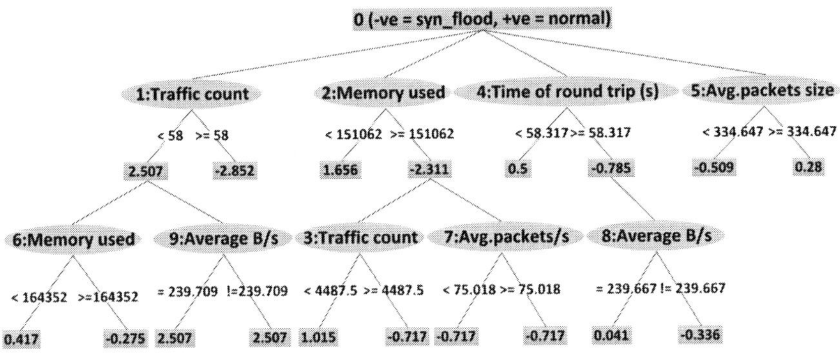

Figure 5. A result of ADTree.

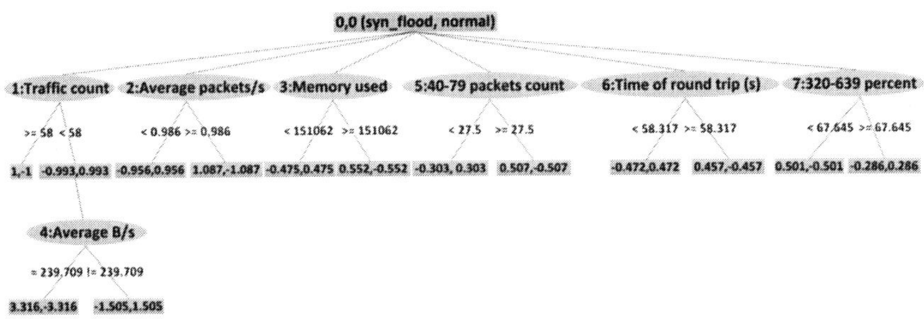

Figure 6. A result of LADTree.

Next, all possible mining algorithms are performed with selected key attributes, using LADTree in the previous procedure; traffic count, average packets/s, memory used, 40–79 packets count, time of round trip (s), 320–639 percent, and average byte/s.

As Figure 8 shows, the results are similar to the results of ADTree. Three algorithms show a 100% detection rate, 29 algorithms show 99.833%, 11 algorithms show 99.667%, two algorithms show 99.5%, two algorithms show 99.167%, one algorithm shows 98.833%, one algorithm shows 98%, one algorithm shows 96.833%, one algorithm shows 96.5%, one algorithm shows 95.5%, and one algorithm shows 87.333%. The overall detection rate is better than before. The results of two algorithms are 54.833%, and the results of eight algorithms are 50%. The results of 10 algorithms are significantly low.

Table 3. SYN flood attack—mining results with ADTree selection attributes.

Detection rate	Mining algorithms
100%	functions.RBFNetwork, lazy.IBk, lazy.IB1 (3)
99.833%	bayes.BayesNet, bayes.NaiveBayesUpdateable, bayes.NaiveBayes, lazy.LWL, functions.SimpleLogistic, functions.SMO, functions.Spegasos, meta.AdaBoostM1, lazy.KStar, meta.Bagging, meta.AttributeSelectedClassifier, meta.Dagging, meta.ClassificationViaClustering, meta.FilteredClassifier, meta.RotationForest, meta.MultiBoostAB, meta.RandomCommitte, meta.RandomSubSpace, rules.Jrip, rules.DecisionTable, tree.ADTree, tree.DecisionSutmp, tree.RandomForest, tree.LADTree, tree.NBTree, tree.LMT, tree.FT, rules.DTNB (29)
99.667%	meta.OrdinalClassClassifier, meta.nestedDichotomies.ClassBalancedND, meta.END, meta.nestedDichotomies.DataNearBalancedND, meta.nestedDichotomies.ND, meta.Decorate, rules.PART, rules.Ridor, tree.J48graft, tree.J48 (10)
99.5%	misc.VFI, rules.ConjunctiveRule (2)
99.333%	meta.ThresholdSelector (1)
99.167%	functions.Logistic, meta.MultiClassClassifier (2)
98.5%	tree.RandomTree (1)
98%	rules.NNge (1)
96.833%	tree.REPTree (1)
96.5%	misc.HyperPipes (1)
95.5%	meta.ClassificationViaRegression, rules.OneR (2)
86.333%	functions.VotedPerceptron (1)
54.833%	tree.BFTree, tree.SimpleCart (2)
50%	meta.CVParameterSelection, meta.RacedIncrementalLogitBoost, meta.Grading, meta.Stacking, meta.StackingC, meta.Vote, meta.MultiScheme, rules.ZeroR (8)

Figure 7 depicts the result after key attributes selection using ADTree.

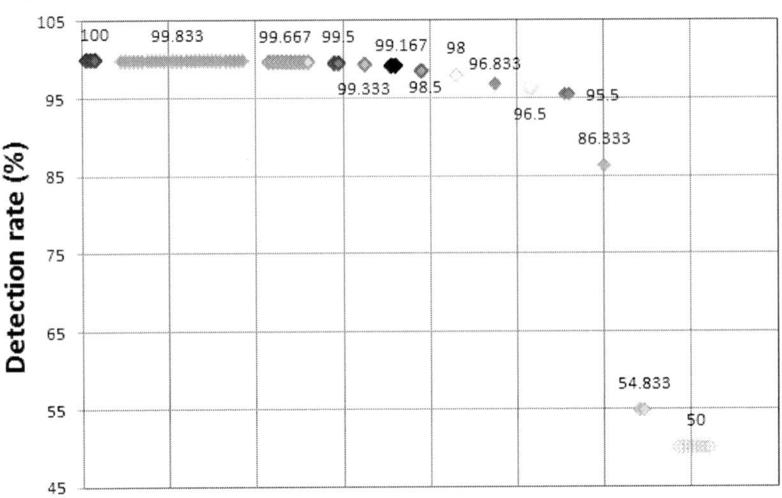

Figure 7. SYN flood attack—detection rate (after ADTree).

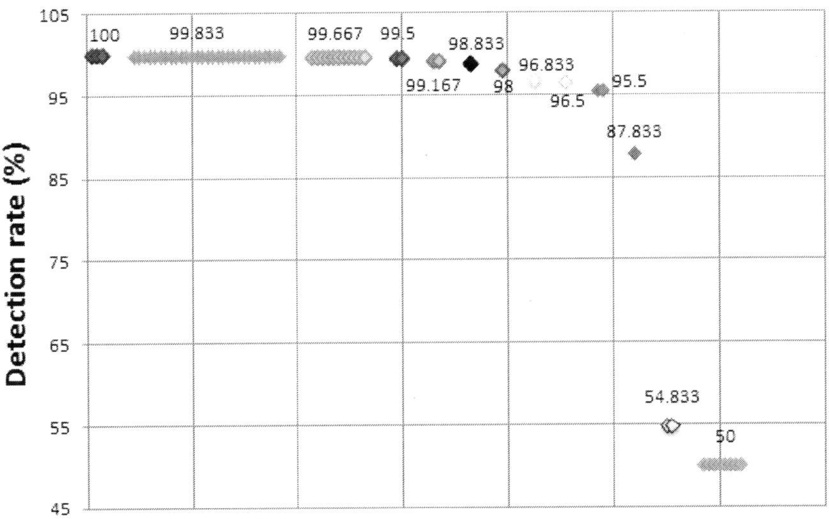

Figure 8. SYN flood attack—detection rate (after LADTree).

5.2. Buffer Overflow Attack

A buffer overflow is an attack that could be used by a cracker to overruns the buffers boundary and overwrites adjacent memory while writing data to a buffer. Buffer overflow attacks can be triggered by inputs that are designed to execute code, or alter the way the program operates. This may result in the DoS to undermine the availability, including a modification of data to compromise the integrity and confidentiality. In this experiment, we focus on the denial of service attack causing the buffer overflow. An attacker transmits a malicious code to a target intelligent electronic device (IED) system that randomly writes oversize data due to insufficient bounds checking. We collect the data necessary for the detection of attacks.

5.2.1. Data Attribute Selection

The following details the selected attributes after we analyze the buffer overflow attack.

- Traffic count, Time of round trip(s), Average packets/s, Average packets size, Total transmission packets (bytes), Average B/s, Average Mbit/s, 40–79 packets count, 40–79 rate, 40–79 percent, 320–639 packets count, 320–639 rate, 320–639 percent, CPU percent, Memory used (kB), Buffer used (kB), Transmission payload size (bytes).

Two kinds of attributes, buffer used (kB) and transmission payload size (bytes), are added when compared with the SYN flood attack.

5.2.2. Attack Trial and Data Gathering

The attacker tries 100 times to attack the victim IED. The attacker transmits a malicious code to the victim IED that randomly writes oversize data due to insufficient bounds checking, and run the malicious code. When the attack trial starts, the data relevant attributes are captured one time, once every minute, and thus a total of 100 data are collected. Normal data is also captured once every minute, and thus 100 normal data are captured. As a result, 100 normal state data and 100 attack state data are collected.

Table 4. Buffer overflow attack—data mining results.

Detection rate	Mining algorithms
100%	tree.RandomForest, tree.LADTree, tree.FT, tree.LMT, tree.J48, tree.ADTree, tree.J48graft, tree.DecisionStump, tree.REPTree, tree.BFTree, tree.SimpleCart, rules.DecisionTable, rules.Jrip, rules.DTNB, rules.Ridor, rules.PART, rules.NNge, rules.ConjunctiveRule, rules.OneR, misc.VFI, meta.AttributeSelectedClassifier, meta.Bagging, meta.AdaBoostM1, meta.ClassificationViaRegression, meta.END, meta.nestedDichotomies.ClassBalancedND, meta.RandomCommitte, meta.LogitBoost, meta.OrdinalClassClassifier, metalnestedDichotomies.ND, meta.RandomSubSpace, meta.MultiBoostAB,meta.nestedDichomies.DataNearBalancedND, meta.RotationForest, meta.FilteredClassifier, functions.SMO, functions.Spegasos, functions.SimpleLogistic, functions.MultilayerPerceptron, lazy.LWL (40)
99.5%	meta.MulticlassClassifier, lazy.IB1, lazy.IBk, functions.Logistic (4)
99%	tree.NBTree, tree.RandomTree (2)
98.85%	misc.HyperPipes, functions.RBFNetwork (2)
97.5%	meta.Cecorate, lazy.KStar, bayes.BayerNet (3)
97%	meta.Dagging, bayes.NaiveBayesUpdateable, bayses.NaiveBayes (3)
96.5%	bayes.BayesianLogisticRegression, bayes.NaiveBayesMultinomialUpdateable, bayes.ComplementNaiveBayes, bayes.NaiveBayesmultinomial, meta.ClassificationViaClustering (5)
96%	functions.VotedPerceptron (1)
90%	meta.ThresholdSelector (1)
50%	rules.ZeroR, meta.CVParameterSelection, meta.Grading, meta.MultiScheme, meta.Stacking, meta.RacedIncrementalLogitBoost, meta.Vote, meta.StackingC, bayes.DMNBtext (9)

5.2.3. Data Mining

The 100 normal data and 100 attack data generated in the previous step are input into the WEKA, and then the available data mining algorithms are run to obtain the detection rate. The results are show in Table 4.

A total of 70 mining algorithms are performed and 40 algorithms including a tree. RandomForest show a 100% detection rate, followed by four algorithms that show a detection rate of 99.5%, two algorithms show 99%, two algorithms show 98.85%, three algorithms show 97.5%, three algorithms show 97%, five algorithms show 96.5%, one algorithm shows 96%, one algorithm shows 90%, thus 61 mining algorithms show a good detection rate. However, nine algorithms including rules.ZeroR show the lowest detection rate of 50%. Figure 9 depicts all detection rates of the buffer overflow attack.

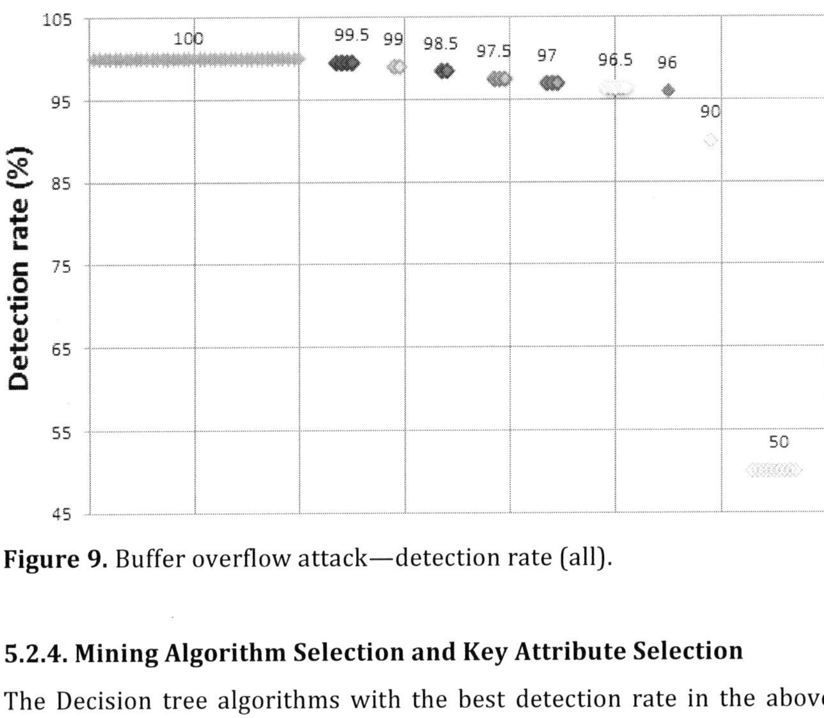

Figure 9. Buffer overflow attack—detection rate (all).

5.2.4. Mining Algorithm Selection and Key Attribute Selection

The Decision tree algorithms with the best detection rate in the above procedure are selected, and those algorithms show the decision tree as a result. Tree.ADTree, tree.RamdomTree, tree.REPTree, tree.J48, tree.J48graft, and tree.LADTree are chosen.

RandomTree [25] is a class for constructing a tree that considers K randomly chosen attributes at each node. REPTree [26] is a fast decision tree learner. It builds a decision/regression tree using information gain/variance and prunes it using reduced-error pruning (with backfitting). J48 [27] is a class for generating a pruned or unpruned C4.5 decision tree. C4.5 is an extension of Quinlan's earlier ID3 algorithm. The decision trees generated by C4.5 can be used for classification, and for this reason, C4.5 is often referred to as a statistical classifier. J48graft [28] is a class for generating a grafted (pruned or unpruned) C4.5 decision tree.

Figure 10 depicts the result after key attributes selection—average packets size—using ADTree, RandomTree, and REPTree. Figure 11 depicts the result after key attributes selection—total transmission packets—using J48 and J48graft. The key attributes of LADTree are selected with average packets size and total transmission packets. The result is as shown in Figure 12.

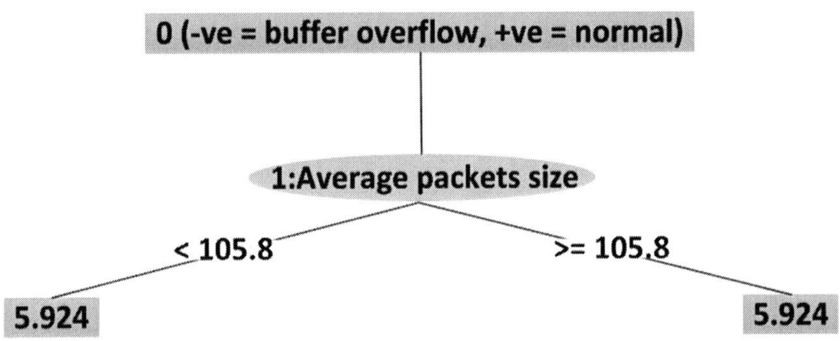

Figure 10. A result of ADTree.

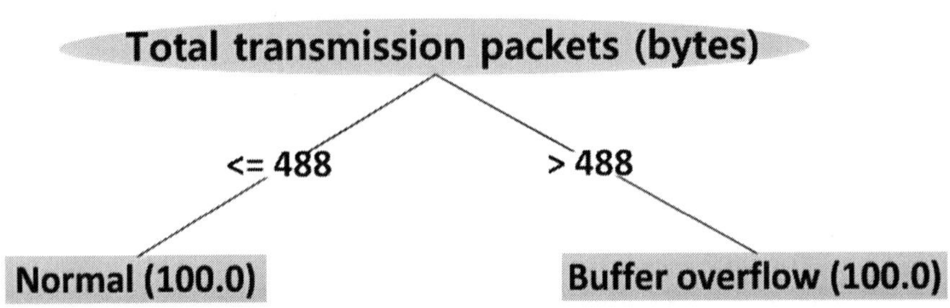

Figure 11. A result of J48.

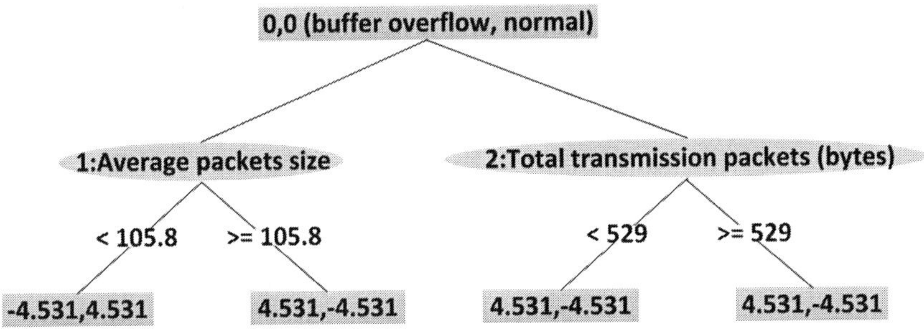

Figure 12. A result of LADTree.

5.2.5. Data Mining

All possible mining algorithms are performed with average packets size, selected key attributes, using ADTree, RandomTree, and REPTree in the previous procedure. The results are as shown inTable 5. 57 algorithms show a 100% detection rate, 14 algorithms show 50%. The overall detection rate is better than before.

Table 5. Buffer overflow attack—mining results with ADTree, RandomTree, REPTree selection attributes.

Detection rate	Mining algorithms
100%	tree.RandomForest, tree.LADTree, tree.FT, tree.LMT, tree.J48, tree.ADTree, tree.J48graft, tree.REPTree, tree.SimpleCart, tree.BFTree, tree.NBTree, tree.RandomTree, rules.DTNB, tree.DecisionStump, rules.DecisionTable, rules.Ridor, rules.Jrip, misc.VFI, rules.PART, rules.ConjunctiveRule, rules.NNge, rules.OneR, misc.HyperPipes, meta.OrdinalClassClassifier, meta.AdaBoostM1, meta.Decorate, meta.END, meta.AttributeSelectedClassifier, meta.Bagging, functions.SMO, meta.ClassificationViaRegression, meta.FilteredClassifier, meta.MultiBoostAB, meta.ClassficationViaClustering, meta.multiClassClassifier, meta.RandomCommitte, meta.nestedDichotomies.ClassBalancedND, meta.LogitBoost, meta.RandomSubSpace, meta.nestedDichotomies.ND, meta.Dagging, meta.ThresholdSelector, functions.Logistic, meta.nestedDichotomies.DataNearBalancedND, meta.RotationForest, bayes.BayesNet, functions.MultilayerPerceptron, functions.SimpleLogistic, functions.Spegasos, functions.RBFNetwork, bayes.NaiveBayes, lazy.IBk, bayes.NaiveBayesUpdateable, lazy.KStar, lazy.LWL, bayes.NaiveBayesSimple (57)
50%	meta.MultiScheme, meta.CVParameterSelection, meta.Grading, meta.Vote, bayes.BayesianLogisticRegression, functions.VotedPerceptron, meta.StackingC, bayes.ComplementNaiveBayes, meta.RacedIncrementalLogitBoost, meta.Stacking, bayes.NaiveBayesmultinomialUpdateable, bayes.NaiveBayesMultinomial, rules.ZeroR, bayes.DMNBtext (14)

After selection of key attributes bayes.NaiveBayesSimple is run in addition. Figure 13 depicts the results of this execution. Next, all possible mining algorithms are performed with total transmission packet, selected key attributes, using J48, J48graft the previous procedure. The results are as shown in Table 5. Fifty seven algorithms show a 100% detection rate, 14 algorithms show 50%. The overall detection rate is better than before. Finally, all possible mining algorithms are executed with average packet size and total transmission packet size. The results are similar to those in Table 5.

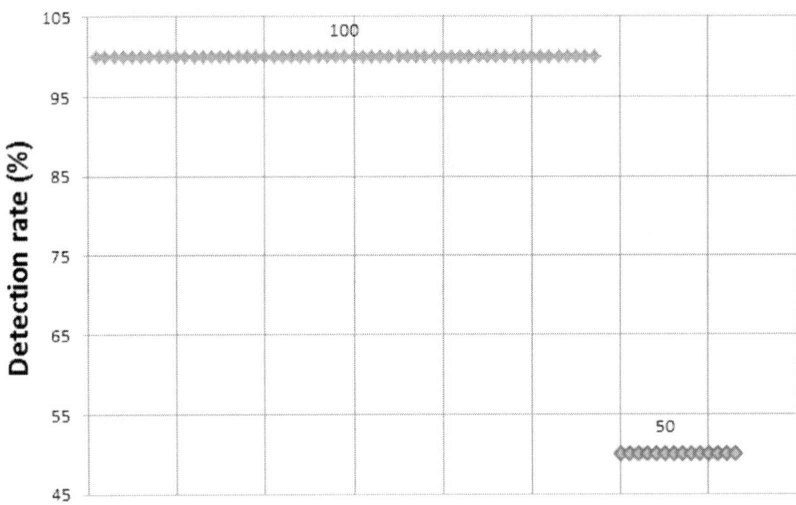

Figure 13. Buffer overflow attack—detection rate (after ADTree, RandomTree, REPTree).

5.3. Discussion for Scalability Issue

This paper's main contribution is to propose a way to make a detection model using two mining algorithms to improve the efficiency and performance. The first algorithm selects key attributes among candidate attributes. Next, the second algorithm actually makes the detection model with data for selected key attributes outputting from the first algorithm. The final detection model improves detection performance because it is made with data for only a few key attributes, and modeling time reduces through modeling with data for a few key attributes. After that, detection can be performed through detection model in real time.

In our methodology also, the scalability issue is related. The more attacks that are considered to be detected, the more candidate attributes are input in the first algorithm. However, as shown in the experimental results, our methodology can reduce modeling time that can take a lot of time, through selecting a few key attributes among candidate attributes. As experimental results, the average three key attributes of the average 16 candidate attribute was selected. Moreover, this modeling is irrelevant to the detection time because of performing in the offline. If the detection model is made, the detection is performed in real time. As a result, our proposed methodology is not strongly influenced by scalability problem.

6. CONCLUSIONS

This work analyzed Network and System Management (NSM) requirements and NSM data objects for intrusion detection in power systems. We analyzed a SYN flood attack and a buffer overflow attack to cause a DoS attack, as described in NSM. We proposed the data attributes for the SYN flood attack and the buffer overflow attack, and the detection process to find efficient data mining methods for those attacks. In our experiments, several data mining methods showed good detection rates. Moreover, after key attributes selection, the overall detection rate is better than before.

In case of SYN flood attack, a total of 64 mining algorithms are executed with the selected key attributes. Thirty algorithms show 99.833% detection rate and 54 algorithms show more than 90% detection rate. Next, the decision tree algorithms with the best detection rate are selected, and those algorithms show the decision tree as a result. Sixty four algorithms are performed with selected key attributes using result of decision tree. Three algorithms show a 100% detection rate, 29 algorithms show 99.833%.

As similar with SYN flood attack, a total of 70 algorithms are executed with selected key attributes, and 40 algorithms show 100% detection rate. Sixty one algorithms show more than 90% detection rates. Again, the decision tree algorithms with the best detection rate are selected, and key attributes also selected as a result. A total of 71 algorithms are performed, and 57 algorithms show 100% detection rate, 14 algorithms show 50%, the overall detection rate is enhanced after selection of key attributes. We prove that our selected attack attributes and the proposed detection process are efficient, and suitable for intrusion detection in smart grid environments.

ACKNOWLEDGMENTS

This work was supported by the Power Generation and Electricity Delivery of the Korea Institute of Energy Technology Evaluation and Planning (KETEP) Grant funded by the Korea government Ministry of Knowledge Economy (No. 2011101050001B) and in part by the Ewha Global Top 5 Grand 2011 of Ewha Womans University, and World Class University Program (R33-10085) through National Research Foundation of Korea funded by the Ministry of Education, Science and Technology. It was also in part supported by Basic Science Research Program through the National Research Foundation of Korea (NRF) funded by the Ministry of Education, Science and Technology (2012-0004279).

REFERENCES

1. *IEC 62351-7 TS Ed.1: Power Systems Management and Associated Information Exchange—Data and Communications Security—Part 7: Network and System Management (NSM) Data Object Models*; International Electrotechnical Commission (IEC): Geneva; Switzerland, 2009.
2. *IEC 62351: Power Systems Management and Associated Information Exchange—Data and Communications Security*; International Electrotechnical Commission (IEC): Geneva; Switzerland, 2007.
3. Wikipedia. SYN Flood. Available online: http:// en.wikipedia.org /wiki/Syn_flood (accessed on 12 October 2012).
4. Wikipedia. Buffer Overflow. Available online: http:// en.wikipedia.org /wiki/Buffer_Overflow(accessed on 12 October 2012).
5. *IEC 61850: Communication Networks and Systems in Substations*; International Electrotechnical Commission (IEC): Geneva; Switzerland, 2003.
6. *IEC 60870-6-503 Ed2.0 : Telecontrol Equipment and Systems—Part 6-503 : Telecontrol Protocols Compatible with ISO Standards and ITU-T Recommendations—TASE.2 Service and Protocol*;

International Electrotechnical Commission (IEC): Geneva; Switzerland, 2009.

7. Liu, Y.; Ning, P.; Reiter, M.K. False data injection attacks against state estimation in electric power grids. *ACM Trans. Info. Syst. Sec.* 2011, *14*, 13:1–13:33.

8. Dán, G.; Sandberg, H. Stealth attacks and protection schemes for state estimators in power systems. In Proceedings of 1st IEEE International Conference on Smart Grid Communications, Gaithersburg, MD, USA, 4–6 October 2010; pp. 214–219.

9. Kosut, O.; Jia, L.; Thomas, R.J.; Tong, L. Malicious data attacks on the smart grid. *IEEE Trans. Smart Grid* 2011, *2*, 645–658.

10. Zhang, Y.; Wang, L.; Sun, W.; Green, R.C.; Alam, M. Artificial immune system based intrusion detection in a distributed hierarchical network architecture of smart grid. In Proceedings of IEEE Power and Energy Society General Meeting, Detroit, MI, USA, 24–29 July 2011; pp. 1–8.

11. Chen, T.M.; Sanchez-Aarnoutse, J.C.; Buford, J. Petri Net modeling of cyber-physical attacks on smart grid. *IEEE Trans. Smart Grid* 2011, *2*, 741–749.

12. Yuan, Y.; Li, Z.; Ren, K. Modeling load redistribution attacks in power systems. *IEEE Trans. Smart Grid* 2011, *2*, 382–390.

13. Xie, L.; Mo, Y.; Sinopoli, B. Integrity data attacks in power market operations. *IEEE Trans. Smart Grid* 2011, *2*, 659–666.

14. Mohsenian-Rad, A.H.; Leon-Garcia, A. Distributed internet-based load altering attacks against smart power grids. *IEEE Trans. Smart Grid* 2011, *2*, 667–674.

15. Lu, Z.; Lu, X.; Wang, W.; Wang, C. Review and evaluation of security threats on the communication networks in the smart grid. In Proceedings of IEEE Military Communications Conference (Milcom 2010), San Jose, CA, USA, 31 October–3 November 2010; pp. 1830–1835.

16. Kundur, D.; Feng, X.; Liu, S.; Zourntos, T.; Butler-Purry, K. Towards a framework for cyber attack impact analysis of the electric smart grid. In Proceedings of 1st IEEE International Conference on Smart Grid Communications, Gaithersburg, MD, USA, 4–6 October 2010; pp. 244–249.

17. Fries, S.; Hof, H.J.; Seewald, M. Enhancing IEC 62351 to improve security for energy automation in smart grid environments. In Proceedings of 5th International Conference on Internet and Web Applications and Services, Barcelona, Spain, 9–15 May 2010; pp. 135–142.

18. Mohaghi, S. A fuzzy cognitive map for data integrity assessment in a IEC 61850 based substation. In. In Proceedings of IEEE Power and Energy Society General Meeting, Minneapolis, MN, USA, 25–29 July 2010; pp. 1–7.

19. *IEC 61850-7-2: Communication Networks and Systems in Substations—Part 7-2: Basic Communication Structure for Substation and Feeder Equipment—Abstract Communication Service Interface (ACSI)*; International Electrotechnical Commission (IEC): Geneva; Switzerland, 2010.

20. Engler, F.; Kern, T.; Andersson, L.; Kruimer, B.; Schimmel, G.; Schwarz, K. IEC 61850 based digital communication as interface to the primary equipment. In Proceeding of the International Council on Large Electric Systems (CIGRÉ) Sessions 2004, Paris, France, 29 August–3 September 2004; pp. B3-205:1–B3-205:8.

21. Ozansoy, C.R. *Design & Implementation of a Universal Communications Processor for Substation Integration, Automation and Protection*; Victoria University Press: Melbourne, Australia, 2006.

22. *Weka 3: Data Mining Software in Java*; University of Waikato: Hamilton, New Zealand, 2005; Available online: http://www.cs.waikato.ac.nz/ml/weka/ (accessed on 12 October 2012).

23. Freund, Y.; Mason, L. The alternating decision tree learning algorithm. In Proceedings of the 16th International Conference on Machine Learning (ICML-99), Bled, Slovenia, 27–30 June 1999; Volume 54, pp. 124–133.

24. Holmes, G.; Pfahringer, B.; Kirkby, R.; Frank, E.; Hall, M. Multiclass alternating decision trees. In Proceeding of the ECML 13th European Conference on Machine Learning, Helsinki, Finland, 19–23 August 2002; pp. 161–172.

25. Amit, Y.; Geman, D. Shape quantization and recognition with randomized trees. *Neural Comput.* 1997, *9*, 1545–1588.

26. Su, J.; Zhang, H. A fast decision tree learning algorithm. In Proceeding of the AAAI 21st National Conference on Artificial Intelligence, Boston, MA, USA, 16–20 July 2006; pp. 500–505.

27. Quinlan, J.R. *C4.5: Programs for Machine Learning*; Morgan Kaufmann: San Francisco, CA, USA, 1993.

28. Webb, G.I. Decision tree grafting from the all-tests-but-one partition. In Proceeding of the IJCAI 6th International Joint Conference on Artificial Intelligence, Stockholm, Sweden, 31 July–6 August 1999; pp. 702–707.

12

CHAPTER

A NETWORK INTRUSION DETECTION MODEL BASED ON IMMUNE MULTI-AGENT

Nian LIU[1,2], Sunjun LIU[3], Rui LI[3], Yong LIU[4]

[1]*College of Computer Science, Sichuan University, Chengdu, Sichuan, China*

[2]*School of Electrical Engineering and Information, Sichuan University, Chengdu, Sichuan, China*

[3]*The software engineering college of Chengdu University of Information Technology, Chengdu, Sichuan, China*

[4]*Chengdu Institute of Computer Applications, Chinese Academy of Sciences, Chengdu Sichuan, China*

ABSTRACT

A new network intrusion detection model based on immune multi-agent theory is established and the concept of multi-agents is advanced to realize the logical structure and running mechanism of immune multi-agent as well as multi-level and distributed detection mechanism against network intrusion, using the adaptability, diversity and memory properties of artificial immune algorithm and combing the robustness and distributed character of multi-agents system structure. The experiment results conclude that this system is working pretty well in network security detection.

Keywords: Artificial Immune, Intrusion Detection, Multi-Agent System,

1. INTRODUCTION

Along with the rapid development of network technology and fast upgrade of network attack technologies network security has become the focus of this age. However, current intrusion detection technologies [1,2], like statistical analysis, characteristics analysis and expert system etc, can not meet well all the needs. Firstly, the lack of adaptability makes it difficult to detect unknown attacks; Secondly, the lack of robustness leaves each part isolated without communication. Therefore, the building of a detection system with adaptability and robustness is in pressing needs.

Biological Immune System [3] identifies and eliminates foreign bodies intruding into the organism by immune cells. From the aspect of information processing, BIS is a distributed autonomic system and its selflearning, adaptability and robustness serve as important inspirations for the solving of network security problems. In 1974, Jerne [3] brought forth the first mathematical model in immune system, later in 1994, Forrest [4] put forward the concept of computer immune system for the detection of network intrusion, and up to now the artificial immune system based on biological immune theory has been applied extensively in network security.

Agent [5] refers to such entity as possessing perceiving, analyzing and reasoning mechanism. Multi-agent [5,6] system, with fairly strong distributed character, robustness and coordination, realizes problem solving under complicated environment by harmonizing the interaction and cooperation among various separate Agents.

In this article, a new network intrusion detection model based on immune multi-agent (NIDIMA) is established and the concept of immune multi-agent is advanced in the building of logical structure and running mechanism of immune multi-agent to realize multi-level and distributed detection mechanism against network intrusion. This model provides a new way in network safeguard and proves to be an effective solution to network security detection throughout the experiment.

2. SYSTEM PRINCIPLES OF THE DETECTION MODEL BASED ON IMMUNE MULTI-AGENT

Apart from inheriting the original characteristics of Agent, immune agent also has the characters of evolution, diversity, tolerance and detection [7,8] properties etc.

1) Evolution: Following the evolution law, IA activates antibodies, which can effectively recognize antigens, into higher form, while eliminates the inefficient one. In this way, the self-learning ability of detection is realized.

2) Diversity: The matching of antibodies and antigens adopts fuzzy matching [9], with just the need to meet the preset value. The incomplete matching, which realizes the diversity of recognition, enables immune antibodies to recognize various kinds of antigens and in this way, it can produce antibodies covering the whole form space in theory.

3) Tolerability: Immune tolerability refers to the non-response status of immune cells towards the peculiarities revealed by certain kinds of antigens [10]. The tolerability of IA is of great significance in the maintaining and balancing of the model.

4) Detection property: The immune system transmits the produced immune cells within each organ in vivo to increase immunologic competence. Network security model based on this mechanism is of great detection ability.

Combined with multi-agent and AIS technology, the detection model constitutes a multi-direction and multi-level intelligent network security model, with its mapping relationship with BIS model as shown in **Table 1**, and its system structure diagram as shown in **Figure 1**.

The model adopts large-scale and distributed system structure, and a series of network situation awareness agents and a network security situation evaluation agent is deployed in target networks and its host computer firstly.

Security situation evaluation agent gathers information about the security situation of subordinate subnets and host computers from each security situation awareness agent to evaluate about the whole integrated risks to the whole network, and the information includes the type, quantity, strength and harmfulness of the attacks.

The network security situation awareness agent shown in **Figure 1** is itself a sub-network security situation awareness system, defined by recursion, and it mainly monitors on the sub-network security situation within its control, and specifically speaking, real-time monitor on the type, strength and harmfulness of attacks suffered by sub-network. Because there might as well be subnets under subnets, sub-network security situation awareness agents may be composed of sub-network security situation awareness agents at lower level. Eventually, security situation awareness agents, that monitor the specific host computer, are made up of intrusion detection and security situation evaluation of the host computer.

In this architecture, IA distributed at host computer node starts to recognize the intruded events at first, and in case unknown attacks are discovered through learning and memory, information will then be sent to corresponding SMC, while vaccines that has identified new attacks will be distributed to each node within the same network segment to improve the intrusion defense capability of each node. SMC makes analysis on the intrusion information sent by each IA in the network segment and SMC of suffered network segment will send vaccines to other non-intruded network segments for early warnings for the realization of whole detection.

Table 1. The relationship between the BIS and the NIDIMA.

Biological immune system	Network intrusion detection system
Organism	Network
Organ	Network segment
Cell	Host computer
Vaccine distribution	The transmission of intrusion information
Antigen	The binary character string feature-extracted from IP packets
B Cell, Antibody	Antibodies represented in binary character string
Cell clone	Duplication of antibody

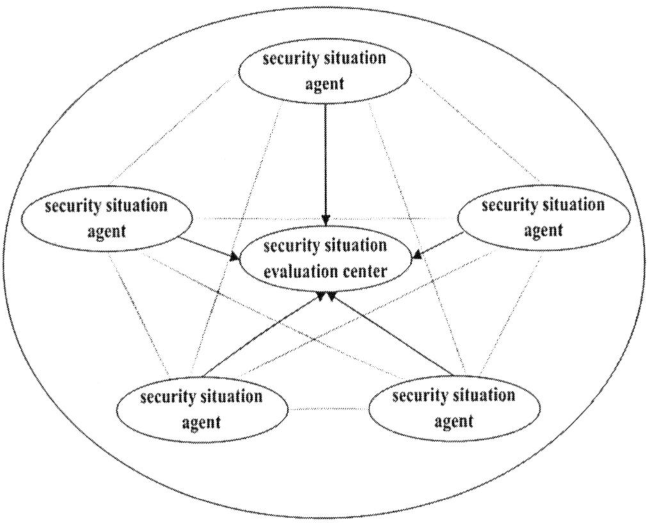

Figure 1. Architecture of NIDIMA.

3. SYSTEM MECHANISM OF THE NETWORK INTRUSION MODEL BASED ON IMMUNE MULTI-AGENT

In **Figure 2**, the logical structure of IA is shown, which includes self antigens, immature immune antibodies, mature immune antibodies and memory immune antibodies etc. The working procedures involve two interplaying and concurrent circulations, which are the circulation of immune antibodies' detection of external antigens and the circulation of immune antibodies' evolution.

3.1. The Definition of Immune Elements

Definition 1: Antigens are binary character strings in the length of l that are feature-extracted from network IP data packets. Let $U=\{0, 1\}^l$ $(l>0)$, antigen assembly Ag Ì U, it mainly includes IP address, port and protocol type etc.

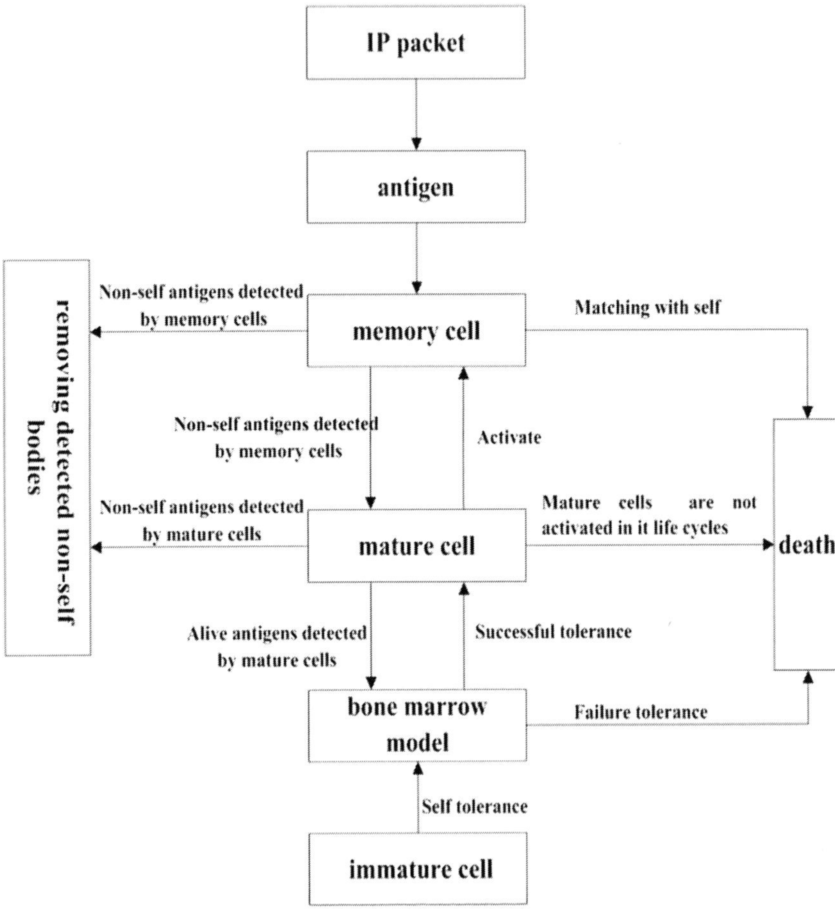

Figure 2. Architecture of immune agent.

$$Ag = \{<a,b>| a \in D \wedge b \in \Psi \wedge |a| = l \wedge a = APCs(b)\} \tag{1}$$

Definition 2: The antigen assembly Ag is classified into two substes of self assembly Self (normal network behavior) and non-self assembly Nonself (abnormal network behavior):

Self È NonSelf = Ag, Self Ç Nonself = Æ

Antibodies and antigens have binary character strings of the same features and length, the definition of antibody assembly B Ì U :

$$B=\{Ab|\ Ab=<s,age,count,ag>\} \tag{2}$$

Antibody Ab is a quadruple, among which s means binary string in the length of l, age is the age of antibody, count is the quantity of antigens matched with antibodies, ag is the antigens that are detected by the antibodies. Antibodies are classified into three categories: mature antibodies, memory antibodies and immature antibodies. Mature antibodies, tolerable to self bodies, refer to the antibodies that are not activated by antigens, mature antibodies assembly T_{Ab} Í U; memory antibodies evolve from mature antibodies that are not activated, memory antibodies assembly M_{Ab} Í U; immature antibodies are antibodies that have not undergone self-tolerance, immature antibodies assembly I_{Ab} Í D.

Definition 3: Affinity serves as the main evidence to judge the matching state between antibodiesand antigens, and the calculation formula is as Formula (3), equaling to 1 means matching, or else non-matching. In the formula, x Î Ag, y Î B, x_i, y_i are the i-th characters of x, y respectively, l is the length of character string, q is the threshold value of affinity matching.

$$f_{match}(x,y)=\begin{cases}1, & (f_{h\_dis}(x,y)/l)\geq\theta \\ 0, & otherwise\end{cases} \tag{3}$$

$$f_{h\_dis}(x,y)=\sqrt{\sum_{i=1}^{l}(x_i-y_i)^2}$$

3.2. The Changing Process of Immature Antibodies

Let I be the number of immature antibodies included in I_{Ab} at certain time, the dynamic changing formula of immature antibodies assembly is:

$$I(t+\Delta t)=I(t)+I_{new}\cdot\Delta t-(\frac{\partial I_{mature}}{\partial x_{mature}}\cdot\Delta t+\frac{\partial I_{dead}}{\partial x_{dead}}\cdot\Delta t \tag{4}$$

The Formula (4) indicates that the changing process of I_{Ab} assembly is divided into 2, that is, inflow and outflow. Inflow is the process of newly produced immature antibodies' joining in I_{Ab}assembly: $I = I_{new} \times \Delta t$, I_{new} means the production rate of immature antibodies per unit of time. Outflow is the process of removing immature antibodies from I_{Ab} assembly, and there are two directions of outflow: the quantity of immature antibodies decreased out of successful tolerance and evolution into mature antibodies is presented by

$$\frac{\partial I_{mature}}{\partial x_{mature}} \cdot \Delta t \text{, and } \frac{\partial I_{dead}}{\partial x_{dead}} \cdot \Delta t$$

presents the quantity of immature antibodies decreased out of tolerance failure.

In order to avoid matching between antibodies and self bodies, newly produced immature antibodies can only match with antigens after passing self tolerance. The tolerance process is shown as in Formula (5), and 1 means passing self tolerance, 0 means failure of self tolerance, $x \in I_{Ab}$.

$$f_{tolerate}(x) = \begin{cases} 0 & \exists y \in Self \wedge f_{match}(x, y) = 1 \\ 1 & otherwise \end{cases} \quad (5)$$

3.3. The Changing Process of Mature Antibodies

Let T represent the number of mature antibodies included in T_{Ab} at certain time, and the dynamic changing formula of mature antibodies assembly is:

$$I(t + \Delta t) = I(t) + I_{new} \cdot \Delta t - \left(\frac{\partial I_{mature}}{\partial x_{mature}} \cdot \Delta t + \frac{\partial I_{dead}}{\partial x_{dead}} \cdot \Delta t\right) \quad (6)$$

the Formula (6) indicates that the changing of T_{Ab} assembly is divided into two processes: inflow and outflow. The inflow is the process of antibodies' joining the T_{Ab}, and there are two ways: The number increased out of immature antibodies' successful tolerance and evolution is represented by

$$\frac{\partial T_{tolerate}}{\partial x_{tolerate}} \cdot \Delta t \; ; \; \frac{\partial T_{clone}}{\partial x_{clone}} \cdot \Delta t$$

means the number increase out of clonal selection of memory antibodies. Outflow is the process of removing mature antibodies, it also has two directions: the number of memory antibodies that have been evolved from activation is presented as represents the number that die from failed activation.

$$\frac{\partial T_{active}}{\partial x_{active}} \cdot \Delta t \quad \text{, while} \quad \frac{\partial T_{dead}}{\partial x_{dead}} \cdot \Delta t$$

The mature antibodies assembly T_{active} that have been activated and evolved into memory antibodies is shown in Formula (8), and the mature antibodies assembly T_{dead} that have failed in activation is shown in Formula (9), among which b is activation threshold, and l is the life cycle of mature antibodies.

$$T_{active} := \{x \mid x \in T_{Ab} \wedge x.count \geq \beta \wedge x.age \leq \lambda\} \tag{7}$$

$$T_{dead} := \{x \mid x \in T_{Ab} \wedge x.count < \beta \wedge x.age > \lambda\} \tag{8}$$

3.4. The Changing Process of Memory Antibodies

Let M as the memory antibodies quantity contained in M_{Ab} at certain time, and the dynamic changing formula of memory antibodies assembly is:

$$M(t+\Delta t) = M(t) + \frac{\partial M_{active}}{\partial x_{active}} \cdot \Delta t + \frac{\partial M_{bacterin}}{\partial x_{bacterin}} \cdot \Delta t \tag{9}$$

Because memory antibodies have infinite life cycle, the change of M_b assembly only has the process of inflow, without the outflow process of dead memory cells. The inflow of memory antibodies is conversed by activated mature antibodies T_{active},

$$\frac{\partial M_{active}}{\partial x_{active}} \cdot \Delta t = \frac{\partial T_{active}}{\partial x_{active}} \cdot \Delta t$$

3.5. Immune Surveillance

During the detection process of IA on network behaviors, it mainly adopts mature cells and memory cells to detect antigens, and it is capable to detect non-self antigens efficiently and rapidly, what follow are the detailed steps:

1) Antigen presentation: The feature information of IP packet is extracted from actual network data flow to constitute a binary string in the length of l, which is then put in the antigen assembly Ag as antigen regularly.
2) Using memory antibodies M_{Ab} to detect antigens: Non-self bodies that match with memory antibodies are removed, and memory antibodies that have detected self bodies in are also removed.
3) Using mature antibodies T_{Ab} to detect antigens: The non-self antibodies that match with T_{Ab} are removed, and the T_{Ab} that has detected enough antigens in the life cycle is then activated and evolved into memory antibodies M_{Ab}; The M_{Ab} that has not been activated or detected self elements in life cycle will die.
4) Self body assembly upgrade: After detection, the left antigens will join in self body assembly, maintain dynamic self body upgrading, undergo self tolerance with immature antibodies and maintain dynamic evolution of antibodies.

4. SIMULATION EXPERIMENT AND RESULT ANALYSE

4.1. Experiment Environment and Parameter Settings

The experiment environment is classified into two network segments of A, B, and composed of 20 host computers of the same configuration. A_i, B_i ($1 \le i \le 20$) means the i-th host computer in A, B segments respectively. The experiment applies part of the data from KDDCUP99 [11] in MIT LINCOLN lab as training and test data. The training set is normal network data without any attack, and the test set includes normal data and attack data. The attack data is classified into 4 categories: DoS, Probe, U2R, R2L. The test data I includes guess_ passwd, buffer_overflow and other attacks, 7 in total, and the test set II includes the attacks in test set I and other 10 attacks or more, e.g. land, spy, perl.

Antigen data architecture is composed of source, destination IP address, port number, protocol type, IP tag field, IP packet length and TCP/UDP/ICMP domain etc, $l = 172$, affinity matching threshold value$\theta = 0.7$.

Table 2. Experiment data list.

Attack Type	Training set		Test set I		Test set II	
	Attack Times	Attack Type	Attack Times	Attack Type	Attack Times	Attack Type
Normal	18300	0	17500	0	14400	0
DoS	4580	1	5140	2	5580	5
Probe	1250	1	2700	2	4240	4
U2R	560	1	650	2	420	4
R2L	290	1	300	1	360	3

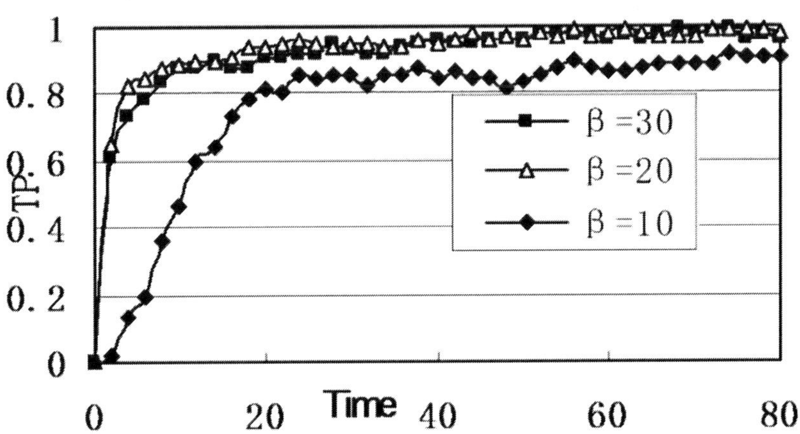

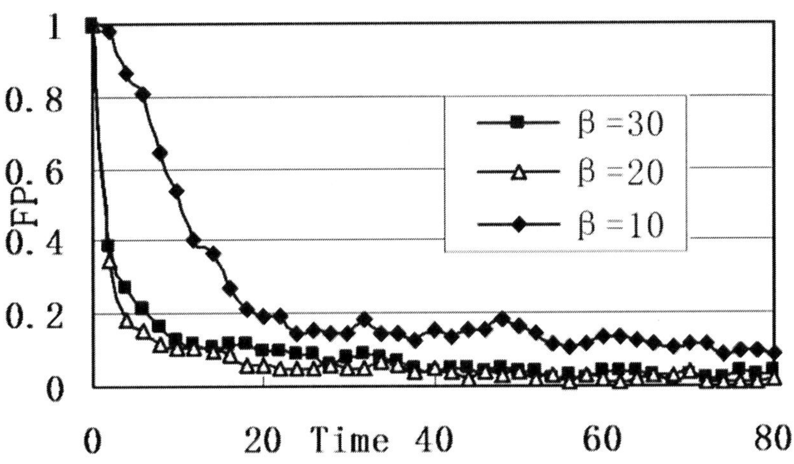

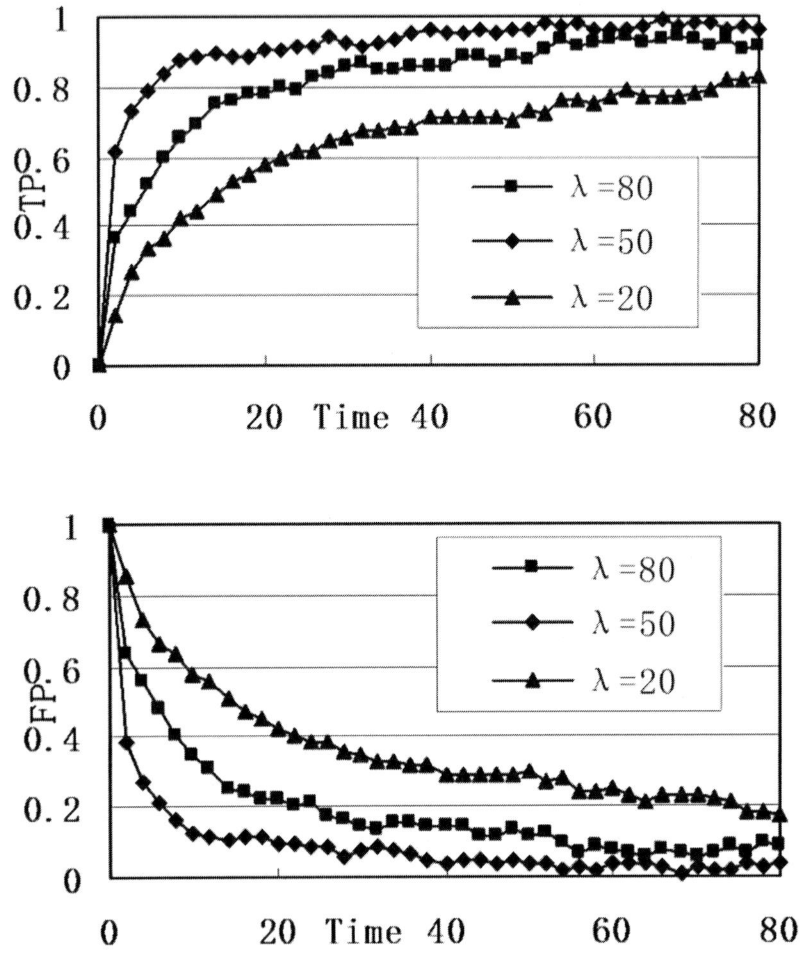

Figure 3. Effect of the activation threshold β and the lifecycle λ.

4.2. Experiment Results and Performance Analysis

Activation threshold value βand life cycleλbear large influence on TP and FP, the test performance of ADNIIMA, therefore, optimization test should be carried out. The experiment results are shown in**Figure 3**, when activation threshold value β is relatively small, and the mature antibodies are activated without thorough learning, FP is relatively bigger; when the life cycle λ is relatively small, the mature antibodies will die without activation and the memory antibodies will be scarce, which in total may cause TP lower. Along with the increase of β and λ, TP increases and FP decreases. However, when βandλare too big, TP decreases instead and FP increases. After through analysis, it is found out that when$\beta=20$, $\lambda=50$, FP<6%, TP>93%, the effect is better.

Table 3. Detection results of ADNIIMA model experiment.

Attack Type	Test Set I			Test Set II		
	Recognition Type	TP (%)	FP (%)	Recognition Type	TP (%)	FP (%)
Normal	0	98.6	0	0	97.2	0
DoS	2	97.2	2.8	5	97.1	2.9
Probe	2	96.5	3.5	4	94.3	5.7
U2R	2	94.5	5.5	4	95.4	4.6
R2L	1	95.2	4.8	3	94.3	5.7

Table 4. Detection results of BRO experiment.

Attack Type	Test Set I			Test Set II		
	Recognition Type	TP (%)	FP (%)	Recognition Type	TP (%)	FP (%)
Normal	0	97.5	2.5	0	97.2	2.8
DoS	1	73.3	26.7	2	53.6	46.4
Probe	1	72.2	27.8	2	52.1	47.9
U2R	1	68.5	31.5	1	45.6	54.4
R2L	1	94.5	5.5	2	63.5	36.5

In **Table 3** and **Table 4**, the comparison test results of this model and the detection tools matched with the patterns based on, BRO [12], are listed, and from the tables we can infer that the detection model is of higher TP and lower FP, and the types of recognized unknown attacks are more than that of BRO, which demonstrates that this model is of high self-learning and adaptability.

In **Table 4**, TP and FP curves of host computer A_2 with self evolution and detection, and the host computer A_3, using vaccines emitted from A_1 for detection, are list respectively, and from the table we can conclude that in the later phase of experiment, the TP and FP curves of A_2 and A_3 are almost coincident. But in the early phase of the actual experiment, A_2, that relies on itself for detection, has low detection rate due to a lack of antibodies, and the attacks have made severe damage to the during this exact phase, which is unacceptable for key network node.

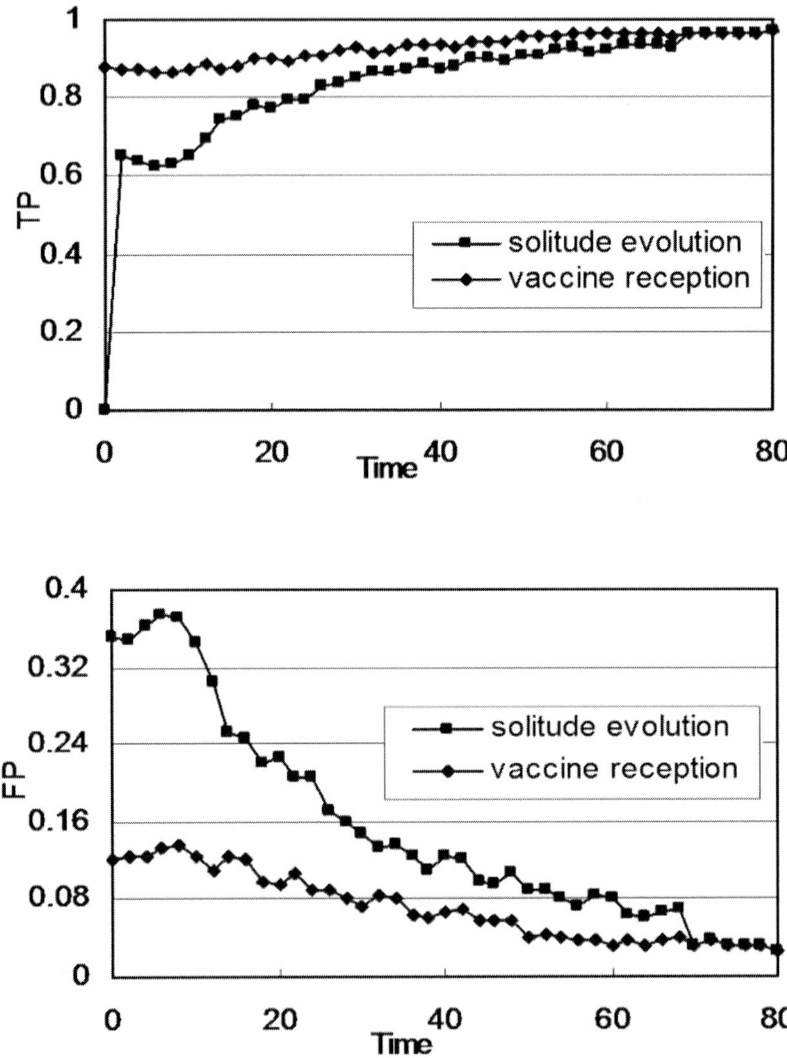

Figure 4. Comparison of detecting effect between solitude evolution and vaccine reception.

4. CONCLUSIONS

The active defense model for network intrusion based on artificial immune multi-agent put forth in this article has following advantages compared with other network intrusion defense techniques: 1) Self-learning; The memory mechanism and antibodies generation mechanism can not only detect well-known attacks, but also bear recognition ability towards unknown attacks. 2) Multi-level; The model has introduced in the concept of vaccine, which can strengthen network nodes and connection between each network segment. 3) Robustness; The model applies distributed system structure so that a single node under attack does not impact the detection abilities of other nodes. In a word, the experiment results reveal that the model differs greatly from the isolated and passive defense situation of traditional network security model, and it is a better solution to network security detection.

5. REFERENCES

1. Y. Bai, and H. Kobayashi, "Intrusion detection systems: Technology and development," IEEE Advanced Information Networking and Applications, pp. 710–715, 2003.
2. A. Pilz and J. Swoboda, "Network management information models," Aeu-International Journal of Electronics and Communications, Vol. 58, pp. 165–171, 2004.
3. Y. L. Dong, J. Qian, M. L. Shi, "A cooperative intrusion detection system based on autonomous agents," IEEE CCECE 2003, Vol. 2, pp. 861– 863, 2003.
4. P. D'haeseleer and S. Forrest, "An immunological approach to change detection: Algorithm, analysis and implication," in Proceedings of IEEE Symposium on Research in Security and Privacy, Oakland, pp. 110–119, 1996.
5. J. Kim and P. Bentley, "The artificial immune model for network intrusion detection," 7th European Congress on Intelligent Techniques and Soft Computing, 1999.
6. P. K. Harmer and G. B.Lamont, "An agent based architecture for a computer virus immune system," Proceedings of the Genetic and Evolutionary Computation Conference, Orlando, Florida, USA, 1999.

7. F. Esponda, S. Forrest, and P. Helman, "A formal frame work for positive and negative detection schemes," IEEE Transactions on Systems Man and Cybernetics Part B-Cybernetics, Vol. 34, No. 1, pp. 357–373, 2004.
8. I. M. Hegazy, H. M. Faheem, T. Al-Arif, and T. Ahmed, "Evaluating how well agent-based IDS perform," Potentials, Digital Object Identifier, IEEE, Vol. 24, 27–30, 2005.
9. P. Ballet and V. Rodin, "Immune mechanisms to regulate multi-agents systems," GECCO 2000, Las Vegas, Nevada, USA, July 2000.
10. Z. Z. Shi, "Intelligent agent and its Application [M]," Science Press, Beijing, 2000.
11. A Hofmeyr and S. Forrest, "Architecture for an artificial immune system," Evolutionary Computation, Vol. 7, No. 1, 2000.
12. N. K. Jerne, "Towards a network theory of the immune system," Annual Immunology, Vol. 125, 1974.

INDEX